"Sisters are my heroes, and this marv
portrait of an absolutely remarkable
torian's skill and a writer's talent for storytelling. Janice Farnham, RJM,
demonstrates tremendous flair as she delves through the history of one
of the most incredible of all women's religious orders and, in the process,
brings to life centuries of pioneering spirits and generous hearts."

—JAMES MARTIN

SJ, author of *Jesus: A Pilgrimage* and *Learning to Pray*

"In *Weaving Hope*, historian Janice Farnham recounts the saga of her
congregation's American mission, starting with the immigrant sisters
who educated countless immigrant children with minimal resources, and
continuing into the twenty-first century. The unique experience of the
Religious of Jesus and Mary in the United States is also a significant chapter of a larger American story involving the tens of thousands of women
religious who have made an enormous contribution to our social fabric."

—LESLIE CHOQUETTE

Assumption University

"Sr. Janice Farnham, RJM, serves up a moving narrative of the ministries
of the Religious of Jesus and Mary undertaken in the US over the past
140 years. Peppered with illustrative anecdotes, *Weaving Hope* brings to
life an inspiring story that needs to be heard, the story of the courage,
perseverance, and fidelity of the daughters of St. Claudine in serving the
gospel in changing times and needs."

—THOMAS D. STEGMAN

SJ, Boston College School of Theology and Ministry

"*Weaving Hope* offers a lively and eminently readable close-up look at
two realities that largely defined the world of nineteenth- and twentieth-
century Catholicism in the United States: women religious and the dense
network of Catholic schools that significantly shaped the lives and worldview of millions of Catholic school children. Farnham's book now consti-
tutes required reading for students of the American Catholic experience."

—MARK MASSA

SJ, Director, Boisi Center for Religion and
American Public Life, Boston College

"This is a magisterial study by a first-rate historian. Based on years of archival research, Janice Farnham has woven a compelling account of how the Religious of Jesus and Mary women's order crucially shaped Catholic culture within the United States. With deft precision, she chronicles the order's educational and ministerial outreach among multiple ethnic groups. Crucially, Farnham's in-depth study also illuminates the larger landscape of Catholicism and religious women across the United States."

—CATHERINE M. MOONEY
Associate Professor of Church History,
Boston College School of Theology & Ministry

Weaving Hope

Weaving Hope

The Religious of Jesus and Mary
in the United States, 1877–2017

Janice Farnham

WIPF & STOCK · Eugene, Oregon

To all weavers of our story—past, present and future

Each of our threads runs its course, then
joins in life together. This magnificent tapestry—
this masterpiece in which we live forever.

PARKER J. PALMER

Contents

Acknowledgements

Traditionally, weaving is known to be labor-intensive. *Weaving Hope* has adhered to that tradition, taking over twenty years to complete. While I cannot name all who have made the book possible, I happily acknowledge with gratitude the small army of "weavers" who have helped me along the way. Above all, I thank our loving God for weaving a tapestry with the threads of all the Religious of Jesus and Mary who have lived and served in the States. "May the Lord write your history," Pope Francis once said, and I pray that this work reveals God's hand and love at work in our sisters' stories.

In 1995, I was invited to write this history by our province leader, Sr. Eileen Reid. The project presented unique geographic, linguistic and administrative challenges. Initially, a team of researchers, fifteen sisters from East and West, gathered regional information, and met regularly for four years as "The Weavers." To each of them, I am grateful for the necessary and useful groundwork: Sisters Alice Aubé, Yvette Beaulieu, Irene Castonguay, Patricia Dillon, Anne Egan, Lorraine Genest, Mary Kenny, Catherine McIntyre, Rosemary Nicholson, Shirley Leveillé, Alice Ouimette, Irene Rhéaume, Kathleen Scanlon, Mary Scanlon, and Josephine Vargas. Among them, I want to highlight Sisters Yvette Beaulieu and Irene Rhéaume, province archivists when we began working; they provided essential documents from the archival collection when it was housed in Maryland. I am deeply grateful as well to our province leaders who have supported this effort from its inception.

As a historian, I have long appreciated, and learned from, the skills and generosity of archivists. My special thanks to Sr. Doris Bissonnette, province archivist form 2013 to 2017, and Dr. Denise Gallo, who replaced her in 2017. Sr. Louise Turmel, archivist for the Canadian Province, contributed important information on the founding sisters from Canada.

In 2007, the historical section of the province collection moved to the French Institute at Assumption College, Worcester. Dr. Leslie Choquette, professor of history and Director of the French Institute, has my deep and lasting gratitude. She encouraged and welcomed our request for space, rearranging her office to house part of our collection. She has supported me throughout the writing process, reading chapters, commenting, making editorial suggestions. To Leslie and her able assistants, Ms. Elizabeth Lipin and Ms. Nina Tsantinis (+2020), *reconnaissance profonde.*

A group of colleagues and friends offered resources and expertise of all kinds, keeping hope alive when it foundered. My heartfelt thanks to Deans Mark Massa, SJ, and Thomas Stegman, SJ, and to my longtime friend Richard Clifford, SJ, at the Boston College School of Theology and Ministry, for making available the rich resources of the university libraries, as well as reading chapters, making suggestions, and giving me the impetus to keep going. To another dear friend, James Martin, SJ, of *America Media*, my debt is huge. Jim gave the book its title, suggested an editor and publisher, read selected chapters, and supported the effort with his prayer and good humor. Thanks from my heart to dear M. Cecilia Gaudette, RJM (+2017) for her precious notes and knowledge of our Congregation and its history.

An effective editor is a precious asset and a blessing. I found one in Ms. Vinita Hampton Wright, senior editor at Loyola Press; she agreed to be my content editor, carefully reading the manuscript, correcting grammar and offering positive critique for improvement. She has contributed greatly to bringing the book to light. At every stage of writing, I have also counted on the memory and insights of my close friend, Rosemary Mangan, RJM. She read every chapter carefully and critically; I welcomed her fact-checking, incisive comments, helpful suggestions. Her support and wisdom have been invaluable. My RJM sisters at St. Timothy's, Warwick, Rhode Island, provided me with a caring, prayerful community and office space in which to work. They helped me persevere when writing energy waned. To each one I offer heartfelt thanks.

The competent team at Wipf and Stock assisted me at every step of the publishing process. I am grateful to Mr. Matt Wimer, my editorial manager at Wipf and Stock, and Ms. Rachel Saunders, for their professional advice and understanding with my concerns and questions.

The final chorus of the Broadway musical, "Hamilton," asks in its moving refrain: "Who will remember your name? Who will tell your story?" With *Weaving Hope,* I have told one story of our sisters in this country, realizing that it is imperfect and incomplete. Much of their rich legacy has passed with them into God's silence. I hope that this narrative gives them new voice and life as it re-members them into the future. Any factual errors or historical inaccuracies readers may find are all mine, for which I ask their indulgence.

Praised forever be Jesus and Mary!

Author's Note

As a historical study, the research and writing of *Weaving Hope* relied on a number of sources. Primary documents and materials were researched in the General Archives of the Congregation's headquarters in Rome, as well as the historical collection of the Province Archives, housed in Warwick, Rhode Island and at the French Institute of Assumption College in Worcester, Massachusetts.

At the beginning of each section, the primary archival material for citations has been indicated.

I have translated all citations from sources in French or Spanish. Accents were omitted when common usage indicated they should be.

Part One

Framing a Loom

1

Nation, Church, and Congregation in a Century of Change

E Pluribus Unum. One from many. From diversity, unity.
From many peoples, one nation. From many provinces, one province.
De plusieurs peuples, un seul peuple.
De plusieurs provinces, une province.
De muchos pueblos, un solo pueblo.
De tantas provincias, una provincia.

THE RELIGIOUS OF JESUS and Mary in the United States now form one province, but once were three provinces.[1] They form a tapestry woven of many cultures, a province with origins in Europe, French Canada, and Mexico. Multi-cultural and multi-lingual, from their origins they have mirrored the diversity of our vast nation and its Catholic population. The history of their first century in this country reveals the changing contexts and challenges in their evolution as an apostolic congregation within the larger cultures of church and nation in the United States. It also recounts how that congregation has been shaped by its larger history and has in a unique way contributed to its development.

Like the United States itself, the Religious of Jesus and Mary are one from many. Originating from European, Canadian, and Mexican settings, they present a rich tapestry of customs and cultures. This chapter frames its unique and compelling story from 1877 to the years following World

3

War II. It provides the "loom" on which the fabric of its community and apostolic history has been woven. It gives an overview of the immigrant populations to which the congregation was sent, the challenges faced by the American church, and the role of schools and teaching sisters as the "institutional face" of Catholicism in a rapidly developing nation.

US Growth in the Immigrant Century[2]

It is no exaggeration to say that the late nineteenth and early twentieth centuries were a period of critical change and challenge, both for the nation and the Catholic faith community, including women's religious life. The country itself was growing by leaps and bounds. In the mid–nineteenth century, there were twenty–five states and the total population of the United States was over thirty million. A hundred years later, the numbers would grow to a total of forty–eight states and two territories, with a population of 130 million. This tenfold expansion was largely due to the massive influx of Catholic immigrants from Europe, particularly Ireland, Italy, and Germany. Diverse in cultures but one in their desire to make a new and better life for their families, they created new ethnic identities that blended loyalty to ancient traditions with appreciation for the opportunity United States citizenship promised. "The interaction of these immigrants with the customs of their new home would change America forever and usher in the century of the 'immigrant church.'"[3]

The Largest Group: Irish Immigrants

With the potato famine of the mid–century (1845 to 1852), well over a million Irish Catholics emigrated to the United States on the infamous "coffin ships"—disease–infested vessels overrun with vermin. More than ten percent would perish en route to their new homeland. In 1865, over 350,000 Irish immigrants had settled in New York, one quarter of its population, often in crowded slums where disease and crime were rampant. By the 1920s, more than four million Irish immigrants swelled the larger cities of the East Coast as well as the Midwest and the West. Because they had skills in English, Irish immigrants were quickly hired in a variety of industrial and rural areas, and they often rose to leadership positions in labor unions. In fact, the Irish would become the chief source of labor for the growing economy of the country. Like other ethnic immigrants, all members of the family—including women and children—were ex-pected to find work. For women and girls, the area of domestic service dominated: in some cities, over three-quarters of Irish women workers were employed to cook, clean, and serve as "nannies" to the children of upper-and middle-class families.

Prior to mid-century, anti–Catholicism and deep prejudices against the foreign-born were rampant, developing into a movement known as nativism. Because of this and other anti–Catholic movements in many large cities, the Irish immigrant applying for work might be confronted by a sign marked NINA (No Irish need apply). In some cities, hostility to the Irish was bitter enough to erupt into church burnings, riots, and armed street fights. Poverty among the Irish was widespread, as was alcoholism and its effects on family life. As early as the 1830s, the temperance move-ment rallied Catholic clergy and laity, so that one historian wrote that it was "the most enduring reform movement that Catholics sponsored in the nineteenth century."[4] While they may have been unpopular among some people, Irish immigrants were assisted by powerful and flamboy-ant church leaders—like Irish-born "Dagger John" Hughes (1797-1864), the first Archbishop of New York—who defended their flocks mightily and militantly, calling for public funds for educating Catholic children, founding colleges, and building cathedrals, along with supporting the labor efforts of Irish union bosses for better wages and conditions. Along with Hughes, Irish ecclesiastical leaders such as James Gibbons (Balti-more), John Ireland (St. Paul, Minnesota), and John Keane (Richmond, Virginia) came to dominate the American Catholic hierarchy and make a major contribution to the Church's culture in the United States.

Slowly, attitudes towards the Irish began to change. The Civil War was probably the turning point; many thousands of Irish–Americans actively participated in the war on the Union side, gaining respect and acceptance from other Americans as a result. Some second-or third-generation Irish Americans were moving up the social ladder; because of their deep interest in education and their tradition of literacy, many entered professional positions. Yet this was not the lot of the majority. The 1900 census recorded hundreds of thousands of Irish immigrants living in poverty, mostly in urban slums. Economic circumstances would slowly improve life for a significant number during the twentieth century. As a group, the Irish managed to secure footholds in the workplace, especially in the labor or trade union movement, the police, and the fire service. Their numbers helped. In Boston, Chicago, and New York, the Irish could

elect their own candidates and develop an Irish–American political pow-
erhouse that would culminate with the election in 1960 of the first Irish
Catholic president of the nation, John Fitzgerald Kennedy (1917–1963).

A Major Port of Entry: New York City

New York was a primary port of entry for most immigrants, with Ellis
Island established in 1892 as the chief immigration center of the East.
Along with the potato famine, British land policies in Ireland had forced
many to leave their cherished homeland for what they hoped was a land
of freedom, opportunity, and prosperity. Once arrived, Irish immigrants
who had hoped to travel further west had no financial resources and were
forced to stay in the city to find lodging and work. They were soon to
discover that the streets of New York were not quite paved in gold!

At the turn of the twentieth century, one of every six New Yorkers
was born in Germany. Waves of Italian, Jewish, and Eastern European
immigrants followed, coming through the New York port to swell the
population of the city; their presence, too, was often met with contempt
and apprehension. Yet all these immigrants transformed New York into
a vibrant cosmopolitan city by the richness and diversity of the cultures
and traditions they contributed.

The impact of waves of unregulated immigration was rapid and
chaotic. The city's population went from about 40,000 in 1838 to almost
800,000 in the 1860s. One historian describes New York in this period as
"dirty, fetid, disease–ridden . . . subject to outbreaks of typhoid, cholera,
and smallpox."[5] Decent lodging was often impossible to find, and poor
people ended up in alms houses, sixty–four percent of them Irish immigrants. By 1900, there were over three million people in New York
City, and its urban economy was booming. It had more people within
its boundaries than all but six states and was home to many of the nation's millionaires. Municipal boundaries were set in 1898 to cope with
New York's expansion, creating the five boroughs: Manhattan, the Bronx,
Queens, Brooklyn, and Staten Island.

A potent symbol of the impact of Catholics and their dedication to
the Church was St. Patrick's Cathedral, dedicated in 1879 and attended by
thousands who had contributed to its erection. By the end of the century,
New York had become a major center for Catholics, who accounted for
fully one–third of its population. This was the pulsing metropolis where

the Religious of Jesus and Mary settled at the turn of the twentieth century, hoping to undertake apostolic work while providing accommodation for sisters traveling to and from Europe, Mexico, or Canada.

The rise of New York's Catholics is reflected in the distinguished if unsuccessful run for national office by its governor, Alfred E. Smith (1873–1944). Nominated in 1928 as the Democratic candidate for President of the United States, Smith personified the rise from poverty, the ethnic diversity, and the immigrant roots of the city. His grandparents were German, Italian, Irish, and English. His own formal education ended at the age of fourteen, when he took on a series of unskilled jobs; politics for Smith would serve as a way up and out of dead-end labor. And while he did not win that election, Smith made it possible for Catholic immigrants to believe in the political promise held out to them in their adopted nation. While Irish immigration diminished significantly in the twentieth century, a large number of Irish ethnic neighborhoods—such as the mission of the Religious of Jesus and Mary to St. John's, Kingsbridge, in the Bronx—continued to nourish the faith and culture of generations in thriving parishes, schools, and civic institutions. Numerous vocations to the priesthood and religious life, along with vibrant lay associations and parish groups, bore witness to the profound religious convictions of immigrant forebears who sowed the faith in tears and would certainly have welcomed the harvest of their struggles in joy.

Immigrant Italian Communities

In southern Europe, harsh economic realities connected to the unification of their country in 1870 prompted a great wave of Italian immigration, especially in the early twentieth century. Before the 1870s, there were relatively few Italians emigrating to America; but in the decade before 1890, close to a million came, primarily to work in the large industrialized cities of the Northeast. "Little Italys" sprang up in cities wherever these immigrants settled. These were marked by devotion to family and to various saints, and by an array of Marian piety that spawned popular processions and feasts. Italians also shared deep bonds of belief and regional ethnicity. Many American Catholics are familiar with the most famous of Italian immigrants, Mother Frances Xavier Cabrini (1850–1917), the first naturalized American citizen to be canonized, whose service to her own people and others in New York extended well beyond the confines of the Catholic community.

By 1920, Italian Americans numbered over four million, some of whom had also found work in the mining regions of the Midwest. The majority had been farmers, skilled tradesmen, or unskilled laborers, mostly from rural villages in southern Italy. Like other immigrants without language abilities in English, Italians had to compete for jobs and often found themselves marginalized and unemployed. They cultivated a style of Catholicism in their new country that reflected both their Mediterranean roots and their immigrant experience. One historian writes, "Where the Irish invested great spiritual authority in the priesthood, Italian–American spirituality was oriented toward a devotion to family rooted in the peasant villages of the homeland."[6] The Religious of Jesus and Mary came to know the richness and goodness of Italian families early in the twentieth century, when they served at Loreto, a poor parish community in lower Manhattan, and later, with a thriving parish in upstate New York.

German Immigration Patterns

German–speaking peoples numbering over a million also migrated to the United States in the nineteenth century, running a close second to the Irish in terms of Catholic numbers. They generally came from more prosperous and skilled backgrounds than other immigrant groups and were concentrated in farming communities of the Midwest. They were determined to maintain their German customs and language. To achieve this, like many other immigrant groups, they sought to establish "national parishes" designed to serve the unique religious needs of their ethnic community. In fact, by the dawn of the twentieth century, the national parish was a primary institution to serve the needs of diverse immigrant Catholic groups. Most of the parishes to which the Religious of Jesus and Mary first came were French–Canadian national parishes. This reality sometimes caused conflicts with the Irish–dominated leadership of the American Church, but it also showed strong pride in ancient heritages that would contribute to the special character of American Catholic faith and life.

French Canadians in New England

Immigrants from French Canada were the first and most important ethnic group served by the Religious of Jesus and Mary. They would generate the largest number of vocations to the congregation from the United States. Therefore, it is appropriate here to present a brief history of their evolution in New England, as well as their unique challenges and contributions. Their story provides a context for the mission of the Congregation in its founding years.

From its original colonies of the Revolutionary era, New England in the mid–nineteenth century comprised six states. The Industrial Revolution, with its factories and mechanized machinery, brought workers into New England in large numbers, many of them French Canadians. Anglophones migrated to New England during these years as well, but their numbers were eclipsed by French–speaking compatriots. Between 1840 and 1930, nearly a million French Canadians left Québec to immigrate to the United States, two–thirds of them to New England. Considering that the population of Québec was only 892,061 in 1851, this was an exodus of major proportions.[7] The shortage of land in Québec had become critical in the nineteenth century, and agricultural work was insufficient for its growing population. Because of geographic proximity, economic opportunities, and a growing textile industry, New England was the choice for two–thirds of Québécois who chose to move to the United States. With the arrival of railroad transportation in the 1880s, their journeys became easier and less expensive.

These women and men came, not because of religious oppression or persecution, but to improve their financial lot and their families' lives. The vast majority of French Canadians ended up employed as factory workers in mill towns of New England, living in neighborhoods known as "*petit Canadas.*" Major centers of French–Canadian culture included the cities of Woonsocket, Rhode Island; Lewiston, Maine; Worcester, Massachusetts; and Manchester, New Hampshire. In 1850, French–Canadian immigrants to New England probably totaled less than 20,000 persons, 62 percent of whom had settled in Vermont. During the second half of the century, however, that figure rose to more than 106,000 French Canadians settled in the six–state area. By 1900, they were concentrated in northern Maine, western Vermont, and upstate New York as well as in central and southeastern New England. Between 1840 and 1930, about 900,000 French Canadians left Québec to labor in factories, mills, potato fields, and logging camps throughout New England. Many immigrants worked in the flourishing textile industries of the region, including the towns of New Hampshire, Massachusetts, and Rhode Island, where the Religious of Jesus and Mary would center their earliest apostolic work.

Three of these "factory towns" were foundation sites for the Religious of Jesus and Mary in the United States. Like those they served, they had recently emigrated from France or French Canada, foreigners to the language and customs of this new world. New England Franco–American culture provided the socio–religious context with which the community would be identified well into the twentieth century.

In 1885, the census report for Massachusetts listed French Canadians as comprising sixty–two percent of the Fall River, Massachusetts work force; by 1900 their numbers were still on the rise. Massachusetts would account for the greatest number of French Canadian immigrants. In New Hampshire they represented over fifty–four percent of the labor force at the textile mills of Manchester. Working in factories offered employment to various members of families; the extensive use of women and young children—up to sixty–three percent in cotton mills—characterized French–Canadian immigration to New England. A Fall River census for 1900 reveals that over eighty percent of its textile workers were female. An interesting aspect of French–Canadian migration was its fluidity. During the last quarter of the nineteenth century, economic and natural crises often kept French Canadians moving back and forth between the United States and Canada, and sometimes from one state to another. Nevertheless, by 1912, seventy–two percent of all permanent settlers among French Canadians were in New England.

The French–Canadian contribution to Catholic life in America reflects a people's struggles to preserve the language, traditions, and faith they brought from Québec and venerated as the root of their culture and identity. Historically, French Canadians were accustomed to being a Catholic minority in a Protestant land, resisting any attempts at assimilating into the majority culture. In the United States, they were perceived as undesirable by both Protestant Yankees and the Irish–American immigrants who were their competition for work and jobs. French Canadians were even referred to as "the Jews of New England" and "the Chinese of the eastern States" because of poor treatment, discrimination, and dangerous work assignments they often received. With time, French Canadians developed a strong sense of their unique culture in a new land: defined by language, determined by faith, and dedicated to the family. Their vocal leaders called for a unified fight for Catholic and French survival, *"la survivance catholique et française."* The means to attain this *survivance* were the safeguarding of their faith, their language, and their traditional family customs.

The experience of French Canadians in New England was similar to that of other immigrant groups. A period of early hardship and discrimination was followed by gradual acculturation and rise to a higher social and economic position. Drawn to New England for economic gain, primarily in the burgeoning textile industry, these immigrants relied on certain character traits to endure and prevail: a sense of independence, a willingness to work hard, tenacity, frugality, and patience. Rather than become assimilated, however, many French Canadians tended to isolate themselves in tight–knit communities, remaining socially distant and defensive vis–à–vis American society and labor practices. For example, when the labor movement was initiated and factory workers began to organize for higher wages and better working conditions, French Canadians in Fall River did not join the unions. They were often hired to replace their striking co-workers, mostly Irish, creating tensions in the workplace as well as in their civic communities. However, their compatriots in factories of labor strongholds like Woonsocket and Manchester benefited from union memberships and the benefits of organizing.

To safeguard their faith, French Canadians relied on strong parochial cohesion, and they aggressively sought Franco–Canadian priests to be their pastors. The clergy's presence and leadership assured the organization of French–Canadian *survivance* for the bewildered cultural strangers they served. This dynamic corps of dedicated priests helped them recreate a unified socio–religious world in a new and sometimes hostile environment. A common goal of French–Canadian national parishes was to build churches and schools where the French language and their own customs would be preserved. Members of several dozen apostolic congregations sent priests, brothers and sisters from France and Québec to establish schools, orphanages, hospitals, and charitable works of every kind. At the turn of the century, more than 400 clergy and 2,000 women religious—among them over100 Religious of Jesus and Mary—were engaged in apostolic work among French–Canadian communities in New England. One historian has stated that "as with no other group, a rapidly increasing corps of clergy and religious was available to help recreate the French–Canadian kind of faith within the American environment."[8] In 1907, Rev. Georges–Albert Guertin (1869–1931), was appointed as the first French–Canadian bishop of the United States in Manchester, New Hampshire.

Schools were considered a major factor in *survivance,* and they were at the heart of the parish educational endeavor to maintain the language

and faith of its children. By 1910, there were 133 French–language parochial schools in New England, which accounted for more than forty
percent of all parochial schools. By 1912, the Religious of Jesus and Mary
directed and staffed seven bilingual parish schools in which French–Canadian language and culture were a priority. Sometimes, as we shall see,
because of their insistence on French instruction in the classroom for a
half day, these institutions became a source of conflict between French
Canadians and the predominantly Irish hierarchy, as well as with civic
and educational leaders in various cities.

The experiences of French Canadians in the United States helped
them develop strong ethnic loyalties, a deep attachment to cultural expressions of faith, and a sense of themselves as a group "that respected
the distinctiveness of its special membership."[9] The central place they
gave to parish life and lay leadership would help shape part of a post-
Vatican II model for the whole church. Their solidarity with one another
and their deep attachment to family life and values wove a tradition that
transcended national borders.

Resisting Assimilation[10]

Like other immigrant communities, French Canadians encountered
some friction with the New England Yankee population, especially during the anti–Catholic crusade of the Know Nothings (1854–1856), an
anti–immigrant political movement. They were not helped by their isola-
tion from other immigrant groups or by the hostility of Irish–American
Catholics. In fact, French Canadians in the nineteenth century experienced their bitterest controversies with the predominantly Irish–American hierarchy. Though their faith was the same, major differences in
religious customs and parish life made it appear to some that God might
have to separate them even in heaven!

The acquisition of French–Canadian clergy was dependent upon the
local bishop, who was not always sympathetic to the cause of *survivance*
or to the foundation of national parishes. One theory supported by the
American episcopate was that assimilation of immigrants should occur as
quickly as possible in order to reduce the possibility of nativist discrimination. Thus, many bishops opposed the desire of French Canadians to
have national parishes and French–language schools because this would
make them appear less American and separate them from the rest of

mainstream America, as well as from their co-religionists. Other bishops thought it wiser to encourage the preservation of ethnic traditions and supported French Canadians in their belief that "to lose your language is to lose your faith." This conflict of views formed the basis of a larger complex of tensions between the French Canadians and the Irish, created by cultural differences, the language barrier, and rivalry among workers.

Several rifts occurred between the French–Canadian communities in New England and their Irish–American hierarchy. One such eruption, known as the Flint Affair, took place in the French–Canadian "Flint" section of Fall River, Massachusetts. In 1884, Bishop Thomas F. Hendricken (1827–1886) became involved in a struggle over the appointment of someone to replace the recently deceased Rev. Pierre Bédard, founding pastor in 1874 of Notre–Dame de Lourdes Church. From the outset, Bédard had implemented the French–Canadian concept of a lay corporation, or *fabrique*, for his parish, in order to bypass the bishop's control of parish finances. When Bishop Hendricken first tried to name a French–speaking Irish priest to replace Bédard, the congregation rose up in protest, refusing to attend church services or make further contributions. They eventually appealed to Rome and demanded the installation of a French or French–Canadian priest. After putting the parish under a ten-month interdict, Hendricken bowed to Vatican pressures and compromised by appointing an Irish pastor and a French–speaking curate. The effects of this parochial crisis on the Religious of Jesus and Mary are discussed in the next chapter.

A few years later, from 1894 through 1896, Danielson, Connecticut was the scene of angry outbursts from French Canadians who were the majority ethnic group at St. James Parish. They refused to contribute to the construction of the parish school because they claimed the Irish pastor had reneged on a promise to provide French instruction to the children. Even though peace was ultimately restored, the memory of the refusal of the French Canadians to come to an amicable solution in Danielson remained to haunt the memory of the hierarchy. Similar clashes occurred in Brookfield, Massachusetts in 1899 and in Brunswick, Maine in 1906.

The last significant challenge to ecclesiastical authority and the climax of ongoing tensions occurred with the Sentinelle Affair of the 1920s in Woonsocket, Rhode Island, the fourth largest French–Canadian town in New England, accounting for sixty percent of its population. There were five French–Canadian parishes in the city by the 1920s. The third

Bishop of Providence, William A. Hickey (1869–1933), took up his responsibilities in 1921, during a period of xenophobic assaults on parochial and foreign–language schools across the nation. A proponent of
Catholic assimilation, he hoped to centralize the control of parish funds
and to emphasize the teaching of English in the schools of his diocese. To
support the schools and other proposed programs, he called for fund-
raising in the parishes. Clergy, religious, and laity were sharply divided
over Hickey's fund–raising campaign. Opposition forces were led by
Elphège Daignault, a lawyer and president of the *Association Canado-
Américaine*, a mutual aid society for French Canadians. In 1924, the
group began publishing their opinions in a journal, *La Sentinelle*, which
supported the idea that parish property was inviolable and that Hickey's
campaign was illegitimate. It called for more national parishes, in direct
opposition to the Americanization policies of Hickey and the National
Catholic Welfare Conference. Futile appeals were made to Rome and to
Rhode Island's Superior Court, which upheld the bishop's levies as legitimate. *La Sentinelle* was banned in April 1928, and more than sixty
members of the faction were excommunicated.

The challenges of assimilation and identity would affect the lives
and service of the Religious of Jesus and Mary in several New England
missions. They sometimes found themselves in conflict with clerical
authority because of their language, customs, or culture. Through their
struggles they learned to adapt to new situations and sacrifice long–trusted patterns of behavior for the good of the whole. If the congregation
was to flourish in the United States, it needed to grow beyond comfortable self–defined cultural borders, and engage in broader, more inclusive
apostolic fields.

A Conquered People: Mexican Americans in the Southwest

By the third decade of the twentieth century, the Religious of Jesus
and Mary would find refuge in Texas from revolutionary upheavals in
Mexico. As aliens and exiles, they shaped a flourishing ministry to their
own people in the Southwest, fulfilling their mission even to the southern
California coast. One historian has rightly noted that "the first Mexican
Americans were not immigrants but a conquered people with deep roots
in a territory in which they found themselves treated as 'foreigners.'"[11]
Mexican Americans are second only to indigenous tribal peoples as the

oldest culture to populate North America. From the sixteenth to the nineteenth century, Mexico was part of the Spanish conquest. It was influenced by a synthesis of cultures and religious practices from indigenous groups as well as their Spanish conquerors. As early as 1610, the *conquistadores* founded San Antonio, one of the oldest cities in North America, in the Mexican territory of Texas, followed by thriving Franciscan missions in California. For centuries, prior to the founding of the United States, Mexicans and indigenous peoples flourished along what is now the southern border of the nation. In 1821, after a decade-long struggle, Mexico won its independence from Spain. For the next few years, it gave land grants to American settlers in Texas.

By the middle of the nineteenth century, a considerable number of Mexicans lived in territories that had been annexed to the United States after the Mexican–American War (1846–1848). Their story is a sad one because the provisions of the treaty ending that war were disregarded by the United States. Economic exploitation and the theft of large tracts of land, along with abuse of other human and civil rights, are just a few examples of how Mexicans lived under yet another form of conquest and assimilation. Still they came, with hopes of finding a better life in "*el norte.*" In 1881, with the construction of the railroad in Texas, there was a rapid increase in Mexican arrivals, especially to the area around El Paso. During the last decades of the nineteenth century, the movement of Mexicans to and from the southwest was unregulated, so crossing the border did not involve any formalities at all. The largest number of immigrants would arrive in the 1920s, with about 1,400,000 reported in the U.S. Census of 1930.

While most Mexicans worked in traditional occupations of subsistence farming and cattle–raising they had known in Mexico, many were lured by the attraction of new enterprises such as railroad construction north to Kansas, mining in the southwestern states, or cotton farming in Texas. Others were affected by what has been termed the "push and pull" of economic realities. Migrants were pushed out of Mexico by new trade policies of their government, which had a negative impact on their traditional local economies. They were pulled north by the possibility of work and income. Some fared better in the States than they had at home. Without the benefit of the English language, however, Mexican immigrants were often treated harshly and unjustly, and they had little if any recourse to legal assistance. Considered transients and unskilled laborers, they were not admitted as full participants in the capitalist society of the growing nation.

Their neighborhoods—*los barrios*—had no paved roads or streetlights. Located near sewage canals, they were unhealthy environments and contributed to serious health problems among the people. Yet, the *barrio* was not an entirely negative environment for these immigrants, for whom seasonal movements imposed by migrant farm labor meant frequent relocations to strange cities. In the *barrios* of these cities, Mexican immigrants found havens of familiar sounds, tastes, and sights. *Barrio* life reinforced for them a sense of identity, "nurturing a tradition that valued family, nationality, and cultural continuity . . . even as they struggled to deal with an aggressive Anglo mainstream."[12]

Education was a major area of discrimination for Mexican immigrants, posing a key problem for local and state officials. In the first decades of the twentieth century, only about 30 percent of Mexican children attended school, while their population in the Southwest far exceeded that of Anglo–Americans. Because they spoke little or no English, Mexican children were often refused admission to public schools. By 1918, a majority of schools in Texas had an English–only policy. In other areas, Mexican–American children were sent to schools of inferior quality, where funds, materials, and teachers were scarce. Because their children were needed in the fields for farm work, many Mexican parents kept them from going to school. For several reasons, Mexican Americans were alienated by the discriminatory policies in place regarding public education. Attitudes and biases contributed to the belief among some Americans that "Mexicans were disloyal to the United States because of their 'obstinacy' in maintaining their language and culture."[13] To these people on the periphery of a larger society, an exiled community of Religious of Jesus and Mary would offer support and understanding as well as an alternative educational opportunity.

During the Great Depression of the 1930s, Mexicans in the United States became scapegoats to blame for economic shortages and joblessness; they were deported in very large numbers by federal authorities. When World War II broke out, however, with so many men off to battle in Europe and Japan, there was a growing need for farm laborers from Mexico. Known as *braceros*, migrant workers ensured the production of U.S. food supply through the war years. While Mexican immigrants have made an essential and rich contribution to the country, patterns of legal marginalization, deportation, and neglect created an ethnic group that was largely unassimilated and impoverished until well into the twentieth century. Mexican Americans were a class of forgotten citizens and neglected Catholics. Not until the 1960s would they begin to assert themselves as a distinct and visible social ethnic group, asking for a rightful place in the nation's political and cultural life. Theirs is the promise of a vital future as they increase in numbers and in leadership.

Issues and Challenges for the Church

In 1859, Charles Dickens began his novel, *The Tale of Two Cities,* by describing the era in now–famous phrases: "It was the best of times, it was the worst of times, it was the age of wisdom, it was the age of foolishness, it was the epoch of belief, it was the epoch of incredulity, it was the season of Light, it was the season of Darkness." These lines apply well to western society and Christianity in the nineteenth century, when both were rebounding from the devastation of the French Revolution and other European upheavals that followed. For the Catholic Church, it was a period marked by crises, chaos, and confrontation within a world forever changed by Enlightenment and post–revolutionary thought, socialist ideologies, the new sciences, and the promises of democratic and republican political movements, including the new American Republic. This was an era of liberty, equality, and fraternity. The power held previously by monarchs and religious leaders had declined. Change was in the air, and progress in technologies and human sciences seemed assured. People could look forward to a future unshackled by the restraints of the past, whether from political regimes or ecclesiastical prohibitions. But change also brought fear that the stable order of the past might be once again overthrown, leading to confusion and chaos.

Ultramontanism

The culture of modernity, with its emphasis on freedom and liberal ideas, emerged as a symbol of much that seemed antagonistic toward traditional Catholicism. In response to perceived threats to the Church from rationalism, socialism, and various republican movements in Europe, a form of Catholicism emerged to become the hallmark of this era: Ultramontanism. Coined in France, the term refers to going "over the mountains"—to Rome and to the papacy—where Catholics could turn with confidence for the truth, stable authority, and religious freedom in a world of uncertain ideas and unstable political contexts. Confrontation with the modern world marked the Church's official position in the decades prior to the Second Vatican Council (1962–65). Its characteristics included authoritarianism and loyalty to the Pope and to Roman decrees, a Roman style of worship, and fervent participation in sacramental life and devotional practices. This was an era of militant, defensive Catholicism, offering a strong sense of Catholic identity to a besieged community of believers. In many ways, ultramontanism contributed to the papalization of the Catholic Church, where the figure of the pope became central to the way Catholics would define themselves as they defended their faith in an increasingly secularized world. Catholics were those who believed in, and obeyed, the pope. Historian John O'Malley writes, "The cult of a papal personality began to take shape for the first time. Pius IX (pope from 1846 to 1878) . . . boldly advanced the claims of his office through the first papal definition of dogma, the Immaculate Conception, and by being the pope under whom the dogma of papal infallibility was defined."[14]

The challenge to defend the Catholic faith while remaining faithful Americans dominated the ecclesiastical scene in the United States throughout the long nineteenth century. It informed the struggle to "baptize" the American democratic experience of church–state separation and the efforts of some leaders to Americanize the Catholic Church by including more democratic structures. Some wanted to revert to the styles of Catholicism they had known in the "old country" of Ireland or Europe. Bishops and laity often found themselves at odds over issues of lay leadership and stewardship in parishes, or how best to defend and promote education in the faith—through the parish school or the family? With few exceptions, the hierarchy and clergy remained on the defensive when it came to confronting the American republic and its approach to free speech, religious liberty, and democratic patterns of political life. They wanted to protect their immigrant flocks from the dangers of secularism, rationalism, and the other "isms" that could endanger the faith of their flocks, who were often uneducated and unchurched.

Ultramontanism found expression in various forms of popular piety and devotion that characterized Catholic life in the nineteenth and early-twentieth centuries. As one historian has written:

> The ultramontane temper affected church life in the United States from workings of the hierarchy to details of the Catholic home, where a devotional revolution shaped patterns of prayer

and religious sensibility from the middle of the nineteenth century until the dawn of Vatican II. That milieu, which many older
Catholics remember as 'traditional,' was intimately connected
with a specific and very Roman understanding of Church, one
that came to be synonymous with 'Catholic'.[15]

Ultramontane Catholicism showed signs of extraordinary renewed
vigor in Europe, especially in France, where church structures had been
almost completely destroyed in the wake of the French Revolution. Vocations to the priesthood and religious life, almost extinct in France by
1800, grew in unprecedented numbers. New religious congregations
multiplied, especially for women: there were more than 400 French
foundations in the early nineteenth century. The majority of these were
apostolic in nature, dedicated to works of charity and piety and to service
of the poor. Many would be at the forefront of the massive missionary
movement of the century, as women religious accompanied priests to
evangelize Asia and Africa in unprecedented numbers. They answered a
missionary call to North America as well, joining immigrant communities to establish charitable institutions in the New World. The Religious
of Jesus and Mary are one example of this outpouring of missionary zeal
and activity. Founded in 1818 in Restoration France, they had well–established missions in India, Spain, and Canada before coming to the United
States.[16] One of the most visible signs of renewed fervor and vitality could
be seen in the programs of catechetical instruction set up everywhere,
especially in Catholic schools and universities. The result of this massive
effort, as one historian has noted, was that by the mid–twentieth century, Americans were the "best catechized Catholic population in the
history of the church."[17] For the majority of Catholics, and certainly for
those in the United States, the most important and lasting expression of
Ultramontanism was the evolution of a devotional piety that sometimes
became sentimental, anti–intellectual, and politically conservative. This
style of personal piety focused Catholic spirituality on a loving God, as
seen in the devotions to the Sacred Heart, the Immaculate Heart of Mary,
St. Joseph, and the saints. There was a strong reawakening of Marian piety, supported by the nineteenth–century accounts of apparitions of Our
Lady to the poor and young people. The 1858 apparitions of Mary to a
poor and unlettered Bernadette Soubirous in Lourdes, France, confirmed
the papal decree proclaiming the dogma of her Immaculate Conception
four years earlier, helping to make of Lourdes the pre–eminent European
shrine of the era, a renowned mecca for the sick coming to its healing

waters. These expressions of devotion thus served to enhance papal pres-
tige and reinforce fealty to the pope, They also provided immigrant communities with reassurance, a sense of certainty, and justifiable pride.[18]

The Impact of Vatican I (1869 to 1870)

In response to the massive changes issuing from the Enlightenment,
European revolutions, and scientific advances, Pope Pius IX decided in
1869 to call a church council, which came as a surprise. Two tendencies
had arisen as responses to new cultural conditions. One was to examine
the good in the movements and see how the church could be enriched
by them and reconciled with their ideas. The second, a more suspicious
and confrontational position, opposed change and emphasized the importance of taking a strong stand in proclaiming the Catholic doctrinal
message. Pius had already issued his Syllabus of Errors (1864), condemning many recent currents in Catholic intellectual circles, and reaffirming
papal authority against a need to reconcile and adjust to modern civi-
lization. There were 700 bishops in attendance at Vatican I. Most came
from Europe, but there were representatives from all five continents, the
only truly ecumenical council since the fourth century. For the first time,
forty–five bishops attended from the United States. The council was able
to discuss and issue only two decrees before it suddenly adjourned: *Dei
Filius,* on faith and reason; and *Pastor Aeternus,* on the Catholic Church,
emphasizing papal primacy and infallibility. The proclamation of the
Franco–Prussian War meant that the French soldiers guarding the pope
against Italian republican forces were withdrawn. Rome was invaded by
Garibaldi's troops on September 20, 1870. The forces of social change had
charged into the Vatican, and the council was left unfinished.

What most Catholics remember of this council is its definition of
papal infallibility, a doctrine often misunderstood and misinterpreted.
Reflecting the promise of Jesus to be present to the Church in the Spirit
and protecting it from error, ecclesial infallibility has been a consistent
belief of Catholics. In the decree from Vatican I, however, the development of papal primacy includes the "infallible teaching authority" of the
pope alone, without the Church's consent. Put simply, it gives the pope
sole authority to "define doctrine concerning faith and morals." Such
papal pronouncements are believed to be without error and "irreform-
able." While much scholarly ink has been spilled over papal infallibility,

its use has been restricted since its proclamation to clarifying one Marian doctrine, the Assumption (1950). Understood in a positive sense, papal infallibility can be viewed as reassuring the faithful of "God's promise to stay close to and guide the church, in which the bishop of Rome has a special place."[19]

The controversial consequences of Vatican I provided a backdrop for shaping much of Catholic life until Vatican II. Most Catholics knew that the "pope is infallible" even if they had no idea what that really meant! They understood that the pope was a special authoritative figure in Catholicism, a guarantee of unity in a world beleaguered by social upheaval and religious doubt. Ultramontanism, paired with the devotional revolution of this period and Vatican I, transformed the Catholic Church of the nineteenth century. From a decentralized and loose grouping of local churches in communion with Rome, it became a vast, uniform, papal-centered institution. Ironically, Catholicism emerged from a near-death experience early in the century to become a strong religious body, more unified and surer of its identity than ever.

Handing on the Faith: Building a Catholic School System[20]

In 1884, the Third Plenary Council of Baltimore affirmed the bishops' authority in America as strongly as the First Vatican Council had affirmed that of the papacy. More importantly for the ordinary Catholic, it mandated parochial elementary schools as an "absolute necessity" for every parish throughout the nation. This decision created one of the enduring hallmarks of the American Catholic Church, giving special impetus to the vital role of Catholic sisters in the construction of an alternative to the public school. One of the major fears of some nineteenth-century bishops was the leakage of believers from their folds into the secular environment of the American common school. They believed it often reflected a Protestant worldview and supported nativist and anti-Catholic sentiments. Immigrant people were already separated from the cultures and practices of their homelands. For church leaders, it seemed imperative not to alienate them from their religious, ethnic, and family heritage by surrendering their education to the state. All agreed that "Catholic schooling was a necessity if the Church was to survive and flourish in Protestant America."[21] Some episcopal leaders, primarily in the Midwest, supported a compromise approach, with religious education for Catholic children being offered within the public school system. They believed this solution would alleviate the financial toll exacted on pastors and families in building separate schools for their children. Such a moderate view had considerable merit, but the majority of bishops supported the construction of a separate network of schools in their dioceses. How well this was accomplished depended on the individual commitment of bishops and pastors, as well as support of the laity.

The number and population of Catholic parochial schools grew at a pace equal to the taxpayer–funded public elementary schools. In some areas, demand exceeded supply, and school construction was inadequate to the needs. By 1900, there were 3500 Catholic elementary schools, usually under the auspices of the local parishes. Twenty years later, that number more than doubled, with 1.8 million students taught by 42,000 teachers, most of them women religious. Similar, if smaller, growth patterns occurred in secondary education. At the turn of the century, there were fewer than 100 Catholic high schools; by 1920, more than 1500 secondary schools were in operation. It is no exaggeration to say that the Catholic school was one of the "wonders" of immigrant America.

Role of Catholic Teaching Sisters

The major factor on which the development and success of American Catholic schools depended was the availability of teachers. In the mid–nineteenth century, elementary education was the preserve of women, and Catholics found in women religious a large pool of available candidates. Some sisters were native–born or belonged to congregations founded in the United States specifically for education. A major example of such a group was the Sisters of Charity of Emmitsburg, Maryland, founded in 1809 by the convert–saint, Elizabeth Seton. Their numbers in 1900 exceeded 1600, and they "became the framework for the growth of Catholic schooling" in succeeding decades. Twenty or more indigenous congregations were founded by American women; many of them developed unhampered by the constraints of European traditions. As part of the century's massive immigration, Catholic sisters were pouring in from Europe to the United States, providing a much needed workforce for the Church's social services to its immigrant communities. In the 1920's, more than 100 European women's congregations were actively serving as the backbone of a massive social welfare infrastructure. Their schools, hospitals, orphanages, homes for working women and the elderly, and centers of charity of every kind testified to their competence, compassion, and care. As the twentieth century dawned, about 40,000 sisters from more than 400 teaching congregations were staffing parish schools: "sister–teachers were the single most important element in the Catholic educational establishment."[22] Because they were willing to work for low wages, teaching sisters made it possible to keep the costs of Catholic education within a parish's financial means. Their ministry in the schools was a heroic response to an urgent need.

Challenges Faced by Teaching Sisters[23]

As they tried to meet their serious responsibilities as educators in sometimes primitive situations, sisters faced several distinct but interrelated challenges. First of all, how would they maintain the balance between the demands of "Americanizing" the education of immigrants in their care with the need to preserve customs, language, and instructional traditions from their countries of origin? This was a source of tension and misunderstanding at many levels for teachers who were themselves foreigners, along with well–meaning pastors whose ethnic origins differed from those who staffed their schools. A second challenge was one of professional competence. Sisters were expected by local authorities to be of equal competence with their public school counterparts. Until the early twentieth century, however, the staffing of Catholic classrooms took precedence over the training of competent teachers. Sisters with diverse levels of experience often came directly from foreign countries and were assigned to teach with little or no training. Women teachers with college degrees were the exception until after World War I, when programs were set up for certification and professional training. Until then, a "normal school" certificate or some mentoring by more experienced teachers was the best many communities could offer their novices. Yet, Catholic schools grew and flourished, the sisters making up in sacrifice, dedication, and persistence for their limits in professional training.

While there were scattered efforts to provide part–time programs for sisters in a few colleges, it was not until 1941 that Sr. Bertrande Meyers, DC, issued a clarion call for an integrated curriculum that would train women religious to take their place as equals with their secular counterparts in public schools.[24] Her dissertation, "The Education of

Sisters," analyzed the outcome of part–time attendance by sisters at colleges and universities. The results were dismal and discouraging. "In the majority of cases," she wrote, "the experience seems to have destroyed rather than nurtured any love of learning."[25] Three years later, Holy Cross Sister Madaleva Wolff inaugurated a graduate school of theology for the preparation of religion teachers in Catholic schools, at least twenty–five years before women would be admitted in other faculties of theology. At a panel for the National Catholic Educational Association convention in 1949, Wolff presented a paper later published in booklet form as "The Education of Sister Lucy." Her basic premise was that "sisters were treasures, not machines, and that an integrated, well–paced, clearly–designed training program was necessary."[26]

In 1950, Pope Pius XII convoked the leaders of women religious worldwide and issued a mandate for improving sisters' professional qualifications, calling for changes in antiquated customs and adaptations in dress and customs. Juniorates and other educational endeavors were gradually integrated into initial formation programs for young sisters, especially in larger communities. These were the seeds of the Sister Formation Conference (SFC), founded in 1954 to promote cooperation among congregations. Its founder is generally acknowledged as Sr. Mary Emil Penet, IHM (1916–2001). While attending the teacher education session at the National Catholic Education Association (NCEA) Conference in 1952, Penet galvanized some in the group with her call for integrated sister education. She asked for a committee of volunteers to initiate a national survey of pertinent data on the topic from religious congregations. This group became the core of the Sister Formation Conference, divided into six regional areas. While the primary focus was to promote programs for teaching sisters, the group recognized an equal need for sisters in nursing and social work. As it evolved, the SFC was recognized for its integration of the spiritual and intellectual training needed to respond to modern needs, a preparation equal to that of their secular counterparts, while adhering to American teacher–training standards. In 1954, the Conference began to publish the influential *Sister Formation Bulletin*, a major tool of communication and grassroots education for about 400 congregations. Four years later, it reported over 4500 subscribers in 3700 countries. This collaborative self–evolving effort, the work of sisters themselves, laid the foundation for post–conciliar efforts among women religious.[27]

On November 24, 1956, a sisters' committee of general and provincial superiors of pontifical communities gathered in Chicago to discuss the formation of a national conference. By unanimous vote, the Conference of Major Superiors of Women (CMSW) was launched. Its purpose was three-fold: to promote the spiritual welfare of the women religious; to ensure greater efficacy in their apostolates; and to foster closer cooperation among all sisters with the hierarchy, clergy, and Catholic associations. A year later, more than 300 congregations of sisters were members of these conferences and programs. Thanks to this period of visionary leadership and creative formation programs, American sisters were primed for change more than a decade before Vatican II. As a group, they were better prepared than many of their lay peers to undertake the reform and renewal the council called for. By the 1960s, many sisters had been educated in secular universities. Most were receiving college degrees as a matter of course in their forma-tion programs. A challenging decade later, sisters were learning from new feminist movements and burgeoning civil rights and peace groups. They gradually confronted the need to redefine themselves in the face of global and ecclesial transformation. In some instances, renewal became radical-ization, as sisters joined others on picket lines of protest, even going so far as choosing imprisonment as a form of witness. The impact of the civil rights and anti–war movements, as well as liberation and feminist theolo-gies, was for many sisters significant and transformative.

The third major challenge to teaching sisters was a recurring call to adaptive change. When they first arrived, women religious often had to adapt their customs and constitutions to situations that differed widely from their European contexts. If they were to establish themselves successfully in a democratic, secular republic, they needed to abandon former patterns and customs. In some instances, communities faced the challenge of competition from other congregations for resources (includ-ing the best potential candidates), advantageous situations for academies and schools, and the financial support of benefactors. Pastors who fa-vored a certain teaching congregation might easily dismiss one group already in place and invite another to take over the school. In a very real sense, the teaching sisters' security in a parish could be tenuous. Their decision to leave parish schools was at times dictated by the whims of temperamental prelates or pastors.

Of all the problems facing Catholic educators, however, the most consistent and serious was the issue of financial support. Struggling pastors were eager to have teaching sisters, but sometimes they had no proper residences or schools for them. Sisters were often temporarily housed with another community or in a former rectory. They also found themselves in primitive teaching conditions. Until classrooms were available, there might be hundreds of children to teach in church basements or temporary locations without books or desks. Sisters managed on very low wages; in some instances, they received no remuneration for services other than board and room. Throughout the twentieth century, issues of debt and insufficient funds plagued women's congregations, especially those with smaller numbers, foreign headquarters, and less influential establishments. Nonetheless, the school system developed by sisters' labors became the envy of the Catholic world. Their lives and service were admired, attracting large numbers of young women as candidates, for whom the religious life was a highly respected calling. Moreover, it offered them social status and a respectable profession, along with a meaningful vocation in a universe of need.

Challenges of Vatican II and Beyond

Enrollment in Catholic parochial schools climbed through two generations until the mid-1960s, when it reached a peak of 4.5 million elementary students, with over one million registered in secondary schools. Demographic and socio-cultural changes affected the nation and Church, as more affluent Catholics moved into suburbs with high-quality public or private schools. Enrollment figures in Catholic schools declined steadily, as did the number of teaching sisters. The need to hire lay faculty grew, resulting in higher costs for pastors. These issues coincided with the Second Vatican Council called by Pope John XXIII (1881–1963), inviting the Church into a journey of theological rediscovery and pastoral renewal that he called its "new springtime." Vatican II offered a message that was "traditional, while at the same time radical, prophetic while . . . soft-spoken."[28] Phrases like "*aggiornamento*" (updating) and "return to the sources" became part of Catholic vocabulary, especially for women religious. They pointed to deep and transformative change, which the sisters were more than ready to embrace. "It has been said that John XXIII opened the windows of the church with Vatican II, but American sisters were already there and burst through the door ahead of most priests, male religious, and laity."[29]

The number of sisters in the United States reached its peak of nearly 200,000 in 1965, just as the Council was adjourning. Their specific apostolic ministries in the church, however, remained fairly static and institutional, dedicated to teaching, nursing, or pastoral care. They had focused creative energies on the *quality* of their service and concentrated more on formal professional education than before, resulting in a competent and highly-trained corps of women religious at the time of the Council. Sandra Schneiders has suggested that the combination of theological and liturgical renewal movements in the 1940s and 1950s, along with the impact of Vatican II and socio-cultural events, such as the assassinations of political leaders and the student anti-war and civil rights movements, contributed to the renewed prophetic character of apostolic religious life. These events, together with the emergence in the seventies of a new wave of feminism, helped redefine for women religious the meaning and expression of their lives and service. A deeper understanding emerged that the primary object of their service was the people they served, not the institutions. They came to see themselves as disciples of Jesus called primarily to share the good news of his life and message, especially to the poor.[30] With a growing awareness of the "universal call to holiness" and the priesthood of all the faithful, ministerial opportunities for lay women offered attractive alternatives to consecrated life in community. As Catholic sisters shaped another vision of their role in the late twentieth century, the economic impact on their institutions was significant. The post-conciliar years resulted in a massive exodus of sisters from stable Catholic institutions. For teaching sisters, the numbers paint a stark picture. In 1950, over seventy percent of teachers in Catholic schools were sisters; three decades later, they represented only twenty percent of elementary school teachers in the system. While the increased presence of a trained laity was welcomed by many, the decline in sisters' numbers required significantly higher wages for lay faculty. Schools that had served almost all children in a given parish at nominal tuition were forced to increase fees, limiting the number of families who could afford a Catholic education. The center of gravity in parish life had shifted from the school to other activities.

The following chapters develop how the Religious of Jesus and Mary served the Church faithfully through many changes, challenges, and hardships. They helped transform a nation of immigrant American children into good citizens and faithful Catholics. Their parish schools and academies shared in the shaping of an American Catholic ethos, preparing women and men of faith to serve a secular society with the skills and competence they needed. In the heady period following the Second Vatican Council, they learned that the task of weaving hope in changing

times required a painful but life–giving surrender of long–cherished patterns, styles, and fabrics woven into their past. Above all, it mandated a
gradual transformation of the weavers themselves. That call to ongoing
conversion by a pilgrimage into the unknown challenged them to move
beyond boundaries and to grow as weavers of hope for a new century.

2

Mission to the United States

First Foundations

The Congregation from 1877 to 1947[31]

In the panorama of religious life, where did the Congregation of Jesus and Mary find itself during its first seventy years of existence in the United States? What was the geographical and cultural world in those critical years that saw the beginnings and growth of its presence in this nation? When the founding sisters arrived, it had been only forty years since their foundress's death. Many sisters from the first generations could recall the early years of the Congregation in France. They were collecting documents and oral memories for what would become the initial history of the Congregation, published in Lyon in 1896.[32] As the Congregation entered its eighth decade, what issues, concerns, and challenges did it face? Who were the congregational leaders, and how did they relate with the sisters they had sent to the New World? More importantly, who were these intrepid missionaries, and what did they experience as they undertook new apostolic communities in the non–Catholic and secular world that was the United States? This chapter explores these questions through the stories of the first mission foundations and the women who gave them life in a nation of diverse people, languages, and customs.

The Congregation's process of adapting to new situations had been underway since 1842, when the first group of missionaries arrived in Agra, India. They were little prepared for the climates, peoples, religions, and cultural patterns they encountered, which were unlike any they had known in France. Moreover, they realized that for their own survival as well as their mission, they needed to change. Before the Religious of Jesus and Mary came to North America, successive General Chapters in France had already made changes to their religious habit, customs, and daily schedules, asking for modifications to the Constitutions "because of difficulties experienced in India." One of these was a perception of class distinctions and titles for the sisters, which seemed to distance them from people.[33] Another change to their constitutions and "way of proceeding" took place in 1890, when a decree from the Holy See addressed freedom of conscience in matters of confession for religious orders and congregations. Earlier editions of Constitutions had an Ignatian–inspired rule entitled "Of Direction," by which a sister was able to choose a spiritual director within the community, with whom she met to "reveal her conscience" and to discuss her spiritual, community, and apostolic life.[34] To prevent abuse, the decree forbade superiors from interfering with sisters in conscience matters or inviting such confidences from their subjects. The rule of spiritual direction disappeared from subsequent editions of the Constitutions. Its spirit remained in the monthly interviews sisters had with superiors and the visitations of their Superiors General and Provincial.

Another novelty introduced by the Holy See early in the twentieth century permitted nuns to receive daily communion, an uncommon practice in many religious communities. By the end of the nineteenth century, the question of temporary vows became a topic for Chapter discussions; until then, at their first profession, sisters made vows for life in most cases. In 1890, the General Chapter made the following determination: "Given the precarious [political] situation of our time and the challenges of knowing and forming subjects in just two years, along with vocational uncertainty in some cases," they would present to the Archbishop of Lyon the proposal to make final vows only "after probation of ten years." First profession was for two years, renewable for two periods of three years. Eventually, a period of five years became the norm for temporary profession, followed by profession for life. Wearing a ring after perpetual profession began early in the twentieth century, after the French Law of Associations (1901) required the secularization of all teaching sisters, and occasioned a massive dispersion of sisters from France to many other countries, including the United States. The ring may have been a safeguard against unwanted male attention. For the

Religious of Jesus and Mary in France, this was a devastating time: more than 100 choir religious, auxiliary sisters, and novices were sent to various European countries. Two of the exiles, M. St. François de Sales Bertrand (1862–1924) and M. St. Augustin (Marthe) Ferbeyre (1854–1926), came to the States, arriving in New York in 1903.[35] This political–religious crisis in France provided the original impulse for the Congregation to open its first house in Rome in 1895. In 1902, congregational leaders transferred the headquarters to Rome.

Challenges and Difficulties

With the promulgation of the Code of Canon Law in 1917, the Church officially acknowledged the vowed commitment of apostolic women as "religious life." That meant setting in place a more homogenous and regulated lifestyle than in earlier times, one that emphasized the importance of cloister, common life, and closely guarded ways of relating with the world. The openness and flexibility of the founding years gave way to a "template" of accepted structures for apostolic women religious that were determined by ecclesiastics in curial offices. While making necessary changes required by the new Code, the Religious of Jesus and Mary continued to face challenges arising from missionary expansion and corresponding cultural adaptations. This in turn affected the self–understanding of the Congregation and of its relationship to multiple political, religious, and socio–cultural situations. Likewise, it propelled changes in structures that had supported the mission at its beginnings.

As they sought to make Jesus and Mary known in nations that were not French, Catholic, or even Christian, missionaries found it necessary to adapt and change as circumstances dictated. Such flexibility assured the growth and vitality of the Congregation, with the sisters finding themselves transformed by new lands, peoples, and ways they came to know. In some situations, the Religious of Jesus and Mary found it difficult to adapt. They tended to identify with the European roots from which they had come. The continental model of teaching girls in urban boarding schools area was the default mode for the Religious of Jesus and Mary, even as they undertook other educational ministries in rural situations and in parish schools. As their mission developed in the northeastern United States, the sisters maintained the ideal of directing boarding schools for "young ladies" like those in Europe and Canada,

while remaining faithful to parish–centered missions that were flourishing and numerous. In later years, emerging from an experience of forced
exile, the sisters coming to the American Southwest developed more flexible and diverse opportunities for education and Christian formation to
Mexican communities on the margins.

For superiors general of this period, there were challenges of every
kind. These included the ongoing problem of erratic communication
across vast distances; disturbing political developments in various regions; difficulties with bishops and local pastors; formation and education of the sisters; and, not least, concerns for the health and well–being
of the sisters in unfamiliar circumstances. Until World War II, there were
constant requests for expansion to new places, but where to find the personnel? Because of hardships suffered from the two World Wars, many
plans for the Congregation and its provinces were deferred in hopes of
better times. A turbulent nineteenth century became a tumultuous twentieth century; sisters in some provinces endured the trials of civil war
and anticlerical persecution. Financial worries were never absent. Travel
over long distances improved with the expansion of railway systems in
Europe, India, and North America. During the founding years, personal visits from the superior general or her assistants were unusual and
unregulated. With time, the evolution of modern technologies like the
telegraph, telephone, and airplane facilitated travel and communication
between the provinces and the general leadership in France or Rome.

On the ecclesiastical scene, major superiors had to deal with church
authorities whose ideas about how sisters should live and serve sometimes
conflicted with rules and customs of the Religious of Jesus and Mary. As
a pontifical congregation with Ignatian characteristics, autonomy and
self–governance were prized traditions. Its authority structure was centered on a superior general, who appointed province leaders and whose
approval was required for major provincial decisions. This created occasional difficulties with bishops, who found it problematic in their own
decision–making to await permissions from Europe. A recurring example
of their different priorities concerned the sisters' teaching of boys, not allowed by their constitutions. Modeled on European principles of education, the Congregation's rules mandated that the sisters limit themselves
to girls' education. Their reluctance to teach boys in the American mission caused occasional difficulties in local parishes and even triggered the
community's withdrawal from some schools. Clearly, the bishops were
concerned about the faith and schooling of young boys as well as girls,

given the dearth of teaching priests or brothers. For many struggling pastors of North America, separating children by gender was a luxury they could not afford, especially when it came to elementary education. With special permissions, the Religious of Jesus and Mary did welcome boys and fostered many a religious and priestly vocation by doing so.

Fidelity to the founding inspiration in new apostolic circumstances sometimes required allowing for cultural differences and abrogating certain points of the Rule, never an easy decision. The question facing the general leadership was how to preserve the Congregation's identity in situations that demanded flexibility. In her Christmas letter to the Canadian provincial in 1881, the superior general stressed this point: "The houses must be set up according to our rule. Otherwise, our Congregation will not be recognizable."[36] If the General Chapter report for 1886 indicated that the territories of Canada and the United States were doing "*très bien*," it also noted that the strict rules of enclosure and going out had to be relaxed in those same places. The sisters were "to conform themselves to the customs of those countries when the diocesan ordinaries so determine."[37] Some bishops must have been making noises! Geographical distances in the Congregation were contributing factors to tensions between the center (generalate in Europe) and the periphery (the missions). The challenge to the general superiors was balancing the need for strong, centralized leadership while allowing provincial leaders to exercise autonomy in the governance of their mission territories. Misinformation and misunderstandings created stress, especially when important decisions were made at a distance of several thousand miles without real experience of what was happening "on the ground."

Minutes of General Chapters and General Council meetings, along with lively exchanges of letters between superiors general and provincials, throw some light on the first seventy years for the sisters in the States. These documents reveal numerous pleas for sisters from bishops and pastors. From the American mission, there are reports of plans to build and/ or expand; requests to borrow funds or spend them, to move to new cities and towns; and always, pleas for more sisters to meet the ever–growing needs of swelling immigrant populations. The hopes and concerns of these times reveal the ardent zeal of superiors to make foundations that would glorify God, "make him loved and served as much as we are able" and help the people wherever the sisters were.[38] But it is likewise clear that for the founding leaders, there was a desire to "establish ourselves" in large urban situations where there were better resources, more affluent

families, and possibilities of setting up girls' boarding schools. This form
of educational service had become the preferred educational ministry of
the Congregation in other countries, including the mission in India. The
same hopes were expressed for the American mission. Rather than focus
on smaller towns and rural situations, leaders believed it was important
to make foundations in urban centers in the United States, as the Congregation had done in other nations.

The dream of a house in New York City took shape as early as 1885,
when the possibility of a parish school on the Upper East Side seemed
to offer what the provincial hoped for. It would provide a convent where
sisters traveling from Canada or Europe might be able to stay. It would
also be a means of contact with young women whose education and social status would provide vocations to the "first class" of choir professed.
Finding appropriate sites for communities was an ongoing concern for
the leaders, as was the challenge of obtaining funds and personnel. These
matters came up regularly in correspondence with the superiors in Lyon,
as well as repeated invitations to "come and see" the vast new territory
into which the Religious of Jesus and Mary had established themselves
as missionaries.[39]

Rapid Growth, New Life

Despite some difficulties, the new mission grew and multiplied. The
report of the General Chapter of 1903 marveled at the work done in the
first six foundations in the States. Sisters were teaching and catechizing
more than 3000 children. The report exclaimed: "What a vast field that
God our good Father has entrusted to his daughters and workers in
Jesus and Mary"![40] In the spring of 1911, at the end of her visit to the
houses of Canada and the United States, Reverend Mother St. Clare
Bray held a three-day meeting with provincial and local superiors.
The set of "recommendations" noted in the minutes reveals the issues
discussed in these sessions. There is clearly a realization of the need to
adapt and adjust to the North American style while remaining faithful
to the spirit and rule of their common life. Many of the suggestions pertain to convent discipline and good order, yet stress the importance of
charity and moderation for good leadership. Some of the major points
include the following:

- The need for superiors to care for the sisters, to meet with them monthly; when possible, to offer weekly interviews for the younger sisters;

- A call for respect among the sisters, charity to all, and abstaining from rash judgments;

- A reminder that sisters should not be going out to shop or visit, except for serious reasons, and should limit their use of the tramway;

- The need to maintain the "family spirit" among the sisters; they should refrain from fault–finding and appealing to the bishop concerning local matters;

- Preserving the "pious custom" of a visit from family and/or correspondence only once during Lent;

- Ongoing education for the teaching sisters, with lessons in pedagogy;

- Limiting later hours for bedtime; not allowing the sisters to visit other communities.

The discerning reader will guess that some of these items had already become problematic. One interesting recommendation concerns the subject of what today is "vocation promotion" in the schools, including criteria for judging who would be an apt candidate for the novitiate. The sisters were to require that a prospective applicant be from a "respectable" and good family; that she be pious, of sound judgment, and good health. In cases where the young woman needed more "refining" and time, allowance would be made for a one–or two–year stay in one of the rural houses of Canada before sending her to the novitiate in Sillery.

Several recommendations referred solely to the houses in the States. Because their residences were generally urban and lacked space for large gardens, the sisters had permission to take walks near their convents early in the morning. In New York, until a country house became available, sisters might take boat rides to get fresh air. They were, however, to be polite and appropriately behaved on these occasions! As a concession to the missionaries, they had permission to spend holidays in Canada after five or six years in the States. We see an example of forward–looking general leadership early in the twentieth century in the bold plan to set up a province house of studies in Washington, DC, near the newly founded Catholic University of America, where a Sisters' College was offering degree programs and summer courses for women religious from teaching congregations. In October, 1913, the General Chapter discussed this "work of the highest importance," which M. St. Clare was eager to promote. "To insure the continuance of these courses and to promote a comprehensive pedagogical formation, the University [Catholic University of America] has purchased a large piece of property that could be subdivided into lots where different congregations could build their own houses. In this way, the religious could continue to live in community while pursuing their studies." Each congregation would assume responsibility for the building construction.

The capitulars discussed the possibility and agreed that "we accept under the condition that funds be found in order not to deplete the finances of the province."[41] Plans were made to set up a house of studies; in April 1914, the General Council discussed having the novitiate nearby. The minutes indicate that an unnamed trusted friend advised against such a move. While the councilors believed that "at a future time there might be advantages to such a move," they decided to remain with their original decision to transfer the novitiate to Washington.[42] That decision never materialized. It would seem that the outbreak of World War I (July 1914) and its consequences diverted the attention of the Congregation to other urgent matters. Finances and administrative concerns of the growing province may have also been issues. In April 1915, M. St. Croix (Artemise) Tanguay, the provincial in Québec, wrote to Rev. Thomas Edward Shields, director of the project, postponing the Congregation's plans "for another year." The reasons given were "the state of affairs in Europe" and the installation of a new heating system at the provincial house. In 1917, a few sisters did attend the Sisters' College and summer school in Washington, affirmed as a "necessary and indispensable preparation" for their teaching profession.[43] With time, it seemed more practical to send sisters to Fordham University in New York, where the community had houses. The project of building a house of studies in the nation's capital was left unrealized until decades later in 1955, when the provincial house relocated to Maryland.

Before the Great War, statistics of the Congregation were promising: more than 1300 sisters were serving in sixty houses on three continents. Among the thousands of students in their schools, about 6000 were in the United States. Describing the growth and dynamism of the mission in New England for its first four decades, a contemporary writer painted a bright picture:

Today our Congregation counts ten houses in the United
States—boarding schools, colleges (girls' academies), parochial
schools where boys and girls muster by thousands, the boys
meek as lambs with the Sisters . . . The record of these forty years
has been a bright one . . . Perhaps the Children's Mass on Sunday
morning would impress a stranger most . . . To see the great
church filled with hundreds of children; girls on one side, under
the care of the sisters; boys on the other, in the charge of more
sisters—or, in some places, of Brothers; to hear nearly a thousand sweet childish voices — they are naturally musical—sing
the praises of God and Our Lady, is surely a delight to all who
love Christ's little ones.[44]

Later in that same text, the author mentions the ongoing challenge
of bilingual education. In 1920, of the 100 Religious of Jesus and Mary
serving in the States, seventy–six were "foreign–born," and not always
fluent in English. State school boards, along with more demanding pastors, required that the major and essential subjects be taught in English,
and the sisters were expected to be proficient in both French and English,
making for "heavy demand upon the staff." Writings such as these open a
window into the world of these missionaries, their concerns and desires
to live as fully as possible their consecrated life in unfamiliar and sometimes unfriendly surroundings. They also reveal that the primary focus
for leaders was to maintain charity, unity, and affection among the sisters
and communities for which they were responsible, while promoting the
educational ministries to which the sisters were sent, and protecting their
health as well as the interests of the Congregation.

In 1931, as the United States entered its years of Depression, the
Religious of Jesus and Mary gathered again in General Chapter. They
listened to reports from mission areas, and took first steps toward the
introduction of the foundress' cause for beatification. The Canadian
report (including its seven foundations in the United States, all in New
England) noted with satisfaction that devotion was growing toward their
foundress, Claudine Thevenet, among the sisters, students, and families;
many favors and graces were attributed to her intercession. Statistics of
the province were impressive in their vitality and number: 370 choir-
professed, 145 auxiliary sisters, sixty in the novitiate, and eleven sisters
serving in Europe/India. In their several boarding and parish schools, the
Religious of Jesus and Mary were teaching 7300 students.

Tapestry of Three Cultures

In addition to the New England foundations, by 1931 the mission included a newly established "American Province." With two New York
houses — St. John's in the Bronx, and Thevenet Hall, Highland Mills—it
had a total of thirty-seven choir professed, eight auxiliary sisters, two
novices, and two postulants, serving the needs of close to 1000 students.
The formation of this province fulfilled one desire of some congregational
leaders and missionaries to move beyond identification with the French
language and Canadian culture of the origins and grow into a truly
"Americanized" community. That endeavor proved to be a difficult and
long-term trial. Despite various efforts to establish an English-language
province in New York, the Religious of Jesus and Mary were perceived as
foreigners, with their French-Canadian origins, language, culture, and
religious expressions. Attracting vocations and keeping them was often
an uphill challenge. Patterns of growth were strongest in the New England
houses, where the Congregation had first established itself and had the
backing—with personnel and finances — of the Canadian Province. The
small American Province struggled to attract vocations in a geographical
area where larger and well-established congregations were better known
and supported by diocesan authorities. Unless and until they could stand
on their own, the Religious of Jesus and Mary depended on the influx of
new members from New England and/or Canada.

By the 1920s, Religious of Jesus and Mary in Mexico had become
exiles, refugees of the persecution during that country's twenty-year
revolution (1910 to 1929). Founded from Spain in 1902, the sisters ran
an independent school in Merida, Yucatan, for over a decade. They
also directed several parochial schools in that region. By 1904, the
Congregation had made a foundation in Mexico City, but it closed in
a few years due to religious persecution, reopening in 1921. For two
years (1924 to 1926), the novitiate was set up there, but the political
situation brought severe financial difficulties and anticlerical uprisings.
These erupted into full-blown civil war in 1926. The Spanish provincial
decided to send the sisters to Argentina, Cuba, Spain, and the United
States. Thanks to kind benefactors and the support of exiled Mexican
Jesuits whom the sisters knew, a request was made for hospitality in El
Paso, Texas, where the novitiate was transferred in the summer of 1926.
Despite its fragile and uncertain beginning, this small but heroic com-
munity would flourish on the southwestern border, where sisters offered

educational ministry and pastoral service to Hispanics in various towns and missions, eventually expanding to include establishments in New Mexico and California. In 1938, the four houses of the Southwest became the "Hispanic–Mexican" independent province, which continued until 1955, when they were absorbed into the newly formed Mexican province. Five years later, almost all the southwestern houses formed an autonomous Western–American province.

Congregational Leadership: 1877 to 1947[45]

For the Congregation's leaders, the situation in North America for the first half of the twentieth century foreshadowed the multicultural, diverse ethnic patterns that came to characterize the situation of Religious of Jesus and Mary in the United States. It made for a period of growth, struggle, union, and separation that marks the "missionary phase" of the Congregation. Faithful to a tradition already well in place for the Congregation, the seven Superiors General who encouraged and supported the mission of the United States in its first seventy years were exemplary in their courageous leadership. This next section provides an overview of their individual contributions to the development of the Institute, with emphasis on the North American situation.

M. St. Pothin (1867–85) and M. St. Eulalie (1885–91)

The fourth superior general, M. St. Pothin (Antoinette Cholle), had lived for ten years with the foundress and was an eyewitness to the turbulent events in the city of Lyon during the 1830s and 1840s. As one of the first sisters sent to the Spanish mission in 1850, she was familiar with the challenges and difficulties of missionary life, as well as its joys and accomplishments. Faithful to the founding inspiration, she was responsible for enlarging the Congregation's mission territory—with houses in India, Spain, Canada, and England — to include the United States. Soon after her election, the Congregation celebrated its golden jubilee (1868). Statistics prepared for this event revealed the growth and extent of the institute. There were at that time 332 Religious of Jesus and Mary in five countries worldwide, serving in twenty-three communities.

M.St.Pothin wanted to preserve the founding spirit of the early years, which she believed might be dissipated by vast distances and difficulties in communication. Shortly after her election, she appointed as provincial of Canada the intrepid, strong, and capable M. St. Cyrille Reynier (1823–1904), who became the founding provincial of the U.S. mission. M. St. Pothin was careful to select provincials who knew the true spirit of the origins and would maintain that spirit wherever they were in leadership. She consecrated the Congregation to the Sacred Heart, one of its traditional devotions; she encouraged all the sisters to study Claudine Thevenet's life and virtues. As one who knew the foundress firsthand, she inspired the sisters with her recollections. In a letter to M. St. Cyrille written on July 30, 1879, denying a request to open a new house in Canada, she recalled:

> I witnessed the problems our founding Mothers had, especially the first of them . . . How our worthy M. St–Ignace suffered! Her zeal had led her to take on this work for poor children and she never gave up, despite the difficulties. Her confidence was in God who sustained her; her intrepid soul never weakened . . .[46]

M. St.Pothin died on February 15, 1885, diminished by age and illness but admired for her fidelity to community exercises to the end. Her death brought to a close the first generation of leaders directly formed by Claudine Thevenet.

Having made profession in 1852 and served for several years in the Spanish mission, M. St. Eulalie (Basilide Marcorelle) de Roquefort was a refined and cultured woman known for her common sense, energy, and educational gifts. She returned to Lyon in 1870 and became mistress of novices until her election in 1885 as superior general. She oversaw the foundation of apostolic centers in Europe, especially in Spain and England. She also approved the expansion of the North American mission to include several new houses in New England. The problems she faced were largely concentrated on the internal life of the Congregation. Sensing that she did not have sufficient skills and energies to confront these and other complex issues in an international situation, she refused reelection in 1891, at the end of her first term. M. St. Eulalie continued to serve as a local superior in France and then returned to Spain, where she died in Barcelona on October 27, 1910.

Mother St. Cyrille (1891 to 1903)

The American mission owes its original fire to M. St. Cyrille (Irène) Reynier, a fascinating woman who had inherited the leadership qualities of her father, an officer in Napoleon's army. He resisted her desire to enter religious life. Trying to convince him of her call to the Religious of Jesus and Mary, she wrote: "I've never met these sisters, but they have missions in India. Since I can't serve in the military, I want to be a missionary." She probably could have commanded an army or a kingdom without difficulty, and she would exercise leadership at various levels in the Congregation with foresight, intelligence, kindness, energy, and boldness. She entered the Congregation in Lyon in 1845, at the age of twenty–two. As a novice, she had asked to be sent to the new mission of India, but superiors thought it best to defer her request. After profession, she taught in Lyon and Rodez, France. She did become a missionary, not to India, but to Spain, where she was the local superior in Tarragona. In 1869, M. St. Cyrille sailed to Canada as the second provincial appointed to the Canadian houses, replacing M. St. Cyprien (Rose) Eynac, who had died a year earlier. For the next twenty–two years, she administered a growing number of ministries in two very different nations.

In 1870, shortly after her arrival in Canada, she transferred the provincial house from Lauzon (Lévis) to the newly constructed convent and boarding school at Sillery. Tenacious and forward–looking, M. St. Cyrille saw that the future of the mission depended on its success with the middle classes of Québec. Within a few years, thanks to the quality and labors of the teaching staff, the convent school at Sillery had acquired a well–earned reputation for instruction in the classics and humanities, in civility, and in the Christian formation of women who would contribute to both church and society. When she wanted to move the novitiate from Lauzon in a rural area to the provincial house at Sillery, as the Constitutions indicated, M. St. Cyrille met with resistance from the local pastor, Rev. Honoré Routier, who believed that the "mother house" and novitiate should remain in Lauzon, site of the first Canadian mission. In fact, both houses were taking novices, which caused some clerical consternation. Some priests and a bishop wrote letters of complaint to M. St. Pothin, who counseled moderation, tolerance, and flexibility. M. St. Cyrille felt that the autonomy of the Congregation and fidelity to its Constitutions were threatened. In a letter to her, the superior general admonished: "You are too hasty, too rigid . . . Prudence is needed! We must not lose the good graces of Fr. Routier, who has been very helpful to us. Everyone is on our case because of this! Please help the foundation house to flourish . . ."[47]

With customary directness, M. St. Cyrille responded by recounting her own problems with the same pastor. She had found life in Lévis difficult to begin with. Her conflicts with Routier made it hard for her to lead the new communities as she saw fit:

> He thinks that I want to move all the sisters [to Sillery]. O Reverend Mother, how good God is to have saved me from the misfortune of being married! These men are impossible! To make peace, one always has to bow to their wishes, and in the process, one's conscience can be compromised.[48]

Headstrong, determined, and energetic, M. St. Cyrille never suffered fools gladly, nor did she find it easy to negotiate with some church leaders, despite the complicated nature of the missionary situation. With time, the arc of history bent toward the provincial's wishes. Within months of the death of the problematic pastor, in July of 1873, she was able to transfer the novitiate to Sillery.[49]

With a true missionary's heart, M. St. Cyrille began to send sisters from Canada to serve in India, France, and England. The foundation in the States was simply another expression of her desire to extend the Congregation's mission wherever God's glory and the needs of people seemed to call. Fearless and tenacious in the face of many trials, she was remarkable as well for her compassion towards the poor and sick, her prayerfulness, and an original approach to many problems. Little wonder that the General Chapter of 1891 unanimously elected her to become the sixth superior general of what had grown into a global religious family. Due to the political troubles in France, M. St. Cyrille opened houses in Switzerland and Austria for the exiled sisters, as well as a first community in Rome (1895), which moved several times in a few years. One can only imagine her anguished decision to close the foundation house at Fourvière as a result of the repressive French laws against teaching congregations. As a consequence of their expulsion from France in 1902, M. St. Cyrille had to send the sisters off in many directions, with the hope that they might someday return to France and take up the apostolate begun by the foundress and her first companions. The General Council moved definitively to Rome that year.

Undaunted by the setback, M. St. Cyrille accepted a new foundation in Mexico, entrusting it to the province of Spain. She realized an earlier dream to have a house in New York with the founding of the women's residence on 14th Street in New York City. Within another year, the sisters were opening a convent and school in the parish of St. John's, in the Bronx. M. St. Cyrille continued to lead the Congregation with vision and energy at the age of eighty. Still, the stress and fatigue of years had taken their toll on her health. Having served two terms, the valiant woman refused a third, saying, "It would be cruel to elect someone as old as this!" She undertook a return journey to Sillery after the Chapter, where she hoped to spend her remaining years. Landing in New York, she visited 14th Street, and then went on to greet the communities in Fall River and St. Charles, Providence, where she rested for a few days before her journey to Canada. While there, on June 3, 1904, she suffered a stroke during Mass that left her paralyzed on one side. Her death on June 15 in one of the communities she founded seemed fitting. It is no exaggeration to give this remarkable missionary the title of North American foundress, a woman whose vision, courage, and bold enterprises marked the Religious of Jesus and Mary well into the twentieth century.

Mother St. Clare (1903 to 1931)

With the dawn of the twentieth century, the Religious of Jesus and Mary had spread to three continents. With the election of M. St. Clare (Emily) Bray, the first election held in Rome, the General Chapter inaugurated a truly international phase of the Congregation's history. Orphaned as a toddler and raised by her devout Anglican grandparents, Emily Bray grew up in rural Cornwall, England, learning about the Bible, gardens, and agriculture. One of her aunts had converted to Catholicism. In 1865, at the age of twelve, Emily followed her into the Catholic faith, living with her after the death of the grandparents. The aunt lived near the Jesus and Mary Convent in Ipswich, so it was there that the young convert went to boarding school to be educated in letters and to explore her desires for religious life. Admitted as a postulant, she remained in Ipswich, completing her formation there as the only novice, and making profession in 1876. For the next twenty years, the Ipswich Convent would be her home. As a teacher, assistant to a French superior who knew no English, and later as the local superior, she showed a depth of intelligence and insight that led to her appointment in 1899 as novice mistress in Lyon. Elected as a general councilor in 1901, M. St. Clare learned firsthand the trials experienced by the dispersion of the French sisters. She traveled to make a general visit of India, the first of many to the vast country she came to know and love so well, where she undertook ambitious educational projects. As the first superior general of the new century, M. St. Clare embodied a "modern" style of leadership for the next twenty–eight years. A tireless traveler and visionary administrator, she expanded the institute's horizons to take in Mexico, Argentina, Cuba, Ireland, and Germany. She served five terms, all marked by breadth of vision and passionate devotion to education, placing great store in the importance of studies and the professional training of the sisters and teachers. One of her conferences on the teacher's calling, published by the Congregation posthumously, presents her vision of the educational ministry. "The teaching vocation," she wrote, "yields to none in dignity and usefulness. If a cup of cold water given in Christ's name to the thirsty body will not pass without reward, what can we say of a cupful of Living Water brought to a parched and thirsting soul?"[50]

Shortly after her election in 1904, M. St. Clare returned to India to establish there the first college of the Congregation. St. Bede's, in Shimla, was undertaken to offer higher education and teacher training in the Punjab, a ministry that continues today. That same impulse led her two years later to open an international finishing school, *Stella Viae,* on Via Nomentana in Rome. Its aim was to provide a safe and congenial atmosphere for young women who came to study and explore the cultural and religious riches of the Eternal City. She moved the general headquarters to a new property she purchased on Via Flaminia, in what was then a very poor section of Rome. M. St. Clare loved the people, the children, and the various apostolic works the sisters began there. While she had not spent much time in Lyon, she developed a deep interest in and love for Claudine Thevenet and the early history of the Congregation. In 1917, M. St. Clare wrote and published *Cameos,* a brief history in English of the Religious of Jesus and Mary. Encouraging the communities to learn about their foundress and promote her cause, she initiated the beatification process at the General Chapter of 1925 and assigned a Spaniard, Mother Eufemia (Rosa) Mandri, to begin collecting pertinent documents. In her many visits to the Congregation over the years, M. St. Clare spoke warmly of Claudine, brought portrait reproductions to be displayed in communities, and promoted prayer for cures and favors through Claudine's intercession. Recognized within and beyond the Congregation for her remarkable intelligence and leadership, M. St. Clare continued to inspire the sisters to the fullest development of their gifts as educators and women religious. In 1925, despite her tearful protests citing advanced age, she was elected once again to lead the Congregation for the next six years. Finally relieved of that charge in 1931, she became provincial of England and Ireland. While her capacity for work and physical energies diminished with failing health, M. St. Clare insisted on traveling to the Chapter of 1937, which marked the centenary of Claudine's death. While in Rome, she contracted pneumonia and died at the age of eighty–five, in the house on Via Flaminia that she had founded and loved so well. Her memorial prayer card summarizes an extraordinary life and mission:

> A great lover of God, her Congregation and souls, she devoted her whole life and exceptional talents to their service. A pioneer always, her zeal was only equaled by her courage and trust in God . . . She died in harness, as she had always desired, unmindful of self, thinking of others.

At her death, the Congregation had seventy–two educational centers in many parts of the world. To this holy and visionary woman, the mission of North America owed a lasting tribute of gratitude. M. St. Clare saw what it might become, believed in that vision, and helped it flourish and grow.

M. St. Borgia (1931 to 1945) and M. St. Thérèse (1946–1947)

The first Spaniard to be Superior General, M. St. Borgia (Teresa) Mas de Xexas had been a student in the Religious of Jesus and Mary school at San Andrés. She entered the novitiate in Barcelona, but moved on to Lyon, where she made profession in 1893. Her first apostolic mission was at the boarding school and women's residence in Lyon. At the dispersion of the French sisters in 1902, she returned to Spain; a year later, she became superior of the new mission of Yucatan, Mexico. The Mexican political difficulties and religious persecution resulted in the community's move to Havana, Cuba. There she began an educational apostolate and expanded the mission. In 1919, she went to Rome as a general councilor and mistress of novices. Believing the worst of the troubles to be over, she returned to Yucatan once again until her election at the Chapter of 1931.

Mother St. Borgia was another great traveler. Within three years of her election, she had visited most of the Congregation. In 1936, a violent civil war between nationalist and republican factions erupted in her native Spain. This was a conflict that severely affected the Catholic Church and its institutions. Many Religious of Jesus and Mary had to flee their houses in haste, wearing secular dress for fear of reprisals or imprisonment. Some were able to cross into Italy and took refuge at Stella Viae or Via Flaminia, where M. St. Borgia had constructed additions to the buildings to make space for them. Some sisters were welcomed in Lyon, where a small community resided. M. St. Borgia entered her own beleaguered country in disguise to visit sisters who were still there and to plan for their future once the conflicts ceased. A missionary like her forebears, M. St. Borgia continued to send sisters to India, a mission that was rapidly expanding. In the eight years before World War II, twenty-five Religious of Jesus and Mary from several provinces were assigned to various parts of the Indian mission.

She also gave much attention to the "New World," especially the Mexican territory where she had labored. In 1934, she visited El Paso, Texas, where the sisters had taken refuge during the religious persecutions in Mexico. She was pleased to see that what began as a place of temporary exile had become the center of a thriving apostolic work. The sisters had opened a secretarial school in El Paso, tending to the needs of Mexican students coming across from Juarez, Mexico. By 1939, there were communities in San Diego, California, and Carlsbad, New Mexico, along with several summer missions in outlying desert areas. That year M. St. Borgia encouraged the independent growth of the southwest with the canonical erection of the Hispanic–American Province.[51]

During the hazardous years of World War II (1939–45), this zealous leader had to curtail many of her journeys. With anxiety, she followed whatever news came from Religious of Jesus and Mary in various parts of Europe, including the sisters in Germany, whose house in Dresden was completely destroyed by the Allied bombings. These years marked various anniversary celebrations for the Congregation. M. St. Borgia managed to get a pass into Lyon, France, to be with the sisters for these occasions. By the end of the war, her health had weakened. She continued to write to the houses and provinces, reminding the sisters of the importance of the Rule and of their task of education. At the General Chapter of 1946, M. St. Borgia resigned and returned to Spain. She died in Barcelona in July of 1948. She left her mark as a woman who led the Congregation with a steady hand and head in turbulent times.

M. St. Thérèse (Laure) Chapleau was the first North American elected to lead the Religious of Jesus and Mary, becoming the ninth superior general. She had been the assistant to the previous two Mothers General and the local superior of the generalate community. Prior to her apostolic work at the general level, she was provincial of Canada from 1918 to 1926. During those years, M. St. Thérèse founded a much–needed teacher training school (*École Normale*) at Beauceville in Québec. She presided over the founding of the Villa Augustina School in Goffstown, NH, and oversaw a catechetical mission in Chester, NY, near Highland Mills. In 1921, she admitted to postulancy a young musician, Dina Bélanger, known in the community as Mother St. Cécile de Rome, whose mystical experiences revealed a unique vocation. M. St. Thérèse permitted the local superior at Sillery to invite this gifted young sister to write her spiritual autobiography, published after her death as *Canticle of Love*.[52]

As the first post–war congregational leader, M. St. Thérèse laid plans for the celebration of the centenary marking the pontifical approbation of the institute. She visited sisters of the houses in Switzerland and France. The first superior general to travel by air, she took a flight from Paris in May 1947, to begin a visitation of Canada. During that visit, she authorized the separation of the eastern houses in the States to form an independent Franco–American Province. Despite a heart condition, she continued to travel by air, unaware of the danger to her health. On August 11, she boarded a flight back from a visit to Gravelbourg, at the far western reaches of the Canadian mission. She suffered a fatal heart attack on the plane. Stricken in mid–voyage, she died a true missionary, not yet having completed a full year as the general. In her spiritual journal, she had written, "All for my Congregation . . ." Her sudden death was the seal of that self–offering. The following December, a special election was held by correspondence, at which M. Luisa Fernanda (Clementina) Sagnier became the tenth successor to M. St. Ignatius.

Founding Stories and Storied Founders

In 1876, Rutherford B. Hayes became president of the United States, which had a population close to forty million. Colorado was admitted to Statehood. Alexander Graham Bell had just invented the telephone; within several months, it would become a public service. Two years later, Thomas Edison invented the light bulb, transforming night into day and changing the rhythms of life and work for the nation. The Catholic world was still digesting the impact of Vatican Council I, and Pope Pius

IX, aged eighty-six, was in his last year of the longest papacy in history. Leo XIII (1878–1903), his successor, seemed more open to the modern world; he was the first pope to raise awareness of the need for social justice toward workers rather than traditional charity. The next pontiff was Pius X (1903–14), a theological and liturgical conservative; he mandated the revision of Canon Law (1917). Pastorally engaged, Pius promoted First Communion at an early age. The papacy of the scholar–pope Pius XI (1922–39) was marked by the growth of totalitarian movements. Pius issued strong protests against both Communism and Nazism as demeaning to human dignity and violations of basic human rights. He accused the Western democracies of a "conspiracy of silence" in the face of totalitarian regimes. His strong promotion of Catholic Action as a model for lay participation in the Church served as the groundwork for Vatican II.

By the early twentieth century, the Catholic population of the United States had swelled to over four million. There was a growing need for churches, schools, and various social services. Bishops welcomed the arrival of numerous teaching and nursing congregations to provide educational, social, and pastoral services, lending assistance to overworked pastors. At their Plenary Council in 1884, they mandated a Catholic school in every parish, which meant enlisting an army of teachers for the daunting task.[53] In New England, where the Religious of Jesus and Mary undertook their first mission work, a growing Catholic community from diverse ethnic backgrounds was pouring into the region, seeking work in the factories, hoping for a better life and possibilities for their children. They wanted as well to preserve the cultural and religious identities they had known in the lands they had left behind, and they looked to the church for leadership.

For the Congregation and its mission provinces, the new century brought significant changes in leadership, along with the deaths of some pioneer missionaries to the States. The founding provincial, M. St. Cyrille, had resigned as general in 1903 and died a year later on her way to Canada. Her successor, M. St. Clare, made an initial visit to the American missions in the fall of 1904. Earlier that year, the Canadian provincial, M. St. Augustin (Adelaide) Hatschemberg, one of the earliest Religious of Jesus and Mary missionaries in Manchester, NH, died suddenly in New York. Maintaining a vital, growing presence in North America was never without its balance of gains and losses. Moreover, as the mission developed, the first Religious of Jesus and Mary to die on its soil were buried where they had given their lives and service so far from home. Clergy and laity in the communities and schools where they had served would remember these intrepid spiritual leaders with affection.

Diocesan territories were expanding and multiplying. The diocese of Boston was established in 1808. The influx of New England immigrant populations called for the establishment of several other New England dioceses, including Portland (1853), which took in the territories of Maine and New Hampshire. In 1872, the diocese of Providence was created, comprising the whole state of Rhode Island and a portion of southeastern Massachusetts. Manchester, New Hampshire became an independent diocese in 1884; Fall River followed as an autonomous diocese in 1904. When the pioneer Religious of Jesus and Mary arrived in Fall River, Massachusetts, Thomas F. Hendricken, bishop of Providence, was their ecclesiastical superior. In 1881, when the sisters journeyed to serve in Manchester, NH, their first episcopal authority was the bishop of Portland, James A. Healy. These were years of growth, change, and challenge for New England Catholics, their priests and religious, many of whom were fellow immigrants to the United States. This section introduces the founding stories of Religious of Jesus and Mary in New England. It presents their storied founders and leaders whose courage matched their unshakeable trust that God would weave for them a future they would never see.

First Foundation: Notre-Dame-de-Lourdes Parish, Fall River, Massachusetts (1877)[54]

> I left Sillery on December 13, 1876, with Madame St. Benoit, to see about a foundation in the States, as Rev. Mother St. Pothin had requested. We needed a house where we could send those sisters whose health could not withstand the rigors of Canadian winters, but who might be able to offer some service in a milder climate.[55]

This account of the origins in the United States, written by M. St. Cyrille, makes it clear that the Religious of Jesus and Mary came to the United States not in response to an urgent call from the outside, but from their own need for "*survivance*." It had become a matter of survival for the mission; growing numbers of sisters were contracting tuberculosis and other illnesses because of the rigorous climate in Québec. Some had returned to Europe, their constitutions unable to withstand Canadian winters. Having obtained permission from the General Chapter held in the summer of 1876, Mother St. Cyrille decided to make an exploratory visit to Fall River, accompanied by Mme. St. Benoit (Mathilde) Fournier in December of that year. She wanted to make a new foundation "down south" for sisters whose health was too frail to endure harsh Canadian winters but who would be able to minister to the children of the growing numbers of immigrants who were employed in the cotton and wool factories of Fall River, Massachusetts. By the time of the founding, over 30,000 workers labored in more than 100 cotton mills in "Spindle City," situated in the southeastern part of the state. Besides, there were family connections that made Fall River attractive. Madame St. Benoit had parents and a sister, Virginie, living there.[56] The family were well known for their hospitality and outreach to the immigrant community. The provincial and her companion received a warm welcome with the Fournier family, where they stayed on that initial visit. But would they find a welcome in a parish? Bishop Hendricken suggested to the sisters that they first meet with Rev. Paul Adrien de Montaubricq, the French missionary and first priest to serve French Canadians in Fall River. The founding pastor in 1870 of St. Anne Parish, he was unable to receive the community, and discouraged the sisters from making a foundation.

Undeterred, they presented themselves to Rev. Pierre Jean–Baptiste Bédard (1842–84), first pastor of the new parish of Notre–Dame de Lourdes, known already to the Fournier family. A missionary from Montréal, Bédard had bought land and built a wooden church within months of his arrival in 1874. It was situated in Flint Village, a neighborhood of French Canadians employed in several textile mills recently set up in the city. Notre Dame, as it was known, served a mixed population of about 300 Canadian families and over forty families of Irish origin. An enterprising leader with organizational skills, energy, and vision, Bédard labored strenuously to preserve the national spirit and religious customs of his people. He wanted to recreate in his parish a microcosm of French–Canadian parish and culture, especially with regard to education. As one historian has written: "To Bédard and those . . . who shared his convictions, the wish of their neighbors to see the Canadian children quickly learn English in preference to French, and become culturally integrated was the equivalent of denying the value of French–Canadian history and tradition."[57]

Interpreting the visit of the Religious of Jesus and Mary as an answer to prayer, Bédard warmly welcomed the sisters, inviting them to establish themselves in the parish, where he hoped they would help promote his vision and ministry. In a written note to M. St. Cyrille, he promised to give the Religious of Jesus and Mary some of the vast property he owned near the church and to build them a convent on the grounds. He also gave them two pianos, a reed organ, the use of barns on the property, and the offer of regular Masses and spiritual counseling. Clearly, he wanted to impress the sisters to come, and to stay. Early in May 1877, a pioneer trio arrived to take up temporary residence as guests in a house that later was known as the *"petit couvent."*[58] By the end of the month, construction was completed on a new, three-story convent at the corner of Mason and Notre Dame Streets, large enough to house the sisters and the school for the next ten years. On May 31, the founding trio moved into their quarters, eager to begin their mission. Who were these three courageous women?

- M. St. Xavier (Louise Gosselin, 1842–88), aged 35 and professed five years, superior of the mission;

- Mme. St. Benoit (Mathilde Fournier, 1845–89), whose family was known in the parish;

- Sr. St. Sabine (Philomène Marion, 1844–1917), an auxiliary sister who was healed of a serious illness after she promised Our Lady to spend her life in the missions if restored to health.

Sr. St. Sabine's name is included in the list of foundresses of several mission houses in New England from 1877 through 1889: Fall River; Woonsocket, Rhode Island; Manchester, New Hampshire; Providence, and Centreville in Rhode Island. An unsung hero, Sr. St. Sabine indeed had recovered her strength. Despite a brush with death in 1885, she lived to be seventy-three. Remembered as kind, self-effacing, and dedicated, she proved equal to every challenge presented. The earliest account of the Fall River foundation states: "There isn't a corner of the convents [where she was sent], not a patch of the ground, that she hasn't watered with her sweat and tears."[59] Sr. St. Sabine stands as the forebear and icon of countless auxiliary sisters who were indispensable pioneers in the apostolic work of the Religious of Jesus and Mary until the mid-twentieth century. Little noticed and for the most part invisible, they set up the kitchens and laundries; they cooked, cleaned, and oversaw the practical life of each foundation. Deeply apostolic women, they were living witnesses of the

Gospel call to humble service. Without their practical intelligence and hidden labor, the mission would have faltered.

A month after arriving, the Religious of Jesus and Mary welcomed 200 boys and girls who had registered for the parish school. They took up a strenuous schedule that consumed most of their waking hours. Once classes were over for the day, the sisters began night sessions for eighty young women who had spent long days at factory work. They also offered piano lessons to thirty-five other students. Throughout the summer months, six more sisters from Canada and France arrived to support the mushrooming educational enterprise. October brought the consolations of a first Mass in their little chapel, and a month-long visit from M. St. Cyrille. If these women were weak and ailing, their strength of spirit compensated. Within the first year, they had set up a flourishing boarding school in September; in 1878 they opened the first Catholic orphanage for girls in Fall River. In all their ministries, they wanted to help children preserve their faith and culture in a land where differences and religions were many, but where, in the hearts of those who came, hopes for a better life were the same. The first Religious of Jesus and Mary in the United States were women of steely resolve, zeal, and bold determination, eager to carry out the pastor's dream of a self-sustaining Catholic community that addressed the needs of the weakest among them. The secular press was lavish in its praise of their early accomplishments:

> Forty-three pupils now board at the Convent . . . The Academy is in the charge of thoroughly educated ladies and is open to Protestant as well as Catholic girls. Non-Catholic pupils are not held to conform themselves to any exterior religious act practiced in the institution. Liberty of conscience in matters of religion is complete.[60]

The article went on to describe the course of studies "in all branches of a useful and Christian education" in English and French. Monthly board and tuition was ten dollars. By 1880, the convent was enlarged to provide space to house young working girls without families.

The orphanage of St. Vincent de Paul reflected the tradition of the Religious of Jesus and Mary to continue the apostolic work begun by their foundress in favor of girls who were without parental support or family resources. Its doors opened on December 7, 1878, to welcome a four-year-old Irish orphan, Mary Kate Cox. A month later, five-year-old Rose-Anne Descoteaux arrived, followed a few weeks later by her sister,

Virginie. By 1880, fourteen children lived with the sisters; that number grew to over thirty in another year. In 1882, seeing the need for larger accommodations, Bédard bought a house in another part of the city and had it moved adjacent to the convent as lodgings for forty girls aged two through twelve. Its new name was Notre Dame Orphanage, and its reputation grew along with its swelling numbers. A new directress, Mme. St. Gabriel (Celina) Lavoie, oversaw the undertaking for the next seven years. Financial support came from charitable collections, fairs, concerts, and other activities organized by the pastor and the sisters. Undated promotional news clippings describe the apostolic style of the establishment:

> If a homeless girl is accepted and has friends or relatives who can afford it, the charge is about $1.00 a week. Where friends or relatives cannot afford to pay and the case is a desolate one, the girl is taken without charge, and there are several such destitute ones. Girls who are admitted from Catholic families and who have had no other training are taught in the Roman Catholic faith. Where a girl from a Protestant family is received, she is taught morals, good behavior, reading, writing and arithmetic; and her religious training is left to be decided by her friends. No question of nationality, locality or creed interferes with the admission and management of the institution."[61]

This was the only orphanage the Religious of Jesus and Mary would ever direct in the eastern United States. The instructional needs of schoolchildren and the limited personnel required a concentration on the boarding and day students in their care. Orphanages were not a primary focus in the States, with the leaders' eagerness to become "established." Yet they stand as examples of continuity with the first ministries of the Congregation, as well as an expression of its traditional preferences for the poor and weakest of God's "little ones." In 1890, after twelve years of service there, the Fall River community transferred the direction of the orphanage to the "Grey Nuns," (Sisters of Charity of Québec). The pastor at the time wanted to have boys and girls housed in the one edifice, a change contrary to the Rule and customs of the Religious of Jesus and Mary.

Their work begun in poverty and weakness was thriving and growing rapidly. Four years after the Fall River foundation, another house opened in Manchester, NH. Late in 1881, M. St. Pothin wrote to M. St. Cyrille with her compliments and concerns:

We rejoice over your hopes for the United States. Four hundred students in so few years: how beautiful that is! Let's hope that God will bless it all. It seems that the other house [St. Augustine's, Manchester] is also doing well. However, you will need more sisters for Manchester, if you only have four there now. Because the [sisters'] constitutions are not strong, it might be better not to make too many foundations. People are worn out and the work that could be accomplished doesn't get done . . ."[62]

Resistance and Growing Pains

On August 24, 1884, at the age of 42, Bédard died of a massive stroke, leaving behind a thriving network of charitable institutions and good works. In addition to the parish school, orphanage, and boarding school already in place, he had opened a boys' collège—a commercial school where over 200 French–Canadian youth learned the basics of economy and industry in view of their future. The loss of their shepherd was a massive one for the parishioners and the sisters. The community annals mourn the death of their friend and father: The convent annals note that "the whole parish is thunderstruck and saddened, for Father Pastor was beloved by rich and poor alike." At Bédard's death, his successor faced mounting debts and several unfinished projects. Fear grew among the parishioners that Bédard's dream of providing pastoral care and education in their native tongue would die with him. Throughout New England, tensions had grown between bishops who wanted immigrants to learn English to facilitate their assimilation to American life, and church leaders who felt that "to lose one's language is to lose one's faith."

A series of disagreements and misunderstandings known as "the Flint Affair" led to some decisions on the part of Bishop Hendricken that were met with active resistance in the parish.[63] Even before the pastor's death, there had been a series of conflicts with the diocese concerning the pastoral care of French Canadians in Fall River. To protect the autonomy of his parish, Bédard had set up a lay corporation to oversee and administer its financial affairs, with some Religious of Jesus and Mary as members. This approach to parish administration did not sit well with Bishop Hendricken, who was hard–pressed to attend to their demands, and whose relationships with Bédard had proved difficult. After several unsuccessful meetings, the bishop became frustrated with the parishioners' angry refusal to accept several associates and a temporary pastor,

Rev. Samuel McGee, an Irish–Canadian priest who spoke fluent French. Some parishioners boycotted or disrupted church services. They rudely interrupted the priest during his sermons, evicted him from the rectory, and refused to let him officiate at baptisms and weddings. On February 12, a frustrated Hendricken placed the parish under interdict. All sacramental and pastoral services ceased until the recalcitrant group agreed to come around. Notre Dame Church had to close its doors to parishioners from February through August 1885. In a public letter, the bishop gave the cause as "insubordination of some who . . . wish to dictate to him on matters which pertain to his rule."[64] A few days later, a curate of the parish removed the Blessed Sacrament from the sisters' chapel. Two of the sisters went to Providence to intercede with Hendricken, asking him not "to deprive us of this one consolation," but the prelate proved inflexible to their tearful request. It was not until September that the convent chapel again housed the Blessed Sacrament.

This "affair" led to an appeal all the way to Rome. It focused on the authority of the bishop versus the autonomy of the parish. It raised the question of whether parishioners had a right to a pastor of their own nationality. Late in 1885, the Vatican decision arrived bearing a compromise solution. While it acknowledged the bishop's right to appoint pastors as he saw fit, the document suggested a French–Canadian appointee for Notre Dame to resolve the dispute. Ten months to the day of the interdict, a French Canadian, Rev. Joseph Laflamme, was appointed associate pastor and took over the pastorate. It brought satisfaction to the parishioners who felt their voices had at last been heard. They had won a battle in the name of ethnic pride and *survivance* of their way of being Catholic. Healing and peace came gradually to the Notre Dame Parish community. When Laflamme returned to Canada in 1888, Rev. Jean–Alfred Prévost assumed the pastorate, a position he would hold for thirty–seven years. To him can be attributed the renewal and restoration of trust in the parish community, which counted close to 1000 families. With their generosity and donations, Prévost rebuilt the original parish church, destroyed by fire in 1893, and constructed a magnificent edifice for worship, noted for its artistry, stained glass, and church bells. At its blessing in 1924, over 15,000 joined the celebrations. One of the outstanding priests and administrators of his day, Prévost was hailed as the second founder of Notre Dame de Lourdes. He paid off its heavy debts, organized many religious organizations, and promoted the growth of the orphanage and schools. On a broader level, he successfully joined the

French–Canadian and American traditions, according the laity a voice in temporal affairs while strengthening relations with the bishop when it came to financial accountability.

New Convent, New Parish School

In the midst of the Flint Affair, the sisters continued their educational ministry and proceeded with the construction of a new convent–school building on St. Joseph Street from their own resources, at a cost of $50,000. At the administrative level, the parish problems had created concerns for M. St. Cyrille, who felt it might be time to move some of their ministry away from Fall River to "greener pastures." At the end of April 1886, she wrote at length to the superior general about the situation, stating that it would help the mission very much if the general and/or her councilors came personally to evaluate the situation. The letter indicates that earlier plans for a house in New York had fallen through, but that an offer was in place to open a foundation in Newport, RI, where the boarding school might find a more suitable site and population:

> In any case, we have to leave the house in Fall River where the sisters have been living to move to our new property nearby. Instead of building a big, expensive convent to attract American students who probably would not want to come to that neighborhood . . . we could move our day schools and orphanage into the existing houses we already own on the property. The boarding school could then be transferred to Newport, where Dr. Storer has been preparing the way for us over the past three or four years. Reverend Mother, come and see for yourself"![65]

The transfer of the boarding school never took place. The Newport foundation in 1886 was contentious and short–lived. Construction of a new Fall River convent was completed in June 1888. It opened that year with forty boarders and over 300 day–students. At the turn of the century, the new bilingual parish school, Notre Dame, opened its doors to 1200 girls and boys whose previous instruction took place in a number of parish buildings. Twenty–one sisters and several lay teachers served as staff and faculty. The neighboring *Couvent Jésus–Marie* housed the academy for young women, with fifty–one boarders from all parts of the diocese. Beginning in June 1906, an alumnae association undertook activities to support the sisters' schools. At the twenty-fifth anniversary celebration in May of

1902, the *Fall River Evening News* reported that the institution, complete with chapel and infirmary, was "a model of neatness from the well-kept . . . dormitory on the fourth floor to the cozy refectories on the first."

In the spring of 1912, the community celebrated a spectacular healing of their assistant superior, M. St. Philomène Lemieux, aged sixty-three, from a malignant tumor. When doctors advised surgery, she sought the prayers of Brother André Bessette, CSC, the "miracle worker" of Montréal, whose devotion to St. Joseph had brought him fame as a healer.[66] After applying the oil he had sent her and praying to St. Joseph, M. St. Philomène noticed her tumor shrinking; shortly after, the doctor declared her fully healed. To offer thanksgiving, she wrote to former students to join a fund-raising drive for a statue of the saint to be erected in the convent garden. Beginning in June 1913, the statue welcomed all visitors, reminding them to "go to Joseph" as she had. M. St. Philomène lived for eighteen more years, dying in Fall River at the age of eighty-one.

In early December 1916, seventy-two former students and friends of the community gathered for an inaugural meeting of *L'Amicale*, an alumnae group affiliated with the parent group in Sillery. Thereafter they met once or twice a year and were actively involved in planning for fundraisers and social activities to support the sisters' work. Meetings included lunch, a spiritual conference, and Benediction of the Blessed Sacrament. Members helped organize the convent's jubilee festivities, card parties, and raffles. By the 1940s, the Fall River group numbered over 500 women, some of whom went to Sillery for meetings of the International Federation of Catholic Alumnae.

Marking the First Fifty Years: A Golden Thread

The sisters celebrated the golden jubilee of their foundation in 1927 with concerts, literary presentations, and several Masses of thanksgiving. For this first-born "daughter" of the Canadian province, it was a time of grateful remembrance of all whose service had contributed to its growth. Over 500 attended the solemn Mass on October 12, celebrated by Bishop Daniel Francis Feehan (1855–1934). His sermon included thanks to the Religious of Jesus and Mary "for all the good you have done through your educational influence." When the academy began to admit day students in 1927, their numbers were such that the sisters had to add a four-story wing to their main building. Two years later, a secondary school curriculum was offered for girls from the parish; with time, the high school accepted students from all parishes. A new auditorium/ gymnasium opened in 1939, proving beneficial for parish activities as well as school functions.

Notwithstanding the crisis they had endured, the Religious of Jesus and Mary were grateful to God and the good people of the parish for the success of their first ministry in the United States. The valiant trio of the early years had woven a lasting tapestry of dedicated educational service that honored their faith and culture. A report for the General Chapter of 1937 presents the Fall River community as a thriving apostolic center with forty–two choir–professed, eight auxiliary sisters, and three lay teachers. They were ministering to 900 children (boys and girls) in the parish school of Notre Dame, 200 externs and thirty–five girls in the boarding school, known as Jesus–Mary Academy. In addition to the regular classes and services to the boarders, the community directed catechism classes for public school students, as well as a variety of confraternities, missionary activities, and an alumnae association. While the Second World War brought financial struggles to the parish and the community, a report to Rome in 1948 indicated over 700 students in the parish school, fifty–four boarders, and 300 day–students in the Academy. The community numbered fifty sisters, all involved in a multi–faceted apostolic venture at the heart of an industrial city. Sisters offered extracurricular lessons in violin, piano, drawing, and painting, as well as annual closed retreats for alumnae.

By the 1950s, students published a bimonthly newsletter in French and English, *Thevenet*, and edited *Echo*, the senior yearbook. There was a thriving chapter of the Sodality of Our Lady, begun in the first decade of the school's existence. The Sodality was a positive expression of Ignatian spirituality and Catholic Action for young people throughout the network of the Congregation's schools, and it became a seedbed of many vocations to religious life. Almost fifty young women from Notre Dame School and/ or the Academy chose to enter the Religious of Jesus and Mary in the twentieth century. Twenty–five entered other religious communities.

Adapting to New Times

In 1959, a significant and welcome change for the summer holidays was the province purchase of its first and only summer residence, in Swansea, Massachusetts, about five miles from Fall River. Formerly the Lajoie property, it cost $11,000. An imposing stone building on the Lee River, "Stella Maris" offered a swimming area, respite, and relaxed schedules for sisters from the East until it closed in 1977. The lives and ministries of the sisters in Fall River were deeply affected by postwar social change and again with the Church's renewal after the Second Vatican Council (1962–65). Declining enrollment in the boarding school led to its closing in 1962. There remained 200 day–students in the high school program. Demographic changes in the city and diminishing numbers of sisters signaled economic challenges that were difficult to overcome. Following much discussion, deliberation, and consultation, Jesus–Mary Academy merged in 1971 with two other institutions, Dominican Academy and Mount St. Mary's Academy, to form the Bishop Gerrard High School for Girls. The last graduation exercises marked the official closing of the Jesus–Mary Academy in June of that year. The large building, with airy rooms and spacious halls, offered ideal space for other educational uses in a Headstart program and instructional projects for disabled children. The community continued to live in the convent space; some sisters taught at Notre Dame School or elsewhere. The third floor underwent major renovations in 1975 to create a fully equipped infirmary with elevator, for the aging and ailing sisters of the region.

In 1977, as the Religious of Jesus and Mary celebrated their first century in the States, the foundation house provided a retirement center for the whole province. That year, however, a disastrous dormitory fire at Providence College resulted in more stringent fire codes for Catholic institutions throughout New England. Fire officials came to inspect the facility on St. Joseph Street and judged it inadequate, even unsafe, for elderly or ailing residents. Meeting the new fire codes would incur additional, exorbitant expenses. These considerations led to the relocation of the infirmary to North Providence, RI, at the Jesus–Mary Cenacle, where active retired sisters had been in residence since 1973. For sisters who continued to minister in the Fall River area, two options in the city were available: one in a large property purchased on Highland Avenue (1977), and the other on Eastern Avenue (1982).

On May 11, 1982, tragedy struck the parish in a fire that destroyed the beautiful historic church building of Notre Dame, along with several homes in the neighborhood. While there was no loss of life, the fire was a symbol of historic and profound loss for the Religious of Jesus and Mary. That June, the remaining sisters closed the doors of their foundation house for the last time. Later in the year, the complex was put up for sale at an estimated value of $525,000. In December, a developer bought the property to transform it into Lafayette Place, a housing development with 125 units for senior residents. One of the sisters, M. St. Eugenia (Irene) Castonguay, a Fall River native and alumna, served as its assistant managing director until 1995. In 1998, province leadership initiated a two-year process that concluded in an agreement with a non-profit group, Sakonnet Associates, to use part of the house on Highland Avenue for an early-child-learning center to be called Thevenet Center for Children. It opened on February 6, 2000. Two years later, the Sakonnet group was unable to sustain its part of the financial commitment. This led to the decision of the Religious of Jesus and Mary to terminate the project in August of 2002. The house continued to serve as a residence for six sisters, Thevenet Mission Center.

Notre Dame School continued to thrive as an elementary school for boys and girls in a changing environment. By 1980, to provide for working parents, extended-care programs were established. The school's first lay principal, Ms. Anne Conlon, was hired in 1995. While a few sisters continued to minister at Notre Dame, most of its teachers were laywomen and men. New academic and extracurricular programs enhanced the regular school program, but enrollment figures continued to decline, resulting in the school's closure in June 2008. The last Religious of Jesus and Mary had left their residence on Highland Avenue in 2004, bringing the Congregation's presence to a quiet close after 127 years of uninterrupted service to the good people of Flint Village and the parish of Notre Dame.

St. Augustine's Parish, Manchester, NH: 1881[67]

"I hope you continue to feel the same way concerning a settlement of the religious in Manchester. I will come to gather the 'little regiment' in August."[68] These lines were penned to the provincial by Rev. Joseph-Augustin Chevalier (1843-1929), founding pastor of St. Augustine's Church, Manchester's first French-Canadian parish. Ten years before, and only four years after his ordination in Montréal, the young priest had offered himself to the first bishop of Portland, Maine, for ministry in that new diocese. With Manchester's growing population of French Canadians—close to 2500 in 1870—it presented a fertile ground for Chevalier's zeal and abilities. Manchester, the "Queen City" of New Hampshire, was home to a network of factories for weaving and manufacturing, including the largest cotton mill in the world, with 4000 looms. This attracted large numbers of workers from Canada and propelled a population explosion of the city's immigrants. Late in the nineteenth century, sixty percent of the textile workers in Manchester were French Canadians. By 1900, 23,000 French Canadian immigrants would live and work there.

Arriving in May of 1871, Chevalier first offered Masses in a small rented hall, with a modest table set as an altar; later the parishioners worshipped in a rented Protestant church nearby. He soon purchased property at the corner of Beech and Spruce Streets for the planned parish buildings and oversaw the construction of the church, completed in 1873. The first services were celebrated in the new edifice in December, with its soaring Gothic spire one of the symbols of the neighborhood. From its humble beginnings, St. Augustine's would become the "mother" of six other national parishes; by 1924, eight other parishes served the needs of French Canadians in the area. As was the case in Canada, the parish unit and personnel provided newcomers with pastoral and social services, including education for their children that would preserve both the faith and language of their homeland.

Enter the Religious of Jesus and Mary, the second group of sisters to settle in Manchester. In 1858, five Sisters of Mercy had arrived to undertake a network of educational works in St. Anne's Parish, including a girls' boarding school and adult evening classes.[69] Next to arrive, the Religious of Jesus and Mary would be the first sisters to provide educational service for the city's growing French–Canadian populace. In 1881, Chevalier formulated his plan to build a much–desired parish school for St. Augustine's. He had been impressed with the sisters' good work in Fall River: "the spirit and methods of Claudine's daughters coincided with his own aims."[70] With the permission of Portland's Bishop James Augustine Healy, Chevalier wrote to M. St. Cyrille, who gave a resounding "yes" to the new mission and to his desire to have sisters there as soon as possible. The priest had purchased land to build the convent and school but was finding it hard to get suitable temporary housing for the "little regiment" he expected to welcome in a few weeks. With a Christian courtesy reflected in his surname and personality, Chevalier—a true knight—was eager that the new building conform to the sisters' needs and educational requirements. At the beginning of August, he wrote of his disappointment that no lodging had yet been found:

> I shall have to hurry to build a house as soon as possible. I
> wanted to wait until the Sisters arrived so that the construction
> would proceed according to their plan and under their supervi-
> sion, conformable with the instructional needs . . . I want above
> all to build an establishment that will please you, and am un-
> comfortable proceeding without your approval.[71]

Going even further, the good pastor invited M. St. Cyrille to visit
the site and offer her own ideas.[72] Energized by these challenges, four
volunteers—all under age forty — prepared to give themselves to the
new mission: M. St. Norbert (Caroline) Pouliot, its intrepid and generous
leader; M. St. Jean de la Croix (Anna) Maguire, the community treasurer
and sacristan; Mme. St. Ferdinand (Marie) Goulet; and Sr. St. Geneviève
(Louise) Bureau, essential companion for the community's kitchen and
household needs. Having first traveled to Fall River, the quartet left with
Bédard for Manchester, arriving the afternoon of August 26, in the afternoon. An account of the foundation transcribes one of the letters of M.
St. Norbert describing their first hours:

> Here we are in Manchester! We bless the hand of God who has
> called us here, and the land that we shall water with our labors
> . . . While we did arrive today (the 26th), we will mark the foun-
> dation date as the 27th, vigil of the feast of St. Augustine, patron
> of our institute, of the parish and of our worthy pastor. We have
> placed our apostolate and work here under the special protec-
> tion of the Sacred Heart of Jesus.[73]

Chevalier's "regiment" was welcomed with joy and treated to a festive supper. The next day, they moved into their temporary convent, a
small house near the rectory, which the pastor had fully appointed for
their use until the larger convent school was built. At 9 AM on September 5, in a driving rain, the Religious of Jesus and Mary opened their
school to 350 children, and by afternoon added eighteen more. Classes
took place in the church nave because the basement was too damp. While
it may have seemed a consolation to think of teaching in the presence
of the Blessed Sacrament, the reality proved less positive. In a letter the
next day, M. St. Norbert wrote with news of the "factory" in which she
and M. St. Ferdinand were teaching: "not easy to inspire these fidgety
girls and boys with any respect for the holy presence! Poor children! But
we haven't given up. Piety and good behavior will grow with work and
education."[74] On the second day, with 400 in attendance, the teachers divided the children into two groups, girls and boys, at opposite ends of the

"classroom," giving lessons as best they could in the catechism, prayers, and some reading. Two teachers, hundreds of lively children! Such large numbers may indicate how eager the French–Canadian parents were to have an alternative to the public schools in the area, which suffered from a sudden drop in enrolled students. Beginning on September 6, the sisters also taught evening classes for working girls. Thirty–five young women presented themselves, paying $1.00 per month for twelve lessons. Within a week, Bishop Healy visited the church–school. By the end of September, Mme. St. Gabriel (Celina) Lavoie arrived to help with the teaching. At the New Year, the pioneers had added three more to their "regiment": Mme. St. Ignace (Rose) Dumas, Sr. St. Léocadie Corcoran, and Mme. Marie de la Salette Nolin.

Construction of the three–story convent/boarding school on Spruce Street was completed in January 1882. Most of the schoolchildren were able to move into their new quarters. Without teachers' desks for six months, however, the sisters had to make do and probably stood a great deal. The children, they discovered, were "rocky soil," resistant to learning and discipline, with the boys throwing peas and marbles while awaiting their turn to recite or read! Despite their emotional and physical fatigue, the missionaries persisted in their efforts, counting on God's grace and the prayers of the community back home in Québec. On March 1, the community moved into their new convent quarters, where the pastor celebrated the first Mass on the feast of St. Joseph. The solemn blessing of the new building occurred on March 23, presided over by Bishop Healy, with the beloved M. St. Cyrille in attendance, along with twenty–five priests, two Sisters of Mercy, and hundreds of parishioners. Célanie Deschamps, the first boarder, arrived at the end of April; there were twelve others within a year. With time, the convent came to be known among the sisters as *"maison du bonheur."* It truly was a happy house, despite its overcrowded refectory and dormitory. Parents and students loved the sisters, and they in turn delighted in serving this people. The gentle, persuasive disposition of their indomitable pastor seemed to permeate the atmosphere of the whole parish complex, extending even to Anglo–Protestants from the civic community.

By June of 1883, St. Augustine's held its first public distribution of prizes in the convent hall. There were now more than 450 students, with three double classes for boys, three for girls, and an academy for a few secondary school students. It wasn't unusual for a sister to have 100 children in her classroom. When a local public school at the corner of Beech and Spruce became vacant, Chevalier was able to lease and later buy the property to house the boys' classes, which got underway in 1885, helping to reduce a crowded and stressful situation. Four years later, Chevalier added a third floor to the edifice. He also obtained the services of the Brothers of the Sacred Heart, from Québec, to direct the boys' education in what would be known as St. Augustine's Academy. Four brothers arrived in September of 1889, to the relief of the Religious of Jesus and Mary, who were happy to "hand over the restless boys who need the hand of a man to bend them to discipline" and probably enjoyed quieter classroom situations![75] As the academic year began, eleven sisters made up the community (seven choir–professed, four auxiliaries), with over 200 girls in the classrooms and twelve boarders in the convent–school.

In 1884, the Diocese of Manchester was established, with Most Reverend Denis Mary Bradley (1846–1903) as its first bishop. In less than twenty years, Bradley established an impressive number of charitable and educational institutions in his diocese, including St. Anselm's College. He welcomed several congregations of women and men to minister to his increasing flock of immigrants. By the turn of the century, there were close to 100,000 Catholics in Manchester, cared for by an army of zealous priests, brothers, and sisters. At St. Augustine's, the house annals make references to Bradley's regular visits to the school, supporting the missionaries, and showing interest in the educational progress of the children.

To commemorate his silver jubilee of ordination, Chevalier wanted to open an orphanage for the children of his parish. He invited the Sisters of Providence of Montréal to direct it and used the gifts received for his anniversary to fund the new endeavor. The first six sisters arrived in December of 1892, opening the doors of St. Vincent de Paul Orphanage to seven boys and five girls, whose numbers multiplied and required a larger building within the year. Over 290 orphans or needy children were admitted in the first three years. Such large numbers reflect persistent problems of immigrant millworkers: outbreaks of contagious disease, deaths in childbirth, overburdened working parents unable to provide adequate care for growing families. The sisters from the orphanage also visited the sick at home and sheltered elderly boarders of the parish. Their institution lasted well into the twentieth century, closing its doors in 1958.

In the summer of 1895, the community welcomed sisters from other houses for the annual retreat. Among them were the sisters from the neighboring convent of St. Mary's, Claremont, where the community had recently terminated its ministry because of misunderstandings with the pastor. The provincial of the Oblates of Mary Immaculate, a Father Guillard, preached the retreat. His instructions were on the need for Catholic schools and the dangers lurking for children who attended public schools. This inspired a comment in the annals that God would inspire the parents to recognize their duty and "send us all their dear children."[76] As a new century dawned, St. Augustine's network of social and educational institutions offered services to 520 girls, 450 boys, and 100 orphans. In May of 1899, the Religious of Jesus and Mary had the joy of a First Holy Communion celebration for 180 children, by all accounts an impressive ceremony. That July, the sisters were happy to host the annual retreat, preached by a Jesuit from Montréal. By that time, their superior was the much–admired M. St. Honoré (Adele) Bourget, who spent more than twenty–five years in all at St. Augustine's. On April 18, 1900, she led the community in mourning the death of her assistant, M. St. Gabriel Lavoie (b. 1844), the first Religious of Jesus and Mary to die on U.S. soil, after a brief bout of pneumonia. One of the founding members at St. Augustine's, M. St. Gabriel left a legacy of fervor and generosity. Her remains were buried in the parish cemetery until 1915, when they were transferred to the community plot at Villa Augustina, in nearby Goffstown.

Growth and Consolidation

M. St. Honoré would oversee a more joyful event with the construction of a new and larger convent school to accommodate the mushrooming numbers of girls at what was now known as the *Académie Jésus–Marie*. Located at the corner of Beech and Cedar Streets, the new edifice was a three–story brick building with modern installations and amenities. There were living quarters for the sisters on the ground and first floors, and ten spacious classrooms on the second and third floors. Built in part with the donations of parishioners and the generosity of the benevolent pastor, the new convent school cost $50,000. The Religious of Jesus and Mary moved in on Sunday, January 18, 1903, and began classes in the new school the next day. Their former convent became the brothers' residence. Due to lack of funds, the chapel of the new convent was left unfinished; but a group of *anciennes,* the school's first alumnae association, organized a number of activities and concerts to raise the money for an altar and wall decorations. Other generous benefactors provided funds for a way of the cross, vestments, carpeting, and statuary.

On June 27, 1906, parishioners celebrated the twenty–fifth anniversary of the sisters' arrival in Manchester at a Mass in the new convent chapel with their beloved teachers, followed by a jubilee banquet. Remembering this event, the sisters regarded that chapel as a monument to the goodness of their former students and benefactors; it was "forever engraved in the heart of the community." The parishioners had challenged their new pastor years before: "You find us nuns; we'll take care of the rest." Now they could look with satisfaction on the good work their faith, generosity, and dedication had built; they could take pride in the sisters' contribution to their beloved parish. They were equally proud of the appointment of the first French–Canadian bishop to the diocese in 1907. Most Rev. Georges–Albert Guertin (1869–1931), a native of Nashua, NH, served as Manchester's third bishop for twenty–four years, through the events of massive industrial changes, World War I, and the Great Depression. Guertin had been a curate at St. Augustine's from 1893 to 1897, and it was a special joy to welcome him back for his first episcopal visit in 1907 to bless the restored and enlarged church, another of Chevalier's accomplishments. He would likewise preside at several celebrations marking anniversaries in the parish.

In 1917, Chevalier, at the age of seventy–three, celebrated the golden jubilee anniversary of his ordination. He continued to be involved in a number of projects, including the erection of a new Religious of Jesus and Mary boarding school, Villa Augustina. During a four–day feast in May of 1921, he presided over the golden jubilee of the parish, surrounded by his beloved flock and the students of St. Augustine's schools and academy. A few weeks later, he suffered a stroke that left him paralyzed on one side. In June 1924, he resigned as pastor, having led the parish he led with great love and generosity for over fifty–three years. Chevalier had shepherded a struggling, small community of poor immigrants and helped it grow into a thriving, debt–free parish, worshipping together in the church he had built a half–century earlier. Selfless and unprepossessing, he had achieved extraordinary results, evidenced by a network of flourishing parish institutions. Respected as a leader in bilingual education, Chevalier showed zealous care to preserve both faith and language among French Canadians. He retired to his residence on the parish property, spending his last years in solitude, rest and prayer—along with some heartfelt singing, which he enjoyed. In 1927, the parish marked his sixtieth year as a priest. M. St. Peter Claver Bilodeau, Canadian provincial at the time, expressed the sentiments of the community on August

5, 1927, in a laudatory letter: "Guide, counselor, benefactor: you have been all these for Jesus–Mary. Above all, you have been a father . . . you have given us your all." Two years later, in February of 1929, at the age of eighty–five, Father Chevalier died peacefully and quietly as he had lived. To the Religious of Jesus and Mary, he had said, "I know you won't forget me." The memory of this great and noble man would long be graven in their hearts, their prayers, and especially in the educational monument to his generosity, the Villa Augustina, where his sowing produced a great harvest into the 21st century.[77]

In 1931, the Manchester sisters celebrated fifty years of ministry in Manchester. The commemorative booklet for the occasion, prepared by grateful alumnae of St. Augustine's, traces the history of the Academy and the role of the sisters in that educational enterprise. The first to inaugurate bilingual education in the diocese at primary and secondary levels, the Religious of Jesus and Mary had fulfilled their mission faithfully, without fanfare or publicity. They had sown the good seeds of Catholic teaching and Franco–American traditions in the hearts of hundreds of girls, graduates of the Academy, who were now handing the same traditions on to their children. For this, the Religious of Jesus and Mary were grateful to God and to the generous families they had served and loved dearly for a half–century. During that time, over seventy choir–professed and seventeen auxiliary sisters had ministered in the Manchester mission; they had likewise nurtured twenty–seven vocations to the Religious of Jesus and Mary.[78] They fondly recalled M. St. Norbert Pouliot, leader of the pioneer "regiment" to Manchester in 1881 and foundress of the Academy there. She had returned in 1914 as superior of the new foundation and boarding school in Goffstown, NH. Her years of ministry spanned several houses and countries of the Congregation, including the American missions of Fall River and Providence. In 1919, at the age of seventy–four, she was elected to serve as a general councilor in Rome and then returned to Sillery to spend her last years. In failing health, but still admired as the indispensable partner of Chevalier, M. St. Norbert enjoyed receiving occasional letters from him with news of the mission. At her death in October 1924, Chevalier sent a message of admiration and sorrow that sums up her contribution to the American mission:

> From the time I first met her, in August of 1881, I often noticed her energy, zeal, and devotion to the success of our endeavor. Her death leaves a void in your house that will be difficult to fill. Her absence is painful for me, as I enjoyed corresponding with

her and reliving our work together in the past, as well as our difficulties and hopes ... I owe her much gratitude for the good she did in my parish, for the comfort she offered in my dark hours, and for all her prayers on my behalf.[79]

M. St. Norbert is but one example of scores of enterprising Religious of Jesus and Mary sent to St. Augustine's to maintain the faith and traditions of its French–Canadian immigrant people. Ever on the alert for new fields of charity, they turned next to an educational need in South Manchester.

St. Theresa's Parish, Manchester (1927 to 1936)[80]

Begun as a mission chapel in 1923, St. Theresa's was one of several daughter churches of St. Augustine's, providing pastoral care for many French–Canadian families who lived a good distance from their home parish. Thanks to the zeal and persistent requests of the laypeople of South Manchester, the bishop agreed to allow services for them in a temporary chapel that they maintained by holding bi–monthly whist parties. In 1924, when Rev. Georges A. Demers replaced Chevalier as pastor of St. Augustine's, he began the construction of a one–story chapel on Mitchell Street. It was solemnly blessed by Bishop Guertin in October 1926, and named after St. Thérèse of Lisieux, canonized the year before. The bishop promised to construct a second story on the chapel to serve as a school, and the pastor invited the Religious of Jesus and Mary to assume the educational work there.

The construction work was finished by summer of 1927, comprising four classrooms and two offices. Early in September, two sisters joined two laywomen to become the first faculty of the mission school, which opened with space for 125 students. M. St. Nathalie Bibeault became director and English teacher for Grades 5 through 8; M. St. Lutgarde Roy led all the French classes. Mrs. Leda Goulet, who had prepared children for First Communion in the parish, taught Grades 1 and 2; Ms. Gertrude Laroche had Grades 3 and 4. Sometime later, M. St. Eloï Gagnon arrived to teach French in the upper grades. The sisters had no residence at the parish and commuted daily from the St. Augustine's Convent.

Father Demers fell seriously ill and retired from active ministry in January 1929; he died the following August. His successor at St. Augustine's was Rev. Aimé–Philippe Boire, who suffered with his parishioners the pangs of economic depression in the 1930's. Nevertheless, he managed to maintain both chapel and school at St. Theresa's, where a growing student population of close to 200 required more classrooms and teachers. On June 14, 1931, the mission school held its first eighth–grade graduation in the parish hall, with eleven girls and one boy receiving diplomas and class rings. Among them was Ms. Florence Lebreux, who would later become a Religious of Jesus and Mary.

With the opening of academic year 1931–32, 190 pupils crammed the classrooms, a number that would drop significantly as factories closed and families moved away during the Great Depression. The number of sisters, however, grew to four, and the graduating class two years later numbered thirteen girls and six boys. Late in September of 1934, St. Theresa's, the seventh and last offshoot of St. Augustine's, became an independent parish, with Rev. Louis A. Ramsay as its resident pastor. For the next six years, he was its spiritual leader and able administrator, founding many parish confraternities and groups and building a much–needed rectory. His also was the unwelcome task of bidding the Religious of Jesus and Mary goodbye when they left the Manchester area in 1936. It brought some consolation to know that from this small mission, nineteen women entered religious life. Four of them became Religious of Jesus and Mary: Thérèse Bénard (Marie de Lorette), Claire Lebreux (Marie de l'Annonciation), Florence Lebreux (Marie du Temple), and Violet St–Cyr (M. St. Flore).[81]

The End of an Era: Leaving the Manchester Schools (1936)

The economic depression that brought so much suffering to immigrant families also impacted parish life. Factories had closed down in Manchester, depleting the population of mill workers. Large numbers returned to Québec. Faced with a crisis in parish finances and pressured by diocesan authorities, Boire decided he could no longer maintain two separate schools at St. Augustine's. Furthermore, city authorities had deemed the boys' building unsafe for school use. In the fall of 1935, Boire asked the three Sacred Heart Brothers to leave, hoping that the Religious of Jesus and Mary would assume the education of the boys in their Academy and move their living quarters to the boys' school. Such a change would call for an increase of eight or more sisters, a number that the provincial and her council could not afford to send. Just before Christmas in 1935, the pastor addressed a strong letter to the provincial, stating in part:

Mother Superior (M. St. Clementine Tetreault) and I would
have wanted to see the Religious of Jesus and Mary maintain
the primary school for both boys and girls at St. Augustine's, as
they did when they first came fifty years ago. Jesus–Mary does
not want to do this. The die is cast: Jesus–Mary should withdraw, as you yourself have indicated. The Religious of Jesus
and Mary have the first choice. The pastor begs them to stay,
but they have refused."[82]

Having received the authorization of Most Rev. John B. Peterson,
appointed Bishop of Manchester in 1932, Boire announced the withdrawal of the Brothers of the Sacred Heart and the Religious of Jesus and
Mary, effective in June 1936. M. St. Borgia, superior general, sent a letter
to the province announcing with regret the sisters' withdrawal, after so
many years of unstinting service and nurturing numerous vocations to
priesthood and religious life. The circular lays out the reason for the community's departure, "a decision imposed upon them by diocesan authority, for financial reasons that we cannot judge. We find it impossible to
send twelve teachers in addition to the present personnel, to replace the
Brothers who will be leaving."[83] The pastor obtained the services of the
Sisters of the Holy Cross of Montréal, who had been his primary school
teachers. They were well known and long established in the diocese, and
they had sisters available for the mission. They would take over both parish schools in Manchester in September 1936. Meanwhile, the Religious
of Jesus and Mary community prepared to leave their "happy house" and
the work they had begun and nurtured carefully for over five decades.
Two of the sisters became seriously ill and died in the spring of 1936,
adding grief to the community's sense of loss.

At the graduation and closing exercises early in June, many parents expressed their sorrow at the departure of their sisters; some cried
openly, unable to speak. On closing day, June 12, usually a joyful occasion, the children were sad and the pastor wept as he blessed them for the
summer. The Religious of Jesus and Mary published an open letter in one
of the French–language newspapers, expressing gratitude to their former
students and reiterating the reasons for their departure. It offers a touching testimony to the sisters' generosity and lack of bitterness:

> With heavy hearts, we leave our beautiful *Académie Notre-
> Dame* and the young school at St. Thérèse, where we appreci-
> ated your excellent spirit, your sincere piety, your work habits,
> and your love for your teachers . . . The sisters coming after us

will soon understand why we loved you so much, why it was easy to dedicate ourselves to such well-disposed children and cooperative parents. Our best wish for them is that they have students like ours to receive their excellent teaching . . . May the happiness you have given us, dear *anciennes*, be returned to you a hundredfold. Remember we will continue to be your neighbors in Goffstown.[84]

One bright chapter of the Religious of Jesus and Mary American mission had closed, but a new future awaited them in rural New Hampshire, where they would move away from parish allegiances to begin an independent educational enterprise, one from which they could not be sent away.

St. Mary's, Claremont, NH (1890-95)[85]

The Catholic community of Claremont, about sixty-five miles northwest of Manchester, traced its roots to a mission church begun by Jesuit missionaries in the early nineteenth century. The "old St. Mary's" was the first Catholic church in the town, built in 1823 by a convert-priest from Episcopalianism, Rev. Virgil Barber, SJ, who had been educated at Georgetown University. By mid-century, with the opening of several cotton and wool mills, immigrants surged into the village of Claremont, seeking better work and a connection with their faith. St. Mary's became an autonomous parish in 1870; several Jesuit itinerant missionaries served their pastoral needs, albeit on a temporary basis. Not until 1881 was Irish-born Rev. Patrick J. Finnegan, SJ appointed its resident pastor. He would serve there for over twenty years, ministering to a mixed congregation of Irish and French-Canadian Catholics.

Finnegan's first order of business was to complete and renovate a new church building, which had stood unfinished for years. The new church was blessed in 1883 by Bishop Bradley. Six years later, Finnegan had bought two properties opposite the church on Center Street, to use as a convent and elementary school, and set about looking for a community of teaching sisters. Why or how the Religious of Jesus and Mary were sought for the task is unclear, and little documentation remains concerning their Claremont mission. A correspondence took place between M. St. Cyrille and Finnegan in 1889, when it seems that the pastor had approached her to request teachers for his new school, with a boarding school foreseen as well. In November of that year, M. St. Cyrille responded to a letter from Finnegan telling him that four of five on her council approved the new mission, but she had to wait for final approval from the General Council in Lyon. She attached copies of the contract agreement between the Religious of Jesus and Mary and Rev. Charles P. Gaboury, pastor of their newly opened mission in Centreville, Rhode Island.

On March 6, 1890, M. St. Cyrille wrote to the bishop from the Manchester convent where she was visiting. In that letter, she stated that the response from Lyon headquarters raised concerns about property ownership. The General Council favored community ownership: "If the property rights are the Congregation's, you may accept the foundation. If this is a school where from one year to the next you can be asked to leave, you already have enough of these situations in the States." The provincial answered that she believed the property would be the Congregation's, but would check it out. Bradley's respectful response, sent the next day, made his position very clear:

> Not knowing the discretionary power that you possess, I am unable to say whether you can consider yourself at liberty to accept the Claremont school under the (present) circumstances. Two things are settled: 1) we are not at liberty to give the sisters the title to the property; 2) Rev. Finnegan accepted the conditions which you kindly sent him . . . there was no allusion to your purpose of requiring a title to the property.[86]

In closing, the bishop asked for a response "at your earliest convenience" under the conditions he reiterated. M. St. Cyrille summoned her own council and sent their decision that very day. They were accepting the mission under a provision of their Constitutions that gave her the authority to do so "when I cannot contact the General Council." Meetings with Finnegan then took place in Manchester, where plans were made for a visit of M. St. Cyrille to the property. The provincial secretary, M. St. Augustin (Adelaide) Hatschemberg, was to act on the provincial's behalf for the necessary negotiations toward opening the school in the coming months.

In mid–March, the bishop and pastor received by post the affirmative decision, as M. St. Cyrille was visiting other New England houses. On March 20, Finnegan came to meet M. St. Augustin in Manchester to say that a visit to the property was not feasible because the buildings were occupied but that all would be ready by September. He had not brought the revised contract he had received, so she produced a copy for him. In it, the Religious of Jesus and Mary had removed an article requiring the sisters to pass an examination if judged appropriate, along with a mandate to teach Sunday school to the parish children for a half–hour weekly. Finnegan was pleased that his strong plea for two Irish or American sisters and one Canadian were accepted. His concern was that the sisters would be able to communicate with the English–speaking members of his mixed congregation, and he hoped that in the future the sisters would maintain this proportion of two to one. In a more positive mood than he had been previously, Finnegan expressed confidence that the Congregation would never regret having come to Claremont, a center where the number of students would multiply and religious vocations were sure to flourish. At his departure, he seemed relaxed and happy, looking forward to welcoming three new missionaries in the fall.

Late in August, the Claremont missionaries arrived in Manchester, where they remained for several days waiting until the convent and school buildings were ready. Rather than the expected number, six Religious of Jesus and Mary made up the founding community. M. St. Jean de la Croix Maguire, aged 41, was the eldest and the superior. The others were M. St. Honoré Bourget, assistant; M. St. Magdeleine de Pazzi Tanguay, for French classes; M. St. Andrew Carlyon and M. Marie du Perpétuel–Secours Hanley for English classes; and Sr. St. Fidèle Corcoran to provide the necessary domestic services for the group. A look at the sisters' surnames makes it clear that Finnegan's stipulations had been heeded! At age twenty–three, the youngest of the community was newly–professed M. du Perpétuel–Secours (Grace Hanley), a native of Boston. As the first Religious of Jesus and Mary born in the United States, the unusual story of her "miracle healing" as an adolescent had circulated in Catholic circles of New England by the time she arrived in Claremont.[87] Her religious life would be cut short by tuberculosis; within two years, she was sent to Fall River, where she died in June 1902.

On August 29, Finnegan eagerly welcomed his pioneer group of sisters to one of the houses he had completely furnished as their convent. There, his niece had prepared and served for them a *souper splendide*. Three days later, the sisters held their opening day of classes for 195 students, boys and girls from a mix of Irish and French–Canadian families. It would be a challenge, one they seemed to welcome. The school building adjacent to the convent had four well–appointed classrooms. The house annals mention the graceful terraced gardens surrounding the property. The Religious of Jesus and Mary looked forward to many years in this pleasant spot. They were eager to help the children "preserve the sacred deposit of Faith in the

heretical environment in which they live." Within several months, however, financial difficulties of an undisclosed nature began to surface. The
provincial felt that there was insufficient income for the community and
thought of closing the house at the end of their first year.

The sisters were persuaded to remain for another year, but new
problems arose, this time concerning the pastor's style of governance.
An undated manuscript states that Finnegan "wanted to run the house,
meet sisters in the parlor under pretext of spiritual direction, insisted on
English–language teaching to the Canadians, etc. etc." There is no way of
knowing whether this perception was accurate or stemmed from ethnic
tensions between the French–Canadian sisters and the Irish pastor. Once
again, the Religious of Jesus and Mary made plans to leave Claremont
in the summer of 1892, offering as a reason that they could not provide
a sufficient number of English–speaking sisters. Once again Finnegan
asked them to stay on. The sister–assistant replaced the superior, and
the community remained in Claremont through July of 1895, when the
provincial decided definitively to withdraw them because of insufficient
personnel. A note in the community annals of the Manchester house is
the only indication of how the decision affected the sisters: "Our Mothers and Sisters of Claremont have arrived, having closed their house for
reasons that are not ours to question. They are happy to see us again,
but saddened that they had to bid farewell to a mission they had for five
years."[88] In 1896, the Sisters of Mercy arrived to assume the educational
task at Claremont, one they accomplished successfully until the end of
the twentieth century.

3

Autonomy and Expansion in New England

Villa Augustina, Goffstown, NH: 1908/1918[89]

"In 1903, Fr. Chevalier had discontinued the girls' boarding school to have more space for the hundreds of parish children. But the long-desired project of a *pensionnat* never left his mind, as it was also the concern of the Mothers. With the acquisition in 1907 of Villa Augustina, the project took a new turn."[90] At her first visit to the Manchester mission in 1905, newly–elected Rev. M. St. Clare had asked the superior, M. St. Honoré (Adèle) Bourget, about the possible purchase of a country house for the community to escape the city, especially in the summer months. While the idea struck the sisters as a luxury they would never have dreamed of, with the encouragement of M. St. Clare they began making enquiries about properties that would be both affordable and within easy travel. Several possible sites were examined and rejected, despite many prayers to St. Joseph, who had been entrusted with finding them an appropriate setting. The well-connected and enterprising Chevalier joined in the search as well. In August of 1907, he learned that the Daniel Little Farm in nearby Goffstown was up for sale. Situated near Manchester, it offered many possibilities. Chevalier invited the sisters to come and see for themselves, assuring them he had found the perfect spot! It was a delightful site, with sloping hills and 125 acres of fields and farmland at the foot of Uncanoonuc Mountain, popular with hikers and skiers. On August 28, the parish patronal feast, eight of the sisters joined Chevalier for a visit to the main house and barns, along with its adjacent white cottage, where they had an outdoor picnic. They found it "charming, enchanting"—an ideal spot for a summer holiday house. The purchase price was $4525. Permissions were sought and granted. Chevalier made a $200 down payment on the property and finalized the sale with Mrs. Little in October.

The parish ladies' group organized a giant whist party to raise funds for needed renovations, which began in January of 1908. Chevalier oversaw the building improvements, including new floors and porches, electricity, hot water, heat, modern bathrooms, and a "jewel" of a chapel that could accommodate twenty-five. In addition, he provided a horse, two cows, two farm vehicles, and farming equipment. He sent his own custodian to plant oats and landscape the area around the houses. Little wonder that the sisters decided to name their new home in honor of their faithful benefactor. When Bishop Guertin arrived early in July to bless the house as the community began its first summer holiday, he commented that it felt like "being at the entrance of a Roman villa." From then on, Villa Augustina honored the memory of a partnership that not only gave the sisters a vacation spot but a site as well for a superior educational experience among French-Canadian *demoiselles* in the area. The Villa welcomed the sisters in August for their first summer retreat there, preached by a Missionary of the Sacred Heart. The next year, three sisters came to live at the Villa as caretakers of the property. The father of one of the sisters gave them a watchdog that they named Carlo. Every summer, the Manchester community spent holidays and made retreats in the Villa's peaceful surroundings.

The sisters continued to hope that a *pensionnat*—boarding school—would rise on its spacious grounds, fulfilling a dream deferred for many years. The Villa served as a summer residence for women in the area, which helped to cover expenses. In 1913, weakened by poor health, the beloved M. St. Honoré came to live at the Villa she had founded a few years earlier. She would die there in December 1919 and be buried in the cemetery on the convent grounds. A valiant woman who had dedicated more than twenty years of her apostolic life to the young people of Manchester, M. St. Honoré was memorialized in the fiftieth anniversary booklet of 1931: "Several generations of students owe her the blessings of a solid and superior formation . . . Filled with tender affection for her sisters, beloved by her students as a mother, this talented educator and distinguished woman religious possessed all the virtues of a model superior."[91]

Building the Pensionnat

In September 1914, M. St. Norbert, foundress of the New Hampshire mission, returned as superior to Manchester after a thirty-year absence. She was seventy years old, but within weeks she found herself in charge of leading the mission to another level. Encouraged by Chevalier and supported by prayers to St. Joseph, M. St. Norbert approached Bishop Guertin with a project to open a *pensionnat* on the Villa grounds. At first he was not favorable to the idea, so the sisters redoubled their prayers, adding a novena. There were concerns about such a project. Other communities already had boarding schools in the state; would building another add unfair competition? Would the Villa boarding school be dependent for financial support on St. Augustine's Parish? There was also opposition from Protestants and others who did not support uniquely Franco-American schools. The sisters were persistent and insistent. They sent the required petitions to the general headquarters in Rome to establish the school; these were approved. Then they waited for episcopal approbation. In April 1915, the Bishop submitted the petition of the Religious of Jesus and Mary to his diocesan council. Having received their approval, he happily granted permission the next day to build the school. M. St. Norbert was to supervise the construction, to begin in May that year. In July, the Religious of Jesus and Mary decided to buy the adjacent Upham Farm, increasing the property to 200 acres. The purchase would resolve boundary disagreements with the owners, who were not happy that Catholic nuns were their neighbors. Negotiations for the purchase were entrusted to a benefactor and friend of the sisters, Miss Elizabeth "Lizzie" Barnes, of Manchester. Much to their surprise, Miss Barnes bought and donated the property to the Religious of Jesus and Mary, with the one condition that they pray for her and her deceased parents. Her generosity to the Villa lasted all her life. In gratitude, the community welcomed her as a guest, cared for her in her last illness, and buried her in the Villa cemetery.

On September 3, 1916, a large crowd attended the blessing of the Villa cornerstone. The Religious of Jesus and Mary signed a legal deed of incorporation in November, with five of the sisters serving as the members. They received substantial loans from the Amoskeag Bank to help cover building expenses. The economic consequences of World War I brought an increased cost of materials and delayed the construction somewhat. Ever the personification of generosity, Chevalier donated more than $15,000 toward the building's foundations. Parishioners and other friends of the sisters organized various fund-raising events and projects to offer their support. Clearly, they saw the Villa as a monument to French-Canadian aspirations that first-class education would be possible for their daughters: "Within its walls our young women (will) acquire, along with knowledge of God, all the abilities needed to become elite Franco-American women."[92] The Villa would stand as a living testament of their attachment to their ethnic roots, preserving both faith and language. Two years later, on July 25, 1918, Bishop Guertin presided at the official benediction of the Villa and its first Mass in the convent chapel. He expressed gratitude to Chevalier and asked for blessings on the sisters and their future students. In appearance, the new school was both impressive and welcoming. As described in a contemporary history of Goffstown, it was "a magnificent brick building with stone trimmings, four stories in height . . . From the upper story of the building, there is a commanding view of the country to the north and west, which is very attractive. This magnificent structure finely finished and furnished, erected at the cost of $125,000 is owned by the Catholic Society and is to be used as a seminary or convent for the education of female students."[93]

Early Years (1918 to 1937)

On September 5, thirty-nine girls arrived as the Villa's first boarders; two weeks later, there were forty-six. Among them was a Manchester native, Marie–Clarisse Gaudette (1902–2017), the first Villa student to enter the Congregation and who later attained legendary status as its longest-lived member.[94] It was an encouraging start, only to be interrupted by the school's closing due to the spread of the dreaded Spanish influenza, which took the lives of over half a million Americans in 1918–19. The Villa closed for much of that autumn season but reopened as the pandemic declined. The bilingual curriculum included a French course of study, with language, French and Canadian history, art, gym, and domestic science. The English section offered literature, Latin, history, mathematics, and science. One prospectus in French stressed the importance of the healthy environment, with opportunities for physical exercise, long walks, and healthy diet. One-piece uniform dresses from "The Brown Sisters" in Philadelphia were required, along with a gym outfit. Student numbers rose to seventy-seven by 1920 and peaked at about 100 in 1922. By that time, the students were grouped into three "sections," a hallmark of Religious of

Jesus and Mary boarding institutions. The "Guardian Angel" section took in Grades 1–5; the "Sacred Heart" section was for Grades 6–8. Secondary school boarders formed part of the "Blessed Virgin" section. It seems that numbers tapered off during the Great Depression and thereafter, so that the total number of girls at the *pensionnat* before 1950 did not exceed fifty. The Villa began admitting "half-boarders" in 1933; they returned home in the evenings but had a noon meal at the school. As a freestanding institution, the convent was entitled to resident priest-chaplains, who lived in a small house on the property (later Emmaus House). The first of these, Rev. Henri Beaudé, arrived in 1911; eleven chaplains followed in that capacity prior to the boarding school's closing in 1968.

On June 12, 1923, the first graduation exercises of the secondary school took place: two for the academic or classical course (Edna Tarte and Alice de Montigny), five for the commercial or business course. As part of the ceremony, each of the graduates received a commemorative silver thimble. That month, the school's Sodality of Our Lady, recently affiliated with the *Prima Primaria*, celebrated its first reception.[95] By 1927, the Villa's Alumnae Association held its first meeting and elected seven councilors. A fascinating note in the Villa Annals reports the school's celebration of the 200th birthday of George Washington, on May 5, 1932. There was singing of the national anthem, a talk on President Washington, and the planting of sixteen spruce and pine trees, in honor of the country's sixteen presidents, including a New Hampshire native, Franklin Pierce. Clearly, the Franco-American Villa community was eager to show patriotism by celebrating the father of their adoptive nation.

Improvements continued on the property, many of them paid for by Chevalier, now aged and in frail health. In the 1920's, the barn was renovated, and construction began on a larger coop for the hens, together with a slaughterhouse. A small bridge was built over the stream—"*le pont Chevalier*"—boasting electric lights on its pillars. Classroom floors were painted, new furniture appeared in library and classrooms, and a motorized well would provide water at any time. The sisters made several improvements to the original building, transforming it into a summer villa for women. Sometime in 1932, they erected an outdoor statue of Our Lady of Lourdes in the rock formation behind the building, where it still stands. On February 3, 1937, to mark the centenary of the death of the foundress, a new organ was installed in the chapel. That evening the students put on a special program, highlighting the global apostolate of the congregation. Many parents and friends of the Villa attended the event.

In May, statistics for the Villa appeared as part of the province report to the General Chapter. There were twenty-five Religious of Jesus and Mary in the community, ten of them auxiliary sisters. Fifty boarders and ten day-boarders made up the student body, complemented by a summer colony of thirty-five "lady boarders" who came to spend a holiday, enjoying the surroundings and helping to defray expenses of a working farm and growing school. The first two decades of the Villa boarding school gave much promise, despite the difficult economic circumstances of the Depression years and their aftermath.

Decades of Growth and Expansion

With the onset of World War II, the number of boarders remained stable, but there was an increase in day boarders. A note attached to the first book of Annals indicates that from 1918 to 1945, the total number of Villa students was 322. Over half the girls—172—had attended the elementary school (Grade 1–8); fifty-three had completed a commercial course at the secondary level, and ninety-seven graduated from the classical course. The school's reputation grew. The Villa became a first-rate convent school offering bilingual education and graduating young women whose training fitted them for the workplace as well as marriage and family life. The content of its course of studies was as impressive as it was extensive. A printed prospectus from the mid-1930's indicates "the electric car from Manchester to Goffstown stops at the convent gate," an enticement for the city families about seven miles away. The particular attraction of the convent school was its "special attention given to the study of French," along with formation in sound Catholic principles, good manners, and "habits of order, thrift, and other domestic virtues." The aim of the sisters was to offer motherly care and vigilance, attending to each girl's moral, physical, and intellectual progress. Regulations were set forth for boarders regarding visits, money, and outside reading material, with an admonition to parents that they not "compromise the authority of the Teachers by yielding too readily to their children's desires." The pamphlet highlighted the lovely natural surroundings of the Villa, along with its peaceful rural setting and opportunities for a variety of outdoor sports. The course of studies outlined in the prospectus aimed at primary, intermediate, and secondary levels. The secondary school curriculum offered business, classical, and "normal school" (teacher-training) tracks.

Emphasis was on the bilingual character of the Villa, with mathematics, history, geography, and the sciences taught in English. Offerings included four years of Latin, physics, and art history, as well as the core subjects. The French course of study was affiliated with Laval University in Québec. Classes in "domestic science" were required for two years at the secondary level. The sisters offered private music and art lessons; business subjects such as typing and stenography added practical training to the curriculum. An extensive list of clear guidelines for the boarder's trousseau included the required black and white uniforms, black and white gloves, as well as high-necked and long-sleeved nightgowns. The Villa boarding fees—payable monthly—were similar to those at the St. Clare boarding academy the sisters directed in Woonsocket, Rhode Island. Tuition and board were $250 annually, with additional fees for private lessons in painting, voice, violin, and piano instruction.

Along with its legacy of cultural formation of many Franco-American wives and mothers, the Villa bore rich fruit in a number of vocations to the religious life. By 1947, seventeen Villa students had entered the Religious of Jesus and Mary; eight had chosen life in other congregations. It would seem that the dreams of its founders had become a reality. A contemporary article in the Manchester French–language newspaper, *L'Avenir,* stated that "the spirit of the apostles who gave (the Villa) birth and helped it to grow seems to be hovering over the sisters, alumnae, students and friends, and saying with a smile: 'We are so proud of you.'"[96]

Post-War Changes: Provincial House and Novitiate

In 1948, a group of seven American novices arrived from Sillery to form the first formation community of the newly established Franco-American Province. A year earlier, the convents of the Eastern United States had been separated from Canada, the mother province. Headquartered in Goffstown, the new provincial, M. St. Peter-Claver (Marie Louise) Bilodeau, took up residence with her council, where they remained until the transfer of the provincial house in 1951. By that time, the community had over thirty sisters in residence, with 153 students registered at the Villa school. The chapel of the Villa opened its doors to the Catholics of Goffstown for their Sunday Masses prior to 1955, when St. Lawrence parish was established. In 1962, through the efforts of the parents' organization, construction began for a new facility to provide additional classroom space and an auditorium for plays and school functions. Known as "Rosary Hall," it served over the years as a gym and cafeteria as well as the site of numerous school masses, concerts, dances, science fairs, and an annual penny sale. In time, it provided rental space for the civic community of Goffstown.

Post-war changes occurred in rural communities of the state as families moved into cities. Catholic school populations felt these changes as well as the larger cultural shifts in the nation. At the Villa, there was a gradual diminishment in the numbers of students, resulting in two major changes. In 1968, the high school closed, and two of the sisters joined the teaching staff at a diocesan high school in Manchester. Elementary–level classes began admitting boys. By the 1970's, the boarding school also closed, but a new kindergarten class opened in response to area need. In the ensuing years, the Villa offered morning and aftercare of the children to accommodate working parents. Beginning in 1985, a summer camp program got underway. In 1989, the first School Board of the Villa was elected to oversee its financial management and plan for its future development. When the school celebrated its seventy-fifth anniversary in 1993, enrollment was at 200 students. Welcoming the new technological era, all students took computer classes. Lessons in music, drawing, painting, and the performing arts were part of the extracurricular program, along with a variety of sports activities. Above all, the Villa offered the children a family atmosphere where Christian values were of the utmost importance. Moreover, Villa families gave generously of their time, talent, and financial resources to support the school's mission through an active Home and School Association and a large team of parent volunteers for extra-curricular programs. With the decreasing number of sisters and growing costs of hiring teachers and operating the school, early in the twenty-first century the Religious of Jesus and Mary faced the possible closing of the Villa and sale of its property. The Board showed courageous leadership with a variety of projects to attract new students and faculty. They hired principals for the first time who were not Religious of Jesus and Mary, including two laypersons. One of the sisters on the convent leadership team acted as liaison with the administration. Hers was the task of maintaining continuity with the mission and spirit of the institution. The remaining sisters, aging and few in number, gathered their belongings, emptied the convent of furniture and treasured mementos, and took definitive leave of the Villa in the summer of 2002, leaving room for expanded educational space in the building. Mirroring a demographic pattern in the area, however, the number of students at the Villa declined.

The school culture had changed. After many meetings and planning sessions, a group of parents and concerned individuals offered to administer the school and move toward its eventual purchase. An agreement with the Religious of Jesus and Mary led to the sale of the Villa and some of its surrounding land to the Villa Board in 2008. The school's name became "St. Claudine Villa Academy." The Board sought creative ways of securing the Villa's future; however, low enrollment figures and growing financial challenges forced its closure in June 2014, four years shy of its centenary. The property was sold for $700,000 in 2015 to RdF [sic] Corp., a developer based in Hudson, New Hampshire.

Parish of *Précieux-Sang* (Precious Blood), Woonsocket, RI: 1884[97]

"From the outset, it was clear to our dear missionaries how much good there was to do. These children are "new" in every sense. Most have no idea who the religious (sisters) are, nor do they have any sense of the most basic rules of polite behavior. They lack any religious knowledge. What a vast field the Heavenly Father has given us to cultivate"![98] Such were the first impressions of the sister-annalist shortly after arriving in their newest mission field. Within a decade of their foundation in Fall River, the Religious of Jesus and Mary undertook a third educational center in the neighboring state of Rhode Island, known for its beautiful ocean beaches and resorts, and for upholding religious freedom from the time of its origins in 1636. Rhode Island had been home to a number of Native American tribes; their influence can be seen in the names of some its towns, such as Apponaug, Cowesset, Conimicut, Matunuck, Pawtucket, and Woonsocket. The smallest state joined other New England states in receiving large numbers of immigrant Catholics as laborers in its textile mills. Established as a town in 1867, Woonsocket was located in the northeastern corner of the state, on the Blackstone River, making it a prime location for textile factories owned by Belgian manufacturers. Like Fall River and Manchester, Woonsocket was a mecca for French-Canadian immigrants looking for work, places of worship, and education for their children. By 1875, French Canadians would account for a full quarter of the town's total population of more than 13,000, and were growing in number. Fifty years later, during the Great Depression, they represented three-quarters of its people. Public conversations often took place in French, with newspapers, radio programs, and movies offered in that language.

Their Own Church and Pastor

Major changes were occurring in the diocesan structures of New England. Since 1843, Rhode Island Catholics had been included in the Hartford diocese. In 1872, the diocese of Providence, which included southeastern Massachusetts, was established, with Irish-born Most. Rev. Thomas Francis Hendricken (1827–86) as its first bishop. Earlier in the century, the Woonsocket parish of St. Charles had provided for the religious needs of the Francophone community. The influx of French-Canadians, however, imposed an increased strain on limited parish resources. Tensions arose as these immigrants demanded to have a separate parish and a pastor who was one of their own. These factors convinced Hendricken to consider the purchase of land and approve construction of a church for the French-speaking. He named Rev. Antoine Bernard as the founding pastor of the first "French church," *Précieux-Sang.*In April 1873, the French-speaking community began holding services in the Harris building on North Main Street, while they collected funds for construction of a new church. That same year, excavations began on the basement of an edifice on Hamlet Avenue. A financial panic that year delayed its construction and sent many Canadians back home. Nevertheless, the basement was completed in October of 1874 and its cornerstone blessed.

A year later, the bishop appointed a Belgian-born pastor for the new parish, Rev. James Berkins. Despite his native knowledge of French, Berkins "found a cold welcome" among the parishioners, with some refusing to attend his Mass or contribute to his support. He was transferred in November of 1875, after some discussion between Hendricken and the dissident members of the parish. A young French-Canadian curate, Rev. Charles Dauray, arrived in December from a temporary assignment in Central Falls to assume pastoral leadership of Woonsocket's contentious flock. Despite chronic ill health and the stress of overwork, Dauray emerged as one of the most highly respected pastors of New England, ministering to the people of Precious Blood with wisdom, humility, fairness, and administrative skill for over sixty years. In a commemorative booklet summarizing Dauray's extraordinary leadership, his gifts were well described:

> From an untilled field, he brought forth a harvest of diverse institutions so necessary for the faith of a people, for its growth and development towards a chosen ideal . . . Primarily a man of God, he gave himself completely to his children. Nothing dear

to them was foreign to him. At all times, in word and deeds, he modeled for them true fidelity to religious faith, civic duties, and the traditions of their forbears.[99]

Within two months of Dauray's arrival, a winter storm raged through Woonsocket, shearing the roof off the nearly finished church building. Undaunted and with fierce determination, Dauray and his parishioners set to repairing the building and completing the structure, despite the heavy debts that would incur. On July 17, 1881, the people of Precious Blood proudly assisted at the dedication of their own impressive church building. Fifty years later, six parishes in Woonsocket would claim Precious Blood as the "mother church" of the city's French Canadians.[100]

New Mission Field

Immigrant children in Woonsocket were subject to a school truancy law requiring anyone under the age of fourteen to attend school for twelve weeks a year. For French-Canadian parents, the options were public schools or Irish Catholic schools, which were less than welcoming. Children were often teased or bullied for being vulgar, crude, and backward, because they were not fluent in English. It was humiliating, and Dauray intended to remedy the situation as soon as possible. Despite the heavy debt already on the parish, he obtained the bishop's approval to invite the Religious of Jesus and Mary to open a parish school. Dauray had learned of their good work in Fall River from his seminary classmate, Pierre Bédard, whose sudden death in August of 1884 delayed the arrival of the first Religious of Jesus and Mary until after his funeral services. When Dauray requested sisters for his new parish, "it was perfectly apparent that he had little in a material way to offer them. But he had faith and hope forecasting a brilliant future in a field bound to produce a fruitful harvest."[101]

His hope was well-founded. On August 28, the first group arrived: M. St. Scholastique Fortier, from the Fall River mission, as superior; M. St. Eloi (Ceduline) Gagnon; M. St. Placide (Marie) Roy; M. de la Nativité (Leontine) Labrecque; M. de la Visitation (Leda) Larochelle (whose arrival was delayed until March of the following year); and the ubiquitous Sr. St. Sabine Marion. Most were under the age of thirty; their youthful vitality would be essential to cope with the uncertain situation, as the new school got under way.

Welcoming as he was, Dauray had neither school building nor convent ready for the sisters. He began searching for temporary rental sites. Meanwhile, the sisters learned to be traveling missionaries. On their first night, and for several weeks thereafter, they would separate every evening after school: two to the rectory, and three to St. Bernard's Convent, where the Sisters of Mercy lived near the church of St. Charles. The Mercy Sisters were the first women religious in Woonsocket, having arrived in 1869. They offered the new missionaries hospitality "with a most cordial charity." An exchange of "gifts" took place between the two communities. The Mercy Sisters asked for French lessons, and in turn taught the Religious of Jesus and Mary some phrases in English, to the mutual enrichment and enjoyment of both groups.[102] This provisional housing arrangement lasted into the third week of October, when Dauray rented a small cottage that the community could call home until their school and convent were built. He provided the furniture and furnishings; bought the community a stove for heating; and was solicitous for all their needs. His mother and sister arrived to help with the move, bringing additional furnishings and cooking some of their meals. On October 25, Dauray came to bless the house and its modest chapel; the community happily resumed its regular practices and customs. For the first Christmas, he arrived with the gift of a piano! All these ministrations were signs to the Religious of Jesus and Mary of God's providence, reflected in the generosity of their pastor and the parishioners. They continued to attend Mass in the parish church rather than their own chapel. This was a sacrifice some found painful. In her New Year letter to the Woonsocket colony, M. St. Cyrille admonished them to remember their high calling: "You form a seedbed that will draw blessings on the Church . . . You haven't yet welcomed Jesus into your chapel? Well, consider the men and women religious who are persecuted in the world, who can neither say Mass nor receive communion, not even on holy days! Do you think God loves them less? On the contrary! Dear sisters, be very happy and courageous."[103]

Tilling the Field: The First Bilingual School

On September 8, 1884, after a solemn Eucharist celebrating Our Lady, the missionaries proceeded eagerly to the church basement, where "a veritable avalanche" of youngsters and mothers awaited the opening of their first school day: 124 girls, 112 boys! The sisters divided them into age groups, where the first lessons were recitation of prayers and rosary. The next day, even more children arrived, and the overwhelmed teachers attempted some instruction. They realized quickly it would be an impossible task, given the circumstances. The children had little discipline or training and were crowded together in cramped space. Many had no chairs, let alone desks. At the end of that harrowing week, the annalist summarized the experience:

> Most of the children in our care have grown up without the benefit of a solid home formation. Some are quite difficult to manage, to the point we had to call in a police officer to talk to the classes and scare those (boys) who behaved most badly. This seems to have worked, as the worst of them are now quite contrite. Not perfect contrition, of course, but they were forgiven and not one was sent away . . .[104]

"Not one was sent away . . ." As the first days grew into weeks, student numbers swelled to 180 girls and 160 boys. Clearly, there was great need and desire on the part of French-Canadian families for Catholic, bilingual education. Some Woonsocket voices opposed the idea as a "foreign institution out of harmony with American practices and ideals."[105] Father Dauray dispelled those doubts in a creative way. He invited some local citizens to form an examination board to evaluate regularly the children's educational progress. His decision revealed beyond a doubt that instruction in French was no hindrance to the students' performance in English or other subjects. Dauray's model of a bilingual school "showed great wisdom and foresight, for it brought about an adjustment which acquainted the children with . . . traditions of American life, while acquiring . . . a familiarity with the language and traditions of their forbears."[106] As the community settled into its temporary domicile, Dauray purchased land near the church on Hamlet Avenue for a three-story building to serve as both convent and school. In the spring of 1885, construction began on the structure of a "*petite maison blanche*" into which the sisters would move by September of that year. Small compared to their familiar Canadian convent schools, it had space for a few classrooms along with sisters' living quarters.

When they returned in August from their annual holiday in Fall River, the house was two weeks' short of being ready to receive the community and students. Unfazed, the Religious of Jesus and Mary spent the time setting up classrooms and furniture. In spite of the fumes of new paint, they enjoyed a meal together in their new refectory. On September 8, 1885, the first anniversary of their arrival, the sisters held classes in the new building and happily took up permanent residence in quarters that were more spacious. A decision was made to separate the girls and boys in the boarding section; fifty-nine boys gathered in the new "Academy," under the direction of Mme. St. Ferdinand Goulet. About eighty girls had classes there as well. The 160 day-students continued to receive instruction in the church basement. The sisters noted with satisfaction that piety and good discipline were on the rise, and that the situation in the church basement had improved with less-crowded conditions. On Dauray's patronal feast that year, the Religious of Jesus and Mary rejoiced to attend the first Mass celebrated in their modest chapel.

"Castel Dauray" (1895)

The new building was an improvement, but growing numbers of children were signs to Dauray that more construction was essential to accommodate the population of his parish, which now included several areas of the city. By the end of July, 1885, he purchased a "magnificent" property at the corner of Carrington and Park Avenues and began to plan for a larger convent and school on the site. However, construction was delayed for several reasons, one being a change of episcopal leadership. After the death of Hendricken in 1886, his successor, Boston-born Most Rev. Matthew Harkins (1845–1921), was concerned over the major debts already incurred by both the parish and the Religious of Jesus and Mary in Fall River. He withdrew earlier permission to go forward with the building project. The sisters would need to manage a difficult teaching situation for the near future and adapt their ordinary methods of instruction. The annals for 1889 report that a few sisters were traveling daily to cramped quarters in two rented buildings, where they instructed more than300 children from the "Globe" and "Social" geographical sections of the city. Without desks or teachers' platforms, the sisters stood all day to give their lessons. In March of 1889, the "Academy" was closed; it could no longer accommodate an ever- expanding school population. Boys' classes moved to the church basement; girls had their lessons in the convent. When the school opened in September of 1892 with more than 500 students, girls and boys were assigned to "mixed" classes for the first time. The next year, the bishop established the parish of St. Anne for French Canadians from the Social district of Woonsocket. Sisters of the Presentation of Mary (PM) arrived in 1893 to direct a parish school there, alleviating the over-crowding at Precious Blood. In 1894, the necessary permissions arrived to proceed with building the new school, and construction began on the site. It opened its doors a year later, on November 4, 1895, as the par-ish celebrated Dauray's twenty-fifth anniversary of ordination. Fittingly, the turreted new brick building was named "Castel Dauray," honoring its founder as well as its noble architecture. It was here that the Religious of Jesus and Mary would live and serve the thousands of students who became their living legacy well into the twentieth century. In July of 1896, a Jesuit from Montréal preached the first annual retreat for the sisters in their new convent. The Castel became a preferred gathering site for large group retreats and conferences over the next seven decades. Recent advances in transportation made the site accessible to many. The city's new electric trams passed directly in front of the building, "*devant notre porte*," which may have proved a mixed blessing for some! On February 2, 1897, the community dropped the title "Madame" for its temporary professed sisters, and every choir sister assumed the title "Mother," by which they would be known until after Vatican II. The auxiliaries contin-ued to be called "Sister."

The first day of school in 1898 brought a major transformation in the student population. Boys from ages eight to fifteen would no longer at-tend the Park Avenue school. They moved to the former "white house" on Hamlet Avenue for their classes. Known as the Collège du Sacré-Coeur, it was administered and directed by five Brothers of the Sacred Heart, who had arrived that year from Canada. At the turn of the century, Castel Dau-ray opened its doors to growing numbers of French-Canadian students and increased its staff of sisters and lay teachers. With more than 800 chil-dren registered annually from 1900 to 1905, the community's population swelled to twenty-eight choir professed and five auxiliary sisters. The con-vent was a site for the annual summer retreats, with student dormitories as sleeping quarters for large numbers of sisters. Generations of sisters from the houses of the Northeast descended upon the imposing building to fol-low the annual exercises of their Ignatian-style retreats, often preached by visiting Jesuits from Canada. Four times a day, conferences in French presented the Spiritual Exercises of St. Ignatius and the life of Jesus, topics on prayer, religious life, and fidelity to its commitments.

In the summer of 1902, a renowned French Jesuit missionary from Montréal arrived to direct the Woonsocket retreat. Almire Pichon, SJ had a global reputation as a spiritual director and retreat preacher to many women religious in France and Canada, including the Religious of Jesus and Mary of Sillery. He had been friendly with the Martin family of Lisieux, and subsequently became spiritual director of St. Thérèse's sister Marie. During the Woonsocket retreat, one of the sisters collected verbatim notes of his conferences, later published as a dissertation in Rome.[107] The book offers insight into Pichon's devotion to the Sacred Heart and his rejection of scrupulosity. His passionate style, flashes of humor, as well as his emphases on the importance of love, trust, peace, and freedom in one's relationship with God endeared him to sisters who had been exposed to more rigid approaches to their spirituality. A special friend to the Religious of Jesus and Mary, Pichon offered his last Mass in North America at their residence in New York City.

In 1902, the diocese established a second "daughter parish" of Precious Blood, and named it for the Holy Family: "Ste-Famille." Four of the community continued traveling daily to instruct roughly 400 children in a house on River Street, rented by the pastor as a four-room school. His hope to provide a convent for the sisters was put on hold until the church building was completed. Nine years later, the Religious of Jesus and Mary moved into their own parish convent. The new century occasioned a change in congregational leadership for the Religious of Jesus and Mary. The provincial of Canada, M. Eufemia Mandri, returned to her native Spain in 1901. She was replaced by a vice-provincial, M. St. Augustin Hatschemberg, who died suddenly three years later in Highland Mills, New York. Her successor was M. St. Croix (Artemise) Tanguay, who led the province for the next fourteen years. After her election in 1903 as superior general, M. St. Clare Bray wasted no time traveling to the far-flung congregation. Her first journey to the States was in 1904, and the missionaries everywhere warmed to her energy and personality. At the end of her visit to Woonsocket, on March 14, 1905, she brought sisters to tears with these parting words: "May we be united, loving one another as true sisters . . . I have been so consoled by the good that you are doing here, and the evident fervor I have found."

The Boarding School (1908) and the New Academy (1911)

At the opening of classes in September 1906, 1000 children registered, creating a sense of urgency for more space. The administrators drew up plans to add a new wing and a fourth floor to the building. The community that year numbered twenty-seven choir sisters and six auxiliaries, under the inspiring leadership of M. St. Etienne (Vitaline) Bilodeau, in her ninth year as the local superior. Following her death in 1908, a niece, M. St. Peter Claver Bilodeau, became superior, a position she would hold three more times at Precious Blood. Her intelligence, competence, kindness, and bilingual fluency were gifts needed and admired by the religious and civic communities at this critical time. She proved an able and much-appreciated partner of Father Dauray, working with him over the years to build up an extraordinary apostolic endeavor. She likewise drew the admiration and respect of ecclesiastical authorities with whom she dealt over the years, both as superior and provincial.[108] Encouraged by their congregational leaders, the sisters had hoped for years to build an independent boarding school. They were now in a position to purchase the convent, along with another property Dauray had found nearby, for the sum of $28,000. While Dauray supported their project, some parishioners and Bishop Harkins questioned the wisdom of the transfer of ownership. The parish had funded the building of the school. According to the American Church's conciliar legislation, the parish corporation owned it. There were other legal irregularities with the Precious Blood Corporation, causing a year's delay in obtaining the necessary episcopal permission. In May of 1907, Bishop Harkins called on five Religious of Jesus and Mary to form a separate corporation representing their Woonsocket schools under the title of "*École Ste-Claire.*" When he attended the funeral services for M. St. Etienne in September 1908, the bishop gave the desired permission for the purchase. To some it must have seemed a providential push from the woman who had been the moving force behind the idea of expansion and a community-owned boarding school.[109] In November that year, before new construction began, the boarding school opened with three admissions: Rose-Alba Beaudet, her younger sister, Eva, and nine-year old Eva Giguère. By January 1909, there were fifteen boarders, and thirty-nine three years later. Their sleeping quarters were the sisters' former dormitory; the community slept in two nearby houses purchased as temporary housing.

When the Religious of Jesus and Mary celebrated the twenty-fifth anniversary of the foundation in November 1909, a community of thirty-one sisters was ministering to thirty-five boarders and well over 900 children in the day school. They hired a staff of several women to help with the cleaning and cooking. Four lay teachers joined the faculties of both day and boarding schools. Groundbreaking for the new parish school building took place late in August 1910, and the cornerstone was blessed by Dauray in November. The convent would house the boarding school for several more years. On September 10, 1911, the *"Académie Jésus-Marie"* was blessed, and three donated bells—Charles, Pierre, and André—rang out to welcome a student body of 900, a dedicated staff of a score of sisters and ten teaching assistants, some of whom were former pupils, under the able direction of M. St. Lutgarde Roy. The community had assumed a massive debt on the building, amounting to $98,000. A new era in Woonsocket was under way. The boarding school held an open house that fall, with increasing numbers of young girls added to the census. At the end of the school year, the sisters inaugurated the "crowning ceremony," a French custom they had brought from Canada to honor virtue and piety among the boarders by distributing crowns of flowers to them. In the States, it melded with the traditional May crowning of Mary practiced in many Catholic immigrant communities.

In late spring of 1915, while World War I was raging, Precious Blood became a temporary refuge for fifteen Spanish Religious of Jesus and Mary fleeing the civil strife and persecution in Mexico. They arrived by train to be welcomed by the New England communities. Five stayed in Woonsocket, where the annalist wrote on June 20: "With what affection and enthusiasm we welcomed them into our arms and hearts! Only one speaks French. Yet, Spanish and Canadian, we are still one." Despite the growing reputation of the schools, financial straits caused by the World War I and their huge debt overburdened the community. In January 1914, M. St. Peter Claver had petitioned Harkins for an increase of $500 to the annual sisters' subsidy of $1500. Help came in the form of gifts from Harkins and others, along with annual fundraisers and many whist parties. In 1918, the sisters decided to keep the boarding school open for their seventy-five boarders during the Spanish influenza pandemic, but they closed the academy for several weeks. That year brought the celebration of the Congregation's centenary, the Armistice for the "war to end all wars," and the announcement of a new provincial, M. St. Thérèse (Laure) Chapleau. In the "shuffle" of appointments, their beloved superior became the mistress of novices and moved to Québec. Their incoming superior, M. St. Elisabeth (Alice) Fradet, arrived a few months later, as did complete electric wiring for the house. An alumnae association for both schools initiated regular meetings, occasional retreats and pious conferences. Statutes for these

"*Anciennes*" were drafted for approval. As the decade closed, space was already a concern: over sixty students had to be refused admittance.

New Bishop, New Controversies: the 1920s

The early 1920s saw the number of boarders reach 100 and beyond, and the Precious Blood Convent began to welcome large numbers of sisters for retreats and educational conferences. There were significant changes at the diocesan level as well. In 1919, given the failing health of Bishop Harkins, Reverend William A. Hickey, pastor of a church in Clinton, Massachusetts, became coadjutor bishop and administrator of the diocese. At the death of Harkins in 1921, Hickey succeeded him as the ordinary. Possessed of business acumen, he had ambitious plans to improve Catholic education. He hoped to organize and unify diocesan finances so that the youth in Rhode Island could have first-rate education, especially at the secondary level. During his episcopacy, Hickey was consistently generous to the Religious of Jesus and Mary, making large contributions toward their high school building campaign and coming to their assistance with debt payments during the Great Depression. While Hickey gained respect in many Catholic circles, his tenure was not without controversy, especially with a group of ultra-nationalist French Canadians who disagreed with his approach to fundraising for education. In 1923, when Hickey announced a million-dollar diocesan high school campaign, this group organized itself to protest the tactic as a potential threat to local parish funds and autonomy in educational establishments. Following the announcement, Mr. Elphège Daignault, a Woonsocket lawyer-activist and acknowledged leader of the dissidents, organized the protestors—known as "Crusaders"—and consulted with canon lawyers in Québec. The next year, the group began publishing a French-language newspaper, "*La Sentinelle*," (The Sentinel), from which the group took its name. Intended to provide a vehicle for their critique and promote organized resistance, the journal resorted to rabid editorials and articles conveying perceived grievances and threats on the bishop's part to French-Canadian customs and language. The group held rallies, raised funds, and organized pew-rent strikes in parishes. It attracted both outspoken and silent supporters from parishes in the diocese, including a few priests. In 1925, the Sentinellists sent a formal petition to the Vatican, asking it to halt the bishop's assessment of parish funds. They felt it was unfair and illegal for their parishes to subsidize the building of English-language schools. The officials in Rome dismissed their petition as groundless.

A war of words ensued in various local journals and newspapers. Because Hickey refused to compromise with their demands, the Sentinellists brought their case to the civil courts, which voted to uphold the bishop's position. By spring of 1928, pastors in all the churches read a letter from Hickey excommunicating Daignault and about sixty Sentinellists. The group's journal appeared on the Index of Forbidden Books. From Rome came documents of suspension for the editor. A Woonsocket pastor, Rev. Achille Prince, an active supporter of the movement, was removed from his parish. Some Religious of Jesus and Mary and their relatives in the area were undoubtedly sympathetic to the movement, yet the annalist refers to it as having "done much harm to Canadians on the false pretext of language issues." In later years, sisters describing the "affair" recalled that because of its sensitive nature, they were forbidden to discuss it in community conversations. In 1927, an undated postscript in a circular from M. St. Peter Claver recommended "extreme prudence . . . in all that concerns 'La Sentinelle.' Let us refrain from speaking about it among ourselves or in community. If it comes up in parlor visits, we should change the conversation. We need to remain loyal to ecclesiastical authority and support it."

Dauray and the congregational leadership were uncompromising in their support of the bishop throughout the controversy. Within a year of their excommunication, all the members of the group had complied with the bishop's conditions for absolution and were readmitted to communion. Having attracted a fair amount of national attention, the Sentinellist Affair revealed how lasting and deep the issue of "*survivance*" was in parts of New England. It had renewed former ethnic misunderstandings and tensions that echoed well into the twentieth century. Interestingly enough, the monies raised in French-Canadian parishes of Woonsocket were used to complete construction of the new boys' high school, Mount St. Charles, named by Hickey for the loyal and intrepid pastor of Precious Blood.[110] Opened with great fanfare in 1924, it was the crowning achievement for the aged Monsignor, now ailing and frail, unable to attend the ceremonies.

The 1920s were a time of increased prosperity in America; most people were unaware that their good fortune would soon take a downward turn. The next decade, the Great Depression, affected the United

States immigrant population in many ways. Banks failed, businesses closed, and farms collapsed. The average income of the American family dropped by forty percent; unemployment for workers rose in some places to twenty-five percent; savings accounts were wiped out; thousands were evicted from their homes. More people began to emigrate from the "land of opportunity" back to their nations of origin. The nation's number of immigrants recorded in 1933 dropped ninety percent from a decade earlier. As early as 1927, Woonsocket manufacturers and textile mills had begun to close. Within the next five years, Woonsocket's economy collapsed. During the worst years of the Depression, half the city's textile workers were unemployed. Several factories, including the Social and Globe Mills, were torn down.

A Light in Dark Times: St. Clare High School (1928)[111]

Economic realities of the 1920s would create financial strains on the community at Precious Blood, who had decided to add two wings to the Castel, enlarging the boarding school and providing space for a new chapel and girls' secondary school. In 1926, M. St. Peter Claver became provincial superior for North America. Familiar with the situation at Precious Blood, she gladly gave permission to undertake another costly but hopeful project. Construction began that July, and the community moved into its new quarters a year later, at which time there were 144 boarders registered. In the fall of 1927, they celebrated the first Mass in the new Chapel of the Sacred Heart. An open house that November attracted even more families interested in high-quality education for their daughters. Housed in a wing of the new building, St. Clare High School bore the name of the visionary superior general who placed a high priority on women's education. In 1928, at the end of a difficult economic year for the community, the sisters met with Hickey, who gave them a check for $25,000 to help with the expenses of their new construction, which totaled over $420,000. By 1931, more than 100 girls were attending the high school as boarders or day students. That January, the alumnae held a whist card party to raise funds for the Religious of Jesus and Mary. Their many tributes praised the "intense labor and selfless devotion" of the sisters: "They have consistently enlarged their institution without fear of the enormous debt they undertook. All this for the sake of our daughters."[112]

An undated prospectus from this period outlines in ample detail the aims, course of study, and a list of expectations for all students, with an emphasis on the secondary school program at St. Clare's. The stated aim of the institution was "to offer girls and young women a superior educational experience in matters religious, literary, social and domestic." The Religious of Jesus and Mary hoped to infuse a girl's intellectual formation with strong moral values in order to help her reach "the end offered her by God: to know him with her intellect, to love him with her heart, to serve him by exercising her free will." Recalling their founder's admonition, the sisters "try at all times to be true mothers to the children confided to their care," using prevention rather than punishment. Special attention was given to the development of good language and manners, habits of order, cleanliness, and economy. Likewise, the school offered personal training in the arts: piano, violin, and voice lessons, oil and watercolor painting classes. Together with courses in domestic arts and physical education, these electives were seen as necessary complements to the intellectual development of a "St. Clare girl." What distinguished the institution from others in the state was its emphasis on bilingual education at elementary and secondary levels. Courses in religion, church history, and language formed part of the French component of each day. In Woonsocket, where Franco-American families were the majority, this approach was appreciated as a link to the language of forbears and the religious practice they valued. Incentives to performance and good behavior in the boarding school were varied. In addition to report cards and examinations, there were weekly sessions of good/bad "notes," color-coded sashes for various "sections," distribution of prizes and "crowning" ceremonies at the end of May. Every aspect of a student's life was supervised in hopes of producing a refined, self-assured, and docile young woman, prepared to move into society with knowledge and grace.

After the boarding students completed the elementary course (K-8), they moved to the secondary level, with a choice of general or classical courses toward high school graduation. Both tracks offered classes in required subjects of English, French, history, mathematics, and sciences. The general course offered "commercial" subjects of typing, shorthand, stenography, and bookkeeping; in the classical course, students could take four years of Latin, ancient history, physics, and the higher sciences. Domestic science was an elective in both groups. As the school grew, a bilingual library, Glee Club, a school paper, *The Clarion*, and a yearbook, *Je Me Souviens*, provided additional incentives. Monthly tuition was $25, with additional fees for all elective courses or services. An active alumnae association, begun in 1931, met regularly and sponsored several fundraising events annually, including evenings of recollection for the members and a May Reunion Day.

A New Era, Golden Jubilee (1930s)

In December of 1930, the parish community celebrated the sixtieth anniversary of priesthood for Dauray, who at the age of ninety-three was frail and unable to attend the festivities honoring his extraordinary life and accomplishments. The commemorative booklet recalls the pastor's qualities primarily as "a man of God." It describes his spiritual and pastoral care of the French-Canadians entrusted to him for over fifty years; his broad and far-reaching contributions to civic society; his proverbial goodness and "generous hospitality that have made of Woonsocket a center welcoming visitors from all nations." A short time later, Dauray succumbed to bronchitis; on February 22, he died peacefully. The Religious of Jesus and Mary formed a guard of honor around his bier at the funeral parlor. Very large crowds attended the funeral services. Dauray was buried at the site he had chosen on the parish grounds, in the shadow of the church he had built and faithfully served over fifty years. His nephew, a curate and close collaborator for eighteen years, Rev. Georges Bédard, became the new pastor. Named as parish administrator in 1929, Bédard was familiar with parochial concerns and finances, which included a considerable debt. Dauray had left no estate, having given away most of his earthly goods during his lifetime. With considerable skill, Bédard would make necessary repairs and improvements to parish buildings and reduce the capital on the parish debt.

This new appointment, however, meant significant changes for the sisters, arriving with the financial crisis of the Great Depression. Their relationship with Bédard proved to be different from their long-standing friendship with Dauray. While the house Annals choose reserved language, they refer to a pattern of financial disagreements with the new pastor, especially about the sisters' income from the parish. Dauray had previously allocated a yearly amount of $2500 to help with support of poor children in the school. Yet, the annalist reports in an undated entry for 1931 that the sisters were "covering the expenses of the parish school without receiving any salaries from the parish." Nineteen of them were teaching in the Academy alone that year, where only eighty students were paying tuition. Bédard no longer permitted the community to organize whist parties or fundraisers to meet expenses on the interest and insurance fees for their building. They finally turned to the bishop for assistance to meet some of their obligations. In November, Hickey sent them the amount for back payment, and things seemed to be settled—for a time. When Bédard gave parishioners a report on the financial status early in 1932, the sisters were surprised to hear that the pastor's figures and theirs did not agree. For example, he announced that he had given the Religious of Jesus and Mary a "gift" of $400. The sisters thought the amount sent them was payment for making the hosts, as well as doing laundry and mending altar linens at the church and at Mt. St. Charles, tasks assumed at their own expense. Several unpleasant discussions ensued, with some disagreement about the terms of debt payments to the parish along with sisters' salaries. At one meeting to which the Hickey was invited, he expressed amazement at the penury of the convent, wondering how the sisters could live on so little income. The superior replied that the community did all its own housework and other chores in addition to running the schools. Hickey angrily reminded Bédard that the parish had first invited the Religious of Jesus and Mary and had an obligation to support them.

Confrontations with Bédard such as these were a challenging trial as the Great Depression continued into the thirties. The pastor was himself in financial straits and trying to save as much as he could. He would send checks to the Religious of Jesus and Mary on occasion "for past due expenses." The strained relationship led to frequent painful and difficult encounters, visits to the chancery for aid with interest costs, and numerous novenas and rosaries of petition. The high school principal and superior, M. St. Pierre (Marie Marguerite) Castonguay, counseled peace, union, and reconciliation. Discreet and devout in assessing the troubled period, the annalist concludes on October 30, 1931: "In this nomination, Providence undoubtedly has its own plans which we adore without understanding them . . . May these trials keep us in the spirit of poverty and help us to save souls." The first diploma and graduation ceremony took place at St. Clare's on June 15, 1932, with the bishop presiding. The ceremony provided a joyful contrast to the hardships the sisters were undergoing. There were four graduates from the classical course; fifteen from the general course; and six from the two-year commercial course. Twenty-nine girls received diplomas from the eighth grade. That

September, 120 day students, or "externs," arrived for the high school course, in addition to the scores of boarders. The following year, there were sixteen graduates from the high school and thirty from the elementary course; total enrollment for the high school held steady at 131. M. St. Pierre was relieved of her duties as superior so she could concentrate on her roles as principal of the expanding secondary school and as supervisor of the sisters' studies.

Encouraged by these signs of growth, the Religious of Jesus and Mary anticipated celebrating their fiftieth anniversary in Woonsocket. In the fall of 1933, however, they received news they described as "a lightning bolt." Their kind and generous benefactor, Bishop Hickey, died suddenly on October 4 of a heart attack. Not until February of 1934 would his successor be named: Most. Rev. Francis P. Keough, bishop of Hartford, a native of Connecticut who had studied with the Sulpicians in Paris. Intelligent and unassuming, Keough would for the next thirteen years oversee continued growth of the Catholic population in Rhode Island, including a 50 % increase in the number of priests. He founded the minor seminary in Providence, worked to reduce the diocesan debt, and was able to ease the ongoing tensions among ethnic groups during a tenure that covered the demanding years of the Great Depression and World War II. By the time the new bishop made his first visit to Precious Blood that June, he was already well liked and admired for his humility and "distinguished bearing." His words to the twenty-six high school graduates at the diploma ceremony at St. Clare included compliments to parents and the sisters. To their teachers' delight, Keough congratulated the graduates on their fluency in both English and French, saying, "Don't be afraid to speak your mother tongue, which you have elegantly mastered. Don't be shy to speak English either, for you have become proficient in it as well." One of the graduates from the secondary course, Miss Jeannette Grisé, received highest honors and the religion prize. She announced her decision to enter the Religious of Jesus and Mary novitiate, hoping to become a missionary. After some time of preparation in Rome, she spent twenty years in India as M. St. Veronica.

Celebrating Fifty Years in Woonsocket: 1934 and 1935

With the celebration of their golden jubilee at Precious Blood approaching, the Religious of Jesus and Mary must have found it hard to believe that their sisters had accomplished so much in just five decades of mission work. A new superior general, M. St. Borgia, made her initial visit to the Woonsocket schools and community in April 1934 and participated in the four-day festivities on the last weekend of that month. A central committee of more than twenty-five alumni and parish leaders had formed five planning groups: reception, banquet, public relations, music, and decorations. Several prominent judges, attorneys, and the mayor himself were among the distinguished speakers at various functions for the occasion. On Friday, April 26, the schoolchildren inaugurated the celebration at a sung Mass and performed a special play they had prepared for guests. Saturday, May 7, was the Alumnae Reunion Day, with a high Mass in the convent chapel, followed by a festive luncheon for the alumnae, speeches for the occasion, and a closing consecration ceremony to Our Lady with Benediction of the Blessed Sacrament. M. St. Borgia presided over the Alumnae Reunion Day, with hundreds in attendance. Her message to the assembly was encouraging: "Your Association, under the patronage of the Immaculate Conception, has as its motto, 'Semper fidelis,' ever-faithful.' In its loyalty and affection toward the Alma Mater, the group enthusiastically moves toward that aim, united and generous." The feast culminated with Sunday's Pontifical Mass in the parish with Keough presiding. This was the formal event for expressions of gratitude to God, to all the alumni and benefactors, and not least, to the assembled Franco-American population of Woonsocket that had supported the endeavor from its humble beginnings in the church basement.

Following the religious ceremonies, some 600 guests filed into the parish hall for the jubilee banquet and its laudatory speeches, followed by a lyrical performance by the high school students. On Monday, the final day of the festivities, a crowd attended the solemn memorial Mass for all deceased sisters and alumni/ae since the foundation. A floral tribute was laid at the gravesite of Dauray, bringing the fiftieth anniversary celebration to a fitting close. Throughout the jubilee year, the sisters held fundraising activities and a festival that brought in profits of over $3000. In the throes of the Depression, however, their financial struggles continued. Many former students came forward to contribute and help the religious community to which they owed so much. The 1935 commemorative "Album-Souvenir" for the jubilee published statistics that point to an impressive harvest of vocations to priesthood and religious life. Alumnae who entered women's congregations totaled 132; sixty-six were Religious of Jesus and Mary (five of them novices) and sixty-seven entered other

French-speaking congregations, most of them with the Sisters of Présentation de Marie, who taught in several Woonsocket parish schools. The Religious of Jesus and Mary could boast as well of twenty-seven priests who had received early education with them and six alumni who became Brothers of the Sacred Heart. In those first five decades, 252 Religious of Jesus and Mary ministered to the parish and boarding schools, dedicating their lives to community service, teaching, and/or administration. The title page of the album presents a descriptive homage from former students: "To these educators who have filled the hearts of the young with a love of the true, the good and the beautiful; to these valiant women whose lessons and example have prepared their students for the challenges of life; to these MOTHERS, whose tender hearts have conquered our own, our tribute of gratitude."[113]

Toward the Mid-Century

Ongoing studies now filled the summers for the teachers in the community. Most went to Providence daily by bus for six weeks of courses at the Catholic Teachers College. Five traveled to New York, attending Fordham University in lower Manhattan. Late in August 1936, twenty-seven sisters took refuge from the ongoing Mexican Revolution in various houses of the Americas: Buenos Aires, Argentina (10); Highland Mills, NY (3); El Paso, TX (12). Two Mexican sisters came from Havana, Cuba, to Precious Blood: M. Trinidad Castilla Samperio and Maria de la Luz Castrejón.[114] Records show that both were in Woonsocket for at least two years and then moved on serve in Texas and California. The exchange reflects a process of "globalization" in the province long before the term was popular. In the province report on the houses sent to the General Chapter in May 1937, impressive statistics added to a sense of satisfaction with the six decades of missionary expansion. At Precious Blood, there was a community of forty-two choir sisters and thirteen auxiliary sisters. Two lay teachers were included in the roster. This dedicated corps of women served 800 children (boys and girls) in the Academy, 100 boarders, and 120 day-students. Their educational establishment now comprised a boarding school, a secondary school with academic and commercial courses, primary and elementary schools, and a kindergarten. In addition, the sisters and some high school students offered catechetical instruction to 215 children from local public schools. They directed

numerous organizations and study groups for young people, both at parish and diocesan levels.

By the 1930s, the sisters were organizing days of recollection and
silent "closed retreats" for high school students, alumnae, and married
women of the area. Directed for the most part by Jesuit priests, these
retreats were offered in French. Not only were they a popular form of
spiritual renewal; they also brought in additional income during the holidays. In June and July of 1941, more than fifty attended the closed retreat
for women. The following November, students were dismissed for the day
while a Jesuit from Montréal preached a day of recollection for more than
300 women. His themes were family life and woman's role in making the
home a happy place. He left them with a spiritual bouquet that reflects
the dominant view of women in Catholic circles of the time, even if it is
jarring to contemporary ears: "For God, the glory, for others, joy; for me,
labor and suffering."[115]

With the bombing of Pearl Harbor in December of that year, the
United States entered World War II, which had already raged in Europe
and Asia for two years. A campaign in the Woonsocket schools encouraged students to buy war bonds and do their part in the war effort that
rallied the whole nation. By November of 1942, students at the secondary school had collected $6000 in bonds, exceeding their taxed amount.
Early in 1943, public schools and the Academy had to close in January
to save on heating costs. Students were enthusiastic in selling bonds; the
combined elementary and high schools raised $55,000. In May of that
year, for the second war bond "contest" among area schools, St. Clare's
took second place by raising $16,000.

The war and its consequences touched the Precious Blood community in a personal way with the arrival of a German sister, M. Pia
(Marguerite) Weisner, a survivor of the terror bombing and destruction
of Dresden, during which the sisters' convent had been obliterated. They
had scattered, but eventually regrouped in Weisman, Germany, hoping
to get to Rome. From 1948 to 1949, M, Pia corresponded with the provincial, M. St. Peter Claver, concerning her efforts to obtain a visa to the
States. Because all their documents had been lost in the Dresden fire, the
German sisters feared they would be locked behind the Russian "iron
curtain." With considerable help from friends and benefactors, M. Pia
eventually traveled to Canada and then to the States. She was sent to the
community at Precious Blood, where she served for many years.[116] After
the war, Keough was able to bring some debt relief to the community. In

April 1946, he transferred the debt of the Religious of Jesus and Mary to the diocese, amounting to nearly $400,000. Henceforth, payments would be made to the diocese, presumably with lower interest rates. It would take decades before the community paid off the entire amount. The schools continued to thrive, thanks to the war effort that brought new life to industry in Woonsocket and its surroundings. A province report for 1949 gives a population of fifty-eight sisters and more than 1100 students. The schools and convent at Precious Blood had entered a new phase of their existence. No longer mission outposts, they were well-established institutions, highly regarded in civic and religious spheres.

The Post-War Years

In December, 1947, the sisters celebrated the centenary year of papal approval of the congregation's Constitutions. They hosted a special program to which they invited the communities of Woonsocket and Fall River. When chapel renovations began, the community held fund-raising evening concerts of sacred music performed by the sisters, especially M. St. John of the Eucharist (Marguerite) Paradis. Known for her operatic training and experience, she gained regional renown as an outstanding musician and voice instructor to several aspiring singers. Well into her later years, she directed a variety of choral performances, including the annual Glee Club concert and recitals by her students. Extracurricular activities at St. Clare's were flourishing: a school orchestra, inter-scholastic sports, debate society, an active and engaged Sodality of Our Lady, and Catholic Mission Club, among others. The parish welcomed a new pastor in 1949, Msgr. Moïse Leprohon. By 1954, a community of fifty-four sisters, including eight auxiliaries, shepherded 673 students in the Academy, 129 elementary school boarders, and 352 young women in secondary school, either as day students or boarders. That year they awarded more than 100 diplomas to the high school graduates, including twenty-one boarders. Quite a change from those chaotic first days in the church basement!

In 1961, the community of Precious Blood celebrated its seventy-fifty anniversary; the elementary school received state certification. A decade later, however, the annals reported diminishing student populations in both schools, while the number of sisters in the community remained stable. The changes in the schools reflected a decline in the demographics of the city, partly due to the relocation of Woonsocket's factories to the South and the opening of new Catholic high schools in surrounding suburbs. They also point to a shift in attitudes toward boarding school education for girls and its rising costs. A roster of teachers in both schools revealed a growing number of salaried lay teachers and a few sisters of other communities. In 1965, there were sixty-six boarders and a dozen "half-boarders" who returned home every evening after a study period. The admission requirements for resident students from 1967 to 1969 show the financial pressures on the school administration. An independent institution, St. Clare's relied on income from tuition for its operational costs. Tuition and boarding fees in the elementary school were raised to $1100 for full-time boarders; the half-day boarders would now pay $300. Despite these attempts to stabilize the economic picture, on May 22, 1969, the superior, Sr. Clarice Dionne, sent a note to parents informing them that resident students would no longer be admitted.

In June 1972, St. Clare High School graduated seventy-four high school students and thirty-four eighth-graders. That spring, at the provincial chapter, there was a discussion about a possible merger of St. Clare's with Mt. St. Charles, the boys' high school. A consultative vote among the delegates favored a merger, but called for postponing it another year. To the dismay of the sisters, the Brothers of the Sacred Heart, who directed Mt. St. Charles, announced unexpectedly their decision to accept girls for the coming academic year. It sounded a death-knell for St. Clare's. On the evening of August 5, an emotional parents' meeting took place. The principal, Sr. Jacqueline Crepeau, announced that St. Clare High would close its doors the following June. Reasons given were the diminishing numbers of students, lack of adequate personnel, and the rising costs of salaries and maintenance. This decision reflected a larger picture for Catholic education and major changes occurring in American religious life. It was, however, a painful one for sisters and lay faculty who had ministered at St. Clare's, as well as for students and their families. The final academic year got underway with 236 registered in the high school. Farewell dinners and final events for alumnae and other school groups filled the last months. Concerts were performed, a last graduation ceremony took place, and a community of thirty-five sisters began the task of packing and moving to other convents and new apostolic work. The doors of both schools closed definitively on June 15, 1973. A closing Mass at the chapel on June 24 marked a sister's final vow celebration, tying past and future together in a poignant ceremony. On July 30, the last sisters left the building, sad to be departing their home and its history, yet grateful to God for nine decades of educational service to parish children and young women of Woonsocket and beyond. Early in November, the province leadership entered an agreement with Living Enterprises, Inc. of Marblehead, MA, for purchase of the property for $268,000, to be converted into independent senior living residences, the Chateau Clare Apartments.

St. Joseph's Parish, Newport, RI: 1886–87[117]

On Saturday, August 21, 1886, the *Newport Journal* reported a sale of the four-acre Hazard property, "situated on the southerly slope of Miantonomi Hill," together with its buildings and "improvements." The buyers were identified as "the French sisters of Jésus-Marie." Fourteen months later, the same property—described as ideal for a young ladies' boarding school—appeared in the *Journal* for sale or lease "because permission was denied to open the school in St. Joseph's Parish." What cautionary tale did that statement infer? What had happened to a promising new venture for the Religious of Jesus and Mary?

The well-publicized problems at Notre-Dame had led M. St. Cyrille to seek a more suitable site for the boarding school the sisters wanted to open in Fall River. She likewise recognized the need to attract students of more affluent families as boarders, pursuing a tradition begun in Europe and Canada. Newport was a better source of students for a boarding school than Fall River and would help to establish the community more broadly in New England. The seaside resort was a popular summer community during this gilded age of the late nineteenth century. Some of the wealthiest families in America built their stately mansions and summer villas on its Atlantic beachfront. They would appreciate and welcome French convent training for their daughters. It appears that the province leaders had initiated conversations with diocesan authorities about their plans. The chancery supported the move but counselled waiting until the Fall River troubles died down. Some years before, the sisters had befriended a prominent physician, Dr. Horatio Storer, who lived in Newport. As an influential Catholic convert, he served as a trustee at St. Joseph's Parish and would be well acquainted with real estate in the area. M. St. Cyrille asked Storer to act as the agent of the congregation in their search for an appropriate and affordable site.[118] Because of some anti-Catholic sentiment at the time, discretion dictated that the sisters not conduct their inquiries in person.

Bishop Hendricken fell seriously ill early in 1886 and died in June of that year. It is assumed that the Religious of Jesus and Mary communicated their designs on a Newport property to the vicar-general, Rev. Michael McCabe. They understood they could not proceed with plans for an academy until they obtained permission of the new ordinary. They would simply offer private lessons and let the house serve as a summer villa for ailing sisters. Storer meanwhile proceeded to negotiate the terms of purchase for the Hazard property, an estate at the outer limits of St. Joseph's Parish. It was an ideal site for their new venture. St. Joseph Church opened in 1885, an offshoot of St. Mary's, the oldest parish in Rhode Island. Its first pastor was Rev. James Coyle, an Irish immigrant who had been assistant priest in the Cathedral parish of Providence until his appointment to Newport. Energetic and ambitious, Coyle purchased the Zion Church property, then remodeled and beautified it as a place of worship for the newly-formed Catholic community. He was zealous for his flock, most of whom were his Irish compatriots seeking a better life. On August 17, 1886, M. St. Paul Frechette, superior in Fall River, signed the deed to the Miantonomi Hill property for the Religious of Jesus and Mary at a purchase price of $15,000. On August 19, she wrote to McCabe informing him of the transaction, "which puts us in possession of that fine estate in Newport of which we have spoken to you during our last visit." She reported that the sisters had later met with Coyle who "received us most kindly." (The truth was very much otherwise, as other documents show). During that visit, they asked Coyle's permission (!) to open the house and "give a few private lessons in music, painting and foreign languages, for according to your advice we shall not open the Academy before the new bishop has taken possession of his see." The letter adds that a few nuns would soon arrive to "put things in order and to answer inquiries with regard to pupils."

An article announcing the sisters' arrival appeared in the Newport *Daily News* on the same day, resulting in a lengthy, emotional exchange of letters between Coyle and Storer, Coyle and M. St. Paul, Storer and various prelates. Storer wrote to Coyle on August 19; the pastor was angry and disturbed by the meeting held without him, along with newspaper articles publicizing the tensions. Storer knew that the pastor had received the sisters rudely, bringing one of them to tears. His letter defends the sisters, reminding Coyle of his own statement that he had "nothing to do with the question." Moreover, "when I told you that the ladies from Fall River were in town and that I wished very much that they should see you, you declined the interview." Apologizing for any embarrassment his actions might have caused the priest or parish, Storer tendered his resignation as a trustee of the parish. When she realized an unexpected clerical temper tantrum had been unleashed, M. St. Paul hastened to write to Coyle on August 20, reiterating the intentions of the sisters in the purchase of the property. She insisted, "Nothing was so far from our views and intentions than the transacting of business without your knowledge and approval." The letter expressed grief, sorrow, and surprise "at the evident displeasure the whole affair gave you" and offered a hope that Coyle would forgive, forget, and welcome the community. Coyle's response, dashed off the same day, gave no indication of a change of heart. He had communicated with unnamed prelates about the affair, he wrote, and they were all "unanimous in terming the affair an 'unparalleled outrage." Whoever "they" were, they agreed—according to Coyle—that this was the first case on record where the pastor had no voice in the choice of a religious community coming into his parish. For this and "many grave reasons, I most emphatically refuse to permit you to locate within the boundaries of St. Joseph's Parish." Unsurprisingly, he did not specify the exact nature of the "grave reasons." Coyle's negative attitude toward the community may seem unexpected but can probably be traced in part to ethnic prejudice. As a close associate of his Irish compatriot, Bishop Hendricken, Coyle was certainly aware of the problems caused by the Flint Affair in Fall River the previous year, which had created a sensation throughout Catholic New England. Perhaps his rejection of the Religious of Jesus and Mary came from misinformation about the role of the sisters there; or maybe it was a move to protect his parish from French-Canadian influence and its "incentive to rebellion." In any case, the Religious of Jesus and Mary now owned a property where they definitely were not welcome.

Formerly a Boston pastor, Most Rev. Matthew Harkins (1845–1921) became the second bishop of Providence in February 1887. Coyle wasted no time penning a lengthy exposé of the sisters' case to the chancery, bolstered by advice he had received from the ordinaries of Boston and Springfield. To vindicate "legitimate authority," he asked and answered two questions: whether the sisters indeed had received the necessary permission to purchase the property and whether their presence might "injure St. Joseph's Parish." To the first question, he offers a clear, un-substantiated "No," inferring that the Religious of Jesus and Mary had dissimulated their intentions and acted without ecclesiastical permis-sion. As to the second, Coyle is even clearer. His plans included a parish school, and the ordinary of Boston had promised him six sisters to teach in it. Coyle also hoped to build his own academy "where the children of the resident and higher population may pay something for education in the higher branches." Having this other academy within his parish boundaries would be "subversive of all order in the parish," not to mention possibly unwelcome competition for students and tuition fees!

Undaunted by the pastor's rude dismissal, on April 16, 1887 M. St. Cyrille wrote to Harkins from Woonsocket. Her letter was a formal request to set up the Newport property as a country villa, "where I can send some of our tired and frail sisters." She also asked for a resident chaplain, able to hear confessions in French. The community would assume the cost of his services. In closing, she petitioned to meet with Harkins to discuss his decision on the matter. That meeting took place on April 23, after which Harkins wrote and signed a summary of his position:

> I stated that my great desire was to establish parochial schools—
> that the establishment of an academy would be an interference
> with that work—on account of drawing support which would
> otherwise be given to the sisters in charge of parochial schools
> . . . Bayview and Elmhurst (academies operated by the Sisters
> of Mercy and Society of the Sacred Heart) supplied all present
> demands . . . for more select pupils . . . I refused application for
> permission to establish a convent at Newport for the Sisters of
> Jésus-Marie.[119]

As expected, Harkins chose not to override the positions of McCabe and Coyle. He would not force the pastor to welcome the Religious of Jesus and Mary, who by this time were eager to abandon their project. As a test case reflecting the policies of his predecessor, the Newport matter reinforced opinions among French Canadians that the new bishop shared the authoritarianism and ethnic prejudice of other Irish clergy. He would have some fences to mend in the future. On May 5, 1887, in a long letter to Harkins, Storer called the matter "bitter race prejudice . . . flagrant injustice" on Coyle's part. Not only he, Storer, but many others also believed that "the presence of these French ladies in the parish would have been of assistance to Fr. Coyle, bringing him into contact with . . . parents of children from outside Newport, who could materially aid him in his projects." It was a futile attempt to get the bishop to reconsider. At the request of the Religious of Jesus and Mary, Storer began seeking a new buyer for the property, without any success. Without ever having settled into their lovely Newport property, the Religious of Jesus and

Mary withdrew with sadness at what might have been, pained by their perceived exclusion within the Church family of the diocese. The following spring, Harkins purchased the property in the name of the diocese. It was known as Eagle Crest until 1914, when it became a diocesan orphanage under the direction of the Sisters of Mercy, the Mercy Home and School.

Part Two

Creating Patterns

4

Parish Schools in Rhode Island

St Charles Parish, Providence, RI (1887)[120]

THE SAYING THAT "WHEN God closes a door, God always opens a window," might well describe the beginning of the Religious of Jesus and Mary mission in Providence. Within weeks of Harkins' refusal to allow them to erect a school in Newport, three Religious of Jesus and Mary arrived to assume the direction of the parish school for French Canadians at St. Charles Borromeo Church, Providence. Bishop Hendricken first established the parish in 1874, under the title of St. Jean-Baptiste, to serve the "French Colony" in the city. For the next four years, the little community held its services at LaSalle Academy on Fountain Street, led by the first pastor, Rev. Napoleon Hardy. The capital attracted a substantial and diverse group of French-Canadian Catholics. They included unskilled laborers for the wool and cotton spinning mills, as well as skilled mechanics and technicians for other manufacturing companies.In August 1878, a year after he took office in the cathedral city, Bishop Harkins appointed Canadian-born Rev. Charles P. Gaboury to minister to the growing French-speaking population. Zealous and dedicated despite many health problems, Gaboury held a fair to raise funds for a new church building for his parishioners. He purchased land at the corner of Lester and Harrison Streets, and construction began. By 1881, Harkins dedicated the wooden church to the honor of St. Charles Borromeo, the pastor's patron saint. Gaboury lived in one section of that original building for the next six years. He praised the support he received from a group of men who formed the core of the community, "mostly all mechanics in good circumstances." Some were property owners, willing to help in whatever way they could. These devout members of the Church, who regularly attended the Sunday services, became the foundation stones for what would evolve into a vibrant faith community known for its dedication to parish life. With their help, Gaboury realized his plans for a parish school.

In 1884, construction began on the first combination convent-school on Harrison Street. That same year, Gaboury wrote to M. St. Cyrille with his request for Religious of Jesus and Mary to staff it. It would be three years before she could respond to his entreaty. Meanwhile, his ailing health made it necessary for the pastor to step down from the leadership of the parish. He was never able to welcome the sisters he anticipated. In the first pages of the founding account, the annalist records: "Fr. Gaboury had to take a leave because of his poor health. So he never had the consolation of seeing the small band of missionaries move into the house he had built." After some time of rest, Gaboury became pastor of the Centreville parish where he would later call the Religious of Jesus and Mary to staff another new school.

The Beginnings

On September 8, 1887, a trio of pioneer sisters arrived from the Hamlet Avenue mission in Woonsocket to undertake the fourth Religious of Jesus and Mary foundation in a decade. Eventually, the fledgling community numbered seven sisters. The superior, M. St. Etienne (Vitaline) Bilodeau, was an experienced and highly regarded missionary. Her first companions were M. Marie de Jésus (Orphilia) Flynn, for English translation and instruction, and the indomitable Sr.Sabine Marion, for whom this was the fourth move in the decade since the Fall River foundation. The sisters' residence was not yet habitable because of humidity in the new structure. For the first three weeks, they were guests at the rectory, received by Rev. E.J. Bachand, the pastoral administrator. The following Monday, classes officially opened with a sung High Mass in the church for parents and new students. The large number in attendance gave proof to the sisters that "these good parents appreciate the gift they have in their parish with the establishment of a Catholic school."[121]

On the first day, 150 were enrolled, boys as well as girls. Like other Religious of Jesus and Mary missionaries, this group learned to adjust to the Bishop's express wish for boys' instruction, at least at the lower levels.

It was a challenge, to say the least: "We need, therefore, to accept this duty as it has been imposed upon us by God, and try to live up to the trust offered us by our Shepherd."[122] Within a week, the sisters were dealing with more than 200 children, whom they deftly organized into classes for English and French instruction. Over the next several weeks, new members of the community arrived to relieve the overcrowded classes: M. St. Raymond (Corinne) Lagarde; M. de la Visitation Larochelle; and in the days before Christmas, M. St. Andrew (Sarah) Carlyon; and M. St. Olivier (Marie-Anne) Therrault. The next year, a young woman from the orphanage of Fall River came to help with the manual work of the convent. The sisters were still organizing things when news came just before Christmas that M. St. Etienne would go back to Woonsocket, replacing the superior who had become seriously ill. Early in 1888, her classes became the charge of a new arrival, M. St. Ignace (Rose) Dumas. Eventually, M. St. Scholastique (Dalila) Fortier arrived as the community superior. Adaptability and change were the norm for this new venture!

Rev. Emile E. Nobert assumed the duties of pastor in November, 1888. While the community annals speak of his paternal affection and interest in the education of the children, notes from the diary of Bishop Harkins, and correspondence from the Religious of Jesus and Mary provincial offer a more complex picture of their relationship. First, there was the issue of Nobert's refusal to pay the sisters' salaries, resolved soon enough by episcopal admonition. In 1895, Harkins received complaints from the Religious of Jesus and Mary that the pastor was "saying insulting things about the community." Later that year, they had concerns about his "strange conduct." Matters worsened for the community after Nobert wrote to the provincial, M. Eufemia (Rosa) Mandri, asking her to remove the superior. Harkins responded that she need not heed the pastor's letter, noting in his diary that he made undisclosed changes "to suit the superior."[123] Three years later, not much had improved for the sisters, who sent the provincial a long letter detailing several complaints concerning Nobert's control of heating, keys, and general access to the school building by teachers. In a letter of April 21, 1899, the provincial appealed to the bishop to help the sisters at St. Charles. Their superior had sent her an emotional plea: "Father Nobert goes from bad to worse. We have witnessed scenes and tantrums. The school doors are closed and locked at 4:30 every day, whether the cleaning is finished or not . . . May God forgive him, and may God also deliver us from him as soon as possible."[124]

Pastoral Problems Unsolved

No answer came from the chancery, so the provincial wrote again in May, insisting that the bishop deal with these matters as soon as possible. She indicated the pastor's behavior had worsened: "It seems that he makes it his business to disturb the sisters in every way, to treat them like slaves, contradict them in whatever they are doing." While she charitably pointed out that the root cause could well be the pastor's ailing health, it was clear to her that the sisters were suffering abuse. They would not be able to begin another scholastic year under these circumstances.[125] The contents of the bishop's response, sent on June 10, are unknown, and his diary entries are missing through 1902. At some point, matters did change, as evidenced from a formal agreement of September 1899, signed by Nobert, M. Eufemia, and Harkins. Similar to contracts signed in other parish missions, the document determines $200 as annual salary for the teachers, fixes class size at sixty, and describes the services of the sisters. It further stipulates that the parish is responsible to provide a man to manage the furnaces of both school and convent. He is answerable in this matter to the superior, not the pastor. Assistant priests had their own grievances with Nobert, including attempted assault and refusal to pay their salaries. One time, Harkins had admonished the pastor "on [his] language in church." There were as well ongoing issues with the church custodian, who was friendly with Nobert and seemed to act on his behalf, giving orders to the curates and sisters and refusing to maintain the furnaces at the school and convent. Harkins made no apparent attempt to remove the pastor or the custodian. Several curates came and went after brief tenures at St. Charles. Despite these relational issues, Nobert proved himself a capable administrator in matters of plant improvement and repairs. He bought a house at 158 Dexter Street to serve as the first rectory. In 1898, he purchased the dwelling at 165 Harrison Street to replace the small house near the school where the sisters had lived since they first arrived. The next year, the Religious of Jesus and Mary pursued plans to provide an "academy" education to some tuition-paying students in their new residence. That convent would serve the community until 1958, when fire ravaged a part of the structure.

In 1900, Nobert took a medical leave and retired, bringing relief to the besieged community. Rev. Louis Octave Massicotte, pastor of St. Dominic's in Fall River, arrived to lead St. Charles as its fourth pastor; he would labor there for the next twelve years. Seeing the growth of the

French Canadians in the city, Massicotte requested that the bishop divide his widespread parish boundaries to accommodate people who lived at some distance. In August 1904, the diocesan board of consultors unanimously agreed to form a new parish. Soon after, Harkins appointed Rev. H. Oscar Mongenais as the first pastor of Our Lady of Lourdes Parish. Nearly 500 French-speaking Catholics in the Olneyville/Mt. Pleasant area were delighted to have a worshipping community closer to home. In time, the Religious of Jesus and Mary would direct the parish school there as well.

A New Era: Arrival of Marist Priests, 1914[126]

Diocesan clergy served St. Charles and its growing population for over two decades. In the spring of 1914, Harkins and his consultors decided to ask the priests of the Society of Mary (Marists), to assume direction of the parish. They hoped in so doing to "strengthen the entire diocese in spiritual work."[127] The Marist Fathers were not new to the diocese. Since 1906, they had directed a parish in Westerly. The propitious decision to bring them to St. Charles, however, was the result of an unhappy confrontation elsewhere in the diocese. Early in 1914, the pastor of St. Ann's, Woonsocket, died. Harkins felt it was time to entrust the parish to the Marists. With a census of about 1200, St. Ann's Church had the largest number of French–speaking parishioners in Woonsocket. They would benefit from the additional spiritual benefits of a French religious order. What the bishop failed to consider was that, unlike other parishes serving French-language communities, St. Ann's consisted mostly of French Canadians, who held that "only a pastor who shared the same mentality and background" as theirs could minister with understanding to their spiritual needs. People were suspicious of religious orders, even French ones like the Marists, believing they would too easily align themselves with ecclesiastical attempts to assimilate French Canadians into the "American Church."

When the Marists agreed to accept St. Ann's some weeks later, they appointed Raymond Plasmans, SM, as the new pastor. A Belgian native who had served in several New England parishes already, he was at the time a pastor in Lawrence, Massachusetts. He announced the news of his transfer to parishioners the following Sunday, and it was carried by local newspapers, including *The Woonsocket Call*. A firestorm of protest

erupted among the trustees and lay leaders at St. Ann's, who organized
a "Vigilance Committee" to discuss ways of persuading Harkins to reconsider. In a series of discussions with Harkins, their leaders informed
the bishop that the people would be unanimous in their opposition to
Plasmans. Harkins let the issue rest for a few weeks, hoping that tempers
would cool; he was not eager to rescind the appointment. At the parish,
the laity took matters into their own hands. Eighteen men volunteered
to watch the rectory night and day, intercept Plasmans should he appear,
and urge him to "keep away from St. Ann's." They encouraged parishioners to withhold the ten-cent weekly pew rent. The next Sunday, the
collection amounted to almost nothing. As usual, money talked. Harkins
consulted with the first French-Canadian governor, Aram Pothier, a native of Woonsocket, about the situation. His advice: "Only withdrawal of
the Marists would return peace in that city."[128] Despite some clerical resistance to that solution, by mid-March Harkins gave the Marists charge of
St. Charles, where Plasmans celebrated Mass, preached for the first time,
and received a warm welcome from his new parishioners. The drama
leading to his arrival among them was resolved. Moreover, a French-
Canadian pastor was appointed for St. Ann Parish, bringing yet another
ethnic confrontation to a close, at least for a time.

Plasmans wasted no time in getting down to the business of erect-
ing new parish buildings. Upon his appointment, he bought the site at
the corner of Dexter and Lester Streets, with an adjoining property on
Harrison Street, allowing for the later construction of the "new" school in
1932. His first objective, however, was to build a beautiful church for the
parishioners. On October 24, 1915, Auxiliary Bishop Doran blessed the
cornerstone for the edifice. Three years later, on May 5, the Romanesque
brick structure was completed and dedicated with impressive ceremony.
Plasmans was tireless in extending and improving parish holdings, thus
providing additional classroom space and a larger rectory. In this way,
he foresaw the growth of his community beyond his tenure and assured
its future. Crippled with rheumatism in 1926, he resigned as pastor but
remained at St. Charles until his death there the following year. This remarkable and generous priest was rightly considered the second founding pastor of St. Charles. He inaugurated an era of vitality, spiritual and
material growth for the parish under the Marist Fathers, who would
serve there for almost fifty years. Plasmans gave the parish a model of
pastoral leadership. In the fiftieth anniversary booklet from 1964, he was
described as "gentle, well-loved by all, capable, priestly . . . an orator, a

builder of buildings and souls." For the Religious of Jesus and Mary, the leadership of Plasmans had offered new hope and courage in their educational aspirations. A new contract drawn up in 1915 between the parish board and the Religious of Jesus and Mary provided for smaller class sizes (50) and annual stipends of $250. However, their struggles with language and cultural expectations in Providence threatened to undermine the good work they were doing. One of the conditions of the contract was that "all sisters will be expected to know the English language," but there were indications that the reality had not kept up with the ideal.

Misunderstandings and Adjustments

With the death of Harkins in 1921, Most Rev. William A. Hickey, coadjutor bishop and administrator of the diocese, became third Bishop of Providence. A Worcester native and graduate of Holy Cross, Hickey had studied at the Sulpician seminary in Paris and was fluent in four languages. As a pastor, he won praise for his eloquence, patriotism, and promotion of the Church's educational mission. As bishop, one of his primary objectives was to ensure that instruction in Catholic schools be equal to that offered in public schools. Early in 1921, some decisions of the local superior at St. Charles prompted negative judgments that reached Hickey's desk, culminating in his request to the provincial for her removal. M. St. Thérèse Chapleau wrote asking for clemency and explaining that the sister acted in good faith, without any false intentions. In his response of March 15, 1921, Hickey pointed to the superior's lack of judgment in sending one of the sisters to a non-Catholic hospital for treatment by "a Doctor who is said to be a Free-Mason (sic)." He did not question her good faith but pointed out that the incident "gave a very peculiar impression to the Catholic public, in view of the fact that we have here an excellent Catholic hospital." At the conclusion of the letter, Hickey stressed the need for English fluency for the personnel of the school: "A word of advice from me would be to the effect that every superior or principal of a parochial school under the care of your Order, as well as the teachers in those schools, should be proficient in the knowledge and use of English." He referred to "severe comments" from secular educators regarding bilingual schools. Citing his desire to preserve and foster parish education, Hickey noted the responsibility of congregational leaders to help him confront the false accusations "now ripening in the minds and on the lips of our educational enemies."[129]

Four years later, the language situation at St. Charles again became a thorny issue. Two sets of inspectors had visited to determine whether the school qualified for state approval and certification. The superintendent of schools in Providence had a reputation as an anti-Catholic, eager to find fault with parish schools. The report from St. Charles confirmed that bias, denying to the school any state approval without significant changes. M. St. Peter Claver described the problem in a letter to the provincial. She had spoken with the Rev. J. Cassidy, who related the bishop's concerns over the matter. The report stated that "the school was not properly equipped, and the sisters did not have sufficient English."[130] Without state approval, graduating students might be denied admission to local high schools the following year. Cassidy requested two or three additional English-speaking Religious of Jesus and Mary to remedy perceived incompetency on the part of lay teachers and sisters, as noted in the report. There is no record of the provincial's response, but within another year there were changes in personnel and in the leadership of the school.

Years of Growth and Flourishing

Beginning in 1927, M. St. Clementine (Alida) Tetreault became the superior and school principal. Born and baptized in the parish and a former student at St. Charles, she was a natural educator with experience in teaching and administration. Kind but firm, M. St. Clementine brought the school up to standards set by both state and diocese. The number of students increased, as did clubs and religious societies: Our Lady of the Sacred Heart Society for girls; Friends of the Sacred Heart, for boys; and the Christ Child Society for primary grades. The school's reputation grew, as did did the numbers in attendance. A larger school became a necessity. Rev. Hernin Pérennes, French successor to Plasmans in 1926, set about collecting funds and renting temporary space for classrooms while construction got underway. Unfortunately, he moved on before the new school was completed and blessed in the fall of 1932. On October 5, sisters and their 450 students began the move to their new quarters. By the end of the month, they had settled into their classes. As early as 1911, the teachers had added a ninth-grade class. By 1936, they were offering secondary school courses for the girls. The first secondary commencement exercises took place two years later, with three graduates. In 1949, thirty students completed the high school program, with its options for classical, commercial, or general tracks. An undated typescript of course offerings in this era describes full Classical, Commercial, and general secondary school curricula. Four years of Latin and modern languages were listed, as well as Greek. Mathematics included algebra, geometry, trigonometry, and physics. Elective courses in typing, music, and drawing were available to students in all three curricula. St. Charles School had emerged from its struggles into an ambitious new era.

In 1937, fourteen Religious of Jesus and Mary were teaching 500 enrolled students at the school. From its small beginnings, the parish had grown to more than 650 families, with several well-organized parish societies and mission clubs. In addition to their regular duties, sisters taught public school catechism, trained high school students to offer catechism in family settings, and directed sewing circles for interested girls. After World War II, the parish demographics changed. The total school population in 1948 was 418; of that number, just over 100 were in the high school. In the following decades, there was a steady decline in the local school population, with fewer children from the parish in attendance. By the 1960's, St. Charles revealed a new profile, with a diverse cross-section of students (over 480) from forty-two parishes in the diocese. In February 1959, fire ravaged and partially destroyed the aging convent building. Parish leaders decided to replace it as soon as possible.

A new pastor, Paul Pepin, SM, arrived just in time to assume both the construction and the debt on the new convent, which included a large chapel and twenty private rooms for the community of sixteen sisters plus guest quarters. Among other modern features, the house boasted a fully equipped home economics kitchen and sewing area for the secondary school program. M. Marie de Massabielle (Irene) Rhéaume, superior and principal since 1954, efficiently organized the sisters' move in December 1960, when the new convent was finished and furnished. Along with preparing the residence for a community of fourteen sisters, she worked to develop forward-looking ideas and methods in the school curriculum. In 1955, she organized the first Parent-Teacher Club. This committed group supported school activities by building up its library, sponsoring fundraisers, and engaging the parents in participation and leadership at St. Charles. They hosted annual Open House events for prospective parents/students, offering a strong example of leadership and enthusiastic collaboration, hallmarks of the parish and its people.

In 1964, the parish celebrated the golden jubilee of the Marists' arrival. The anniversary booklet described the cumulative effect of the community's "fruitful labor" since 1887. Close to 150 Religious of Jesus and Mary had served in the school, with more than thirty auxiliary sisters ministering to their domestic needs. In over eighty years of educational service, they had registered 27,000 students and graduated close to 500. The harvest of vocations from St. Charles to priesthood and religious life was equally impressive: twenty-seven priests, sixty-seven women and men religious, of whom twenty-eight became Religious of Jesus and Mary, and six entered the Marist Missionary Sisters. It signified a joyful golden harvest, sowed in the labor and tears of their forbears. The next decade, however, showed a significant decline in Catholic school populations, resulting in changes to many parish schools and convents in the diocese. More lay teachers were being hired, putting greater financial strains on parishes, especially those without endowments to provide educational resources. By 1969, the diocesan ordinary, Most Rev. Russell J. McVinney, decided to regionalize parish education. St. Charles became a regional school for two other parishes: Our Lady of Lourdes, where the Religious of Jesus and Mary had recently closed the parish school; and Mt Carmel, Federal Hill. Within three years, it was clear that the St. Charles School faced serious administrative problems, largely from lack of personnel and adequate financing. In 1972, the Religious of Jesus and Mary withdrew from the parish and the school was closed. What would become of the lovely convent that parishioners had built hardly more than a decade before? Once again, from an apparent ending, a new beginning blossomed for ministry and community on Harrison Street.

The St. Charles Residence[131]

How the parish convent became a group home for adults with developmental disabilities is a lovely account of new life from the ashes of an earlier ministry. Rev. Gerard O. Sabourin was diocesan director of apostolate to the handicapped and chaplain at the Ladd School, the state's custodial institution for people with intellectual disabilities. Believing in alternative approaches to caring for these persons, Sabourin initiated the project of a group home as a more compassionate and human environment for growth and life. With the bishop's permission, he moved eighteen residents from Ladd, including a married couple, to become the first community in the unused convent, renamed "St. Charles Residence." Beginning in September 1972, Sabourin moved into the building while working full-time as diocesan director for the handicapped, along with Sr. Antoinette Jacques, RJM, a former St. Charles parishioner with a Master's Degree in special education. One account describes Sr. Antoinette's early role as "the heart and hands of the home." In addition to being the cook and house manager, she acted as dietitian, nurse, counselor, therapist and director of the volunteers who had begun helping at the residence on Columbus Day. In recalling her early, difficult years at the residence, Sr. Antoinette learned "to understand, serve, and live with our residents with special needs." Her greatest satisfaction in this ministry surpassed the enormity and challenges of the work: she knew she was "making life better for people who had been institutionalized." While a cook and other staff were hired within weeks that first year, the burden of fund-raising and pastoral care fell to Sabourin and Sr. Antoinette. Thanks to their efforts and pioneer work, the project received access to federal funds that improved and increased services.

Ten years later, Sabourin and Sr. Antoinette moved a small group of residents to a farmhouse in Exeter, RI, to form a smaller group home, while St. Charles continued as a residence for a larger group until 1994, when it closed. The number of group homes multiplied under the auspices of Re-Focus, a non-profit agency founded by a St. Charles volunteer, which continues the ministry in the spirit of the co-founders. The Exeter home evolved into St. Kateri Tekakwitha Parish, formed by five founding families in the area who had attended Sabourin's Masses for the residents in the Exeter farmhouse.[132]

St. Jean-Baptiste Parish, Centreville/Arctic, RI (1889–1900)[133]

In what is now a section of Warwick, Rhode Island, the parish of St. Jean-Baptiste held the honor of being the oldest French Catholic church in the state. It was first established in 1873 to serve the needs of French Canadians in the area, whose numbers were multiplying. Bishop Hendricken placed them under the care of a Belgian pastor, Rev. Henry Spruyt, who built the church and oversaw its dedication in 1880. His successor, Rev. Charles P. Gaboury, arrived in 1887, eager to open a parish school. As the founding pastor of St. Charles in Providence, where the Religious of Jesus and Mary had recently opened a mission, Gaboury admired the Congregation, its educational reputation, and its good work in Woonsocket. Having obtained permission from M. St. Cyrille for sisters to teach in his new school, Gaboury was delighted to know that seven Religious of Jesus and Mary would arrive for the 1889 school year. Three arrived from Providence on August 26: Mme. St. Gabriel (Celina) Lavoie, the directress; Mme. St. Colomban (Marie-Jeanne) Lambert; and once again, the able Sr. Sabine Marion. Four others came within a few days: M. St. Ferdinand (Marie) Goulet, M. St. Eulalie (Eleonore) Beaudoin, M. Marie de Lorette (Clara) Dion, and Mme. St. Madeleine de Pazzi (Leda) Tanguay. When they arrived, they found the construction workers putting the last touches on the new convent/school building, so they stayed in the rectory for several days. Gaboury "was happy to welcome the sisters into his own home and offered gracious signs of hospitality."[134] They spent the first week planning with the pastor for the organization of classes and the purchase of required texts. On the night of September 2, the Religious of Jesus and Mary moved into their own residence under the watchful and caring eye of the pastor, who personally came to see that they had everything they needed.

On Wednesday, September 4, there was a solemn High Mass at 8 AM for sisters, students, and parishioners. It marked the opening of the new school and the first session of classes. Sisters recalled a large crowd at the church, parents and children united in prayer with the Religious of Jesus and Mary to ask God's blessings on the new endeavor. After Mass, teachers and their respective classes went to the school "so the sisters could get to know their 400 students and determine how to separate them into groups."[135] Despite what they described as "*brouhaha*" on those first days, they managed to take in the children's monthly fees, organize them into proper grades, and distribute books and materials. The formal blessing of the building took place on Sunday, September 8, at about 3 in the afternoon. During the "touching and impressive ceremony," the missionaries were struck by the number and diversity in the overflow crowd of more than 5000. Irish, Italian and French-Canadian families were on hand to welcome the sisters, listen to a sermon on Catholic education, and assist at solemn Vespers/Benediction, along with a procession and honor guard of the parish societies. After the blessing, parishioners lined up for the open house of the sisters' quarters, eager to see "their" convent. True to their understanding of the norms of enclosure, the sisters let the good pastor lead the visits of the convent while they locked themselves in the refectory!

Two years later, Gaboury approached the newly appointed Bishop Harkins with a request to set up a mission chapel of the parish in Phenix, higher up the Pawtuxet River valley, to address the needs of Canadians in that area. Once he had the approval, Gaboury got to work on the construction of a combination church-school building, completed in the fall of 1891. It provided a space for Mass on Sundays, and Gaboury opened a school there with laywomen as the first teachers. In 1895, a few sisters from Centreville began traveling daily to teach about eighty children enrolled in the school. They were there until the departure of the Religious of Jesus and Mary in 1900, when lay teachers again assumed the educational task. From this mission outpost would develop the parish of Our Lady of Good Counsel, established in 1903.

New Pastor, Rising Tensions

Soon after the arrival in 1898 of the third pastor, Rev. Joseph R. Bourgeois, difficulties arose on several fronts between him and the community of sisters. It would appear that Bourgeois had specific ideas about the roles and tasks of teaching sisters in a parish, which conflicted with the community's norms and views. An energetic and zealous man, Canadian-born Bourgeois was well educated, civic-minded, gifted, and trained in music. He improved the property of the parish, remodeled the rectory, and installed a Casavant organ in the church. Moreover, he built an acoustically perfect parish hall, the Odéon, for various performances, lectures, and entertainment. His talents and achievements were much appreciated by the parishioners and the general public. As the first Catholic representative on the State Board of Education, Bourgeois gained admiration and respect all around. Within his parish convent, however, tensions were rising. A lengthy correspondence about the issues took place in October 1898 between Harkins and M. Eufemia Mandri, the provincial superior. On October 6, 1898, M. Eufemia wrote to Harkins with her concerns: "This [priest] would like to require our sisters to take care of the sacristy and has threatened sanctions if we do not comply." She noted that there had never been question of sacristy duties in the original community agreement with the parish and that orders from France were clear about not assuming those tasks. It would seem that word had spread from Woonsocket that the sisters there did see to the altar linens; but, as M. Eufemia explained, that was by way of exception. She proposed a compromise solution. The sisters would wash, iron, and mend the altar linens; care of the altar and sacristy could be the tasks of a laywoman hired by the pastor. Bourgeois was not satisfied with this arrangement and made his displeasure known to the local superior. An exasperated M. Eufemia complained in a letter to Harkins on October 28: "What are we to do, Your Excellency, if every new pastor wishes to impose new obligations? True, our sisters in Woonsocket have taken on these duties, but that was an earlier agreement . . . we cannot accept any new charges."

Harkins had earlier suggested that the sisters consider training a group of young women to care for the sacristy. Agreeing to his idea, the provincial indicated that she would inform the superior to proceed and offer to give training to the girls in question on the convent premises. She reiterated her hope that this solution would end the dissension between pastor and sisters. This approach did not resolve the issues. A year later, the Religious of Jesus and Mary and the parish corporation entered into a new contract, with M. Eufemia and Bourgeois signing as representatives, and with the written approval of Harkins. Like other extant contracts, it laid out the rights and responsibilities of both parties. However, this document specifies that the sisters "will, at the request of the pastor, direct a confraternity to care for the sacristy and altar, but will not undertake these tasks themselves."[136] In the section dealing with the annual parish plays that the Religious of Jesus and Mary were to prepare, there is a reference to their strict interpretation of enclosure. At performances of plays they directed and supervised, sisters could be present but "they cannot be visible to the audience; they also need to leave the auditorium by a private exit so that they can be in the convent by 9 PM." On its part, the corporation was to pay each teaching sister $200 annually, along with adequate living arrangements that included furniture, furnishings, and utilities.

Farewell to a Beloved Mission

On March 21, 1900, the provincial wrote again to Harkins of her concerns for the Rhode Island communities, where overwork and exhaustion had led to the need for extended rest and prolonged absence of some teaching sisters. She was not able to supply the needs for teachers in the parish schools, where numbers of students were growing. Given the problems at St. Jean-Baptiste, she suggested to the bishop that perhaps it would be "a service to the Reverend Pastor of Centreville if we were to cede our place to another community." Noting that it would be easy enough to find sisters to replace the Religious of Jesus and Mary, the letter infers that some groundwork had already taken place and that her statement would serve as the six months' notice required before withdrawal. Attached to the back of her letter is a note from Harkins, referring to a suggestion he had made that lay teachers be hired for English and mathematics: "Answered Apr 7, 1900, advising employment of lay teachers." A second note below it adds: "Answered again June 8, 1900—community had been found to take charge Sept. next, 1900." Bourgeois had already contracted with the Présentation de Marie Sisters, who arrived that summer to take over the school in Centreville.

The bishop's final approval of the withdrawal of the community brought the crisis—and the mission for the Religious of Jesus and Mary in Centreville—to a conclusion that signaled their mixed feelings. In her final letter to Harkins, on June 12, 1900, M. Eufemia reflected on the decade the Religious of Jesus and Mary had spent there:

> Please don't think we will leave Centreville without regret. We have loved this mission where our work was often difficult. We loved this corner of earth where dear Fr. Gaboury had called us and gave us so many happy hours. Yes, we have loved the parish of Centreville, but today it is clear that our departure is determined by God's will . . .

She asked that their reasons for termination be kept confidential. Revisiting the sisters' regrets at leaving, she expressed gratitude to Harkins for all his help and gave him the assurance that the Religious of Jesus and Mary would redouble their efforts in the other communities of his diocese.[137] With emotions of both satisfaction and regret, on July 9, 1900, the Religious of Jesus and Mary took their leave of St Jean-Baptiste Parish.

Holy Family (*Ste-Famille*), Woonsocket, RI (1902)[138]

By the turn of the century, French-Canadian families were coming to Woonsocket in numbers far exceeding the capacity of Precious Blood Parish to meet their needs. More than 1700 families (8000 people) lived within the parochial boundaries. They were geographically widespread, making it difficult for many to attend church services or come to the school, which was itself overcrowded. In 1891, Harkins had established St. Ann's Parish; a few Religious of Jesus and Mary taught in provisional classrooms there for two years, awaiting the definitive arrival of the Presentation of Mary Sisters. In late February 1902, at the suggestion

of Monsignor Dauray, Harkins divided St. Ann's into the parishes of St.
Louis de Gonzague and Holy Family, to meet the needs of French Canadians from the Social and Globe/River districts of the city. Rev. Joseph S.
Fortin, until then pastor of a Fall River parish, was appointed to lead Holy
Family, a task he accomplished with great devotion and administrative
skill until his death. While awaiting his arrival, Dauray called an initial
meeting of lay parish leaders in the basement of Precious Blood Church.
At his suggestion, they named two lay trustees, organized two sodalities, and set the structural foundations of their new parish community of
more than 500 families. They gathered again in that location on March 16
with their new pastor, who presided at their first parish Mass.

Following the bishop's directive, Dauray sought and found available property for a church and rectory on South Main Street. After some
discussion with various citizens, Harkins recommended to Fortin that he
purchase the Whitman property, a large house that could serve as a rectory. The parlor would serve as the site for weekday Masses. Precious Blood
Church would continue as the place of worship on Sundays until parishioners had a place closer to their homes. Spurred on by this hope, the people
were generous in raising funds to build their own parish church. By the
summer of 1902, construction of the site was under way. The basement
was completed in a few months and erected as a temporary chapel where
Mass could be offered on Sundays. When Harkins arrived in mid-April to
bless and dedicate the new chapel, he congratulated the people and their
pastor for what they had accomplished so quickly and "urged the people
of Holy Family to take great care of the education of their children."[139]

Acting on that mandate, Fortin rented a property from the parish
corporation of St. Charles in September of 1903 and set it up as a school
with four classrooms, ready to house at least 200 children. It was to this
building—the "River Street School"—that the first Religious of Jesus and
Mary teachers came: M. St. Pierre d'Alcantara (Clephire) Sylvain, the
principal; M. St-Raphael (Louise) Chabot; M. du St-Esprit (Alphonsine)
Fortin; and M. du Précieux-Sang (Marie-Anne) Paquin. Understood at
first as a temporary arrangement, the sisters commuted twice daily from
Precious Blood Convent for the next nine years. Fortin wanted to build a
proper school, but the bishop advised him to finish building the church
first. Construction on that site resumed in 1909; in January 1911, the
blessing of Holy Family Church took place. The pastor bought the neighboring Aldrich property at 404 South Main Street the following summer
to serve as the sisters' residence.

The First Convent and School Extension

No longer needed for worship, the church basement now was the education center for a growing population of children, with an addition of two more classes. On August 28, 1912, the first Holy Family community of sisters moved into the convent that would be their home for the next thirty-eight years. It also served as an extension of the school, offering additional space for classrooms. With M. St. Pierre d'Alcantara as their superior, five Religious of Jesus and Mary formed the founding community of the mission: M. Ste-Augustine Paré, M. St. Nathalie Bibault, M. St. Camille de Lellis Fortin, M. St. Scholastique Fortier, and the auxiliary Sr. St. Frédéric Caron. More than 400 girls and boys appeared for registration on September 3, the opening day of classes. In an undated contract between the parish corporation and the *"Dames de Jésus-Marie,"* the sisters laid down a general principle about accepting boys.[140] An exception to the congregation's Constitutions, the admission of young boys was common in parish schools of the American mission. At Holy Family, boys could register through the age of thirteen. Only with the bishop's permission might they remain another year. Class size was limited to fifty. Instruction was to take place for five hours daily, which did not include time for catechism classes. There were specific references to the question of bilingual instruction, and instructions that all the sisters should have some command of English; the superior and principal should be fluent in the language. The Religious of Jesus and Mary were to oversee the production of annual parish plays. Members of Holy Family Corporation agreed to pay each teacher $200 annually and offer a stipend to the superior for her services. They would likewise provide furnishings, utilities, maintenance and repair of the school/convent property, as well as provide Mass and confessions for the sisters. A six-month notice was required if either party were to withdraw from the contract. Very serious reasons and episcopal approval were the conditions for terminating the sisters' services. Thus did the Religious of Jesus and Mary and the officials of the new parish enter formally into a relationship that would span eight decades.

The early years saw growth in numbers and in Catholic practice, with 178 confirmations in November 1913. With the onset of World War I, shortages and financial struggles were the norm for everyone, and the school was no exception. During the severe winter of 1917–18, classes were shut down a few times due to the depletion of coal supplies. The Spanish flu epidemic took its toll, and the school was closed for the month of October 1918; sadly, four of its students died that month. The parish counted forty deaths from the pandemic, which left many children orphans. On the brighter side, the sisters reported the installation of a telephone in 1917; moreover, they had acquired a convent cat! With the end of World War I, plans for a larger school building got underway. A generous parishioner purchased land near the convent in September 1921 for the new construction. The next year saw the arrival of a new superior-principal, M. St. Anselm (Zelire) Bérard. Once again, generous parishioners held a campaign to raise funds that amounted to $44,000, surpassing the goal set for the project, and construction began. On February 4, 1923, Bishop Hickey blessed the new Holy Family School, with its sixteen modern, "electrified" classrooms. Classes began there the following week. More than 600 students were registered for the following year's courses, which included primary, intermediate, and junior high school (through Grade 9 inclusively). In1926 a pre-school class was added, bringing the total number of children to 735. Fortin had achieved his cherished goals but did not live long to enjoy them; he died in early November 1923, after a prolonged illness. A public school official visited the school in 1928, commending the students for their model behavior, an accomplishment that Rev. Gédéon Laverdière, the second pastor, mentioned in his sermons for the next three Sundays. Sixteen eighth-grade students received diplomas that year, and the sisters laid foundations for an alumni association.

Creating a Parish Culture

Rev. Stephen Grenier, who had led a parish in Phenix, Rhode Island, arrived in 1934 to be Holy Family's third pastor. The next year, he set about expanding the school premises to seventeen classrooms, as well as more living quarters for the sisters. In his long tenure, Grenier demonstrated administrative and financial skills, paying off the parish debt by 1947. A strong advocate of preserving the French language along with the faith, he consistently used French to communicate with the sisters and expected them to know the language. He likewise inspired parishioners to active and devout participation at every level of church life, especially for liturgical and devotional celebrations, as well as social activities. Rev. William J. Raiche, who came to the parish as a curate in 1935, organized an active Boy Scout Troop the next year. In 1944, a newly established parish Drum and Bugle Corps began to play and march at various civic and religious parades. Four different choirs—for men, girls, boys, and the women's sodality—provided a liturgical repertoire in the church from Gregorian chant to polyphony and French cantiques. The training of altar boys, whose number eventually reached 100, was the responsibility of the Religious of Jesus and Mary from their earliest years in the parish. Thanks to Grenier's leadership, the closed retreat movement flourished during summer holidays from 1939 to 1949, with the school serving as a retreat center for the mission priests and laymen who came seeking spiritual renewal.

Attentive to the needs of working-class youngsters who had little access to sports facilities, Grenier looked for an appropriate site to meet their needs. In 1945, he added the Stone House building across the street to the property holdings of the parish corporation, for use as a Catholic recreational center. By the summer of 1950, he had overseen the construction of a new convent at 53 Coe Street, into which the sisters moved on August 4, when Grenier presided at the first Eucharistic celebration. As they reflected on their first fifty years at Holy Family, the twenty Religious of Jesus and Mary in the community were grateful to God and the wonderful parishioners who had supported them and their educational mission from its inception. Their ministry now included a parish school of 618 students, weekly catechetical instruction to about 200 public school children, fundraising campaigns, and several extracurricular organizations. From the beginnings of this mission, the Religious of Jesus and Mary were fully integrated members of the parish at every level, attending and contributing to every church service and function. It was a demanding participation in parish life that required much self-sacrifice. Yet, with the fatigue and struggle came joy and deep satisfaction over the years. Thanks to strong pastoral leadership and the sisters' faithful witness, Holy Family nurtured numerous vocations to the priesthood and religious life well into the twentieth century.

Coping with Social Change

Impacted by demographic and social changes in the city, as well as transitions in Catholic institutions after the Second Vatican Council, Holy Family closed as a parochial school in 1972. That same year, it was chosen to house Grades 7 and 8 as one of the educational centers for the newly- organized network of six Greater Woonsocket Regional Catholic Schools. On May 20 of that year, Holy Family parishioners organized a farewell dinner of tribute for the Religious of Jesus and Mary who had taught at the school. The remaining sisters continued to live in the parish convent, from which they served various educational and pastoral needs in the city. With time, sisters grew older and fewer; the convent needed major repairs and renovation. In 1989, the province leadership offered to purchase the property and adapt it to the needs of senior sisters. They made a proposal to Rev. Maurice L. Hazebrouck, who had replaced Grenier in 1969. After consulting his parish council, he decided the building would be kept for future parish needs. In August 1989, grateful for more than eighty-five years of fruitful apostolic service, the remaining sisters closed the doors of Holy Family Convent. Four sisters continued to live in Woonsocket in a rented house. The other members of the community relocated to several newly opened residences in Providence, North Providence, North Smithfield, and Warwick.

Our Lady of Lourdes Parish, Providence, RI (1906)[141]

In the first two years of its existence, Our Lady of Lourdes Parish functioned without church, rectory, or school. Olneyville French-Canadian parishioners gathered for worship in a rented hall on Manton Avenue. Sometime in 1904, bowing to the pressure of several laymen, Bishop Harkins asked Fr. Massicotte, pastor at St. Charles, to find a suitable property. In August the diocese purchased a large site on Atwells Avenue and appointed as the founding pastor Rev. H. Oscar Mongenais, then an assistant priest at St. Ann's, Woonsocket. A Québec native who came "south" to the States in 1892 because of the milder climate, Mongenais had a frail constitution. He nonetheless gave himself fully to the building of his new parish community. From its origins, strong lay leadership characterized Our Lady of Lourdes, with zealous trustees who were able to advise and assist Mongenais in managing the affairs of a young parish. The pastor moved into a temporary residence on Atwells Avenue, while liturgical services took place in the St. Jean-Baptiste Hall until a proper church was built. Knowing that the Religious of Jesus and Mary had staffed the school at St. Charles for eighteen years, Mongenais lost no time in requesting their services. The first page of the convent annals for Our Lady of Lourdes reveals that the sisters had "hoped for some time to open a second French and Catholic school, to protect the souls of these hundreds of children," realizing that the distance to St. Charles prevented their attending services or religious instruction there.

In June 1905, Harkins approved plans for a combined church, school, and rectory at Our Lady of Lourdes. That same month, he also signed a contract between the *Dames de Jésus-Marie* and the parish corporation. While much of it repeats other parish agreements, there are certain stipulations that reflect the growing tensions about language at St. Charles. Among them is a strong reminder about giving attention to English, taught with care by sisters who are assumed to be fluent in the language. At least a third of the community should be "of English (American) origin or should be so fluent as to be taken for English"[142] Five hours of class, excluding catechism, were required; the choice of subject matter was determined by state requirements. Included in the course of study were English-language classes in geography, history of the USA, Rhode Island, and civics, as well as language and arithmetic. The corporation was responsible for the sisters' annual stipend ($200), their lodging, furniture, and furnishings as well as the utilities in the convent. Further, it provided services of a caretaker for the school and convent buildings. Additional notes, undated and written in longhand, indicate that the sisters were not reimbursed for catechism classes provided to public school children twice weekly, from 4 to 5 PM. Sisters at Our Lady of Lourdes would not accrue any profit from the sale of pious objects, even if such was the custom in other houses.

Pioneer Commuters

Construction on the church-school had first priority, and part of it was ready for use within a year. Late in 1905, Mongenais moved to a house at 211 Carleton Street to facilitate construction on Atwells. Early in September 1906, three pioneer Religious of Jesus and Mary arrived by horse and carriage from St. Charles to take up their teaching duties. The first "commuter sisters" of the province, they would travel daily to their mission school for the next six years. They later recalled this itinerant lifestyle with humor and a bit of irony: "We were given an old horse frightened by every little thing, along with a driver who was extremely timid . . ."[143] The missionaries later had a store of hilarious incidents to recount. The parish hall served as the sisters' dining area, workshop, and meeting room, according to the need of the moment. The first principal, M. St. Hilaire (Rose) Fortier, with her two companions, M. Marie-Anne de Jésus (Corinne) Monette and M. St. Edmond (Eulalie) Gagnon, prepared to direct the new educational ministry in Olneyville. This was a young, and probably inexperienced, community of teachers. At the age of thirty-two, the principal had made profession four years earlier; the two others, both under the age of twenty-five, had taken vows only one or two years before. They would need the energy of their youth. On Thursday, September 6, the sun shone brightly as they arrived to greet their first students, all 330 of them! With school construction still unfinished, the trio organized the first class sessions in the chapel area. There was insufficient space, so the sisters had to turn away a few of the older girls and all the boys who had already made First Communion. Parents and children were devastated, begging not to have to return to the public school, deprived of religious instruction. It was a trying situation all around. The sisters promised to offer catechism classes to public school students on Sundays after the children's Mass. Once these sessions were under way, more than 150 students participated, including working youth up to the age of eighteen. There were fifty in each group, with smaller sessions for the younger children. The house annalist commented tersely on the degree of religious ignorance: "Many need a lot of help with their prayers."

On September 23, Harkins presided at the blessing of the first parish buildings. Slowly, classes were organized by dividing the students into six groups, to be taught by the Religious of Jesus and Mary and three laywomen: the Misses David (English teacher), Blanchet and Tessier (French teachers). Overcrowding and lack of furnishings became a major challenge. The following year saw the addition of a seventh class, to accommodate the pleas of parents whose boys had been excluded at the outset. The parish hall became their classroom, despite the absence of desks and necessary materials. In March 1909, four years after the parish foundation, Mongenais died. The bishop appointed as second pastor Rev. Jean David Lebel, a native of Québec, then serving at Our Lady of Good Counsel in Phenix. A dedicated administrator, Lebel tackled the daunting task of purchasing additional land to enlarge parish facilities and build a new church for his growing flock. Four years later, he took two months off for a much-needed rest. Under the leadership of his devoted assistant, Rev. C. Emile Roberge, and with their usual generosity, parishioners raised enough funds to build a proper rectory for their pastor. In early autumn of 1912, it was ready for occupancy. The priests moved to new quarters and offered the Religious of Jesus and Mary their former residence. Happy at last to leave commuting behind and live in their own convent, by mid-November the community of seven sisters moved to Carleton Street. The first superior, M. Marie de l'Espérance (Thaïs) Gaboury, had become the school's third principal the previous year. Sr. St. Isidore (Délia) Rondeau arrived to organize and manage household tasks.

New Building, Growing Attendance

In the spring of 1924, Lebel directed the construction on a new red-brick church building, completed and dedicated just a year later, at a cost of $100,000. With a population of 345 students, the school was thriving. In addition to their classroom tasks, the sisters continued to teach religion to more than 200 public school students after school hours. When illness forced Lebel's retirement in 1925, the parish welcomed its third pastor, Rev. Joseph Hardy, a native of Connecticut and founding pastor at St. Lawrence, Centredale (North Providence). Hardy recognized that increasing enrollments at the school were crowding the classrooms. He set to work renovating the school and transforming the former church building into new classrooms. By 1927, more than 400 children were attending the school and participating in a number of confraternities dedicated to various saints: Our Lady of the Sacred Heart (200 members), Blessed Imelda, and the newly canonized Thérèse of Lisieux (for smaller children). Within the next decade, these groups multiplied to include the Eucharistic Crusade (sixty members), the Holy Tabernacle Society for women and girls (thirty members), and a parish choir with fifty members. A Safety Council of thirty boys directed traffic at the opening and closing of the school day. By 1937, the Religious of Jesus and Mary community had grown to thirteen sisters.

The effects of the Great Depression, the closing of factories, and the erection of new parishes for French Canadians were some of the factors contributing to a steadily decreasing enrollment at Our Lady of Lourdes School. After World War II, the total number of students never exceeded 275. Yet, Our Lady of Lourdes had a "cachet" that attracted large numbers of vocations to the priesthood and religious life. In the anniversary booklet marking its seventy-fifth anniversary (1979), two pages refer to vocations to priesthood/religious life from the parish: twenty-one priests and brothers, and sixty Religious of Jesus and Mary.

A Light on the Past

Most of the sisters and their daily lives in the parish missions of this era
have disappeared into the silence of long-forgotten history. However,
a gifted student from Our Lady of Lourdes has left an affectionate, in-
sightful account of his young life and learning in this *petit Canada* of the
postwar years. The American novelist David Plante (b.1940) often writes
about his French-Canadian roots and the religious context of working-
class families such as his own. Recalling the Catholic culture of Our Lady
of Lourdes, he describes going to Mass every Sunday during which the
pastor, "*Monsieur le Curé*," preached his sermons in French. Plante recalls the names of several of the sisters in the school "who spoke only
French" and gives life to a learning environment with mornings given
over to French, taught by M. St. Joseph-de-Nazareth (Léora) Décelles.
English classes took place in the afternoon, under the aegis of M. St. Flore
(Violet) St-Cyr. In the morning, all the children belted out the Canadian
national hymn, "O Canada," in French; they pledged allegiance to the
American flag in the afternoon![144] In his novel, *American Ghosts*, Plante
devotes an entire chapter to his sixth-grade life.[145] The perceptive twelve-
year old describes a day in a safe, closed world where religion and learning intersect at all times. M. St. Flore, the classroom teacher, is assigning
parts for the annual school play. Plante recalls the sister's dark eyes and
lashes, her habit, veil, rosary "hanging against her thigh, rattling lightly
among the black folds," and "stiff bonnet, which was sealed tightly under
her chin with a snap."[146] He describes how she regaled her students "in
our French fortress surrounded by Yankee territory," with religious tales
of *le grand Canada* and the miraculous cures at the Shrine of St. Anne de
Beaupré, miracles that "could never occur in the United States of Yankee
America." Then there is "*Mère Supérieure*," who doles out daily warnings
in French and English about proper school dress (blue ribbons at the
girls' necks, obligatory ties for boys). The pre-adolescent Plante conjures
up in her an authoritarian and fearsome ringer of the school bell, with
her wide sleeves slipping up her arm. He is anxious that she might notice
his little gold tie clip with a plastic ruby in it, ranking him among "the
disobedient." While it presents an imaginative reverie, Plante's recollection brings to life the hidden but influential world of that small parish in
Olneyville, where the convent-school and the sisters were essential to the
formation of ethnic Catholics in New England. It exaggerates the reality
to create effect, but it also reveals part of a hidden story of immigrant

nuns and their charges everywhere in French-Canadian parishes of the early twentieth century.

In 1969, with decline in enrollment and the numbers of Religious of Jesus and Mary, Our Lady of Lourdes School closed its doors. The remaining sisters left after more than fifty years of successful labors in the parish. Little did they surmise that within two decades, the community would return to the original house. When the community sold Jesus-Mary Academy, Fall River, in 1981, the province infirmary relocated to the former convent at Our Lady of Presentation Parish in Marieville, North Providence. Their first home at Our Lady of Lourdes being available, eight sisters took up residence there on August 2, 1982, where they remained for another five years. The school and convent properties were sold in 1987, and the "pilgrim sisters" of Our Lady of Lourdes bade a second and final farewell to Olneyville.

5

New Direction and Growth in New York City

THROUGHOUT THE NINETEENTH CENTURY, the city of New York underwent a major transformation, emerging as major international center for culture, trade, and commerce. Thanks to the newly-opened Erie Canal, New York's port was connected to major markets of agriculture and business of eastern North America via the Hudson River and Great Lakes. State and city politics were controlled by a powerful Democratic Party machine known as Tammany Hall. Offering patronage and employment to immigrants, especially the Irish, the organization won their political affiliation. By mid-century, New York City had grown into a major center of European immigration, as well as a northern hub for a large free-black population, which grew to more than 16,000 in 1840. With their arrival in the metropolis, the Religious of Jesus and Mary would experience their own transformation from immigrants and foreigners into engaged citizens of one of the world's greatest cities.

New York City: Immigrant Mecca at the Turn of the Century

Because of its situation as an important port and its two major immigration centers in the late nineteenth century—Castle Garden (1855) and Ellis Island (1892)—the city of New York became a mecca for the "teeming masses yearning to breathe free." It boasted a population of two million foreigners hailing from a multitude of ethnic communities. By 1900, over three million people filled its streets, most of them Irish, German, Italian, or Eastern European immigrants. Material poverty and lack of education crowded them into ghettoes and slum dwellings, preferably among their own compatriots. At first, they had to settle for low-paying jobs in garment factories or as domestic workers: cooks, janitors, maids. However, because the Irish knew English and accounted for fully one-quarter of New York's immigrants, they soon organized themselves and set up a political machine, Tammany Hall, that became a powerful force in city life well into the new century. This unusual but effective patronage system helped Irish and German immigrants find lodging and employment. In exchange for their support and votes, it offered them a path to U.S. citizenship. Irish men soon made up the labor force for the new transit system of trams and subways, which gave them status and the leverage of sheer numbers. They likewise became New York's Catholic majority, wielding influence at many levels. A glance at the names of the city's episcopal leaders reveals that predominance. With one exception, all the titular bishops and cardinals of the archdiocese have been of Irish origin.

A *"Gilded Age" for the Church in New York*[147]

At his appointment as New York's third Archbishop in 1885, Most. Rev. Michael Augustine Corrigan had a flock of more than 600,000 Catholics spread over 4000 miles throughout the state, and covering several counties in addition to the city's boroughs. Growth was spectacular under Corrigan's leadership. In 1900, one of his pastoral letters reported that he had founded ninety-nine parishes and blessed 250 buildings in seventeen years. Every two weeks during his tenure, Corrigan dedicated a new church, school, rectory, convent, or institution, vibrant signs of the rapidly expanding community over which he presided. In that same period, he welcomed twenty communities of men and thirty-two of women to work in the archdiocese, where their services were urgently needed. They became the backbone of a large network of charitable services that included schools, hospitals, orphanages, and shelters for the poor of every age. The Sisters of Charity, founded by the New York convert, Elizabeth Seton, had in 1817 opened the first orphan asylum in lower Manhattan. By 1847, thirty-three of her sisters arrived to establish the diocesan congregation of the "New York Charities" and were responsible for nine institutions in the city, including a number of parochial schools. In 1900, more than 1000 professed Sisters of Charity staffed seventy-seven schools and institutions in the archdiocese, including major hospitals and foundling homes.

The increasing wealth and influence of the Catholic community could be seen in the opening of impressive parish churches, one-third of them "national parishes" that welcomed newcomers from eleven different ethnic backgrounds. Not only were the churches imposing architectural structures; they also were a religious home to communities of predominantly poor parishioners, who from their meager resources built the remarkable system of New York's parochial ministries. Dedicated pastors often made allowances for the grueling schedules of their flocks. Some scheduled noontime Masses on Sundays—not at all customary—for people who worked up to seven days a week. Urban Catholicism was writ large in New York, revealing how important the faith was to the lives of its citizens. At the turn of the century they worshipped in 136 churches in all five boroughs, overseen by an army of about 1000 priests. In 1908, the archdiocese held its centenary celebration in the massive St. Patrick's Cathedral, itself a monument to Catholic influence and growth in a world-class city. This event was the apex of Irish dominance in the archdiocese, a truly golden era.

Corrigan died early in May, 1902, just as the Religious of Jesus and Mary were trying to set up a foundation in New York. His successor was Irish-born Most Rev. John Murphy Farley (1842–1918), who had been Corrigan's secretary, then auxiliary bishop and diocesan administrator. He would not take office until mid-September of that year. Described as small in stature, gracious in manner, and dignified in bearing, Farley was an eloquent speaker, fluent in French and Italian, linguistic assets that were indispensable in his multilingual diocese. His even temperament, prudence, and good humor led him to maintain peace among priests and people who could be contentious. During his tenure, the number of Catholic schools doubled in New York, the teachers formed an association "for God and country," and the Propagation of the Faith was established. An ardent supporter of Catholic higher education for women, Farley promoted the founding in 1910 of the College of Mt. St. Vincent in New York; he likewise lent his support to the newly established Catholic University in Washington. Elevated to the cardinalate in 1911, he shepherded the archdiocese in the difficult years of the Great War, dying less than two months before the signing of the Armistice. An obituary in *The Tablet* on October 19, 1918 summed up his leadership: "Peace he imposed and loved it, but when he was required to meet war, whether in the ceaseless contention between religion and secularism, or when it involved his country, he . . . threw all neutrality to the winds."

Preparing the Way (1885–1902)[148]

M. St. Cyrille had long dreamed of a house in New York, which she had described as "the land of true liberty." As early as 1885, the pastor of a new French-language parish of St. Jean-Baptiste on East 76th Street had asked for Religious of Jesus and Mary to undertake a girls' school there. In a letter to Corrigan early in 1902, M. St. Cyrille recalled his visit to Sillery fifteen years earlier, when she requested his permission to respond to that invitation. "Because of various circumstances," which are not elaborated further, that hope was left unrealized. The Canadian Congregation of Notre-Dame (CND) was chosen to open that school, arriving in 1886. As superior general, M. St. Cyrille was eager to try again for an establishment in the city. The political situation in France had caused concern, and new secular laws created difficulties for teaching orders and congregations. When several Religious of Jesus and Mary in France were forced into exile in 1902, the decision was made to relocate the general headquarters to Rome. Seeking refuge and ministry in New York for some exiled French sisters, M. St. Cyrille addressed her needs to Corrigan in January of that year, explaining that while the ministry of the Religious of Jesus and Mary was primarily teaching, if accepted they would be willing to give private lessons in foreign languages or various arts. Toward the end of the letter, she suggested an alternative to a school: "We might also be able to offer board and room to older women or women without families who do not want to live on their own; it would be yet another way to do some good and save a few souls." On February 12, Corrigan responded graciously. While he would not refuse hospitality to the Religious of Jesus and Mary, he expressed some hesitancy: "I do not know where I could place your sisters to advantage." It was a guarded welcome, with a suggestion that they consider "beginning humbly, in some country parish." M. St. Cyrille answered that Corrigan's letter was reassuring, even if it did not seem the time was ripe.

Meanwhile, there were movements afoot to "ripen" that time. Relatives and friends of the Religious of Jesus and Mary in New York joined the search for a setting where the sisters could begin humbly enough, not in a rural setting but in the metropolis itself. There was a flurry of correspondence between Rome, Sillery, and New York in the spring months; all signs indicated there were possibilities, if the Religious of Jesus and Mary acted quickly. On March 22 of that year, Rev. Arthur Letellier, SSS (1862–1921) wrote letters from New York to M. St. Cyrille and his sister in the Congregation, M. St. Euphémie (Catherine) Letellier, who was in Rome at the time.[149] Letellier was superior of the Blessed Sacrament Fathers, who were assigned to the parish of St. Jean-Baptiste. He stressed the urgency of the sisters' coming to New York to make a foundation as soon as possible. Several French congregations had already received permission to set up foundations in the archdiocese, and the request of the Religious of Jesus and Mary might be denied at a later date. "New York offers unique advantages for a religious community," he wrote, explaining that many French sisters were arriving, among them the Ursulines, and were settling in good neighborhoods. In order to find suitable placement, the Religious of Jesus and Mary would have to act soon. He reminded his sister of the Latin axiom: "To the latecomers, only the bones." Meanwhile, M. St. Cyrille had appointed M. St. Euphémie as the founding superior of the New York mission, an appointment she had long resisted and feared yet undertook with strong faith and courage, despite having only $100 in hand. Her brother's advice and support would prove indispensable. The sisters later recalled that without him, the foundation would have been impossible.

The process slowed when Corrigan contracted pneumonia and died on May 5, 1902. Two sisters, M. St. Paul Frechette and the Canadian provincial, M. St. Augustin Hatschemberg, traveled to New York later that month to meet with various contacts and pursue possible sites. On June 9, the provincial sent a long and detailed account of their meetings with church leaders, including Letellier and Bishop Farley, who was kind and welcoming. They also met the French Assumptionist superior, Rev. Thomas Darbois, AA. As the pastor of Our Lady of Guadalupe, a Spanish-language church on West 14th Street, he was eager to have sisters in his parish. Darbois offered to sponsor and assist them with the spiritual services of the resident Assumptionist community. He suggested that at first they set up a school for the Hispanic children of his parish.[150] There were several Irish families in the neighborhood as well. Letellier believed that once the parish school got underway, the Religious of Jesus and Mary might set up an academy; its income would allow them to purchase property at a later date. Best of all, Darbois knew of a large house for rent near the parish buildings on West 14th Street, at the cost of $1800–$2000 annually. It could provide space for the parish school, academy, and sisters' living quarters.

Darbois wrote immediately for permission from Farley to welcome the Religious of Jesus and Mary into his parish. The chancery's response on June 5, 1902, was that the sisters needed to produce the late

Archbishop's note of acceptance and a letter stating "the work to which they intend to devote themselves." As it turned out, the parish school of the Assumptionists closed soon after it opened because of insufficient numbers to warrant the establishment. Darbois would later point out, "What is most needed is English, and English above all!" Spanish or French might be useful as foreign languages, but immigrants were eager to learn the native tongue of the United States if they were to find employment and be assimilated into American life. Limited resources were also a major concern. Yet, on July 16, facing an uncertain future and with no sure residence, M. St. Euphémie, Sr. St. Marguerite (Geraldine) Lindsay, and Sr. St. Côme (Marie) Bernard sailed for New York and their new mission. In her letter to M. St. Cyrille on August 4, M. St. Euphémie indicated that the foundation "will entail many sacrifices, but where there is so much good to be done"

Our Lady of Peace: Founding Years (1902 to 1905)

The trio arrived in New York on July 28, 1902, where they were met by their provincial, M. St. Augustin, and another sister of the founding community, M. St. Ferdinand (Marie) Goulet. While searching for a suitable house of their own, they were offered hospitality with a Mme. Ouellette, former student from Sillery, who had a large home on Park Avenue at 76th Street. On August 2, Farley received the group at the chancery, where he read the letter of his predecessor accepting a Religious of Jesus and Mary mission in New York. Farley reiterated the welcome of his predecessor and the Assumptionist Fathers but made it clear that the sisters were not to undertake an academy in St. Jean-Baptiste Parish, since the Religious of the Sacred Heart had opened one in the area more than twenty years earlier.[151] He expressed concerned about income for the sisters, welcoming the idea of a residence for working girls and women in addition to the small parish school they had proposed. Schools in the archdiocese were forbidden to collect tuition or fees, in order to provide free Catholic instruction to as many as possible. At the end of their meeting, Farley warned the sisters that the path ahead would be strewn with hardships and poverty. Encouraged by his support and blessing, the Religious of Jesus and Mary moved ahead with confidence.

Two days later, M. St. Euphémie wrote her initial impressions to M. St. Cyrille, pouring out both her relief and anxieties. Her instinctive resistance to the New York mission had been somewhat alleviated by a dream-vision of Our Lady she had in Rome after her nomination.[152] While that experience was consoling, it did not mitigate her concerns as she encountered so much that was unfamiliar. She had already begun to look for housing but complained at the high cost of rents in New York: $150 a month and higher (over $4000 today). Living expenses and food were equally prohibitive. In another letter of August 4, she wrote that "I am not lying on a bed of roses, and can barely summon up the courage to see what is ahead." Thankfully, she was spared greater anxiety by her brother's invaluable assistance with his time and experience. He also gave her funds to help with food shopping. Within two weeks, she could happily report that they had found a property to rent from a Miss Margaret Smith, at 251 W. 14th Street, for $150 a month, plus costs for all the furnishings left behind. There were twenty rooms: ten to serve as sisters' bedrooms, two for a school facility, and one for a chapel. Five rooms were selected for future women boarders; a small room would serve as music/art room for private lessons. On August 21, they signed a lease for three years and began to move in. By then, four more sisters had arrived: M. St. Alexis (Augustine) Bernier, an artist who could give painting lessons; another artist from Spain, M. St. Rodriguez Ballester; M. St. Laurent (Elisabeth) Paradis, to direct the little parish school; and a junior professed, M St. Jean-Baptiste de la Salle (Louise) Lessard, for the kindergarten. By the beginning of September, the community of ten was complete with the arrival of M. St. François de Sales (Albertine) Michaud, Sister St. Amable (Rose) Morin, and Sister St. Denis Jobin. Sr. St. Amable would long be remembered as the holy "chauffeuse," revered in community memory as a worker of miracles. She had charge of the coal bin and burner, rising before dawn each day to heat the large house. Her familiar conversations with the Lord were well-known: she prayed aloud for more coal in the midst of one bitter winter when there was neither coal nor money—and it arrived!

The next month was spent cleaning and preparing the premises, which had been left in a deplorable state. The sisters scrubbed the floors, painted moldings, scraped and papered walls that were hiding "droves" of bedbugs. This helped to make the house habitable, if not attractive. At first, they set up the small nursery school, so they could begin as soon as possible. In the evenings, they gave lessons in French, English, painting, music, and embroidery to help cover monthly rental costs. Occasionally, the paintings of M. St. Alexis and M. St. Rodriguez found interested buyers. A first-person account describes those early months as both difficult and joyful. There were privations in terms of food and furniture. Four sisters slept in hammocks scattered in various rooms, while the others "reenacted every night the gestures of the paralytic (in the Gospel): taking up their mats, they found places for the night, and rolled them up early the next day."[153] A corner of the windowless, narrow kitchen served as a refectory, with a shaky table and the need for gaslight even at midday. On the second floor, another windowless room became the chapel. In order to fit the ten sisters into such narrow space, the doors to a hallway had to be opened. These privations invited the pioneers to share in the Lord's poverty while welcoming him to share in theirs. Letellier—their "visible Providence"—and the Blessed Sacrament community made generous gifts to diminish their penury and help them through the first uncertain months.

On September 15, classes began with space for thirty children in the kindergarten, at the cost of one dollar weekly. In the evenings, the classroom space doubled as a community room for the sisters who were not offering private lessons. A week later, one of the Assumptionist priests celebrated the first Mass in the chapel and blessed the house. There was little income from the parish school, which was struggling for lack of students. The sisters decided to charge $160 monthly rent in the residence. It was disappointing that only one woman applied in the first month. With her broad vision, however, M. St. Euphémie understood that any future for the Religious of Jesus and Mary in New York City required a response to a need that was so clearly evident. On October 22, 1902, she wrote to M. St. Cyrille convinced that their mission in Manhattan was "to offer a home to young women employed in offices or shops, who want to live securely and avoid boarding houses that expose them to risky situations . . ." Many young women had approached the superior, begging to be admitted but unable to pay more than a few dollars a week. While she had to turn them down, M. St. Euphémie realized the need to focus on purchasing a property for this purpose in the near future. In that same letter, she stated that a residence would "respond to an urgent need with a work that seems indispensable. We can do good there, and will find adequate funds, because these young girls are numerous and not demanding." For young Catholic women new to the city's workforce, boarding alternatives were either secular or run by Protestants. A Catholic residence would provide a safe and familiar religious atmosphere with opportunities for worship and companionship.

The sisters' first experiences of Thanksgiving and Christmas in New York were improved materially by many gift baskets from anonymous donors. "Great poverty, high spirits . . ." is the way the annalist described their initial holiday season on West 14th Street. Within a few months, things had started to improve. Thanks to the refurbishing and repairs, the value of the house had doubled. The sisters had daily Mass offered by the Assumptionists. They had rented out all available rooms for boarders, including the one dubbed the "Prisoner's Cell" because of its barred windows! The nursery school was thriving, and evening lessons brought in some regular cash flow. Father Letellier continued as their wise counselor and benefactor, anticipating the community's needs and sparing no expense to help them. He provided all the furnishings for their little chapel, along with a painting of Hoffmann's popular "Jesus at Prayer" to hang above the altar. His sister wrote that "without him, we could never have settled in New York; his name should be written in gold letters for the annals of this foundation." He counseled M. St. Euphémie to purchase a property soon. Mortgage payments would total a third less than the monthly rents the community paid out. She lost no time acting on his suggestion and began to search for an appropriate site. At the end of December, seven Spanish Religious of Jesus and Mary en route to make the foundation in Mexico asked for hospitality at 14th Street. M. St. Euphémie quickly went out to rent folding cots and buy blankets on credit, not having the cash on hand. Only later would the travelers realize how cleverly she hid the poverty of her community, receiving the Spanish sisters with her customary warmth and "unlimited charity."[154]

In November, 1903, M. St. Cyrille resigned as superior general. On her way back to Canada, she arrived in New York for a visit; she was also soliciting funds for the new mother house in Rome. At the New York mission, money was typically scarce. But true to her generous self and ignoring the admonition of the treasurer, M. St. Euphémie emptied the cash box to offer the elderly superior a Christmas gift that came to a total of ten dollars! Within days, to the sisters' surprise, that same amount arrived from a parent for the sisters' Christmas celebration. Before the year came to a close, Archbishop Farley paid the sisters an initial visit. In January, 1904, New York City experienced an outbreak of pneumonia that reached into the sisters' community. Some sisters and three of the women boarders became ill. One of the women died, causing other boarders to move out of the house for precautionary reasons. On January 12, M. St. Augustin, the provincial, arrived for a visit and became deathly sick herself. She died ten days later, having spent her final hours on a cot in a poor, small room where there was barely room for the priest when he came to anoint her. The year ahead did not offer much promise. Along with illness and their deprivations, the community got word in the spring that the Assumptionists would no longer be able to offer a chaplain for their convent services. Their priests were few in number, so they suggested that the sisters walk to the parish for Mass, a practice foreign to these semi-enclosed sisters. Letellier provided one of his priests for a convent daily Mass through the summer. In July, the French Jesuit giving the Religious of Jesus and Mary their annual retreat suggested to M. St. Euphémie that she approach the Jesuit rector at St. Francis Xavier Parish in the area about providing a chaplain. The rector accepted the arrangement on a temporary basis.[155]

When the appointed extraordinary confessor, a Mercedarian priest, arrived in December, he was informed that the Jesuits had already heard the sisters' confessions and were attending to their other liturgical needs as well.[156] He promptly reported to the chancery that the sisters had obtained their own chaplain without the bishop's permission. The ensuing minor melodrama was the result of miscommunication. M. St. Euphémie assumed the Jesuits had obtained the necessary authorization; they in turn believed she had taken care of settling the matter. She was called in to the chancery to explain to Farley what had happened. With her apology and clarification, he understood the unintended misstep. Farley settled the matter by assigning the Jesuits as ordinary chaplains to the Religious of Jesus and Mary, while keeping to the extraordinary confessor he had named earlier. The difficult incident was resolved but had been painful all around, especially for a humiliated M. St. Euphémie.

Our Lady of Loreto School (1904 to 1919)[157]

Notwithstanding the trials of that year, a wonderful opportunity arose for the community at 14th Street. The number of children in the kindergarten had decreased; fewer than a dozen registered for September. At the same time, William H. Walsh, SJ, newly appointed superior/pastor of Our Lady of Loreto on Elizabeth Street in the Bowery, wrote to the Religious of Jesus and Mary, asking for some to serve as teachers in his mission school there of more than 100 children, mostly from poor Italian immigrant families. Permission was slow in coming from the provincial of in Québec because so few sisters were available. Walsh made his needs known to Farley, who advised M. St. Euphémie to "let the kindergarten go," making room for more women boarders and freeing two sisters to take over instruction at the Loreto School.[158]

The first two sisters sent to Loreto, M. St. Laurent (Elizabeth) Paradis, and M. St. Jean-Baptiste de la Salle, traveled by public transportation daily to the school, as would all the teachers in the ensuing years. In 1905, M. St. Antoinette (Flora) Monette arrived as principal, a post she kept through 1911. A fine educator and administrator, she was known as a "woman of great tact and ability." Under her direction, the number of teachers increased from ten to fifteen, and they became known for their high standard of efficiency and performance. When M. St. Antoinette was assigned to the new mission of Highland Mills, her own sister M. Anne de Jésus (Corinne) Monette, who had been teaching eighth grade, took her place. "With the same love and zeal for the work, and with the same ambition to make Loreto School equal to the best in New York, she carried on the good work until 1914, when she was replaced by M. St. Pierre (Marie Marguerite) Castonguay . . . who for two years has been keeping the school up to its high standard."[159] An unexpected and welcome experience for Loreto children came once M. St. Antoinette was at Highland Mills: she invited groups of students to enjoy brief stays there in the summer months.

An undated typescript contains a few recollections of the early days on Elizabeth Street. M. St. Pierre, then thirty years old, recalled that the large brick school building was infested with rats and mice that often appeared in their cupboards or in the teapot. The older boys would be called in to dispatch the rodents. Sometimes cultural and language differences made for misunderstandings in this struggling part of the city. Yet, Loreto left a lasting and loving impression on the sisters who served there: the generosity, warmth, and goodness of the families were counterpoints to the poverty and ignorance that challenged them daily. In 1917, the Jesuits turned the parish over to Italian diocesan priests, who invited some Italian sisters to teach in the school two years later, when the Religious of Jesus and Mary withdrew.

New Buildings, New Focus (1905 to 1915)[160]

Within a short time at 14th Street, space was made for twenty-two new women boarders, who moved into the updated residence, while many applicants had to be turned away. The three-year lease on the house was about to expire, giving the intrepid superior an excuse to explore the purchase of a larger property. With approval from the superior general, M. St. Euphémie surveyed properties in the area. Providentially, she found two adjacent houses for sale near their own, at 225/227 W. 14th Street.[161] On April 10, 1905, she wrote a letter to Farley requesting permission to buy the larger property; he gave approval four days later. As always, the question of funding was paramount. These buildings, repaired and renovated, would cost well over $30,000 (close to $1 million today). The community faced large bank loans and would carry a considerable mortgage for many years. Generous benefactors came forward with large gifts toward the project, but the sisters in the community were hesitant and divided. M. St. Euphémie led them in what today would be called a process of discernment: a novena to "hear the Lord speak." During the novena, a retired governess arrived, asking to live in the residence for the rest of her life. The house had no provisions for this type of arrangement, so M. St. Euphémie proposed that she apply to St. Joseph's Home, a residence in the area for elderly women, directed by the Daughters of Charity. The woman refused to hear of it: "This is where I want to come." With some reservations, the superior acceded to the woman's demands and took her in. Five weeks later, the resident became mortally ill, withdrew all her funds—about $12,000—and gave the total amount to M. St. Euphémie because she wanted no family dissension after her death. This unexpected gift served as the sign to go ahead with plans for the new building.

By summer's end that year, there were accommodations for fifty boarders, with a long waiting list of interested women. In order to maintain the educational aims of their institute, the sisters initiated religion classes and gatherings for the residents at Our Lady of Peace, a ministry that continued for several decades. With the years, they would witness several conversions to Catholicism, inspired by the humble and affable service of the sisters. At last, the New York mission began to prosper. With the success of the residence, an ever-growing number of women had to be turned away. By 1908, it was evident to M. St. Euphémie that time had come to enlarge their quarters yet again. In September, she was informed of two decrepit buildings for sale on 15th Street, just behind the residence. The site was ideal to build an annex to their property. By November she put the matter before Rev. M. St. Clare. In her petition to Farley on January 23, 1909, she mentioned the superior general's enthusiasm for the project. The letter described M. St. Clare as one "who also realizes the pressing necessity of enlarging the house. She encourages me to go forward leaning on the Providence of God."

Before writing to the chancery for final approbation, M. St. Euphémie sought funding for the bold enterprise. She inquired about taking out a loan from Emigrant Bank, and was assured of generous support from friends and benefactors. One wealthy woman, identified only as Mrs. D., offered to help in the new enterprise and was ready to contribute up to $100,000 toward the new construction. She appreciated the apostolic style of the sisters' ministry and wanted to contribute to the growth of the work. This was an appealing offer, and a sign to the superior that it would not be foolhardy to proceed further with limited funds. However, Mrs. D. soon had second thoughts. She did not like the Chelsea neighborhood and wanted "her" new building situated further uptown. M. St. Euphémie rejected that proposal outright, especially since the Religious of Jesus and Mary had recently renovated the 14th Street house at great expense. She proposed to Mrs. D. that her gift be put toward the erection of a completely modern building on 15th Street, with private rooms, running water, a large chapel and other amenities.

After a few days' reflection, Mrs. D. agreed to the superior's proposition. M. St. Euphémie sought out an architect and moved ahead with the plans. The two houses on 15th Street were demolished and plans laid for a ten-story building, with room for 120 residents. On the day set for signing the transaction, with attorneys for both parties present, Mrs. D. withdrew her offer because she still disapproved of the location. She asked that the community instead accept an outright gift of $10,000 and free her of any further obligation. Shocked and disappointed, after a few moments of discussion with her companion, M. Euphémie agreed to accept ten percent of what she had been expecting. This test of her faith and courage only strengthened her resolve to move ahead. By January, she wrote to Farley for episcopal approbation of the project, which he readily gave. In May 1909, under the supervision of the architect, Mr. John Kearney, and a general contractor, construction began on a ten-story, fireproof building, at an estimated cost of $250,000 (over $6 million today). Faced with more debt, more work, and financial insecurity, some in the community who had harbored concerns and hidden resistance to the plan were now openly critical. Word spread around the American houses that M. St. Euphémie's project to build a state-of-the-art residence, with the best furnishings and modern conveniences, was reckless and imprudent. They might even lead to bankruptcy. What about religious poverty? Above all, what about the Congregation's constitutions that mandated education as their apostolic work? Once again, M. St. Euphémie encouraged the local community to trust in Providence, which had helped them thus far and would not fail them. Fr. Letellier advised her to proceed with confidence in God, who had already blessed the work and promised support. He came forward generously with several loans when payments came due. The communities in Canada sent contributions, and area banks agreed to advance bonds on credit toward the mortgage. Slowly, the building began to take shape.

On September 19, 1909, the vicar general presided at the blessing of the cornerstone, at which the convent chaplain, Francis McNuff, SJ, preached. There were delays in construction because of several strikes. By the summer of 1910, the building project was advanced enough to place notices in various newspapers that an annex to Our Lady of Peace would open in October with 170 rooms. An undated typescript of that era notes that the expansion was meant to attract "ladies of the literary profession, retired teachers, bookkeepers, stenographers, and others desiring a peaceful abode." In a later newspaper article on the residence, mention is made of "representatives from many walks of life," including two physicians and an "enthusiastic suffragist"! All faiths and nationalities were cordially received.

The Religious of Jesus and Mary invited guests to an open house and Mass in September; early in October, Farley presided over the blessing of the house. With its nine floors of modern facilities, 112 single rooms and fourteen suites, applications were swift in coming. Soon most of the rooms were occupied. A descriptive prospectus details the advantages of living at Our Lady of Peace. The costs were competitive for the era: $2 daily for transients, $8–12 weekly for resident boarders, including meals (about $250–$300 today). The structure was completely fireproof, with running water, electricity, and an elevator. It housed a spacious dining room, a large chapel open to all the women, a library/reading room, offices, and parlors to receive guests. In each hall there were telephones and individual mailboxes; for every five rooms, there was access to a white-tiled bathroom. A rooftop sun parlor and garden offered respite from the noise and bustle of the city below. Unique in New York City, the new

Our Lady of Peace was built to offer accessibility, warm hospitality, and the comfort of a religious environment to working women. Lessons in music, art, and foreign languages were also available. The indomitable M. St. Euphémie had a hand in every detail of planning, constructing, and furnishing the state-of-the-art building. It can be said she was both visionary and architect, showing great practical wisdom and foresight. She had gone through a baptism of fire in those first years, but her strong faith and bold, enterprising spirit never failed. At the celebration of her golden jubilee in 1922, one of the tributes described Our Lady of Peace as a "great miracle rising from the faith of its foundress." That faith, along with the labors of the sisters, brought the rewards of respect and admiration from their residents, the local clergy, and civic authorities.

An anonymous personal anecdote describes the care with which each sister crafted her tasks to provide an atmosphere of welcome and peace for the residents. The first unidentified guest mistress, assigned to welcome and assist new residents, arrived in 1909. She later recalled her inexperience and need to learn from others in an apostolic setting that had neither rule nor tradition, but was home to their 140 guests. To prepare for her service, the sister consulted visiting clerics and read articles about similar homes in New York. In a visit with Farley, she asked the archbishop for his advice, which came in two words repeated four times: "Amuse them"! She drew up her own "Duties of a Guest Mistress," having studied the Benedictine custom of "receiving all guests as Christ" by showing cheerful hospitality. She aimed to "make the residence a true home" placing the interests of the guests before all else, encouraging them and praying for them. On the last page of her narrative was advice she received from a local chaplain, insisting that she keep the parlors open until 10 PM so the women would be encouraged to visit with friends at home rather than "in cheap places of amusements." Three years later, that sister left the residence, leaving as well a rare personal account of the careful attention given to each woman who came through its doors.[162]

Within two years, the residence functioned like a well-oiled machine. Clear guidelines were in place for behavior of staff and boarders alike. The chapel was open to all residents for private prayer, attendance at Mass and all the services, including the weekly First Friday adoration and benediction. Annual three-day retreats were offered, along with instruction in the faith or other religious-formation classes. A plan was underway to organize a group for aid to the poor. In the dining room, residents were assigned to seats at fixed tables according to their floors.

Women could invite guests to lunch and/or dinner. There was a system for leaving one's keys, staying out beyond 9 PM, receiving mail and phone calls; the house had a safe for residents' valuables. Rules for behavior in the rooms were quite specific. Auxiliary sisters were assigned to clean the rooms regularly, but each resident was asked to make her own bed and keep her room tidy. Food, laundry tasks, and ironing were forbidden in the bedrooms. Reflecting the convent atmosphere, there was to be "no loud talking or laughing . . . in the elevator or halls," especially late in the evening and early morning.

In the spring of 1911, Rev. M. St. Clare arrived for an official visit. She was able to see for herself the growth and success of the New York Mission, which then included the Academy at St. John's, Kingsbridge, in the Bronx. A true Englishwoman, she wanted the sisters to have a summer villa where they might escape from their intense labors and the heat of the city. With her encouraging leadership, that year the sisters acquired the sprawling summer property of former Senator Thomas Platt in Highland Mills, NY. M. St. Clare's plans for a truly American Religious of Jesus and Mary presence included setting up a novitiate in Highland Mills for women from the States. M. St. Ignace (Emma) Matthieu, one of the founders at St. John's, was appointed the first Mistress of Novices. One year later, on April 12, the chapel at Our Lady of Peace was the site of a joyous clothing ceremony for two of the first entrants for the United States mission: Marie-Aline Gendreau, of Fall River, MA, to be known as M. Marie Eymard; and Irish-born Bridget Glacken, who received the name of Sister Julia. A small house near the residence was purchased in 1913 for $18,000. It provided living quarters for the lay domestic workers hired to supplement the sisters' work, providing full room and board to more than 100 residents.[163]

In August of the following year, mounting anti-religious sentiment erupted into full-blown civil war in Mexico. Our Lady of Peace offered a refuge for scores of Religious of Jesus and Mary who were ordered out of their country. The cable sent to them from M. St. Euphémie echoed the hospitality she had offered twelve years earlier: "We are waiting to welcome you with open arms." The house was readied to receive thirty Spanish missionary exiles; most were sent on to Cuba. Another wave of several dozen Religious of Jesus and Mary arrived sometime later from Merida. While M. St. Euphémie would gladly have kept them all in New York, the provincial dispersed them temporarily to houses in the East, where they were warmly welcomed. They helped with teaching and other tasks in the

communities until they returned to Europe or Mexico. Through the early
decades of the twentieth century, scores of Religious of Jesus and Mary
exiled from France and Spain found a temporary home at the residence.
Years later, sisters from the Spanish province wrote with lasting gratitude
of the legendary generosity and motherly attention of the New York superior. Like the metropolis they called home, the community of sisters
at Our Lady of Peace witnessed to the value of internationality and the
richness of many cultures sharing the same quarters.

Life and Ministry in the "House with a Heart" (1915 to 1931)

The annals of Our Lady of Peace's first forty years read at times like a roster of important visitors—clerical, religious, and lay. Because of its location, Our Lady of Peace was a hub of hospitality, especially for Religious
of Jesus and Mary traveling or returning from abroad. As a community of
the Canadian province, it relied on the French-Canadian auxiliary sisters
to perform the core services essential to its residential ministry, apart
from administration. Unlike the other mission houses, this community
of over twenty consistently included a majority of auxiliary sisters. A few
sisters who had spent long years at the residence were interviewed in
their senior years. Their memories of M. St. Euphémie included her business skills, generosity to all, caring, and maternal leadership. The sisters
recalled long hours and backbreaking work, with very little personal
time or recreation. A few felt they had been treated as servants and were
looked down upon by the "mothers" in charge, whom they obeyed in
fear. Others held fond memories of "good feeling in the community," the
kindness of superiors and the appreciation of the women they served. Sr.
St. George (Josephine) Sauvageau spent twenty-one years at Our Lady of
Peace, serving the residents in the dining room. She described generous
gifts of money and personal items the ladies would give "their" sisters
at the holidays and for other occasions. Sr. St. Rita (Louise) Richer, who
cleaned the women's rooms for over four decades, stressed the united efforts of the community and remembered M. St. Euphémie as a "beautiful
Mother." She recounted in great detail personal stories of the residents,
some of whom became very fond of Sister, lavishing gifts upon her well
into her old age.[164]

There are no extant annals of the house during the Great War (1914–
18). Cardinal Farley, whose support and encouragement of the foundation

had meant so much, died in September 1918, just before the war ended. The next spring, his successor and auxiliary was appointed, Most Rev. Patrick J. Hayes (1867–1938). A son of Irish immigrants, Hayes demonstrated great concern for the poor, founding Catholic Charities of New York. He was what today would be called a pro-life bishop, condemning abortion, contraception, and divorce, yet opposing the prohibition campaign. Hayes was a strong advocate for the unemployed, endorsing relief services on their behalf during the Great Depression. During those years of hardship, the Catholic population in New York reached more than one million, with 1300 clergy ministering in more than 400 parishes.

For the Religious of Jesus and Mary, the period marked the stay of a resident who became memorable in their Congregation and in the Church. Dina Marie Bélanger (1897–1929), a young pianist with a teaching certificate from Québec, arrived in New York to study advanced piano and harmony at the Institute of Musical Art, located on 12th Street and Fifth Avenue. The Institute was the origin of what became the Juilliard School in 1926. Arriving at Our Lady of Peace with two friends early in October 1916, Dina had hoped for a private room. With none available, she was assigned a double room with one of her traveling companions, Bernadette Letourneau. The arrangement worked so well that when single rooms were offered to them the next month, they chose to stay together. They enjoyed similar interests and the musical richness of New York, as well as the home-like atmosphere of the residence. According to Dina's frequent letters to her parents, the trio laughed and joked a good deal. Having shared their accomplishments and love of music, they became lifelong friends; all three would enter religious communities.[165] Their studies completed, they returned home to Canada.

Armed with certifications to teach piano/organ, Dina and Bernadette joined the Religious of Jesus and Mary novitiate at Sillery in 1921 and professed first vows together two years later. Dina received the name of M. St. Cécile de Rome, patron saint of musicians; after her profession in 1923, she spent a short time teaching music. Bernadette became M. St. Omer de Luxeuil, earning a lifelong reputation as an accomplished composer and organist at the women's college in Sillery. Dina's journey led her inward, as she struggled with illness and the apostolic limitations it imposed. Her profound mystical prayer experience was marked by inner suffering, along with intimate revelations from Jesus that were a call for her and a source of misunderstanding in the community. In 1924, one of her superiors requested that she write about her inner life and

spiritual experience. After her death in 1929, the Canadian province published her spiritual memoir, *Canticle of Love*, revealing the depth of her
intimacy with God. More than her music, Dina's writings would reach
thousands. Who would have suspected any of this when she lived at Our
Lady of Peace?[166]

End of an Era, Years of Change and Challenge (1929 to 1967)

Twenty years after arriving in New York, M. St. Euphémie celebrated
her golden jubilee of profession at Our Lady of Peace early in 1922, with
festivities that brought accolades from everywhere in the congregation.
M. St. François de Sales had replaced her as the house superior two years
previously and would serve four more terms in the ensuing years through
1952. As one of M. St. Euphémie's first companions in the mission, she
had shared the hopes, poverty, joys, and struggles of the founding years.
An accomplished musician and natural leader, M. St. François de Sales
carried on the traditions of hospitality of the residence until age and illness brought her back to Sillery, where she died after a brief illness. In the
summer of 1929, M. St. Euphémie became ill with stomach cancer. For
the next month, the sisters tended to her until August 29, when she died
in the home she had built on faith, in poverty. It was her living legacy. The
residents and community gathered for a wake service in the Social Room
before her body was taken back to Sillery for burial.

The city of New York underwent a period of expansion and growth
in the 1930's, becoming a world center for trade, commerce, and communication. The decade saw the rise of skyscrapers—the Empire State
and Chrysler Buildings—that came to define the city's skyline. Its sub-
way system, operating since 1904, underwent major expansion in 1928.
Construction of one of the new lines ran under the house at 14th Street,
causing a sidewalk cave-in that made the sisters fear for their own safety.

In May of 1931, the General Chapter elected M. St. Borgia (Teresa)
Mas de Xexas as its first Spanish superior general. M. St. Borgia had been
acquainted with the "new world" and the U.S. houses as one of the found-
ers of the Mexican/Cuban mission. The month after her election, sisters at
Our Lady of Peace learned of the establishment of a new "American Prov-
ince," taking in the two New York communities (Kingsbridge, Highland
Mills) with predominantly English-speaking sisters. The sisters at 14th
Street were to remain part of the Canadian province.[167] It alone could

provide personnel for the necessary corps of auxiliary sisters. French continued to be the spoken language of the sisters of the community. A formal contract was drawn up between the provinces, assuring Our Lady of Peace of continued services with auxiliary sisters from Canada, in exchange for financial support and contributions from the residence.[168] This new arrangement did nothing to reduce the numbers of sisters coming for visits, conferences, or studies at Fordham University. Foreign visitors and former students from Québec often stopped to visit. Well into mid-century, large groups of students from the congregation's American high schools arrived for Sodality conventions such as the Summer School of Catholic Action. The Chapter Report for 1937 lists the personnel of the residence: eight choir-professed, seventeen auxiliary sisters, and 150 women boarders. An active "social works committee" was meeting regularly under the direction of a Jesuit to respond to needs in the area.

When Europe suffered the ravages of World War II, the celebrated generosity of Our Lady of Peace continued in the form of care packages sent weekly to sister-houses in Italy, France, and Germany. Cartons of food supplies, medicines, and clothing left from New York ports and brought relief not only to the sisters but also to families and school children who were in great need. After the War, social and cultural changes affecting the nation and the Church also affected the American mission of the Religious of Jesus and Mary. A decision made by the General Chapter resulted in the separation of all the eastern houses from Canada to form the "Franco-American" province in 1947, with a provincial house at Goffstown, New Hampshire. A second novitiate was set up in Goffstown for the formation of Franco-American candidates. Six American novices moved from Québec to become the pioneer formation community in New England. Two years later, both provinces in the States were reunited as the "American Province," with transfer of province headquarters to Highland Mills, NY. This new configuration would affect Our Lady of Peace in major ways.

For one thing, most young women from the States resisted entering a congregation with "second class" sisters. The number of applicants to be auxiliary sisters dropped significantly through the 1950s. As senior sisters retired and returned to Canada, Our Lady of Peace hired larger numbers of lay staff for domestic service. The expanded costs of this change, along with major repairs and maintenance of the aging buildings, were added to substantial mortgage payments on the property. Secondly, the war had given women new independence and autonomy in the workforce, with

better salaries and more living options, especially in a city like New York.
There was less need for residences like Our Lady of Peace, which gradually
took on the character of a home for elderly residents. The community still
hosted sisters or students for meetings and summer studies. In 1954, the
community entered the electronic age with the arrival of their first televi-
sion set. Their sister foundation in the Bronx boasted a very large parish
school, new convent, young community, and the promise of many vocations. The expansion of the province's headquarters in the mid-Atlantic
region, near the Capitol, was a promise of renewed life and hope. In 1956,
fire broke out in a third floor bedroom of the 15th Street building, causing
extensive smoke damage. For the next decade, it became clear that the
residence faced an uncertain future. Sixty-five years from its inception,
faced with rising costs, diminishing personnel, and an outstanding mortgage of $45,000, Our Lady of Peace prepared to close its doors. In January,
1967, the superior sent a petition to sell the convent and residence, citing
the dearth of sisters for the work, as well as the exorbitant costs to renovate the building. The property was appraised at a value of $550, 000. In
November, 1967, it was sold to a developer, the "159–29 Jamaica Avenue
Corporation," for $175,000.[169] There were plans to convert it into a men's
hotel. Looking back on a vital and prosperous past, the community at Our
Lady of Peace was among the first to face a new and challenging era for the
church and the Religious of Jesus and Mary.

St. John's Parish, Kingsbridge: Bronx, NY (1903 to 2017)[170]

The dream of having an academy in lower Manhattan had been deferred, but news came from "uptown"—in the semi-rural borough of
the Bronx—that the Religious of Jesus and Mary might soon transform
their dream into reality. Within a year of undertaking the mission at 14th
Street, M. St. Euphémie engaged in a flurry of correspondence toward
the educational undertaking that would become St. John's School in the
growing Irish immigrant quarter known as Kingsbridge. Today it is hard
to imagine the Bronx as a region of fields, farmlands, and streams once
inhabited by various Native American tribes. By mid-nineteenth century,
many of New York's immigrants had moved north from Manhattan to
escape the overcrowding and high costs. The "King's Bridge," connecting the East and North Rivers was first constructed in the seventeenth
century to accommodate farmers and tradesmen. Rebuilt several times,

it disappeared in 1916, buried by landfill as part of urban expansion and development. Originally part of Yonkers, Kingsbridge was established as a town in 1873. The Bronx was the last of the five boroughs annexed to New York City, in 1898, with a population of over 200,000. Bronx neighborhoods were friendly to various ethnic groups; Kingsbridge quickly became a magnet for Irish Catholic immigrants.

Prior to having their own parish, Kingsbridge Catholic families worshipped at St. Mary's Parish, Yonkers. They were subsequently served by the Jesuits as a mission of St. John's College, now the Rose Hill Campus of Fordham University. In 1870, property was purchased by the archdiocese on Kingsbridge Avenue and work began on a frame building to house the first Catholic Church in Kingsbridge. By 1886, St. John's had a resident pastor, Rev. Edward O'Gorman, who bought additional property, removed the former wooden church, and began constructing the basement of the church at its present location on Kingsbridge Avenue, costing $21,000. He labored heroically in the parish before his transfer in 1903. With the appointment that year of Rev. Daniel H. O'Dwyer, renovations to the church were completed, followed by the construction of the upper church for the sum of $200,000. O'Dwyer developed many clubs and activities for the parishioners; he converted the former church building into St. John's Hall, a social center for parish groups and sodalities. Within months of his coming to St. John's, he would welcome the Religious of Jesus and Mary into the parish as teachers and evangelizers of the faith so dear to his parishioners.

Interestingly, the first request for sisters and a school came not from the clergy but from the laity who expressed the "pain and anxiety we are obliged to suffer as a consequence of having no Catholic school." In a letter to Archbishop Farley on May 25, 1903, a parish committee of thirty-seven men and eight women signed an impassioned petition for sisters while they acknowledged the pastor's inability to provide revenues from the parish. "[The pastor] told us that if we could secure an order of Sisters who would undertake [the school] at their own expense," without expecting financial aid from him, he would offer no objections. The fifty signers indicated their willingness to contribute to the support of the community. Furthermore, they had already contacted the Religious of Jesus and Mary at 14th Street, possibly through Mr. A.S. Rhéaume, the only member of the committee with a French name. By June, Farley sent the parishioners a favorable answer. They invited the Religious of Jesus and Mary to visit the parish and begin seeking a suitable property for school and convent. On June 16, M. St. Euphémie wrote to the provincial with the "astonishing" news that Farley had approved of Religious of Jesus and Mary at St. John's. "We, French Canadians, admitted into an Irish parish to teach Irish-Americans . . . with Protestant [public] schools in the neighborhood." By then, the new pastor had arrived and was eager to have the school underway. In her letter of thanks to the archbishop on June 20, M. St. Euphémie emphasized that the Religious of Jesus and Mary looked forward to working in a parish that offered such a wide scope for apostolic work and hoped it would prosper "for the greater glory of God and the salvation of souls."

On June 23, Farley responded graciously, adding an emphatic caveat: "I wish to impress one thing on you and on the sisters in charge of the school . . . that I desire it to be a parochial school, free for all children if possible." This articulated clearly where Farley's priorities for Catholic education lay, as "these are the children that need the care of the sisters most of all." It was likewise a mandate, one that the Religious of Jesus and Mary could not then fulfill financially. A day later, M. St. Euphémie responded with some clarifications, referring to the fact that the citizens of Kingsbridge "have come several times to ask if we would be willing to open an establishment in their parish, at our own expense, viz., a paying school (with kindergarten and academy)." The sisters were willing to ask for financial help from their general and provincial headquarters. For the time being, their school would need to require fees from families who could afford to pay, which would contribute to helping those families unable to do so, until the sisters could open a free school for all. To take on a second mission in the city at considerable expense with very little capital was an underlying concern, although it is not mentioned in the correspondence. The original agreement to hire the Religious of Jesus and Mary, dated July 28, 1903, stipulates that the pastor would cover the annual fee of $15 from a fund established for the expenses of children whose parents were unable to pay. By the end of July, Farley had given the needed approval for "St. John's Academy, under the direction of the Ladies of Jesus and Mary." The establishment would function at the expense of the congregation, with some of the students paying fees and others provided for by the school fund described above.

The next task was the purchase of suitable property to include a convent and educational unit large enough for 200 children. Initially, the sisters were interested in a certain "Weber property" on Broadway, but that plan fell through. By mid-August they had met an Irish widow,

Mrs. Ellen Murray, who was willing to sell her property on Kingsbridge Avenue, between 231st and 232nd Streets. It had two houses that might serve as convent and academy; a third house on "Church Street" nearby was purchased as a small boarding residence for women. Advertising their institution, the Religious of Jesus and Mary wrote that the Academy would offer "instruction in the arts, religious and moral training, and preparation for an active business career as well as the quiet and refined accomplishments of social life." The residence was foreseen as a peaceful place for "those who seek quiet, rest, and comfort, secure from the noise and confusion of the city." It would also be an essential source of income in a financially precarious new mission. The total price of purchasing the properties was over $40,000. The provincial house in Canada sent more than $12,000, donations amounted to several thousand, and money was borrowed from Emigrant Bank to pay the mortgage. On the first page of the house annals (all written in English by one hand at a later date), mention is made that in August "the contract for the purchase of the Murray estate was signed." With school set to open its classes within two weeks, there was a bustle of activity as the first sisters arrived and preparations got under way for a new venture "uptown."

Trials and Triumphs: Early Years (1903–30)[171]

Early in September, M. St. Ferdinand, one of the founders at Our Lady of Peace, arrived from 14th Street to become superior of the new community, some of them newcomers to the States. M. St. Alexis (Augustine) Bernier, M. de la Colombière Bilodeau, M. St. Angela (Mina) Broster, M. St. Andrew Carlyon, M. St. Ignatius (Emma) Matthieu, and M. St. Anacletus (Delphine) Trudel were assigned as teachers in the kindergarten and elementary school, tutors of private lessons in music and art, or staff for the women's residence. Assisting them with domestic services were Sr. St. Seraphine Fontaine and Sr. Thaïs Savard. Eventually, their first convent home would be named "Sacred Heart House." On Friday, September 11, 1903, classrooms were set up with the help of several men of the committee. Some moved desks and furniture; others contributed in kind, including a complete set of Encyclopedia Britannica, books on the Bible, and other literature to inaugurate a school library. Sunday school was organized in the church basement, with 200 children present. The following Sunday, the Religious of Jesus and Mary were welcomed with these words by O'Dwyer: "Jesus has come among us in the person of the Sisters whose only aim and purpose will be to make the souls of your children strong by faith, and help those who may have lost the state of grace to recover it."

The first school day, September 14, opened with Mass attended by sixty-five children and their parents, who then crowded in to see their new schoolrooms. Once they separated the students into grades, sisters began "regular class-work" that same afternoon. Notwithstanding their fatigue and language difficulties, they were encouraged by the "bright prospect" of satisfied parents and enthusiastic children, as well as the pastor's visits. They were likewise challenged by the intricacies of Bronx building and fire codes, about which they knew little or nothing. Fire escapes were needed for two of the buildings in which lessons would be given; the sisters narrowly escaped a fine for converting a private home into a school without city permits. Within a month, they would learn the importance of fire safety in buildings that were predominantly wooden structures: a raging fire destroyed a haystack and some neighboring build-ings, narrowly missing the convent property. An unexpected blessing of this tragedy was the rental of one of the barns on the sisters' property to the local fire team, assuring $25 of regular monthly income.

The ensuing weeks offered signs of welcome and appreciation that reassured the missionaries: a visit from Farley in early November; the gift of a Thanksgiving turkey and ice cream treats from parishioners; 4 AM Mass on Christmas Day, the first in their little chapel, which had been furnished by the thoughtful pastor. A few days later, despite bad roads and winter weather, the sisters prepared and produced a Christmas entertainment performed by the children in full costumes for their fami-lies, who provided an audience of 500 to cheer them on. The program included singing, piano and mandolin performances, a play, declama-tions, and choral pieces: no small achievement in so little time! At its conclusion, O'Dwyer exclaimed: "If the Sisters have accomplished as much in ten weeks, what may we not expect in ten months!" Whatever the expectations, the sisters had little time to breathe or rest in the ensu-ing months. Early in 1904, O'Dwyer set up classes for First Communion and Confirmation to be taught by the sisters. More than fifty boys met on Friday afternoons, sixty girls on Saturday mornings. One of the best-known traditions at St. John's began on March 17 that year, when the first St. Patrick's Day parish play took place, honoring the beloved patron saint of Ireland, homeland of most of its parishioners. Children wore costumes representing the "four green fields" of the Irish counties, performed Irish dances, and led the audience in a nostalgic rendition of "Come Back to Erin." This tradition grew with time and the swelling student population, delighting thousands for almost seven decades.

By the end of June and the first school year, the Religious of Jesus and Mary had prepared 125 children for First Communion and Confirmation; received them into the League of the Sacred Heart (boys) and the Sodality of Our Lady of the Sacred Heart (girls); and led Sunday School students in a procession for the celebration of Forty Hours. Summer that year did not provide much rest. There were students for music lessons, a source of financial support; "teacher training" in new methods, such as the Palmer Method of penmanship; and on August 4, a fundraising game day on the convent grounds for more than 400 children. Two large classrooms were being built behind the second house. The nine women in the residence also needed household services, ably provided by two sisters from 14th Street while the Kingsbridge sisters went to Woonsocket for their annual retreat. Looking back on their first year with gratitude and exhaustion, the sisters could not foresee the rich and lasting fruits of their generous labors. The pattern they had set of hard work and generous involvement in parish life became a model for generations to come. They had likewise learned from O'Dwyer to expect respect and large-hearted kindness from the succeeding pastors. Most of them admired the zealous commitment of the sisters to St. John's and regarded them as true partners in their ministry. After hearing one of his inspiring sermons early in 1904, the annalist wrote of O'Dwyer: "The more we see of the kind Father the more we find cause to be grateful to Providence . . . for so holy, zealous and kind a pastor."

Despite great strides in academic, cultural, and spiritual life at St. John's Academy, an undercurrent of tension grew around the issue of the pastor's hopes for free parish education. Sometime in 1906, O'Dwyer communicated with M. St. Croix Tanguay, then the provincial in Québec, requesting that the Academy become a parochial school. Her candid letter of response, dated September 2, 1906, laid out the financial status of the Religious of Jesus and Mary, with annual expenses amounting to more than $5000, an exorbitant cost for the community, which was responsible for the upkeep of buildings, heat, hot water, and janitor's fees in addition to food and lodging for the four sisters. The provincial proposed annual remuneration of $2000 from the parish for four classes of students (fifty per class). That amount would include a $300 annual stipend

for the teaching sisters. The letter refers to a building fund for the new
church and argues that the people would grow in generosity with assurance of a free parish school in the future. Her proposal was accepted on
a temporary basis.

Three years into their new mission, on June 9, 1907, the Religious of
Jesus and Mary joined the parishioners for the laying of the cornerstone
of a new church building and celebrated the first four graduates from the
Academy. Two years later, sadness struck the parish community with the
death of O'Dwyer in November. As he had spent so much energy toward
providing a beautiful edifice for his people's worship, it was fitting that his
funeral Mass was the first service in the new upper church at St. John's.
The sisters mourned the passing of a good father who had done so much
to help them in their first years at the parish. A month later, St. John's
greeted a new pastor, Rev. Francis X. Kelly, a zealous and capable priest
who would spend the next twenty-six years expanding educational and
pastoral services for his growing flock. Early in the spring of 1910, Kelly
must have been pleased to receive a positive report on sisters' school,
as indicated in a letter from Mr. Michael Larkin, of the Catholic School
Board in New York. He complimented the school on its methods, on
"gratifying results in all the branches," fine discipline, and neatness. Religious instruction was "a credit upon the faithful and devoted Sisters in
charge." He complimented the teachers for the quality of English lessons
in grammar and writing, a special commendation to a community perceived by some as foreign. He further noted with surprise the teaching of
algebra, Latin, and other subjects usually included in a high-school curriculum. These signs of hope pointed to a bright future for the school that
he hoped would be able to welcome every child.[172] To this end, a Builders'
Society for the school was formed, along with a Ladies' Auxiliary composed of thirty parish women, to raise funds for a new school building.
With breadth of vision, the group foresaw a school that would serve as a
social and recreational center, and offer modern facilities for instruction.
Plans for the new building included a gym and auditorium to serve both
parish and neighborhood.

That same year, the annals record that two sisters began a weekly
journey to St. Elizabeth's, a neighboring parish, where for a few years they
would teach Sunday school to between 200 and 400 children. By 1913,
new troubles multiplied for the sisters' community, which now included
the novitiate.[173] M. Adelaide (Georgina) Colfer, the school principal who
was fluent in English, wrote a long letter to the superior general early

in March concerning various problems, including discontent with the superior, M. St. Luc LeBoutillier, whose approach several parishioners disliked. The letter describes ethnic tensions between some of the sisters and parents who considered the Academy as "too Frenchie." The superior seemed to embody a "French spirit" that the principal felt was holding back the progress of the U.S. mission and creating problems with the pastor. M. Adelaide felt isolated: "I do wish I had someone to look after things in English and have English ways."

At the end of March, she penned a sad few lines to Rev. M. St. Clare from a steamer on the Fall River line, bearing the body of M. St. Luc back to Québec. The superior had collapsed and died on March 27, two days after the clothing ceremonies of a novice, M. St. Etienne Bilodeau, at the Kingsbridge convent. Kelly officiated at the funeral services where the children sang a Gregorian chant high mass. Expressing the shock and grief of the community, M. Adelaide lamented, "We are sorely tried." Her trials multiplied later that year. They came from false and unkind "reports" from the sisters that her relationship with the pastor was "too friendly." On September 26, 1913, she wrote in French to the provincial who had received the negative information from community members. M. Adelaide defended herself, claiming her innocence before such accusations. She wrote that if Kelly "knew what the sisters were saying about him, he would feel terrible." To conclude, M. Adelaide confessed that she felt "useless" because of things said about her, along with the corresponding suspicion surrounding her actions. While there are no extant records of the superiors' responses, issues were evidently resolved in M. Adelaide's favor. The next year, she was appointed the new leader of the mission. At the end of her term in 1919, M. Adelaide would be remembered as a fine educator and visionary who encouraged academic excellence in the students and moved the new parish school project toward fulfillment. She encouraged the formation of various clubs as well as an alumnae association, with by-laws and dues of one dollar per year. At their meetings, the alumnae would wear a "blue and white ribbon, similar to that worn by other alumnae" of the sisters' congregation, to which they were affiliated.[174]

From Academy to Parish School

While the Academy multiplied its educational and social programs for an expanding body of students, it remained an independent institution, owned and operated by the Religious of Jesus and Mary. Their ongoing concerns included the urgency of mounting debts and the need for a parish free school with additional space. The mortgage on their property was $27,000; the community was barely able to meet interest payments, while nothing had been paid on the capital. By January 1916, there were 170 students at the Academy. One-third of these were received free of charge, ten percent paid the monthly fee of $2.00, and the remaining students paid what they could. There was some respite with the pastor's raise of their annual income to $800 and the amounts raised by parish fund-raisers. The sisters continued to give private lessons and take in a few boarders. Nevertheless, the expenses exceeded their capacity to make ends meet, leaving them with an operating deficit of $1700.

In a forthright letter to Farley on January 31, 1914, M. Adelaide requested his approval to move forward with plans for expansion: "With assessments cancelled and the sum of $50,000, we could begin a new school building, thus extend our work and do more for the parish."[175] She proposed this sum as his donation toward beginning construction on their property to replace the school that was "too small, very old and past repairs." She noted that restricted space made it impossible for them to have gatherings in the school for alumni/ae, Sodality functions, or proposed Sunday conferences for young women. Returning to the original desire of the community, the principal suggested a boarding school that would respond to the hopes of many, and offer more advanced instruction in business and other branches of study. The letter went on to describe the success of teachers and students at St. John's. Three of the boys were training for priesthood, while others were doing well at area secondary schools. One of the girl graduates was already a teacher; others were in training as educators. In conclusion, M. Adelaide laid out the need once more: "Plans are in place for the carrying out of these propositions; but we have no money to proceed. 'Give a man power and you will see what he can do.'" Unfazed that she wasn't a man, this intrepid woman with vision described what could be done for good if the Cardinal gave her the power—and funds!—to realize the idea of a bigger, better St. John's. There are no records of Farley's response, or any donation.

Two unrelated events occasioned a six-year delay of her ambitious plans: the economic straits following the Great War, and the death of Farley in the fall of 1918. In March of the following year, Auxiliary Bishop Patrick Hayes became New York's fifth Archbishop. As the son of immigrants, his pastoral interests focused on family life and helping the poor, along with condemning abortion, contraception, and divorce. A year after his appointment, Hayes founded the archdiocesan Catholic Charities as an organized response to pastoral needs. Having sought and received his permission on June 12, 1922, the St. John's Builders' Society purchased a new piece of property at 3030 Godwin Terrace, for over $35,000. Student population was over 200, with more than 400 being turned away for want of space. It was high time to realize M. Adelaide's dream! Hayes sent his blessing with encouraging words for the fund-raising drive, calling it "gratifying and consoling" to see such fervor for Christian education. Under the direction of Mr. Thomas Larkin, the Builders' Society wrote a statement of purpose with breadth and vision: "The Catholic school today is the foundation of our Catholic faith tomorrow . . ." They planned for an auditorium with a fully equipped stage; ample space for lectures, movies, and meetings; a combined recreational hall and gym. The new school would fill a neighborhood need, offering a public hall open to everyone. Overruling the pastor's desires, they planned as well for a new rectory building, decrying the sparse conditions in which their priests lived.

Construction began soon afterward. From the pulpit on September 13, 1925, Kelly announced the opening of the building for the following day: "there will be room for all our children in the new school." It was twenty-two years to the day from the founding of Jesus-Mary Academy. Close to 500 children enrolled in the St. John's Parish School that day; decades later, their number would exceed 1200, from pre-kindergarten to eighth grade. The school was a living monument to the generosity of parishioners, sisters, lay teachers, and staff. At last, a promising and secure future for the school and sisters was assured. There were, however, signs of dark financial clouds over the sisters' property in Kingsbridge. An undated typed French memo—probably written in the 1920s to province leaders in Québec—indicates there was ongoing discernment regarding whether the congregation should keep or close the mission. Annual expenses and mortgage costs exceeded annual revenues, preventing any payment on the capital debt. Reasons for closing included, strangely, an unhealthy environment (reference to malaria) and a lack of support on the part of some parishioners. A petition was sent to Rome from Québec to "abandon the work," given the community's precarious financial status. At their meeting on December 4, 1925, the General Council discussed the issue and concluded: "Reverend Mother (St. Clare) and we disagree with this proposal. Given all our efforts to assure the school's success by sending it two fine English-speaking subjects, we propose rather that two of the houses we now own be sold . . ." They suggested the income from such a sale could cover the mortgage on the third building, freeing the community from its heavy interest payments. They concluded with the hope that the school and mission at St. John's would continue to flourish.[176] To allay concerns about providing proper English instruction, the superior general appealed to the congregation's sisters in Ireland, who sent three young "missionaries" to Kingsbridge, where they were known and loved for many years: M. St. Charles (Ellen) Collins, M. Mary Camillus (Catherine) Mannion, and M. St. Gabriel (Josephine) Burke.[177]

In spite of this additional help, within three years M. St. Winifred McMahon wrote to the provincial saying that the priest-director of the school, Rev. Thomas Temple, needed more sisters. He complained that it was easier for him to get sisters from another congregation than to petition the provincial every time he needed more teachers. To save money, Kelly had proposed letting go of all but two lay teachers, leaving the sisters with a critical lack of staff. With the numbers of children increasing every year, plans were in place for fifteen classes in September of 1928. A plea for help in the spring that year brought the promise from the provincial of two more sisters, a promise that evoked praise and gratitude from Temple. In his letter to the provincial, M. St. Peter Claver, on July 5, 1928, he wrote: "The past year has been crowned with success in every respect. The nuns have really done wonders with the children." The founding of two new parishes from St. John's—Visitation in 1928 and St. Gabriel's within a decade—helped to absorb the overflow of students. In July 1935, the parish purchased the Möller Mansion, a large three-story house across from the school, at 3029 Godwin Terrace, to serve as the sisters' much-needed convent. Spirits were high as the community moved into new quarters and anticipated a better academic situation.

New Pastor, New Convent:
Years of Consolidation and Growth (1935 to 1965)

Early in August 1935, sad news arrived that the pastor had died at sea when returning from a holiday trip. A year earlier, he had celebrated his twenty-fifth anniversary as pastor and golden jubilee as a priest. Having served the parish alone for many years, he now had three younger curates to assist him with the ministry. Much mourned, Kelly left a legacy of a fine new school and a large church. Above all, he was remembered for a priestly life, dedicated to serving his parishioners and their needs. For his jubilee, the school children had given him a large crucifix, which hung on one of the church walls in his memory for close to thirty years. By Christmastime, a new pastor arrived whose mark on St. John's would be as remarkable as the man himself: Irish-born Rev. Martin A. Scanlan. The second of seven siblings, four of whom were ordained priests, Scanlan would lead the parish through the lean years of the depression and World War II with skills in financial administration equaled only by his faith, enthusiastic spirit, and ability to build morale in hard times. He set high goals for himself, the parish, and the school. He worked tirelessly to plan, organize, and accomplish them. In a parish bulletin notice reviewing Scanlan's attendance at three patriotic dedications on a single Memorial Day, the writer wondered "what kind of vitamins Monsignor Scanlan takes." By 1940, the parish was cleared of its debt. Scanlan then acquired a new church organ and a large stained-glass window for the loft. In the midst of World War II, a new sanctuary and communion rail were installed in the lower church.

Scanlan purchased property at 230th Street and Corlear Avenue in 1945 as a site for a much-needed new convent. He modernized the school and added another floor. With the opening of the academic year in 1947, eight bright new classrooms welcomed over 900 students, taught by eighteen sisters and two laywomen. Many of the sisters would spend Saturdays pursuing degrees or taking advanced studies at Fordham University. Scanlan's appreciation of the Religious of Jesus and Mary was reflected in plans for a new three-story convent, large enough to house a community of twenty-six, at an estimated cost of $350,000. By this time, twenty-two sisters were crowded into the Godwin Terrace convent. Groundbreaking ceremonies were held on May 7, 1949; by April the following year, the community moved into their first spacious, modern convent, complete with a lovely chapel, library, parlors, infirmary quarters, and twenty-seven bedrooms with sinks and connecting baths. A fully-finished basement provided storage space as well as activity rooms for extracurricular activities. At the back of the property was a garden with Marian grotto, a peaceful shrine in the heart of the Bronx.

Scanlan offered the first Mass in the convent chapel on March 27, 1950. On April 2, over 6000 parishioners visited the new convent, built largely on their generous contributions and on considerable gifts from outside benefactors to the congregation. They were especially proud to know that beneath the altar rested a list of 1445 names of those from the parish who had served during World War II. Ten days later, Scanlan presided and preached at the dedication of the building. In a warm welcome to the visiting Religious of Jesus and Mary, including the provincial, he mentioned in particular the support of M. St. John of God and "Mother Good," (Mary of Good Counsel), recently deceased in Highland Mills. He described the beginnings of the school, its expansion and growth, and the need for new sisters' housing as the community itself grew. He spoke of his desire since 1935 to build a new convent and considered adding a third floor to the school for the community. That plan was scuttled for the new property. "I had decided that . . . the chapel would be a unit by itself," he added, an additional expense that the parishioners gladly assumed. "No money was spared in making it one of the finest convents in the Archdiocese," Scanlan announced, adding that "the parish and the nuns will be repaid in the abundance of vocations." To the sisters, Scanlan gave a closing word of counsel: "Your 'Glory' is in a beautiful mosaic on the altar. You will see it many times and it will tide you over many a difficulty."[178]

In June, Francis Cardinal Spellman came to St. John's to bless the convent. By September 7, the first community of Brothers of the Christian Schools moved into a remodeled Godwin Terrace house, initiating their ministry to the older boys at St. John's.[179] After decades of crowding and penury, the new sisters' residence must have seemed like a palace. A lasting tribute to Scanlan's abilities as builder, provider, and visionary, St. John's Convent served as a house of hospitality and welcome to traveling missionaries, visitors, summer and year-long students for more than four decades. Sisters who lived there would recall frequent drives out to LaGuardia and Kennedy Airports to greet or wave off sister–travelers. With time, their involvement with the parish would extend beyond the school into pastoral and liturgical ministries, religious education, and work with the senior Leisure Club. Untiring and enterprising, Scanlan continued to expand the parish educational services to meet its growing

post-war "baby boom." Property was bought for a second school building at W. 232nd and Kingsbridge Avenue, and by 1953 construction was
moving forward. At a cost of $550,000, the school opened its doors to 586
students on September 13, 1954, with twelve classrooms and a cafeteria
upper class girls and boys. Total enrollment at both schools now came to
1700, and they remained tuition-free. By 1957, the community counted
twenty-six sisters, only one of whom was an auxiliary.

Flourishing Supportive Groups: the "Mission Club" and the "Friends"

The post-war years saw the beginnings and development of two groups at
St. John's dedicated to strengthening the mission of the sisters by fostering vocations, as well as contributing to the financial development of the
Religious of Jesus and Mary. While the documentary material on these
groups is sparse, they left an important legacy during the years when the
province entered an era of expansion.[180]

The "Mission Club," for girls from Grades 7 and 8, had its first meeting in October 1948. The founding moderator, M. Mary Regis (Anna)
Henkel, gave talks on prayer, describing it as something "that comes from
your heart." She shared information about the foreign missions of the
Religious of Jesus and Mary, the sister-missionaries in India and the need
to pray for vocations. On the first page of the Minutes are included a few
"rules": compulsory attendance at weekly meetings on Wednesdays or
Thursdays after classes; one monthly Mass and communion offered for
religious vocations as well as for missions and missionaries. Heavenly
patrons were Our Lady of Perpetual Help and M. St. Ignatius (Claudine)
Thevenet, the Congregation's foundress. The order of meetings included
prayer and a moderator's talk, along with various present and planned
activities for the group. Three officers were elected at the first meeting
of each term. Numbers in the Mission Club are difficult to determine,
as extant reports are sparse and sporadic. Where the records report attendance, between twenty and sixty girls came to the meetings. One of
the few remaining newsletters mentions a high-school group that met
on Friday evenings, implying that the girls continued as members after
leaving St. John's. In the absence of any clear numerical statistics, we can
safely assume that in a ten-year period, hundreds of girls participated in
the Mission Club. It was a significant contributor to the discernment of
those exploring religious or missionary life. The young women developed

strong bonds that transcended classroom friendships. Their social gatherings at the convent, replete with Irish dancing, provided additional benefits of membership. They came to know the sisters outside of the classroom setting. Of the 240 Religious of Jesus and Mary listed as having served at St. John's in its first century, twenty-one were girls from the parish. Several recall the importance of the Mission Club as empowering girls to recognize their ability to make a difference with prayer and mission outreach, as well as fostering their interest in religious life as an alternative lifestyle. The members regularly collected medical supplies and made small "prizes" to send to the missionaries in India. Two of them, M. M. Gertrude (Beatrice) Jalbert and her sister M. Bernadette (Cecilia), were well known at St. John's; M. M. Gertrude was there for over twenty years before leaving for India in 1955. Both corresponded regularly with M. Regis or the members. Their letters were read at Mission Club meetings, offering insight into foreign cultures and describing the challenges of foreign missionary life. In a descriptive letter of March, 1953 to the Mission Club members, M. Bernadette wrote from the mission of Mariampura, India: "The country is full of stray dogs, monkeys and cows, all starving, and still no one will kill them, as they are sacred to the Hindus . . . on big feasts, we buy a chicken." She encouraged them in their missionary zeal. "If ever you feel you would like to do something for the missions, send donations big or small to pay for postage . . . Americans are certainly generous." Clearly, the Mission Club contributed to a developing awareness of a global church and invited the students into social ministry beyond their parish horizons. Missionary life was part of the idealistic romanticism of this period in American Catholic life.

The "Friends of the Religious of Jesus and Mary," another example of the ample generosity identified with St. John's parishioners, were organized shortly after the construction of the new provincial house and high school in Hyattsville, Maryland (1955). This group was loosely organized and left no record of regular meetings or projects; programs of annual fund-raisers contain sketchy information. Early in 1956, an amateur performing group known as "The Funny Fathers Minstrel," put on a show for the benefit of the novitiate, where several young women from St. John's were in training. Under the leadership of Mr. Thomas Finnerty, "its founder and president," the Friends included parishioners and parents of novices and Religious of Jesus and Mary from St. John's. They were active in fund-raising for building and formation projects undertaken by the sisters in Hyattsville. Plans for a new novitiate building were under way because of growing numbers in formation. Over time, annual contributions from the Friends were sent to the provincial superior, usually from the proceeds of an annual autumn dance held at Gaelic Park Casino. The group was most active when M. Mary Catherine (Patricia) Kenny, a much-loved former superior and principal at St. John's, was the province leader, from 1965 to 1972. An undated list of contributors in the 1960s names 375 donors at various levels. The proceeds of Friends' activities often amounted to over $1000 annually.

St. John's High School for Girls (1962–63)

One project remained for the good Monsignor to fulfill his educational dreams for St. John's: opening a long-desired high school for girls in the parish. As early as April 1936, the New York provincial had petitioned the General Council to approve the sisters establishing a secondary school in the parish because "the pastor did not want to turn it over to others" but hoped the Religious of Jesus and Mary leadership would accept it. The General Council was unanimous in approving the idea. For unknown reasons, hopes for the project went unfulfilled until the spring of 1962. In a typewritten contract drawn up on June 21 that year, and signed by Scanlan and the American provincial, M. St. Conrad (Leona) Normandin, the "Articles of Agreement" established St. John's High School for Girls and laid out ten norms regarding the administration and functioning of both schools at the Kingsbridge Avenue address. The high school, opening in September 1962, occupied eight rooms on the second floor; the boys' upper school moved to the third floor. Administrative offices of the first floor would serve both institutions. Elementary school girls and boys transferred to the Godwin Terrace School. The high school had accommodations for two home rooms with forty ninth-graders in each one. The principal, stipulated as distinct from the elementary school principal, was M. St. Rite de Cascia (Cora) Mercier. The faculty consisted of four young sisters: M. Janet Clare (Boisvert,) for English and Science; M. St. Lionel (Claire) Brodeur, for Algebra; M. St. Jane de Chantal (Claudette) Prévost, Religion and Social Studies; M. Mary Ellen (Patricia) Scanlon, Latin. The contract foresaw a complete secondary school staff by 1965, with six sisters and four lay teachers for grades 9–12. It also provided for the state-required librarian and teacher in physical education, as well as coaches for sports. A school fund would serve to "defray the expenses of general administrative functions" and all extracurricular activities, including travel. Both schools and facilities were to be maintained by the parish, which maintained its generosity and largesse.[181]

This ambitious program for the new high school was short-lived. At the end of a year, about eighty freshmen and their families were sorely disappointed by the announcement in church that the high school would close in June.[182] With his death after a lingering illness in July 1963, the 84-year-old Scanlan left an extraordinary legacy and a sense of deep loss. He had shepherded St. John's through good times and bad for twenty-nine years. For the Religious of Jesus and Mary, Scanlan had been father, pastor, friend, and supporter, especially of their educational mission in the parish. The parish moved into an era of upheaval and transformation.

"Signs of the Times" after Vatican II

The impact of Vatican II, various social and political movements, and a shift in Bronx demographics would account in part for significant changes at St. John's. In 1966, Msgr. Louis Stryker, the pastor appointed after Scanlan's death, oversaw massive renovations to the church to accommodate the liturgical requirements of the Council. The arrival in 1971 of Msgr. John T. Doherty as pastoral leader coincided with conciliar renewal in the parish. To accommodate a growing Hispanic population in the neighborhood, Spanish-language Masses were introduced A parish Leisure Club for seniors was organized, with a good number of Religious of Jesus and Mary as active participant-leaders. "*Ecclesiolas*," composed of small groups of adults, met in various homes to pray and reflect on the Scriptures and post-conciliar theology. Engaged, informed, and articulate, Doherty encouraged and led an enthusiastic team of clergy and laity to active participation in all dimensions of parish life as understood by the "signs of the times." Assisted by four young, energetic curates, Doherty served St. John's as priest, pastor, ecumenical leader, and neighborhood activist for twelve years. In his testimony to Doherty at his retirement, Deacon Donald Quigley stated: "His view of being a pastor to his parish extended beyond the walls of his church and his ministry extended to all he met." All these changes occurred as the area developed a new population profile for the school and the parish community of sisters.

Once the Brothers left St. John's in 1972, the Godwin Terrace house stood empty. In April 1974, six sisters from the larger community

obtained permission to begin a post-Vatican II "experiment" of small–
community living in the empty convent, with the approval of Doherty
and the sisters of St. John's. This was in part to respond to the norms in
the congregation's "Documents" from the 1971 General Chapter. In a letter of August 8, 1975, they wrote with gratitude of their discovery: "Our
life as members of a small community is constantly creating us anew
from within . . . Personally and communally, our present life-style has
enabled us to live as apostolic women with an even deeper conviction."
While each member gave time and energy to live a more authentic community life, the turmoil of the era took its eventual toll on this group. By
the summer of 1977, all had left the Congregation except Sister Estelle
Gravel, principal at the Middle School, who remained in the house. Godwin Terrace then became the site for another post-conciliar experiment
in community, an outgrowth of the province's Quest Volunteer Program,
directed by Sr. Janice Farnham. With the approval of Doherty and the
province leadership, four laywomen joined four Religious of Jesus and
Mary to undertake the first Christian Community.[183]

The decade of the '70s brought a surge of Hispanic students to St.
John's, mirroring the changing ethnic profile of the neighborhood and its
"white flight" to northern suburbs. And yet, as Sr. Eileen Reid recalls, "as
the parish population shifted, the parish was still a place to find a nurturing faith community, and the school was committed to faith formation
and excellence." Rising costs of tuition and changing demographics in
the Bronx gradually lowered student population. The elementary school
continued to host five classes for each grade, with a growing number of
Latino and Black children. In 1978, St. John's Middle School closed. The
next year, classes in adult education were offered at the Kingsbridge Avenue School. By the time the parish celebrated its centenary in 1986, the
elementary school was also closed and the building eventually sold to the
city of New York, relieving some of the overcrowding in borough public
schools. It was renamed "Public School 7."

The 1990s brought two major changes to the parish and the Religious of Jesus and Mary. In 1994, the archdiocese transferred the administration of the parish to the Order of Augustinian Recollects, with
Edward Fagan, OAR, as pastor. The following year, at the request of the
priests' community, the declining number of Religious of Jesus and Mary
left their much-loved convent to take up residence once more at Godwin
Terrace, after repairs and renovations were completed. The 230th Street
convent became a center for the Cursillo Movement and other parish

activities. The Christian Community members that year relocated to a rented property on Corlear Avenue. The ministerial presence of the Religious of Jesus and Mary at St. John's extended into the 21st century. They marked a centenary of uninterrupted service to the parish in 2003. In 2017, four sisters left the Godwin Terrace house for the last time. Countless numbers of women and men were touched by their 114-year service, adapted to evolving cultural and religious factors. Large numbers of alumni take pride in their heritage as "St. John's students," with scores of them serving as priests, deacons, religious, or lay ecclesial ministers. The efforts and trials of the early sisters in the Bronx bore fruit far beyond what they had dreamed of when they first came to serve the people "by the Bridge."

6

Ministry in Upstate New York

Highland Mills, NY (1911 to 2015)[184]

THE STORY OF THE gray "house in the Highlands" reads like a novel, with its twists and turns, its fascinating characters, and above all, its durability through a century of formidable challenges from weather, economics, social change, and religious authorities. It underwent a series of name changes, multiple apostolic ventures, and cultural transformations. Its long history stands as eloquent witness to the founding spirits of several generations of sisters who made Highland Mills a truly "American" venture for the Religious of Jesus and Mary in educational ministry, formation, and spirituality. Highland Mills lies about sixty miles north of New York City, a rural hamlet in the town of Woodbury, Orange County.

Located in the foothills of the Catskill Mountains, it was one of many early twentieth-century resort areas for those with means to escape the stifling heat of crowded urban streets. Local farms provided stables for horses and raised animals as well as produce. A tannery and flour mill were built during the nineteenth century. Cromwell Lake assured a water supply for surrounding villages and boasted a resort inn on its shores for 150 guests. Nestled high on a hill, Tioga Lodge, summer residence of Senator Thomas Collier Platt, had about fifty acres of land on which stood a modern nine-room residence, tennis courts, a housekeeper's cottage, foreman's quarters, two lakeside buildings, and a stable for ten horses. The main house had hot water and electricity. It was accessible by train from New York, with the local train station just a few miles away. Serving as a Republican in both the U.S. House and Senate, Senator Platt was known as the political "boss" of his party in New York State and would have entertained lavishly at Tioga Lodge, named for his home county upstate. At his death in March 1910, the Lodge became the property of his estranged widow, Lillian Janeway Platt, from whom he had been separated since 1906. In the summer of 1907, the property went up for sale. The listing shows photos of the four original buildings, including a boathouse and cottage on the shores of Lake Cromwell.[185] Mrs. Platt continued to live there with her daughter, and Tioga Lodge was still on the market in 1911.

Enter Rev. Mother St. Clare, who that year was making her second visit to the United States, where her plans for its future were ambitious. While recognizing the invaluable contribution of the Canadian missionaries, M. St. Clare realized it was important to attract vocations from the United States by offering an English-language alternative to the Québec novitiate. She had met with episcopal leaders of the new Catholic University in Washington, DC, and indicated her interest in having sisters educated there. The promotion of studies and learning for the sisters was high on her priorities list. At the General Council meeting of March 9, 1911, the site in Highland Mills was discussed as a possible novitiate location. While the work at Our Lady of Peace in New York had begun to flourish, M. St. Clare bemoaned the lack of a real garden at the 14th Street convent; she resolved to look for a country house where the sisters could get relief from the summer heat and have a holiday home, as well as a place to convalesce from illness. The decision was made to purchase the Platt property at Highland Mills. When M. St. Clare visited the site sometime in February, "she loved it at first sight, the picturesque wooden house with wide, glazed verandahs . . . apples and grapes ripening in the open air, and the peace of God brooding over everything."[186] The cost of the property was $36,000, close to $1 million at today's rates. It was decided to cover the cost by taking out a mortgage and taxing the houses of the province. The American mission obtained loans to cover its contribution, while the Canadian houses contributed a third of the overall cost.

Auspicious Beginning

On May 9, 1911, M. St. Clare led a small group of sisters to their new home, and work got under way to make the best use of the buildings. One house would serve as a sanatorium for the frail or sick sisters, some of whom had contracted tuberculosis; another would become the future novitiate; and the charming lake cottage looked like a fine chaplain's residence. The pioneer group lost no time in settling in, thanks to a good amount of furniture, along with many furnishings and staples that Mrs. Platt had left for them. The first temporary community included M. St. Euphémie, on loan from 14th Street; M. Clement, a German sister from England; and a Canadian, M. St. Celine (Anna) Robitaille. M. St. Clare directed the initial organization of the house. She delighted in cooking, buying the horses and farm animals, and trying (unsuccessfully!) to milk the cows. She was well acquainted with rural life in England and knew what was essential to a functioning farm. The annalist wrote enthusiastically of their first meal: "Reverend Mother had prepared a supper with provisions left by Mrs. Platt. Our first supper at Highland Mills will never be forgotten. How impressive! So many fancy dinners had been served in this room, now our humble refectory."

The following Sunday, the sisters attended Mass at St. Patrick's, one of the mission churches of Rev. Patrick F. MacAran, pastor of St. Anastasia's in nearby Harriman. The annals for May 14, report that the priest welcomed them, anticipating the sisters' service in his parish: "The Good Master has sent the Religious of Jesus and Mary to Highland Mills. Thank God with me! Little children, do not be afraid to go to their school. They will be kind to you." Earlier that year, in communication with M. St. Clare, MacAran had requested sisters to begin a small school in the parish. In August, the provincial, M. M. Ste. Croix Tanguay, gave permission for a group of three to undertake the ministry beginning in September, and reside at Highland Mills. Each one's annual stipend was set for $300; the parish would provide transportation from the train station. School opened with about forty children in attendance. That number would climb to seventy-five in two years.

As planned, M. St. Clare sent a small group of ailing sisters in June to recuperate and gain strength in the little house set aside as a sanatorium, now complete with veranda. On August 18, the first novitiate of the mission opened, with two pioneers: M. St. Jeanne d'Arc (Alice) Fradette, Canadian, and Sr. St. Laure (Wilhelmine) Simard, from Massachusetts. That day, Marie-Aline Gendreau arrived from Canada to become the first postulant in Highland Mills. By the end of September, she had a companion from Ireland, Bridget Glacken.[187] After six successful years as principal of Loreto School in lower Manhattan, M. St. Antoinette Monette arrived at summer's end to be the local superior and teach at the school in Harriman, with M. Mary of the Annunciation (Charlotte) Cullen as its principal. One of the novices joined them to help with class-room teaching. By the end of August, the permanent community of the new mission included M. St. Ignace (Emma) Mathieu, assistant and mis-tress of novices, M. de la Colombière (Gratia) Bilodeau, and Sr. St. Côme Bernard, an early foundress in Manchester and 14th Street, who arrived as community cook. In September, the group was completed by Sr. St. Evariste (Alexina) Gamache, who was assigned to help in the kitchen and with other household needs. Mrs. Platt continued to be attentive to the sisters' needs, making several visits and bringing provisions. On August 31, M. St. Clare made a last visit to the new mission before returning to Europe. Her parting gift to the community was a large photo of Mother Foundress, whose cause for beatification was just getting under way. Clearly Highland Mills held a special place in M. St. Clare's heart; it was one of her own foundations, and she took personal responsibility for its progress. Over the years, she kept Highland Mills in her prayers and fol-lowed its growth with affection. On her return journey to Rome, M. St. Clare took as a companion an American candidate whose future would be entwined with that of Highland Mills. Frances V. Raymond, later known as Mary of Good Counsel, entered in Rome on October 28, 1911, making profession there two years later. Her first assignment in 1914 was at Highland Mills when it reopened as an academy.[188]

The House Closes and Reopens: 1912 to 1914

Their initial winter was frigid, with frequent snowstorms. The sisters suf-fered more than a few privations, including the lack of a regular chaplain to celebrate Eucharist in their small chapel. They welcomed as temporary chaplain a Fr. Brunet, who was unpaid but willing to offer sacramental services. Despite the generosity of kind neighbors and benefactors, illness and food shortages were frequent. There was little income from private lessons, and unpaid bills multiplied. In March, they made a disappointing decision: the two postulants would have their clothing ceremony in the chapel at 14th Street, since the chapel at Highland Mills was inadequate. On the plus side, the Harriman parish school celebrated a successful first year. All through the summer, thanks to M. St. Antoinette, small groups of lively Italian children from the Loreto School came to spend brief holiday time in the countryside. To augment the community's meager income, the sisters offered private summer lessons in French, music, and calligraphy. But the writing seemed to be on the wall: at the end of June 1912, the annalist reported that two sisters had come down from Canada to tell MacAran not to expect teachers from the community in September. She added a laconic sentence: "We probably will close Highland Mills." In fact, M. St. Antoinette had already been reassigned to Fall River for the fall, which was discouraging news for the pastor who had so appreciated the sisters' skills and kindness.

By July, it was generally accepted that the house at Highland Mills was to be sold due to lack of revenue, and the sisters would seek a more suitable site. Nevertheless, from July 25 to August 1, the annual retreat took place, preached by a Canadian Jesuit, Rev. Louis Lalande. After the retreat, sisters of the community received new assignments and prepared to take their leave. The transfer of the novitiate to Kingsbridge occurred in September.[189] Furniture and furnishings were sold or put into storage, bags were packed, and the community dispersed. Three auxiliary sisters stayed behind to oversee the property and finish with the move. On October 1, Mass was offered, after which the little chapel was dismantled. Three days later, the house was officially closed but would remain in use during summer months as a vacation house for the sisters from New York. From his rectory at St. Anastasia's, on February 12, 1914, MacAran wrote nostalgically to M. St. Antoinette, whom he had come to know and admire: "*Deo volente*, your sisters will return to Highland Mills and probably we may again secure their services. Mother, if you were only back again with the good women who opened our school." Clearly, the departure of the community from his school was regrettable, as it now had sixty children, taught by two laywomen. He expressed the hope of many that the house would reopen and the "noble band" of teachers would return.

There were, however, no signs of an impending sale of the property. Moreover, plans were afoot behind the scenes to reopen Highland Mills with a new ministry: a boarding school for girls. On July 16, 1914, M. St. Raymond (Corinne) Lagarde, provincial treasurer, and two sisters from Sillery were delegated by M. St. Clare to undertake a new apostolic venture in Highland Mills, the Academy of Jesus and Mary. To lead the convent and school, they brought M. St. John of God (Ellen) Sutton, a competent educator and former directress of the boarding school at Sillery. As superior and principal, M. St. John of God would dedicate her energies and talents to building the academic reputation of the school at

Highland Mills, living and serving there until her death at the age of 88.[190] By the end of July, M. of Good Counsel Raymond arrived from Rome and soon became house treasurer. In November 1918, she pronounced her final vows; the next year she was named assistant superior. Within two years, M. of Good Counsel was appointed as the local superior, an office she held until being named provincial. She and M. St. John of God would be remembered as close collaborators and leaders in the development of the school and the governance of the little American province after its formation in 1931.

On October 15, 1914, the first students were enrolled. Three were boarders: Adeline and Constance Eldredge; and Florence Hernandez. Two day-students and two music pupils also enrolled. A resident chaplain, Fr. Alva from Mexico, was appointed on a temporary basis and on August 28 celebrated the first Mass for the newly restored community. In mid-December, a severe blizzard prevented registration of students for the second term; two sisters traveling from New York took three days to return. In January of 1916, Cornelia and Marie Etzel registered as students and were slated to take art and piano lessons. Two months later, Frances Raymond, a niece of M. of Good Counsel, registered as a boarder.The novitiate reopened in Highland Mills in July 1916 in the small cottage, "Villa Stanislaus," with M. St. Charles (Laurette) Paquin as Mistress of Novices. There were four new postulants. Their program consisted of spiritual formation, classes in Latin and Christian Doctrine, and various household chores. In February, 1917, they were the first group to receive the habit in the chapel. The annalist described it as "a most beautiful morn," as the four "brides" entered the richly decorated chapel: "Each one's dress was different, but the court trains (!), six yards long, the crowns of orange blossom, and the ample tulle veils were uniform." Lohengrin's "Wedding March" accompanied the entrance procession. Several hymns in Latin and English were sung, and Thomas F. White, SJ, superior at St. Francis Xavier in New York, gave "a most appropriate sermon on the vows." The bridal garb was exchanged for the black habit and white novice's veil, and each one received her religious name: Anastasia di Nicola (M. St. Stanislaus); Marie-Jeanne Jalbert (M. St. Thérèse of the Infant Jesus); Thérèse Labrie (Mary Josephine); and Ethel Molloy (Mary Clement). Family members and guests joined the festivities for the day, happy to celebrate this new sign of life for the church, the congregation, and the restored mission at Highland Mills. Among the guests were members of the neighboring Etzel family, whose daughters were among the first students; one of them, Cornelia, entered the novitiate in 1925, taking the name of M. Mary Adrian. In 1918, M. St. Clare made a brief post-war visit to the States, accompanied by her secretary, M. St. Cuthbert Lindsay, who stayed on as mistress of novices in Highland Mills, a post she held for over a year before returning to Rome.[191] From 1919 to 1932, twenty-nine women would make vows in Highland Mills.

Religious Education in Neighboring Parishes

In the summer of 1915, M. St. John of God and Mary of Good Counsel began twice-weekly trips to Our Lady of Mount Carmel in nearby Tuxedo, NY, to offer religious education to the children, as there was no parish school. An accomplished musician, Mary of Good Counsel trained a children's choir to sing the solemn High Mass in polyphony. With succeeding years, as the number of students increased to near 200, they were assisted by M. St. James (Catherine) Harding, Mary Adrian (Cornelia) Etzel, and Mary Regis (Anna) Henkel. M. St. John of God taught in the parish nearly forty years; in 1952, she reluctantly yielded to a replacement. The pastor, Rev. Patrick Fahy, often visited the Academy with his choir members and parishioners, cementing a strong relationship that extended through 1995, when M. Mary John (Ann) Horan served as director of religious education in the Tuxedo parish. From 1917 to 1919, two sisters went to St. Columba's in Chester, where they offered religious instruction. For decades in the twentieth century, the Highland Mills sisters traveled to Harriman and to Sloatsburg, where they taught catechism to children at the mission church of St. Joan of Arc. They likewise directed summer camps for working girls and sacramental preparation for more than 200 public school students at the convent in Highland Mills

The Academy of Jesus and Mary (1914 to 1931)

The mandate for M. St. John of God had been clear: to establish a boarding school for young women that would offer individual instruction and a course of studies both competitive and comprehensive. In 1917 the community purchased fourteen additional acres of the property, with a cottage to house the chaplain, whose residence had been destroyed by fire earlier that year. Two floors were added to the building annex in 1927, providing space for three classrooms, a recreation room, and fifteen

private rooms for students, along with a refectory for the sisters. The upper floor was destined for the novitiate and remained in that location for
over thirty years. An undated early prospectus for the Academy, complete with photos of the buildings, grounds, and various rooms, details
the objectives and courses of study available to incoming students. The
grounds served to "foster the love of nature, repose of mind, and other
qualities of a well-balanced character, which the happy home life of the
school tends to develop." Parents were assured that the untiring devotion and "motherly care of the nuns" would provide fine intellectual and
moral training. The house and grounds were especially attractive for girls
who were "delicate" in health. There were the modern conveniences of
electricity, central heating, and telephone, as well as outdoor sports facilities. The course of studies stressed a homelike atmosphere and individual
attention, with primary emphasis on religious instruction for Catholic
students by course offerings on Scripture, Christian doctrine, and church
history. Non-Catholics were not obliged to attend religious instruction.

The stated aim of the curriculum was above all to cultivate "unself-
ishness, devotion to duty, sense of honor." Instruction covered primary,
elementary, and secondary grades. Academic courses included an ambitious selection of offerings: English language and composition; American and European History and Literature; Mathematics, Geography, and
Science. French, German, and Spanish language courses were available,
stressing conversation and "a good accent." Elementary and advanced
Latin courses were offered as electives. There were lessons available in
music, art, and singing. During summer holidays "a three months' course
of travel under the care of the Sisters" could be arranged for those interested in European visits. If a young woman wanted to complete her studies abroad, she had assurance that she would be "received by any of the
houses of the Sisters of Jesus and Mary" there. Annual tuition and boarding fees were $500, including instruction in English, French, and Latin.
Additional expenses were added depending on the choice of courses.[192]

There are few extant statistics of the growth of the academy. By 1924,
however, at the last visit of M. St. Clare, a community of sixteen sisters
and thirty students gathered to greet her. The early promise seemed to
bear fruit in the growing numbers. Sisters worked diligently to obtain
the academic degrees needed to qualify the school for state accreditation.
M. St. John of God filled out the required application for accreditation.
In 1925, following an inspection of the teachers' qualifications and of the
classrooms and library, Jesus and Mary Academy was granted its charter

by the State of New York. The Regents' exams were then incorporated into the curriculum. Soon the school boasted several extracurricular groups: the Sodality of Our Lady as well as *The Thevenet Chimes*, a school paper, the annual yearbook, a drama circle, and Glee Club.

New Chapel, New Name: Thevenet Hall (1931)

Thanks to a generous gift of Almeda Raymond, stepsister of Mary of Good Counsel, another dream for Highland Mills was realized: the construction of a new chapel, auditorium, and chaplain's quarters behind the chapel.[193] After several months with builders and masons underfoot, the new chapel dedicated to St. Anthony had its opening Mass on May 29, 1927. Among the five children listed as first communicants was Patricia Kenny, who entered the community ten years later with the religious name of M. Mary Catherine. At the end of October, Patrick Cardinal Hayes (1867–1938) presided at the official blessing of the chapel. For the event, the students were all dressed in white, their heads covered in white silk mantillas. A dozen cadets from Xavier High School in New York entertained the guests on their bugles as they waited for the Cardinal to arrive. At the impressive, two-hour ceremony, Hayes addressed the congregation "in very fatherly and loving words." The sisters and children offered songs and hymns, as well as violin solos. A reception and banquet followed, where the prelate heard recitations by the students and received many gifts. Because of poor weather and lighting, plans to film the occasion were scuttled.

Very little correspondence remains from these years at Highland Mills. However, one incomplete and unsigned letter among the papers of M. St. Clare offers a glimpse into its community and academic life. Given the date and context, its author is undoubtedly M. of Good Counsel. Written on convent stationery on June 18, 1930, it opens with "My own dear Rev. Mother," a reference to the close relationship of both women. The beginning of the letter complains that the "long letters" she and M. St. John had written to Rome were lost in shipping, and the greeting of M. St. Clare sent for her March feast day never arrived in Highland Mills. "It is most discouraging, but I think there are many bags of mail lost swinging in those nets from vessel to vessel," she continued, "so thus we are all in the black books, but not wholly guilty." The text then refers to her improved health, as she had been hospitalized in March for an undisclosed illness. It goes on to describe the end of the school year at the Academy, with some disappointment that the number of students had diminished (probably due to the consequences of the Great Depression the year before). However, the closing exercises were "well attended, everybody pleased." Students were taking the Regents exams. As for the sisters, two were being sent to Fordham for the summer; the academic program was enclosed for M. St. Clare to examine. One of the Fordham professors, whose two sisters were at the Academy, had addressed the graduates at their commencement. "I have succeeded in having three of our teachers here secure their degrees," a positive sign that the professional level of instruction was improving, helping to enhance the school's reputation. "How M. St. John and I long to open a College here. This is our ambition but God knows if we will ever see it . . . we wait and hope." With this wish, the letter comes to its last extant lines.[194]

A disturbing incident took place on a Saturday morning, November 5, 1932, which resulted in the shooting death of a janitor, Mr. John O'Connell, one of the four men employed at the convent. The four-hour confrontation began when Mr. Anthony Churilla, a disgruntled and disturbed former employee, entered the building and barricaded himself in the cellar, "armed to the teeth and determined to shoot us and set fire to the building."[195] State troopers were called in and were eventually able to subdue and kill the gunman, who had begun shooting through the ceiling of the basement intending to injure resident sisters and/or students. With the exception of M. of Good Counsel and her assistant, everyone had relocated to a safer part of the building. Grateful that no greater loss of life incurred, the community and boarding students thanked God and the heroic police officers who had risked their own lives to protect them. The eyewitness account states that the cellar was "riddled with bullets," indicating the violent nature of the incident. It closes with the reassuring claim that "everything is calm on the hillside and the daily routine is going along as if nothing had happened." Perhaps. Nevertheless, this tale of "murder in the nunnery" was a highlight of Highland Mills lore for years to come.

Despite its financial struggles, the Academy looked forward to a future of growth and expansion. It had adopted a new name, honoring the congregation's foundress: "Thevenet Hall Academy." Reports from the next decade show property improvements such as a kitchen enlargement, additional bedrooms for the community, and a separate community room for the auxiliary sisters. Statistical summaries sent to Rome in 1937 report a community of nineteen choir sisters, five auxiliaries, four in the novitiate, with thirty-five boarders and ten day-students at elementary and secondary levels. The decade of the thirties was also promising in religious vocations: twenty-two women made profession in the Highland Mills chapel. At the celebration of the Academy's twenty-fifth anniversary in November 1938, students offered a musical program and drama performance, dedicating it to M. of Good Counsel, who was likewise celebrating her silver jubilee of profession.

From Mission to Province (1931 to 1947)

At their General Chapter in May of 1931, the Religious of Jesus and Mary announced a major decision: two new provinces would be formed for the United States. The Canadian–American Province would comprise all the mission foundations in New England, plus Our Lady of Peace in New York. Headquarters would remain in Sillery. The American Province would consist of the two communities at Kingsbridge and Highland Mills. The latter was designated as the provincial house. The total number of sisters came to about fifty. The reasons given by the Chapter for separating the United States mission were a) differing languages and mentalities; and b) the need to encourage more women candidates from the States by providing formation in their own country. The New York novitiate would continue to be supported financially by the provincial house in Sillery. While foreseen as desirable, setting up a separate province for the New England houses was postponed to a future date. The residence at Our Lady of Peace remained part of the Canadian-American province because it depended on a large complement of auxiliary sisters who originated mostly from Canada and were French-speaking. A formal contract was already in place, stating that Our Lady of Peace would send financial support to Sillery in exchange for auxiliary personnel.[196] The required permissions were obtained from the Holy See; in June, the archdiocesan authorities approved the sisters' petition. M. St. Peter Claver, provincial of Canada since 1926, and Mary of Good Counsel were appointed provincials for the next six years. A new era had begun.

Thevenet Hall continued offering its course of studies to girls from primary grades through high school, with four to seven graduates each year. It kept a homelike atmosphere and was attractive to students from the New York area as well as boarders who came from Latin America to learn English in a safe and welcoming environment. A report sent to

Rome in 1939 stated there were forty-six students at Thevenet Hall for elementary and secondary instruction. At that time the sisters also gave twice-weekly catechism instruction to about 200 children in Tuxedo and Sloatsburg and offered the summer sessions they had undertaken in the early years. They estimated 230 pupils had received First Communion in their chapel. The numbers in the novitiate had grown as well: from 1930 to 1948, twenty-eight women made profession in Highland Mills, raising hopes for greater development of the province.

These signs of growth and expansion were offset by hints of troubled financial situations in the community. The sisters had in 1940 sought permission from the archdiocese to purchase property adjacent to theirs because they were concerned that "objectionable people" might acquire the land, to the "embarrassment" of the school and community. Their request was not granted. Within the next year, the community did purchase that property for $10,000, having half the amount in hand. The agreement stipulated that the balance was to be paid within a year or they would lose the property. They obtained ecclesiastical permission for a loan but were obliged in June of 1942 to ask the chancery for an extension. There were as well unpaid bills for a variety of purchases, some of which the archdiocese was asked to cover because M. of Good Counsel did not seem to have the funds on time. Early in February 1943, there was an outstanding balance of $600 on merchandise purchased for the convent from McEvoy, Inc., over a twelve-year span. The company owner had tried every means to collect on the debt and finally contacted the chancery for assistance in order to avoid legal proceedings. A letter in June from the Vicar of Religious indicated that the debt was still unpaid.[197]

Understandably, these were years of wartime rationing and penury. However, the financial reputation of the house suffered from a pattern of procrastination with debt payments. Meanwhile, the Academy housed forty-four students with a community of twenty-one sisters performing various services. Along with economic difficulties, there were symptoms of mounting discontent and division among the sisters. These were related to perceived authoritarian behavior of the provincial and her assistant, who had been the undisputed leaders in Highland Mills for three decades. The customary term of superiors in the congregation was six years. Until the General Chapter of 1946, however, there was no fixed term for provincials. M. of Good Counsel had assumed leadership early in her religious life and had never moved from Highland Mills. While she was revered as "Mother Good" by numbers of students and sisters, she was feared and censured by others. Anecdotal accounts in letters point to domineering, demeaning, and biased attitudes she and M. St. John of God displayed toward some auxiliary sisters and others who felt marginalized because of ethnic or social backgrounds. An undated report of a visit of Reverend M. St. Borgia refers to a complaint that "some religious feel they are not heard" and indicates there are no recorded minutes of the provincial council meetings at Highland Mills. "Since the American mentality is very different from all others," the report concludes, "that has to be considered for many situations." With the election of a North American superior general, M. St. Thérèse Chapleau, at the Chapter of 1946, some hoped for a better understanding of the issues and concerns of the mission in the United States, including those of the small American province in New York. Delegates at the Chapter had discussed the possibility of creating just one province for the United States but postponed the idea to a later time. The new superior general and her council continued to study the situation and move toward dividing the Canadian province, which now had more than 500 members ministering in two countries.

Province Separation and Reunion: 1948 to 1954

Late in March of 1947, M. of Good Counsel was hospitalized for an undisclosed illness, resulting in surgery from which she did not recover. She died on April 4, a Good Friday. Her passing left the convent and province without a superior. M. St. John of God was appointed as interim provincial and superior, but the issue of naming a new leader for the American province was "to be studied" until a later time. On April 25, a group of five sisters from the community wrote to the archdiocesan ordinary, Francis Cardinal Spellman,[198] with concerns about the indefinite term for a provincial. They requested that he meet with the new superior general who planned to be in New York, to see if "some action may be more easily taken" about shorter mandates for provincials. They signers asked for anonymity. In June 1947, the General Council petitioned the Holy See to divide the Canadian province in two. Twenty houses in Canada had a total of 373 sisters and fifty-one novices; there were 202 sisters serving in seven houses of the United States. Major changes would soon affect the organization, formation, and governance of the province, as well as the lives of the women within its geographical boundaries.

The decision to divide the Canadian province had been finalized and approved before the sudden death of the superior general that summer, so plans went ahead for making the announcement. On August 20, M. St. Charles (Laurette) Paquin, secretary general, wrote a circular letter to the communities of Canada and the United States, stating that the "Canadian-American province will be divided into two distinct provinces: the Canadian province and the Franco-American province." M. St. Peter-Claver Bilodeau, provincial of Canada, would assume leadership of the new province, with headquarters at Villa Augustina, Goffstown, NH.[199] M. St. Antoine de Padoue (Amanda) Talbot became the Canadian provincial. Councilors for both provinces were also named. M. St. Jean-Baptiste de la Salle Lessard would serve as assistant provincial and treasurer while remaining the local superior in Goffstown. M. St. Stanislaus (Vivian) St. Pierre, superior at Our Lady of Lourdes, would spend a year in Sillery as assistant mistress of novices, in view of assuming the responsibility of formation at a new novitiate for the Franco-American province. The houses of Fall River, Woonsocket (two), Providence (two), Goffstown, and Our Lady of Peace, New York, now became officially the Franco-American Province. They were canonically separated from the Canadian mother province to face a future administration in New England, while maintaining strong ties to Québec. In its report to Rome in 1950, the new province numbered 173 choir professed, fifty-three auxiliary sisters, and thirty-eight sisters of temporary vows. It would not be long before the remaining New York houses would be invited to accept the challenge of leaving behind their treasured past for the sake of a more inclusive future.

No Longer Two but One: The "Franco-American Province" (1949)

In the autumn of 1947, Chapter delegates mailed in their ballots to elect a new superior general. Early in December, a cable announced the election of Rev. M. Luisa Fernanda (Clementina) Sagnier, provincial of Aragon, as the tenth congregational leader. Experienced in leading her sisters in the aftermath of the contentious Spanish Civil War, M. Luisa Fernanda was known for her deep spirituality and devotion to the Sacred Heart. She placed her gifts of gentle wisdom and discernment at the service of the congregation, expanding its boundaries in 1951 to include the vast continent of Africa with the opening of a mission in Equatorial Guinea.

Her desire to consecrate the entire institute to the Eucharistic Heart of Jesus was realized in June of 1952. She would be remembered in the United States for her prudence in directing the reunion of the two provinces. She did this, facing unavoidable resistance and obstacles with her customary patience, faith, and a discerning spirit.

For seven months in 1948, an extensive correspondence took place between M. Luisa Fernanda and M. St. Peter Claver. It concerned the need to "regulate" the canonical situation of the two New York houses and begin to move toward a province merger of some kind.[200] Another exchange of letters at the same time between the superior general and M. St. John of God reveals that the latter disapproved completely of the idea. On September 5, 1948, she detailed her reasons for disagreeing. Expressed strongly and consistently, they were focused on French language usage among sisters from New England, differences in mentality, and what M. St. John of God believed was the destruction of "a whole life of privation and hard work" to develop the American province "when things are opening up." These "things" were not specified further, but M. Luisa Fernanda believed that the situation could not remain as it was, and a decision must be made without delay. She suggested to the provincial that if M. St. John of God persisted in her views, she might find life more suitable if she were sent to England. Tensions were high. On July 19, a formal petition to the Holy See asked for the reunion of the two New York houses to the Franco-American Province, with provision for a second novitiate in Goffstown, while maintaining the English-language novitiate at Highland Mills.

On August 4, a letter from the secretary general to M. St. Peter Claver stated that the merger had been effected at the Vatican because of the irregular canonical situation and small number of sisters (forty-one) in the American Province. It was now a matter of making the transition as peacefully as possible. Correspondence continued amid concerns about the "thorny situation" created by the upcoming merger. Following the advice of chancery officials, M. St. Peter Claver insisted that the superior general should come in person to resolve the matter, which was too important to be delegated to another. For unstated reasons, M. Luisa Fernanda instead requested that Msgr. Joseph A. Nelson, archdiocesan vicar for religious, make a canonical visit to poll the sisters in both New York convents.

New Novitiate in Goffstown (1948 to 1955)

Early in the evening of August 23, 1948, the first six novices arrived in Goffstown from Sillery to be the founding group of the Franco-American novitiate. All were New England natives: M. St. Charles (Loretta) Roberts, M St. Thérèse (Irene) Gendreau, M. St. Florence (Jacqueline) Vandal, M. St. Roseline (Thérèse) Marcoux, M. de Liesse (Pauline) Joyal, and M. St. Suzanne (Doris) Bourgeois. They were warmly welcomed by the community, including the provincial and her councilors, before eating a hearty supper and returning to sleep in their new home: the *Maison Blanche*, a little white cottage that stood in sharp contrast to the large buildings of the community in Sillery. In the following days, as the novitiate annals recall, "the novices put on their blue aprons and oversleeves to begin a major cleaning, or *grand ménage* of the house." Furniture was transported and polished, sleeping alcoves were arranged; floors and walls mopped and washed. Thirteen desks and several sewing machines were set up for the coming arrival of the province's first postulants.

On a hot and humid August 28, five young women arrived; they were joined by a sixth a few days later. Donning the lace mantillas of postulants, they began to explore religious life in a peaceful, rural setting. There were spiritual lectures and reading; college-level courses in French, ancient history, English literature, history, and methods in education; and times of meditation before the Blessed Sacrament in the small oratory created by removing a wall between two rooms. It would be November before a tabernacle and suitable decorations were in place to receive the Blessed Sacrament. On February 22, 1949, the six became novices, and two more young women entered. For the next six years, twenty-seven women were received into the formation program in Goffstown, with annual entrance dates in August and February.[201]

The Thevenet Teacher Training Institute, opened in 1950 to provide college-level classes on site, offered the sisters in formation undergraduate courses toward degrees in education. It was affiliated with The Catholic University of America, and its courses were accepted for credit at many colleges. Fresh from high school programs in journalism, some of the novices published *La Maison Blanche*, a bilingual newsletter sent three times a year. It contained spiritual essays, poetry, and short articles on daily life in the novitiate. Photos of ceremonies and of novices at work, study, and play were visual ways of communicating with families, friends, and possible candidates.[202]

A Canonical Visit

On September 12, 1949, Msgr. Nelson arrived for a formal visit to the Highland Mills community, as requested by M. Luisa Fernanda.[203] That day he interviewed twenty-four members of the community: fifteen choir-professed, two of them with temporary vows; five auxiliary sisters, three novices, and one postulant, recently arrived. Their ages ranged from nineteen to eighty-two. A good number had served in other houses of the Congregation. A few were born in French Canada and one in Ireland; several were American citizens from the greater New York area. Of each sister, Nelson asked for information in three areas: 1) her ethnic and national background, and whether she knew French; 2) length of time she had been living in Highland Mills; and 3) her personal opinion about the merger. Additional comments were invited and noted. The overall results exposed underlying hopes and fears, as well as prejudices and division in the community. Eight favored the reunion; six of these were foreign-born. Two professed sisters, the novices, and single postulant were neutral, with no strong leanings either way. The remaining ten opposed the proposal, some very strongly. Among those in favor, comments covered four areas: the "stagnation" in the community, expressed in terms of a "bad spirit," or being "in a rut"; the need for renewed spiritual life; a call for new, more able leadership; the limits imposed by having only two houses in a province. Of those opposed to reunion, many agreed that M. St. John of God's age and management style were problems. Their observations pointed to real or perceived "antipathy" between Franco-American and "real American" sisters. Statements like "the French are narrow," and "Americans [sic] are in the minority," revealed concerns about having to adopt French as a language for prayer and losing one's sense of being "American" without specifying just what that meant. In fact, after World War II, most of the sisters in the States were either native-born or naturalized, and the nationalism decried by these comments appears baseless. While they did not favor the change, many in this group remarked that indecision and "stagnation" were preventing the province from moving forward; most agreed that it was time for new and different leadership. Looking over Nelson's notes, one gets the impression from repetition of words and phrases that community members had conversed prior to his visit, seeking strength in numbers for a given position.

In a letter on September 24, M. Luisa Fernanda asked Nelson for a formal report of his visit and added that "we have been compelled to take some steps" as required by the Sacred Congregation of Religious, which found the size of the American Province too small. In his response three weeks later, Nelson refused to send a written report. Instead, he requested that M. Luisa Fernanda come herself to New York and discuss these matters with Cardinal Spellman. The meeting took place almost a year later, when the superior general made her first visit to the United States. In the long circular she sent to the provinces in October, there is a passing mention of a meeting with Spellman late in August.[204] More importantly, the letter announces the "reunion of the two houses of Highland Mills and Kingsbridge to the Franco-American province," keeping the two novitiates in place. As of October 6, there would be nine communities in the United States, with headquarters in Goffstown. At Highland Mills, M. St. Vincent Ferrer (Flora) Ducharme arrived from Fall River to become the new superior, with M. St. John of God as her assistant. M. St. Theresa of the Infant Jesus Jalbert was appointed novice mistress, replacing M. St. Ignace who was sent to be superior in Fall River.

Back to the Future as Provincial House (1951–55)

Settling into a revised configuration and authority structure gave the communities of the new province fresh hope and surprising challenges. M. St. Vincent Ferrer brought unique gifts of administration and empathic leadership to the sisters at Highland Mills, where she was soon much appreciated. With her customary energy, she set about seeking ways to reduce the mortgage on the house to $25,000 with a lower interest rate. In a letter to the chancery on January 21, 1950, she spoke of her plan to address their financial situation and "budget our finances to amortize our present indebtedness." First, she saw to the placement in a Catholic hospital of a sister suffering from mental illness and living outside the community; she dealt as well with the disturbing and bizarre behavior of another community member. Some concerns were raised after a regular canonical visit in May 1951, including lack of adequate sleeping quarters for the auxiliary sisters. In her response to chancery officials, M. St. Vincent Ferrer stated that the house had received a rescript from Rome to build an extension to the convent and take out a loan for $50,000 toward its construction. Before chancery officials gave permission, they wanted to meet with the provincial in person.

That summer, M. St. Peter Claver, in failing health from chronic cardiac problems, resigned as provincial and retired to Precious Blood, the convent where she had spent so many fruitful years. Hospitalized for a fractured hip from a fall, she never recovered fully and died two years later at age seventy-seven, on September 12, 1953. She had been a respected provincial leader to sisters in Canada and the American missions for twenty-five years. Among the many memorial tributes from clerical and civic organizations was an unlikely editorial from the city's daily paper, *The Woonsocket Call*. Extolling her as one of the city's "most worthy woman (sic) leaders," the editorial noted her intelligence and efficiency, enabling her "to apply the creative, constructive and material instincts . . . to the administration of an educational system whose aim is the formation of girls as good as they are well-educated in the profane arts." It offered high praise for her efforts toward the growth and influence of St. Clare High School, which she had founded and nurtured, as well as her ability to be a "sincere and sympathetic friend" to former students, clerics, and professional or business leaders who visited her. "Woonsocket has lost an educator who has . . . influenced thousands of its citizens toward a better life."[205] The province's necrology stressed this leader's fidelity, faith, firmness, charity, and zeal, as well as her devotion to the Foundress. In her exhortations to the sisters, she reminded them to be "monstrances" for the children, mirroring Christ and echoing their foundress's sentiments: "Remember, no preference for pretty faces"! In a last and fitting tribute, her remains rested in the chapel she had built, facing the outstretched, welcoming arms of the statue of the Sacred Heart she held so dear.

The retirement and death of M. St. Peter Claver brought unexpected changes to Highland Mills. On August 13, 1951, a circular letter from Rev. M. Luisa Fernanda announced the appointment of M. St. Vincent Ferrer as provincial, to begin her term in Goffstown on August 31. The same day, the superior general wrote to Nelson with that news, along with the appointment of M. Mary Aquinas (Agnes) Doyle as the superior of Highland Mills. She indicated that she hoped to meet him in the autumn when she expected to be in New York for her visitation. By the end of November, it had become clear to her that for a number of reasons the site of the province headquarters required a change. On November 26, 1951, while she was in Goffstown, M. Luisa Fernanda announced to the local community that the provincial house was to be transferred to Highland Mills. The same news was privately announced as well to the

Highland Mills community and finally by mail to the whole province at the end of November.

However, due to construction plans at Highland Mills, the move was postponed for several months.[206] Reasons for the change were not stipulated in the letter, but certainly the property in New York was extensive enough for a large educational complex in the future, as well as a new novitiate, teacher-training college for the sisters, and a provincial administration building. Relocating province headquarters back to Highland Mills would also offer positive affirmation of its past contributions and hope for a renewed future—a "consolation prize"—to those who were still grieving what had been lost.

Struggles and Challenges

By spring of 1952, M. St. Vincent Ferrer wrote to Spellman and Nelson asking permission to set up the provincial house and formation programs in Highland Mills. Through April and May, extensive correspondence between Nelson and M. St. Vincent Ferrer reveals that fiscal concerns over Highland Mills were posing difficulties at the Chancery. The proposed building project, amounting to $500,000, was approved by the Roman authorities, contingent on contributions of $47,000 from ten houses of the province, a bank loan, and a Building Fund amounting to $50,000.[207] The convent in Highland Mills still had an outstanding debt of over $38,000. Financial advisors of the archdiocese conveyed their concerns that it would be unwise to consider a mortgage arrangement because of inadequate funds on hand to launch such an ambitious project.[208] On May 6, the provincial wrote again to Nelson with news that the Building Fund was increasing and that the community was seeking good bids to reduce the overall cost. With her customary faith and aplomb, she added that "this is where one of God's miracles will be worked."

On September 4, the provincial and her council took up residence in Highland Mills, still praying for adequate funding to go forward with building plans. Resistance from chancery authorities continued. Late in December, M. Luisa Fernanda died in Barcelona after a brief illness. Five months later, delegates to the General Chapter elected M. Maria del Rosario Araño, provincial of Spain, as their eleventh superior general, one who would make a significant impact on the congregation and the province in the coming decades.[209] She would also intervene within a year to consider alternative sites for the construction of new province headquarters.[210]

New Setting, New Beginning

On December 5, 1953, M.St.Vincent Ferrer met with Nelson. While the report of that meeting is missing, it was the catalyst for a decisive letter four days later. "As a result of our interview with you," she wrote to Nelson, "I am asking if you think it would be wiser for the future benefit of our province to build in a place other than Highland Mills." She offered reasons for this consideration: a desire to "be in a neutral place, affording the chance to forget the past difficulties of Highland Mills"; the need to purchase property near a city "where there is need of a high school academy for girls"; funding from a possible sale of more than 100 acres at Highland Mills. The building fund now had close to $200,000 and the sisters hoped to begin building early in 1954. In closing, M. St. Vincent Ferrer expressed hope that the province headquarters would remain in the archdiocese of New York. Whatever happened in the winter, by March 1954, she wrote to Spellman with their plan to build elsewhere than in Highland Mills.

A difficult meeting took place at the chancery on March 22, during which M. St. Vincent Ferrer proposed other possibilities for building within the archdiocese. Chancery officials raised a number of concerns, among which was the "irregular" situation of two novitiates in the one province—with fourteen novices and six postulants in all—as well as questions regarding the canonical validity of vows made in Highland Mills since 1951. They also indicated that mortgages on various properties exceeded the amount in the building fund. Overall, the meeting offered little hope for the future of the Religious of Jesus and Mary in the archdiocese. Subsequent "crushing" meetings with chancery officials confirmed their sense that "the Lord did not want us to establish our provincial seat in New York."[211] M. St. Vincent Ferrer flew to Rome on April 5 for a meeting with the general leadership. While there, she and the superior general consulted with Vincent A. McCormick, SJ, American Assistant to the Jesuit General in Rome, who advised them to abandon thoughts of New York and counseled Washington, DC as a welcome and hopeful alternative.

In early June of 1954, M. del Rosario made her first visit to the province, beginning with Highland Mills. At a meeting on June 5 with the provincial council, she presented a rationale for transfer of the headquarters to Washington. She mentioned the advantage of being near the nation's capital; the proximity of the Catholic University of America for the professional education of junior sisters; and the great need for new Catholic high schools in a developing area. Moreover, Most Rev. Patrick A. O'Boyle, Archbishop of Washington, had assured her "that the community would be welcome and that all possible assistance would be given," while excluding financial help.[212] The provincial council voted unanimously in favor of the move. On June 6, M. del Rosario and M. St. Vincent Ferrer traveled to Washington for an exploratory visit. On their return to Highland Mills on June 10, the superior general announced that they had met the day before with O'Boyle, who had welcomed them and granted permission to transfer the province headquarters, novitiate and juniorate there.[213] They had likewise visited available properties and settled on a site on Riggs Road in Hyattsville, MD. Architects and contractors were chosen. The superior general shared this good news to the other houses of the province in a quick visit, returning on June 23 to Rome, pleased with two full and profitable weeks in the province.

On June 28, Nelson sent a memo to O'Boyle indicating that "this Institute . . . has had a most unhappy history in this archdiocese." He referred to past cultural/language tensions in Highland Mills but indicated approval that the community was "starting over again in a new milieu" and expressed confidence for its future. On July 1, O'Boyle sent his response: "I must say that these good nuns were most cooperative and are now laying plans to establish their novitiate and a high school" for 500 students. "I shall be happy to assist this Congregation in any way possible." Formal announcement of the move came in a letter from the provincial to Nelson on August 10. It expressed her gratitude, announced the date of the move, and added the sisters' future address in Hyattsville, Maryland. Later in August, another difficult meeting was held at the chancery to challenge the "canonically incorrect" situation of two novitiates in one province. In a letter on August 23 to the superior general, M. St. Vincent Ferrer expressed her frustrations with the chancery officials in New York: "I don't feel the courage to continue this struggle . . . How eager I am to get out from under their power." In his last communication with her, on August 13, Nelson nevertheless thanked the provincial for "the edification you have given me by reason of your patience amid trials that were very taxing . . . you know how to be good to others." At what cost, she alone knew. The move to the nation's capital was imminent.

The status of the Highland Mills community changed yet again. Under the leadership of M. St. John of God, Thevenet Hall Academy continued to receive students and to formulate plans for extension and future growth. In 1951, when the house still served as province headquarters, statistical reports indicate that the Academy had forty-five students, of whom thirty-seven were in the elementary course; ten sisters were listed as teachers in a community of twenty professed and three novices. Improvements to the property were made: fire escapes, dormitory spaces made into private rooms, and a full bathroom added in the convent sleeping area. Updated brochures and a new prospectus were prepared to attract more students. The school advertised its academic programs and accreditations, its Glee Club and music programs, *Thevenet Chimes*, the school paper, and a yearbook, *The Archway*.

In 1955, within a year of the decision to move to Hyattsville, M. St. John of God died on St. Patrick's Day. Beginning in 1956, Thevenet no longer offered an elementary school curriculum and focused on strengthening secondary education, but the number of students remained static. Boarding and tuition fees were raised to $1000 per year for boarders, and $150 for day students. Additional fees were added for supplemental private lessons and other expenses. Several of the boarders were from Mexico or other Latin American countries and had chosen Thevenet to improve their proficiency in English. Despite continued efforts to expand and grow as an educational institution, the community at Thevenet graduated its last senior class in 1971. The ministry and community at Highland Mills were faced once more with an uncertain future. It would take shape later in a creative educational enterprise and spiritual ministry, thanks to the renewal encouraged by the Second Vatican Council.

Auburn, NY: St. Francis of Assisi Parish (1951 to 1969)[214]

Nestled more than 200 miles upstate, the small town of Auburn was home to a large community of Italian-American immigrants. In the early twentieth century they had petitioned the first Bishop of Rochester, Bernard J. McQuaid, to build their own church. The Irish and German communities of Auburn already had national churches. These were not always hospitable to the Italian newcomers. With McQuaid's permission,

in 1907 parishioners began construction on farmland at the west end of
Clark Street. A year later, thanks to a collaborative construction effort of
volunteer parishioners who often came at the end of long days in factories
or agricultural work, it was completed. Auburn's Italian Catholics had
built St. Francis of Assisi Church, a space to worship with their own customs and traditions, and above all, in their own language. A temporary
administrator ministered to them until Rev. Giovanni Robotti arrived
from Italy in 1908 as their first pastor. From that time through 1985,
all subsequent pastors spoke and preached in Italian. Feeling at home
in their new church, parishioners formed religious societies known to
them in Italy, provided social activities such as bocce games and picnics,
and celebrated the Italian Christmas and Easter traditions they held dear.
Like other immigrant groups, the people of St. Francis always hoped for
their own parish elementary school. A local blogger has written that from
1911 to 1917, eight Sisters of Mercy staffed a school at St. Francis. For
unknown reasons, that school closed, and children of the parish attended
local public schools until the mid-century arrival of the Religious of Jesus
and Mary.

In 1949, Rev. John J. Nacca, a Rochester native, came to St. Francis as its third pastor. He had already served there twice as an assistant
pastor. For almost forty years of service to the faith community, Nacca
earned a reputation for holiness of life, love for his people, and generosity. He believed that his primary calling was the care of the people God
gave him. Two principal expressions of that care were the new school
and the shrine to Our Lady of Lourdes that he built in 1950 on the parish
grounds. By May of 1951, he would announce the opening of St. Francis
School for September of that year, to be directed by the Religious of Jesus
and Mary. Rochester Bishop James E. Kearney had given the congregation permission to "start a foundation in this diocese." The reasons for the
sisters' decision to come such a distance from Highland Mills to an Italian national parish are not specified in province or convent annals. It is
possible that the Religious of Jesus and Mary were hoping to direct a high
school in a setting other than Highland Mills and that someone had contacted them with the possibility of a future in Rochester. Whatever their
motivation, they must have welcomed the prospect of a brand new school
building with "the latest architectural features," nine airy classrooms, offices, fully equipped cafeteria, and a large auditorium/parish hall. As their
first mission in an upstate New York diocese, St. Francis Parish offered a
new apostolic horizon for the Religious of Jesus and Mary.

Early Years at St. Francis (1951 to 1956)

On August 22, 1951, feast of Mary's Immaculate Heart, M. St. Vincent Ferrer arrived with three of the founding four, to undertake their new apostolic venture in a "land of promise," as it was described in the convent annals. M. St. Augustine (Gladys) Potvin was the appointed superior and teacher-principal; M. St. Alphonse Rodriguez (Germaine) Lefebvre, M. St. Thomas More (Anne) Wallace, and M. St. Peter Julian (Claire) Rondeau would teach in the school. After a six-hour drive, the sisters were met by the assistant pastor, Rev. Joseph Beatini, because Nacca was away on a sick call. The kindly priest showed the group the church and new school, which they described as a "veritable wonderland," and "the last word in modernity and practicality." They pronounced their cozy convent at 6 Brookfield Place "a gem." It was truly a home that parishioners had prepared for them in every detail with love and devotion. Their generosity was evident everywhere: fresh vegetables and fruit from their gardens complemented ample food provisions from the pastor's mother and sister. M. St. Vincent Ferrer took leave of the community the next day. They welcomed the time and space to settle in and become acquainted with their neighborhood and a new ethnic culture. When they visited the local butcher to buy a chicken, much to their surprise, he brought out a living bird for their approval before he dispatched it, Italian style, and prepared it for cooking!

On September 2, the community joined parishioners for Sunday Mass, complete with the sermon in Italian. An Open House at the school for parishioners followed throughout the day and well into the evening. Everyone was impressed with the new facility and enthusiastic in their welcome of the new sisters. The following day, Labor Day, there were visits from the Mercy Sisters at the Hospital as well as from three Missionary Servants of the Blessed Trinity (MSBT), who were engaged in pastoral work in the parish and had been asked to teach at the new school in the coming year.[215] On Wednesday, September 5, the new school opened to 438 boys and girls, most of whom had transferred—or been netted by the pastor!—from local public schools. Classes for kindergarten and first grade students were delayed a week. While waiting for three school buses he had ordered, Nacca arranged for city buses to transport the students to St. Francis. After the 9 o'clock High Mass, eager students filed out to the click of parents' cameras on "a very happy day in the history of the parish, the opening of St. Francis School." Once settled into their new classrooms, students and teachers met each other for the first time. The four Religious of Jesus and Mary taught grades 1, 4, 6 and 7. The three Missionary Servants took up their assignments: kindergarten (Sr. Louise Marie), grade 2 (Sr. Vincent Marie), and grade 5 (Sr. Thomas Mary). Ms. Florence Scannell (grade 3) completed the staff roster. Early in September, a weekly children's Mass was inaugurated. The children had rich singing voices and learned eight new hymns in three days.

On September 20, the sisters celebrated the first community Mass in their convent chapel. The auspicious month ended with the dedication and blessing of the school by the bishop on September 30, attended by a large number of clergy, sisters, and parishioners. The parish celebration included dancing, singing, and entertainment. At the end of October, staff and students welcomed the visit of Rev. M. Luisa Fernanda, superior general, with addresses in Italian and English. In this year of "firsts" for the Auburn community, the sisters learned the value of intercommunity collaboration as well as the richness of devotional life at St. Francis, especially at Christmas and Easter. The children attended Mass twice weekly during Lent and attended Wednesday Lenten devotions and Friday Stations of the Cross. They participated in regular parish missions, and organized a Mission Club among older students. In the ensuing years, the sisters would prepare large numbers of children for First Communions and Confirmations and organize the celebration of a feast for St. John, honoring the patron of the pastor, who enjoyed them fully. Likewise, they became familiar with regular interruptions in teaching, when Nacca would appear unexpectedly to take the children and/or sisters on "surprise" trips and events. Disruption of the academic calendar did not seem to be a concern for their pastor, the quintessential Italian *paterfamilias*.

M. St. Vincent Ferrer arrived in the spring of 1952 for a series of meetings with chancery officials about "a new high school in Auburn" to be undertaken by the Religious of Jesus and Mary. The leadership of the province was eager to establish another secondary school at this time, perhaps as a source of future religious vocations. Because of plans for further construction in Highland Mills, the idea of building a larger school on that property seemed daunting. The meetings in Auburn continued through the summer of 1952. Province leaders then considered a possible collaboration with the Carmelite Fathers, who were building the new Mt. Carmel diocesan high school and had requested sisters for the girls' section. For several undisclosed reasons, the General Council withdrew its support for the project. The Sisters of St. Joseph of Rochester assumed the direction of the girls' school at Mt. Carmel, which opened three years later.

Two sisters of the founding group left Auburn at the end of the first year, and three others arrived to complete a community of five for the academic year, 1952–53. The services of the Missionary Servants were once again much appreciated, and Ms. Scannell returned to teach grade 3. On opening day, there were 525 students, an increase of 80 over the first year. While this was good news on the one hand, it also meant very large classes of fifty and sixty students, taxing teachers' energies and overcrowding pupils. Notwithstanding these challenges, the second year came to a happy close with the celebration on June 21 of the first graduating class: fifty-one eighth graders. Mass and Communion breakfast were celebrated early in the day; students in caps and gowns received their diplomas and awards later in the afternoon, to the proud applause of their families and friends.

Following the announcement that the Missionary Servants were withdrawing from the school in June, Nacca traveled to Highland Mills to request at least three additional Religious of Jesus and Mary for the following year. To address certain issues and clarify expectations, the community contracted an agreement with the parish on August 24, 1953. It stipulated a non-teaching principal, the payment of diocesan salaries for each teacher, residential support for the sisters, and respect for their rules and customs. Further, it stated that the sisters would not serve as sacristans, do janitorial duties, or count the parish collection. That September, seven sisters made up the community, with four new members. The student enrollment, however, mirrored the national post-war phenomenon known as the "baby boom": 570 students, with two first grade classes and more than seventy children in the second grade. The lay teachers were three in number. In June of 1954, the community welcomed their new superior general for a brief visit. She announced the location of their new province headquarters. She also spoke about a forthcoming spiritual renewal program, or "third probation," to take place for selected sisters in Goffstown, NH, that summer. To their delight, six from Auburn participated in the program. When they returned to take up their ministry in September, the community numbered nine sisters and welcomed a new superior/principal, M. St. Ursula (Wilda) Hamel. Enrollments continued to rise, bringing the total number of students to 650, including two ninth grade classes.[216] Primary grade classes were subdivided, and the sisters welcomed the able assistance of three lay teachers. The following year, their number would rise to seven. One of the enduring characteristics of St. Francis School was its collaborative approach to ministry, honoring the importance of sisters and their lay counterparts serving the parish and school as one educational community.

On September 21, 1955, the community received shocking news. Their beloved provincial, M. St. Vincent Ferrer, had died suddenly in Hyattsville, within a month of opening the new foundation. With his customary kindness, Nacca drove the sisters to Maryland for the funeral four days later. Three months later, a parishioner offered to drive the community down to Hyattsville for the official dedication of Regina High School and the new convent headquarters. Despite a heavy snowstorm and bad roads, they made the 400-mile journey without incident.

Years of Challenge and Change (1956 to 1969)

In December 1956, the community moved from Brookfield Place to 185 Clark Street, a temporary residence while construction of a new church took place. The annals report that "this residence will become the new rectory" once the new building was completed. The former rectory would then serve as the sisters' convent. Christmas holidays that year were spent moving furnishings and belongings into their transitional home. Two years later, after they had closed the house and dispersed for the summer months, the community received another "surprise" from the pastor. In a phone call to M. St. Vincent (Irene) Maynard, the superior, Nacca announced that he was moving shortly into 185 Clark Street. The sisters were to move into the former rectory at 192 Clark Street. This meant another major transfer of personal effects and community furnishings as rooms were painted and refurbished. Three generous volunteers from New England came to assist M. St. Vincent to choose paint colors and arrange rooms, listing needed repairs in each one. When the full community arrived on August 25, 1958, the task before them seemed unmanageable: to organize a new residence while preparing for the opening of school. Counting on the grace of God, prayer, and the help of some school children, as the annals record, "the burden of moving did not interfere with the more important work of education."

By October, a new annex to the nine-bedroom convent was completed with laundry, workroom, and most importantly, a community chapel. Construction of the church was completed in 1958, just before

Christmas. On Christmas Eve, the children, dressed as angels, processed into their new parish church, carrying the Infant Christ to the manger and singing a familiar Italian carol. The following September, school enrollment numbered 539 students, taught by six sisters and three lay women. Some classes were merged, bringing the number in one class to seventy-four. Many extracurricular activities occupied teachers and students: Glee Club, Civics Club, Catholic Students Mission Crusade, Brownies, and Scouts. Fifteen high school girls from St. Francis returned for regular Sodality meetings. More than 100 children received First Communion that year.

In 1961, the parish and school communities were introduced to the Building Campaign of the Religious of Jesus and Mary, who were adding a new "provincial wing" to their building in Hyattsville, enlarging the property and adding a larger chapel. Letters went out to prospective donors for their participation. A layman from St. Francis acknowledged recent claims on parishioners for the new church yet reminded them of their usual generosity: "I know that you will want to help the Jesus-Mary nuns in their time of need." While there is no record of the parishioners' response, it probably was reflective of their reputation for Christian generosity. February of 1962 marked a near-tragedy for the Auburn community, returning by car from a workshop in Rhode Island. Their vehicle skidded on a sleet-slick road and collided with another vehicle. One of the sisters, M. Bernard (Elizabeth) D'Entremont, sustained serious spinal injuries that required prolonged hospitalization; the others, while shaken up, suffered minor cuts and scrapes.

The following year, school enrollment figures began to diminish and by 1966 were down to 380. The faculty, however, had doubled to twelve, divided equally between sisters and lay teachers. Social and cultural changes were felt in the community, along with the Second Vatican Council's call for renewal in the Catholic Church. Named as superior and principal in 1965, Sr. Roseline (Therese) Marcoux set to work with lay and religious teachers to enhance their role as professionals and partners in the ministry of education. By 1966, a Mothers' Club was organized with its members engaged in fund-raising and other activities for the school. On October 6, a special evening event inaugurated the Home and School Association for St. Francis. Many parents attended, along with the Superintendents of Schools for Auburn and the diocese, and M. Mary Catherine Kenny, the newly appointed provincial. At their first meeting the next April, officers were elected and plans for the future were elaborated.

Three new principals served at St. Francis during a six-year period. That turnover in leadership may have had some negative repercussions among faculty and parents, though none are reported in the school annals. For the successive principals, however, the turnover revealed recurrent problems with the pastor that created mounting tension. On April 25, 1966, Sr. St. Roseline wrote to the provincial that without warning, Nacca announced "at all Masses (on Easter Sunday) that the talent show was indefinitely postponed." He apparently disapproved of some dance/ballet costumes. She indicated that the pastor often changed his mind about things and announced decisions affecting the school without first speaking with her. She'd had disagreements with Nacca about organizing the Home and School Association, an attractive project for the parents but one that the pastor found suspect. The next year, another superior wrote of problems with heating, plumbing, and lighting in the school that the pastor had failed to address. He had also promised insulation for the convent, which was very cold in winter, but delayed it for months. When she offered to contact the maintenance people herself, Nacca refused.

Difficult Decision (1969)

In the annual report to the community on January 23, 1968, the provincial wrote: "I am concerned about the situation with the pastor . . . his attitudes and means are a source of tension." She did not elucidate what "the situation" was, but earlier correspondence from principals refers to the pastor's impulsive style of leadership as posing difficulties affecting maintenance and school programs. He also had recurring bouts of illness that resulted in extended absences from the parish. At the end of February, M. St. Edward (Gertrude) Lavoie, newly-appointed principal that year, felt frustrated by several vexing discussions she had with Nacca. On Ash Wednesday, the annals record a "touchy problem." The pastor indicated he wanted *all* the children to attend 8:30 Mass every Lenten morning. The diocesan handbook clearly stated that no teacher should force a child to attend Mass, nor were students to attend Mass during instruction periods unless they were for religion class. Not wanting to confront the pastor directly, the principal decided she would allow attendance during Lent for those who wanted to be at the Mass. She asked the faculty to leave the children free to choose. There is no report of Nacca's reaction, but by early March the provincial visited the diocesan superintendent,

Msgr. William M. Roche, to discuss the problem. He agreed to meet with Nacca during the Easter holiday and proposed a "next step." He suggested a meeting with interested parties about setting up a policy-making board of education for the parish and ways to resolve issues in the future. There is no further information that either meeting took place. Roche seemed sympathetic to the plight of the principal but clearly chose to respect the authority of the pastor.

There were many hopeful signs that year for the future of the school, with a stable student population (325) and an experienced staff of ten, including five teaching sisters. A school board was established, with its first meeting set for August 1, 1968. A school paper, *The Echo*, published its first issue. Various groups and clubs continued to plan activities. Nonetheless, concerns over staffing and ongoing policy conflicts with the pastor prompted the provincial to visit Nacca in October. She gave him advance notice that in June 1969, the Religious of Jesus and Mary would be withdrawing from St. Francis. The reasons she cited were the decreasing number of sisters available for Auburn and the accessibility of other Catholic schools in the Auburn area. Her visit was followed by an official letter on January 19, 1969, stating that a recent Provincial Chapter had voted to withdraw from St. Francis, despite the sense that "all felt very sad to leave a field of apostolate so dear to us." For the parents, such news was met with sorrow, confusion, and anger on the part of some, highlighting a division between those who idolized the pastor and those who felt that his conduct at the school created problems. In a letter to the provincial, a concerned parent wrote that on February 23, the pastor "dissolved the school board of which I am a member." A few parishioners wrote to her in support of Nacca, criticizing the principal's behavior. The pastor's response was a refusal to consider possible alternatives. Instead, he announced from the pulpit that he would close the school, assuring his people that all the children would receive sound educations elsewhere. He also promised to get qualified teachers for religious instruction and use the school facility as a catechetical center: "We are not at a spiritual standstill because of the shortage of nuns," he preached, closing with *Avanti*, the Italian word for "let's move forward."

As the news of the decision spread, the community received expressions of sadness, gratitude, and admiration. On June 13, Sr. Joseph Gilmary, CSJ, wrote that her community regretted the departure of the Religious of Jesus and Mary. "Your presence has added a real measure of love and joy to this community," she wrote. "You have given witness in

a beautiful way . . . remaining steadfast when it would have been easier
to let go." She praised the sisters as valiant women, thanked them "for
all you have been to us." The last day of school was June 14, a tearful
day for parents, students, and their teachers. The sisters were grateful for
eighteen years spent among these generous, warm, and engaging people.
They were sad to leave them but hopeful for their future. The Home and
School Association held a farewell party for the community that same
evening, filling the school auditorium. More than 250 people attended,
and a large number of priests and sisters from the area arrived to express
gratitude and wish the sisters well. At the end of their report, the officers
wrote that "most everyone left the hall with a sad heart," but everyone
also "had a spark of hope in his or her heart." The report indicated that
170 students from St. Francis would attend public schools, and seventy
would go to local Catholic schools. Others were as yet undecided. For
the Religious of Jesus and Mary, there would be new assignments and
communities, but they would keep dear memories of their time at St.
Francis. In 2001, the alumni of St. Francis invited the sisters to return for
the Grand Adult Alumni Reunion. At that celebration, they honored four
Religious of Jesus and Mary in attendance with expressions of gratitude
and mementos of "the place you once called home, Auburn, New York."

7

Textures of Desert Sands

The Southwest

A Community Born of Exile: El Paso, Texas (1926 to 1989)

By 1925, THE RELIGIOUS of Jesus and Mary had a flourishing network
of educational establishments in the northeastern United States. These
included parish schools, boarding schools, academies, and catechetical
outreach. They were all mission foundations of their Canadian province,
headquartered in Sillery, Québec. As part of a growing global congregation, the sisters in New England and New York came to appreciate and
rely on assistance from other provinces in Europe, Ireland, and England.
They in turn were sometimes asked to offer refuge and hospitality to
sisters suffering the effects of civil wars, anti-Catholic legislation, and
forced dispersion from their home provinces. Interdependence and
cooperation were welcome elements for the growing missionary endeavor of the early twentieth century. With the arrival of Religious of
Jesus and Mary almost a continent away in the Southwest, the tapestry
of their American story would be interwoven with the bright colors
and dappled hues of the Hispanic tradition, adding rich texture to an
emerging, multicultural pattern.

Hispanic-Mexican Roots in the Catholic Southwest[217]

Missionaries from Spain were the first to evangelize the southwestern regions of the continent. After the fall of the Aztec Empire in the sixteenth

century, they arrived, introducing Catholic faith and practice to the indigenous peoples of central Mexico. Attracted by rumors of great cities of gold, the *conquistadors* first brought with them Franciscan missionaries to convert indigenous tribes who lived in small villages or *pueblos* along the Rio Grande River. Native and Spanish peoples often intermingled; the Franciscan friars ministered spiritually to both groups. In the early seventeenth century, a diocesan priest was vicar of the region known as "new Spain." By the nineteenth century, several priests who were native to what is now New Mexico staffed a number of parishes, encouraging the rise of a local clergy. This factor contributed very much to a sense of ownership of the church among the communities where expressions of faith and social concerns were naturally integrated. By the time Mexico won its independence from Spain (1821), there was an important and well-established Spanish-speaking population in New Mexico, Texas, Arizona, and California. Tensions and divisions arose between these peoples and other settlers from the United States, resulting in a declaration of independence from Mexico for Texas (1836) and its admission to statehood in 1845. These events in part provoked the Mexican-American war (1846 to 1848), declared by Mexico as an assault on its landholdings. The conflict centered on Texas and resulted in expanding southwestern territories to include California, while decreasing Mexican land holdings almost by half. The Mexican people in these territories often found themselves an oppressed and despised minority, aliens in their own lands. On some occasions, racist and nativist movements incited violence against Mexicans, who were tortured and slain. Their story reveals the dark threads of racism that run through the larger history of the nation.

Vibrant Catholic Popular Culture

What of the rich ethno-religious culture that Mexicans brought to the Southwest? In terms of sheer numbers, most immigrants from Mexico were Catholics with centuries-old traditions. Theirs was a unique blend of Spanish and *mestizo* Catholicism, tried in the fires of centuries of oppression and struggle. Texas offers one example: from fewer than 10,000 Mexican immigrants in the 1830s, by the turn of the century they accounted for almost one half of all the Catholics there. Elsewhere in the Southwest, their presence was equally impressive. In 1848, California was ceded by Mexico to the United States as a result of the war. It enjoyed an open border with Mexico for the first two decades of the twentieth century. Immigrants came and went quite freely, sometimes for short periods, to work and bring funds back to families at home. Statistics from California are not completely reliable, but they do give some idea of the numbers of Mexicans whose presence made an important contribution to the state's culture and Catholic life. Los Angeles, for example, was the largest Mexican city in the United States, growing from an estimated 5,000 Mexicans in 1910 to over 200,000 in 1950. Over two-thirds of these were unskilled laborers, most of them employed in California's farm labor force.

Whatever their work and wherever they found themselves in the new nation, Mexican immigrants experienced their ethnic identity linked to traditional European Catholic practices and traditions. Once established, Mexican parish churches played an important and integral role in *barrio* life, providing a meeting place for groups, a connection with the neighborhood, and a support network for newcomers. Mexicans held to their traditions of prayer, devotional processions, and worship, despite the misgivings of some of their church leaders. A folk form of Spanish Catholicism developed, with its distinct style of religious practice. It was grounded in a strong, popular religious culture distinct from the ceremonies and Romanized cult of European clerical tradition. The parish church of "*el norte*" seemed alien at times to the familiar parochial life Mexicans had known south of the border, where the church was the cultural center of the village; its rhythms of liturgical life were expressed in family rituals, processions, fiestas, and blessings.

Because of a severe clerical shortage in some areas, Mexican parishioners in parts of the Southwest had found themselves without resident priests for decades. They became less dependent on a parish-centered religious experience than were other immigrant groups. What emerged instead was a vibrant alternative, with devotional rituals that did not require the presence of a priest. This style of popular devotion often bypassed ecclesiastical rules and regulations. Devout veneration of Our Lady of Guadalupe, central and powerful symbol of Mexican faith, was at the core of the Hispanic family community, mirroring the compassion of God with the face and heart of a *mestiza* mother. "*La Moreñita*," America's dark virgin, spoke to Mexicans of a tender relationship between their oppressed people and a liberating God who was with them in all their trials. Some Church authorities, unfamiliar with their style of worship, found Mexican Catholics in the American Southwest problematic because of ethnic stereotypes, such as perceived indolence and lack of participation in Mass and the sacramental life. Rooted in cultural prejudice and ignorance, misunderstandings and tensions such as these lasted well into the twentieth century: "Despite the crisis created by the immigration of thousands of Mexicans, the Church continued the . . . pattern of institution building as a priority over serving Mexicans."[218] The institutional church of the United States was slow in advocating for social justice and change on behalf of its Mexican communities. Mexican Americans have stood among the nation's most forgotten citizens and neglected Catholics. Not until the 1960's would they be accepted as a distinct and visible social ethnic group, asserting for themselves a rightful place in the nation's political, religious, and cultural life. The increase in their numbers and leadership offers a bright promise of a vibrant, diverse future for the nation's Catholic community.

Immigrants and Exiles, 1910 to 1929

A wave of immigration from Mexico took place during the Mexican Revolution, which lasted nearly three decades. Violent revolutionary leaders battled for power, using harsh and brutal measures against their people. Almost ten percent of the total population would migrate to the United States during these years, fleeing situations of political unrest and religious turmoil. Some estimates of Mexican casualties are as high as one million deaths. With the Constitution of 1917, new revolutionary laws mandated a virtual persecution of the Catholic Church, which had previously exercised a great deal of power in Mexico. All foreign priests and religious were expelled from the country; religious education and religious dress for members of religious orders were proscribed; public worship and processions were forbidden. Echoing situations in earlier nineteenth-century European revolutions, Mexico's church properties were nationalized, voting rights were denied to clergy and religious, and priests had to register with state and local officials.

Anti-clerical laws were in place through 1938, although they were unevenly enforced in various regions. Some laity undertook an economic boycott in response. Many Mexican bishops complied with government orders to cease all church services. In the central and western parts of the country, resistance movements and insurrections erupted into civil strife known as the *Cristero* Rebellion (1926–1929). The *Cristero* army was made up largely of *campesinos*, those who eked out a meager existence by their manual labor. They were strongly attached to their Catholic faith and way of life. One of the well-known heroes of this movement was the Jesuit Blessed Miguel Pro, executed without trial in 1927, forgiving his murderers and shouting, "*Viva Cristo Rey*"! This painful and difficult period for Mexican Catholicism and its people created the context for the exodus of the Religious of Jesus and Mary from Mexico to El Paso, Texas and other missions in the American Southwest. As exiles, the first sisters of the El Paso mission served not just their Mexican compatriots; they would in time enrich the region and nation into which they were forced to flee with their unique gifts and skills for ministry: "They . . . have been so successful in their work that they can now repeat with gratitude and appreciation their wonderful motto, 'Praised forever be Jesus and Mary.'"[219]

The El Paso Foundation (1926)[220]

With its annexation to the United States in 1845, Texas, once an independent republic, became one its largest and most diverse territories. El Paso is at the far western tip of Texas, on the border of the Rio Grande River. Originally "*El Paso del Norte*," it sits opposite the river from its sister city, Juarez, Mexico. Since the sixteenth century, the area has served as a continental crossroad along a historic route with an international boundary. In the late nineteenth century, the arrival of the railroad transformed El Paso from a dusty adobe village of a few hundred families to a large and flourishing frontier community of over 15,000. The city's population and industry developed rapidly with the influx of refugees from the Mexican Revolution, counting more than 77,000 people in 1925. Its binational and ethnically diverse culture thrived throughout the twentieth century.

When the diocese of El Paso was established in 1914, it covered nearly 65,000 square miles of territory, including southern New Mexico, with an estimated population of 54,000 Catholics, served by a scant thirty-one priests, mostly Jesuit missionaries from the Italian province of Naples. Since 1881, they had ministered in the El Paso area, laying the foundations for more than thirty parishes and fifty–eight missions. The first bishop of El Paso was an American Jesuit, Rev. Anthony J. Schuler, known for his zealous and generous welcome to Mexican immigrants, especially during the persecutions of the Mexican Civil War. He built a number of churches in the city, including the cathedral of St. Patrick. Before 1930, he oversaw the foundation of secondary schools for girls and boys, assuring immigrant children a Catholic education. Schuler was instrumental in bringing several religious orders to West Texas where he gained renown for his support to priests and sisters fleeing religious persecution in Mexico. In 1917, the exiled Mexican Jesuits moved their novitiate to El Paso, providing an opening for the Religious of Jesus and Mary to do likewise.

In 1902, the Spanish province of the Religious of Jesus and Mary had opened its first mission in Latin America with a foundation in southeast Mexico at Merida, Yucatan State. Two years later, they went to Mexico City and founded two flourishing schools there. For twenty-four years, their missionary work intermittently prospered and faltered with changing political regimes. In 1914, they set up a foundation in Havana, Cuba, to accommodate sisters fleeing the Mexican troubles. In 1924, the sisters opened a novitiate in Mexico City for eighteen candidates. During the *Cristero* uprising of 1926, the government forced closure of churches and religious houses and schools. Many women's communities decided to send their novices home until better times. After prayer and consultation, M. Maria de Loyola Zulueta, Spanish provincial of the sisters in Mexico, decided to take a risk. Rather than send the novices away and jeopardize the future of the Mexican mission, she decided to move the novitiate north. The choice of El Paso was, it seems, both providential and serendipitous. M. Guadalupe Maria (Soledad) Perez, one of the future foundresses, was a postulant in 1925. She recalled that at Christmas the novice mistress, M. del Dulce Nombre (Montserrat) Reventós, sent a card to Romualdo Benedet, SJ, in which she asked him—almost as a joke— whether the sisters would be welcome in El Paso.[221] Benedet, however, took the request seriously. He answered that the bishop did not need any more teaching communities in El Paso, because the Sisters of Loretto had assured the direction of its parochial and convent schools.[222] However, he assured her that the novitiate "would certainly receive a warm welcome."

From that time on, he assisted the sisters as their patron, friend, and intermediary with church authorities when permissions were needed. Another friend and longtime benefactor of the community, Señor Luis Perez, father of Soledad, arranged preparations for the initial journey. On May 13, 1926, he traveled with the novice director, a novice (Sr. Genovefa Hernandez), and his daughter, on their journey across the Mexican border into the States. When they arrived, Benedet and several Mexican friends were on hand to greet and encourage them with promises of a fruitful and extensive apostolic future in El Paso. For the first two days, the pioneer trio stayed with a host family. Good friends helped them find a modest house to rent on Upson Avenue, in the neighborhood of Sunset Heights. M. Dulce Nombre described it as "a humble dwelling, poor and simple as the one in Nazareth, where the novices will feel at home with the Eucharist and wearing their holy habit." They purchased beds, chairs, and tables to provide basic furnishings in the house, and on May 15 they moved in. Four days later, ten novices arrived in the company of M. M. Loyola and two other professed sisters. Secure in the assurance that the Jesuits would look after her exiled formation community, M. Loyola returned to Mexico City with its ongoing hostilities, which resulted in the second closing of the school there. Some sisters fled to Havana while others stayed with trusted friends or family. For the El Paso community, this turn of events would affect the financial security they were counting on for their undertaking.

A House on Sunset Heights (1926)

On June 1, Benedet presided at the first Mass in the little provisional chapel of the community. It was clear that larger quarters were needed. Early in June the sisters began the search for an adequate property to establish as a permanent home. They found one in the same neighborhood, at 1401 West Yandell Drive, also known as the Mundy property. Lovely and spacious, the two-story dwelling provided adequate quarters for the growing community, as well as extra space to set up an educational work in the future. The sisters moved into the house on July 1, 1926, and in August welcomed three postulants, two more exiled professed sisters, and an orphan entrusted to their care. Without financial support from Mexico, however, and lacking independent means for their support, the community utilized their other skills to raise necessary funds: sewing, mending, embroidery, photo retouching, and other odd jobs. Their economic hardships were aggravated by the fact that they were also adapting to life in a foreign country and spoke no English. They had petitioned Bishop Schuler to open a commercial academy on the property and waited for his response. Their good humor and confidence in God's providence gave them courage, and they began a novena to Mother Foundress for her intercession in the matter.

On September 12, the bishop made a cordial visit to the community, granting his permission for them to open a commercial academy that would provide Catholic business education for young women from both sides of the border. He also handed them a gift of $500, courtesy of the Chicago Knights of Columbus who had contributed to the needs of exiled women religious. Schuler would visit again at the end of the month with yet another donation for the academy and a kindergarten. The apostolic service of the congregation in southwestern Texas was under way, offering the sisters renewed hope and life. Early in October, three novices made first profession, and four postulants received the habit, adding to the community's optimism for a bright future.

Jesus-Mary Commercial Academy (1926)

On October 15, nine young women, most of them from Ciudad Juarez, Mexico, registered for the course at Jesus-Mary Commercial Academy. They were housed in temporary classrooms until more permanent arrangements were completed. Based on guidelines sent to them by the sisters at St. Clare High School in Woonsocket, RI, the curriculum followed a typical commercial course: language, mathematics, bookkeeping, typing, and shorthand. These subjects, along with daily religion classes, were offered in Spanish and occupied the mornings. Afternoon classes were for other subjects, including French, English, and private piano lessons. The number of students grew and soon included younger girls. With time, the community purchased adjacent property to build classrooms and dormitories that would meet their expanding needs. By 1928, the student population reached 100. Sisters who were not teachers directed the little kindergarten. While they continued to adapt to American ways, the newcomers preserved their beloved Mexican traditions. Among these was the novena before Christmas known as *"las posadas,"* with its traditional *piñata* filled with surprises of sweets and gifts for the children.[223]

In 1931, M. M. Loyola was called to Rome and subsequently was appointed superior of the mission in Havana. This resulted in a major change for the El Paso community. M. Dulce Nombre became superior of the new mission, with M. Maria de la Protección Michel named as mistress of novices. December 5, 1932, was a day of special joy for the sisters. A much-loved statue of Our Lady of the Sacred Heart, hidden with a Mexican family during the persecution, arrived to take up temporary residence in the El Paso house.[224] Fr. Benedet presided over the solemn benediction ceremony on December 8 in the convent parlor serving as a chapel. He reminded the community that Our Lady was among them as a sign of peace and blessing, despite their sufferings and sorrows. As she had protected the embattled community in Mexico, Mary would now be their strong and compassionate companion in exile.

A consoling visit took place in 1934, with the arrival of M. St. Borgia, the superior general who had served in the Mexican mission, and their beloved M. M. Loyola. Both were delighted with the new foundation in Texas. M. M. Loyola had business to conduct in Mexico and was unable to stay very long but promised to return to El Paso after a visit to Havana. On the outbound train journey she contracted pneumonia; while recovering at a convent in New Orleans, her condition worsened. On April 22 M. M. Loyola died, far from her own community but well-cared for by the nursing sisters at the convent and a traveling companion, M. Herminia (Maria-Elena) Rangel. Professed a few months earlier in El Paso, M. Herminia had been missioned to Cuba but never reached her destination. The sisters realized one of their hopes with the construction of their new chapel, begun in October 1935 and completed two years later. During the construction, the community held multiple fundraising events, including Mexican suppers, bazaars, and raffles. On April 25, 1937, amid a crowd of worshippers, Schuler presided at the solemn blessing and opening of the chapel. It was dedicated to Our Lady of the Sacred Heart, and the treasured image was enshrined above the altar to bless and comfort those who would pray there.

Queen of Angels Residence (1936 to 2002)

Ten years after their arrival in El Paso, the Religious of Jesus and Mary rejoiced in a growing educational apostolate, as well as annual pastoral outreach to summer missions throughout the region. Encouraged by the bishop and appreciative Catholic friends, M. Dulce Nombre began to explore opening a residence for working women in the city to provide safety, friendship, and the warmth of a homelike atmosphere. It would also address the issue raised by the sisters' limited knowledge of English, which made it impossible to open a second school at that time. When the Havana mission closed in 1936, a new group of sisters joined the exiled community in El Paso to lend support for its expanding apostolic services.

In her search for an appropriate setting, M. Dulce Nombre welcomed the help of another Jesuit friend and mentor, Rev. Ronald MacDonald, "the soul of this house," according to a later report on the residence.

In January 1936, they found a property not far from the Yandell Drive house, at 536 Los Angeles Street, to which they gave an appropriate name: "Queen of Angels." Five sisters from the Academy community—one Spaniard, three Mexicans, and a Cuban—took up residence. On January 29 they welcomed their first guests, a family from Mexico. At first there were very few residents, so the sisters resorted to their domestic skills to raise needed funds. They made *tamales* to sell weekly, took in mending, and sold embroidery handwork. The guest rooms were attractively prepared; soon several short-term renters arrived. As for the sisters, they endured privations from the cold and a lack of basic necessities. Unfazed by these inconveniences, by mid-February the community sponsored a women's five-day retreat in the house, directed by one of the local Jesuit priests. Many residents were generous with donations and offered their assistance to the sisters in a number of ways that included serving as receptionists. With the financial support of one of the women, in 1938 the community moved to a more suitable house at 119 West Nevada Street, near St. Patrick's Cathedral. This property had twenty-five rooms, two of which were adapted to become the chapel, where guests could find a welcome haven at the end of the day's work. They were happy to have regular access to the Mass and sacraments; some non-Catholics asked for instructions in the faith.

Queen of Angels Residence soon earned a reputation as a center of Catholic Action. Various groups, like the Altar Society and St. Vincent de Paul, held regular meetings in its large living room. When the Jesuits at Holy Family Parish were without a cook for a few months, the sisters prepared and sent meals to their brother community. They held religion classes for the residents and traveled to neighboring parishes for catechetical or pastoral ministry. They spent part of each summer visiting missions to offer whatever services were needed. Without having to tend to the administrative duties of directing a school, the sisters from Queen of Angels had an apostolic freedom to serve the larger mission of the area in numerous ways. When the house in Havana was forced to close, some of the exiled sisters from there arrived to lend support to the staff at the residence. Among them was M. Maria de Jesus Catarineu, appointed superior and principal at Yandell Drive. M. Dulce Nombre took charge of the residence until 1938, when she was sent to San Diego to set up a new mission and a second women's residence, the Joan of Arc Club. The residence on Nevada Street continued its services to women and catechetical outreach, welcoming sisters from Cuba, Mexico, and Spain to assist in its mission. In 1963, as part of a re-structuring plan, Queen of Angels was reattached to the newly formed Mexican province. Because of the aging of the community members and El Paso's shifting demography, Queen of Angels closed its doors in 2002, after fifty-six years of apostolic service to working women and the poor.[225]

A Turning Point:
the Hispanic-Mexican Province (1938 to 1955)[226]

On June 26, 1937, M. de los Angeles (Teresa) Mancheño, a Spaniard, arrived from Rome to assume responsibility for the mission and become the director of the novitiate in El Paso. She faced many serious challenges posed by new foundations staffed with exiled sisters from Spain, Cuba, and Mexico. Her spirited leadership and zeal during the next few decades resulted in three more new ventures for the congregation in the Southwest, reaching all the way to the Pacific coast. In Rome, congregational leaders felt the time had come to separate the houses in the southwestern United States from Spain and/or Mexico. Their reasons for this included the rapid expansion and growth of the communities and the difficulty of communicating with Spanish provincials for needed permissions, especially with the civil war raging in Spain (1936–39). At the end of 1938, the General Council petitioned the Vatican authorities to erect a separate province made up of the four houses in Texas and California, including the novitiate, to be named the "Hispanic-Mexican Province." Permission was granted, and M. de los Angeles became its first and only provincial superior, with headquarters at Yandell Drive in El Paso.[227]

While the new beginning reflected growth and fruitfulness, the sisters of the region were saddened at the separation from their province of origin. They also rejoiced that their new province was enriched by its growing novitiate and by the influx of sister exiles from Cuba. Moreover, they kept alive the hope that the political situation in Mexico would soon become favorable to their return. A zealous missionary known for her serenity and calm, M. de los Angeles hoped to respond to many appeals from former students asking that the Religious of Jesus and Mary renew their apostolic presence in Mexico. In June 1944, the community received news of the death of then-retired Schuler, who had welcomed them two decades earlier. Remembered by everyone for his generosity to Mexicans and Americans alike, he the bishop was mourned as "a true father" to the sisters.

Jesus-Mary Academy in El Paso experienced a period of vigorous growth in the 1940s, expanding its buildings to add classrooms and dormitories. The student population expanded: in 1946, there were sixty boarders and 200 students at the Academy. The problems were, as always, lack of financial resources and personnel. When El Paso celebrated its twenty-fifth anniversary in 1951, the community remembered earlier years of hard work and sacrifice as a time of "great and constant blessings." That occasion was marked by the special visit in June 1952 of the superior general, M. Luisa Fernanda Sangnier, who joined them for the thanksgiving festivities. The sisters' flourishing educational ministry was complemented by their generous dedication to other mission activities in parishes and catechetical centers, where they taught children and adults as part of sacramental preparation. This missionary outreach characterized the service of the Religious of Jesus and Mary in the Southwest, where every summer several sisters traveled to participate in missions at distant places in the diocese.

This vital period of development for the province (1946 to 1953) extended beyond the United States to Mexico and Cuba, where the political situations had improved. The delegates at the General Chapter of 1946 enthusiastically supported the return of the congregation to Mexico, despite the ruling that religious dress could not be worn. Together with former students who had encouraged their return, the sisters planned a reopening of the Academy in Mexico City, which took place in February 1948. A report to the General Chapter of 1953 indicates that a forced absence of twenty-two years and two decisions to close the institution "did not extinguish the fire of love and gratitude, nor dim the remembrance of the virtues and self-denial of our first Mothers." The alumnae had already begun to organize and plan, sponsoring a school for poor children in a nearby residence. M. Maria del Sagrado Corazon Nandin and M. Soledad Murube arrived, both enterprising and courageous pioneers. They sought a temporary building to house the school and outlined plans for a new construction. These sisters were supported by generous donations and labors of their families and former students, who purchased desks, chairs, and classroom equipment for an expected sixty students. The community in El Paso contributed from their meager finances to support the project. To the joyful amazement of the sisters, 120 appeared on the opening day of classes! Five years later, a large and modern edifice had arisen, subsequently becoming one of the best educational establishments in Mexico City, the *"Colegio Regina."*

In 1949, the province assumed responsibility for the San Antonio de Padua Parish School in Los Angeles, California; in Havana, it opened a university residence, marking the sisters' return. By 1951, there was also a return to the foundation city of Merida. These changes created the unique situation of a province based in Texas while it also directed renewed apostolic ventures in Cuba and Mexico. In September 1950, a number of young sisters resided at the San Antonio Convent in Los Angeles while they worked toward degrees at Immaculate Heart College. The novitiate was flourishing with ten members, rich in the hope that the province would be able to send reinforcements to the restored Mexican and Cuban missions. In January 1952, published statistics indicated a total of seven communities with forty-five choir professed, twenty-one auxiliaries, eleven novices, and one postulant. They served in three elementary schools and one parish school (twenty sisters, eleven lay teachers); and in two secondary schools (eight sisters, six lay teachers). They taught over 400 students in the elementary schools, fifty-nine secondary students, and more than 200 in what were named "poor schools." It was an impressive, promising renaissance.

Carlsbad, New Mexico: San Jose Mission (1938 to 1949)[228]

In 1903, the bishop of New Mexico invited the Franciscan Friars to Carlsbad, an agricultural town in New Mexico that had an earlier reputation as a health resort boasting mineral springs. It was also one of the "wild west" towns where saloons and crime abounded. The Catholic situation was dire, and pastoral visits for sacramental life were irregular. Most of the parishioners of San Jose, the Spanish chapel for Mexican Catholics in Carlsbad, were very poor laborers who eked out a living growing corn, cantaloupe, cotton, and other produce on the fertile land. They were little instructed in the faith or practice. By 1907, one enterprising Franciscan pastor built the framework for San Jose Mission Church in Carlsbad, and the Sisters of the Precious Blood presented the parish with an altar and a few pews. A series of collections among the people and friends of the Friars were used to build a small church belfry. Thanks to these efforts and improvements, the people began to sense a Catholic community spirit.

Sodalities and religious societies were established, especially the popular League of the Sacred Heart. Truly, San Jose Mission was among the poorest and most forsaken Catholic communities in the area. In 1917, the Franciscans were still collecting funds to provide a floor, ceiling, and some heating to the chapel.[229] Their pastoral mission extended to neighboring towns within the vast parish boundaries.

At the end of August 1938, Constant Klein, OFM, pastor of San Jose, approached M. de los Angeles, requesting sisters to undertake the catechetical and educational needs of the mission. He had learned of the sisters' summer mission work in neighboring villages. Permission was granted, and in September a group of five sisters left to found a new mission school: M. Salvadora Font as superior; M. del Trinidad Castilla, M. Carmen Rangel, M. Esperanza Dominguez, M. Cecilia Levy, for the school, and Sr. Engracia Rodriguez to manage the household. When M. Salvadora became Mistress of Novices in El Paso, M. Soledad Murube took up the leadership of the small community. Their lifestyle was austere, often deprived of basic necessities, mirroring the condition of those they had come to serve. M. Esperanza recalled that the ministry was "with the children of migrant cotton pickers. Only two of the nuns were prepared to teach. M. Graciela Vargas recalled that what the pastor wanted them to do was 'form the people' . . . to know God so that once out of school, they could go into the cotton fields better prepared." The sisters directed the school of 150 Mexican girls, providing instruction from kindergarten through eighth grade. During the school day the children assisted at Mass and received regular religious instruction. After school, the sisters taught catechism to the public school children of Carlsbad. They cooked meals for the Franciscan community. Weekly they traveled to the villages of Artesia, Loving, Jalisco, and Malaga, teaching catechism and Sunday school religion classes for children and adults. Despite being so few in number, the sisters of this mission offered a cornucopia of pastoral care to the parishioners. They taught in the school and also served as sacristans, directors of song, and organists in the church. At the mission outposts, they offered sacramental preparation to adults and children alike. On occasion, when the Franciscan presider was not fluent in Spanish, the sisters would give the Sunday homily. "And the priest himself listened with attention, trying to understand the Spanish he hoped to learn."[230]

The annals of the mission always included statistics on first communions, adult baptisms, confirmations, and marriages "blessed." The numbers are impressive and include accounts of conversions, return to the sacraments, and enthronement of the Sacred Hearts in homes, as part of the Apostleship of Prayer ministry. There was also a thrift shop available to the parishioners, with clothing and household items sold at very low prices. The sisters found this was another way to get to know the people, to inquire about their families, and to encourage children to attend religious instruction classes. In 1941, a military chief of a Mexican training camp known as the "C.C. Camp" requested someone to offer catechism classes in Spanish to his trainees, all young Mexicans. While the sisters hesitated at first, once they met these young recruits, they were reassured. The men were eager to hear about God and were attentive to the instructions, which resulted in a majority—close to twenty—making their First Communion. Others from the camp returned to the faith and sacraments. It was a deeply consoling apostolic experience. When the river flooded in 1942, the residents of poor hovels and huts fled the inundation to the hillsides outside Carlsbad until they were rescued and relocated temporarily in a public school. The sisters were forced as well to move into a Catholic hospital run by the Sisters of the Precious Blood, while the pastor, Father Stanislaus, OFM, risked his life to help the victims and provide them with basic necessities. When conditions improved, the Religious of Jesus and Mary returned to their heavily-damaged mission and reached out to assist the families who had been displaced. Their experience mirrored that of their people: a flooded basement, furniture and furnishings destroyed, and crowded conditions shared with other evacuees where they prayed the Rosary and shared the deprivation of their people.

By 1945, 253 children were enrolled in the school and hundreds of others received religious instruction in the outposts of Loving, Malaga, and Artesia. The mission offered a hopeful and vital way forward for the missionaries as well as the parishioners. Unfortunately for the missionaries, Father Stanislaus was transferred in 1948 to another mission; the new pastor decided to enforce educational laws of the United States requiring English as the primary language for basic instruction. While dedicated and generous, the teaching sisters were unable to fulfill this requirement. The situation obliged the Religious of Jesus and Mary to relinquish this dear mission to the Sisters of the Immaculate Heart of Mary. On March 30, 1949, the superior general wrote to M. de los Angeles, asking her "to transfer the mission of Carlsbad to Los Angeles, where there are possibilities for a larger apostolic field, more in keeping with our rules and customs."[231] At the end of June, the community of six bid a sad *adios* to a beloved mission. Another horizon beckoned in the sprawling California metropolis.

Summer Missions

The apostolic style of the Religious of Jesus and Mary in the Southwest is reflected in their untiring efforts and effective ministry during annual summer missions where they were sent. Financed by the National Council of Catholic Women, these religious vacation schools were part of their outreach to immigrant children after World War I. Along with the institutional educational ministries they founded or directed, many of the sisters spent a good part of annual school vacation in pastoral and catechetical services to far-flung, impoverished hamlets in Texas, New Mexico, and Arizona. One report describes the varied settings for these ministries: public buildings, small chapels or churches, and at times in the shade of large trees. It estimates that more than 3000 children attended the summer schools of religion. Adult instruction led to the reception of the sacraments of initiation as well as sacramental marriages. Enthronement of the Sacred Heart in homes was a popular religious event in these isolated locations.[232]

The summer mission programs began in 1934, with requests to M. Dulce Nombre from the pastors of Tularosa, Smelter, and Buenavista, all rural hamlets in Texas. They needed sisters to come and assist with the needs of very poor Mexican peasants hired to work the land. Once undertaken, the mission experience was joyful and fruitful for the sisters. While much of the written history of these missions is anecdotal, the annals of the El Paso convent report on their activities regularly. A group of three or four would leave El Paso in June or July to accompany a missionary priest to the mission, acting as indispensable associates of the priesthood: instructing, evangelizing, comforting and healing. The sisters' unique role was catechetical and pastoral, adapted to each mission site with its unique traits and special needs. By 1935, they were traveling to twenty other needy communities in rural Texas and added four more in New Mexico. All sported colorful names: Van Horn, Sierra Blanca, Fort Hancock, Loving, Santa Rita, La Luz, La Union, Tularosa, Cloudcroft, and Clint, to mention a few! The missionaries' first impressions of the communities were mixed. People seemed to have respect for the priest and sisters, but *"no intienden nada"* (they know nothing) about Mass or the catechism, lacking basic instruction in proper behavior at Mass. In some cases, adults were less informed than their children. Yet, the affection and attention of the sisters for these marginalized people mark their annual reports. They welcomed food from the people's gardens. To these women, the children were "like the little shepherds from Bethlehem." In 1940, locations in Arizona were added to the sisters' annual expeditions: Florence, Tiger, Mammoth, and Oracle. In Florence, they prepared fifty-four girls and women for First Communion and 160 others for general communion.

Tiger, a picturesque village with multi-colored huts but no church, was home to families who worked the copper and silver mines in the area. In Mammoth, the sisters came to a very poor and miserable setting for a small community of miners. They felt their vow of poverty keenly. Their "house" had no furniture except for cots and one bad cooking vessel. It did however, have residents such as spiders, cockroaches, and rats, which meant they got little sleep at night. Oracle, on the other hand, was a lovely area in the mountains, covered with vegetation, and it had a church built for summer visitors by an American woman. Sisters' living quarters there were comfortable, despite the constant presence of resident ants. In Arizona, they worked with parishioners to set up Altar and Rosary societies, and the Apostleship of Prayer, groups that were meant to insure continuity of practice once the sisters returned to El Paso for annual retreat and return to their schoolroom duties.

In the summer of 1944, the mission was at Grand Falls, and the sisters were housed in the rectory with a very kind pastor. Their daily schedule was a long one, extending from 9 AM to 4:30 PM, with instruction in doctrine for the children. Evenings were spent giving conferences to adults, many of whom had just come from working the fields all day but who were "eager to learn about religion and moral teaching." The report highlights news of the D-Day invasion by Allied troops on June 6, followed by special prayers in the church. The next summer, the sisters were sent to four different camps in Arizona: Hayden, Winkelman, Mammoth, and Tiger. The challenge was always the same: how to incite the children, and adults, to come to religion classes. At the Augustinian mission of Fort Hancock, where the sisters had earlier served, there were 125 children for catechism classes, a consoling sign that their former instruction had taken root. In July of that year, as they returned to El Paso, the sisters reported a very "holy" vacation time, "spent in mission work for God's greater glory." The community statistics were also encouraging, with eighteen choir professed sisters, eight auxiliaries, and three in formation.

After 1950, a shift occurred in the southwestern missionary outreach. Because there was more emphasis on the development of the Academy and the need for well-trained teachers, summertime for the sisters was given to the study of college courses toward degrees. The number of summer missions gradually diminished, but a new mission field opened up in the poor neighborhoods of Juarez, Mexico, across the river. Destitute children would cross into El Paso at Christmas time, seeking food and clothing. The sisters decided to visit the area and found a ghetto of 600 poor families. They began to offer catechism classes there, in the hope of setting up a school in the future. With time, students and volunteers joined them for the work of these missions. The zealous spirit of the founding exiled sisters continued strong and vibrant, the legacy of those who had lost all and found it again in southwest Texas.

Restoration and Restructuring (1955 to 1968)

At the end of 1955, a major change occurred in the structure of the southwestern mission. Because of improved political and religious relations in Mexico, the Religious of Jesus and Mary had gradually returned to their convents in Mexico. Following a visit to the houses of the Hispanic-Mexican province, the General Council decided to reconfigure and rename it. A new Province of Mexico was established, with headquarters in Mexico City. It would include the houses of Mexico and Cuba, Texas, and California. M. Guadalupe Maria moved to Mexico City from San Diego to become its province leader. From 1955 to 1960, the Mexican Province included the houses of Texas and California, where a majority of the sisters were still Spanish-speaking. The novitiate in Texas remained open, while another novitiate reopened in Mexico City. Some sisters of the Southwest had gone on summer missions in Ruidoso, a village in the hills of New Mexico, a well-known vacation spot. To their delight, the provincial purchased a house there in 1955 to serve as a vacation house for the communities. Nestled high in the pines, it had six bedrooms, space for a chapel, and a large yard. For several years, it offered rest and relaxation from the heat of southwestern summers. Significant changes had marked this period of growth for the province.

The Western-American Province (1960 to 1968)[233]

In August 1960, at her first official visit to the Mexican province since becoming superior general, Rev. M. del Rosario Araño made an unexpected announcement. Communities of the Mexican province were to be divided into two provinces. Thus, the four houses of the southwestern

United States would form a separate entity called the Western-American Province. Reasons given for the division were differences in language of the two countries and the vast distances to travel. To help with the transition and to counter the effects of a diminished number of sisters serving the Southwest, the General Council appealed for help from Canada and the eastern houses of the United States. M. St. Dorothy (Blanche) Boivin, born in the U.S. and serving in Canada, became provincial of the Western-American province.[234] M. Guadalupe Maria Perez continued serving as provincial of Mexico, and M. del Sagrado Corazon Nandin returned to Mexico from El Paso, completing thirty-four years of service at Jesus-Mary Academy, where she would be missed as its animating spirit.

Before M. St. Dorothy could assume her new position, she suffered a heart attack and was on bed rest for some time. M. Margarita del Divino Corazón Rogla, her assistant, assumed the administrative duties of the province until 1962, when M. St. Dorothy was well enough to move to the provincial house in El Paso and take up her post. On December 1, 1962 she sent her first circular from El Paso—in Spanish and English—and mentions a "disobedient" right arm and other signs that she was still in recovery. The past year, she wrote, had been filled with both suffering and joy. The loss of M. Guadalupe Maria, a "devoted pioneer," was keenly felt by the sisters in the Southwest. A province report for the General Chapter of 1965 describes it as "a deep wound" for the sisters of the Southwest, who regarded her as "the heart and soul of the American houses." The letter encourages the sisters to "Americanize ourselves, to study the English language." Referring to a new ecumenical spirit evident at the Second Vatican Council, she closes by asking for harmony among the sisters during the transition.

From 1961 to 1968, twenty-one sisters from the Eastern-American Province were missioned to serve in the communities of Texas and California. The hope was that their presence would facilitate and strengthen bonds among communities both east and west. Likewise, they would strengthen local leadership as principals and local superiors. Some from the East had volunteered and would spend several years in ministry to the missions of El Paso and California; others were appointed as superiors, principals, or teachers, with varying degrees of success. In the first five years of the new province, ten of its fifty-five members were from the Eastern-American Province. The province directory for 1961–62 lists the initial group of nine sisters from the East, including M. M. Aquinas (Mary Agnes) Doyle and M. St. Aloysius (Yvette) Frégeau, named respectively as assistant provincial and province treasurer, who would reside in El Paso. Most had no previous experience of Hispanic culture or teaching in the Southwest, nor were they Spanish-speaking. There was much to learn from one another. At times the challenges of language and culture were painful obstacles to healthy community living and apostolic effectiveness. The number of Easterners remained stable through the ensuing years, rising to a total of twelve in 1966, when the Academy at El Paso was preparing for regional high school accreditation. The postwar years had raised the bar on instructional standards. Teachers and administrators were expected to meet standards for qualification with appropriate certification and degrees; this was one of the area's most serious and urgent challenges.

Thanks to the interprovincial effort, by 1967 Jesus and Mary High School grew from being a commercial academy to a fully accredited secondary school. The academy continued to offer special intensive English programs separately from the high school program. While the course offerings included academic subjects toward college entrance, the focus was on acquiring a commercial diploma, with training in secretarial skills and office practice. Students could also opt for a general course, stressing culinary and practical arts, along with nutrition and child care. Extracurricular courses were scheduled weekly, as were sports activities. Teaching staff included eight sisters, four laywomen, and three laymen. Some parents volunteered time and service to the school in various departments. Open to girls regardless of race or religious affiliation, the school emphasized its Catholic religious philosophy and practice. Among the foundational principles, the prospectus proudly stressed its bi-lingual and bi-cultural tradition. By1973, it listed a projected estimate of about 200 students, including sixty incoming freshmen. Annual tuition for El Paso residents was $260 and $310 for non-residents.[235]

Changing Times: Life and Ministries

At the provincial house, after several months of prayer, the community was able to purchase additional land for a much-desired new high school building. Groundbreaking took place on May 24, 1961; construction was underway by the end of June. Construction managers promised that their site would be completed by October. With the new academic year upon them, the sisters realized that 500 students, sixty of whom were boarders, would begin their semester in an unfinished building. For the first six weeks, classes took place in the auditorium and future cafeteria in an adjacent property of the community. While the teaching staff had anticipated a new instructional environment, they reported that "September was a trying month, as the pupils were not in a class atmosphere." Despite the hardships of those first weeks, the community welcomed with joy the blessing and dedication of a new Jesus and Mary High School on December 17, 1961, by Most Rev. Sydney Metzger.[236] The facility boasted several classrooms, a guidance office, library, and teachers' lounge. Metzger praised the Religious of Jesus and Mary who had "started the work of God with nothing." He congratulated the community, architects, and builders, concluding with the hope that the sisters soon would acquire the lot near the school to extend their ministry.

For the new province, this event pointed to a bright future and renewed its hope in God's loving providence. In May 1962, two houses near the elementary school were acquired for a chaplain's residence and sleeping quarters for a few sisters, along with a furnished bakery in one basement. The following year, the community purchased a corner property with three buildings, to avoid motel construction too near the schools. They understood that this was another financial burden, but it was also another opportunity to expand. In 1963, there were hopeful signs with a registration of 483 girls, 167 of them in the high school. Yet, the province felt the sadness of loss that year as well. Our Lady of Angels Residence reverted to the Mexican province, and the two remaining novices in El Paso left to finish their formation there. One postulant from the West had entered in the East. Adjusting to a new culture as well as adapting to religious life was difficult for many. The province report for 1965 summarized it well: "We must admit that the mentality of southern United States, whether American or Mexican, differs considerably from that of the East." Things had moved so quickly that neither time nor attention was given to the importance of a process of enculturation.

Sadly, applications to the Religious of Jesus and Mary from the Southwest did not produce the much-desired abundant harvest of Latina sisters. The much-loved summer missions sparked new life in these years, with sisters spending a month on the outskirts of Chihuahua, Mexico, catechizing the people in neglected communities. Hundreds of children were prepared for Holy Communion, scores of marriages were regulated, and adults were prepared for the sacraments. In Juarez, Mexico, the Religious of Jesus and Mary directed the catechetical center of San Miguel, one of twenty centers the bishop had undertaken. With their students and lay volunteers, the sisters spent Saturdays instructing more than 300 children; on Sundays, they had competition from the Protestant minister who came around "to spread the Word of God in his own way . . . not forgetting to bring candy"! The high school student-members of the Sodality were also involved in catechetical projects in poor *barrios*. They taught in English and Spanish, preparing children for the sacraments. Not only did they experience the joy of missionary service but they felt they had received a spiritual gift greater than any sacrifice they might have made. In 1965, twelve Sodalists prepared to join the project after participating in a training course.

One of the three priorities for the new province was the intellectual formation of its members, so it reported with satisfaction in 1965 that five sisters received bachelors' degrees and several more were taking courses at various colleges during the academic year or in the summers. Courses in English were difficult for some, as the language was "a tremendous barrier." On the other hand, there were hundreds of Spanish-language centers in the Southwest where Mexican sisters were much appreciated and could receive training while offering some assistance. In 1959, the province initiated its first juniorate formation program in El Paso for newly-professed sisters. It was directed by M. Berchmans (Regina-Graciela) Lowenberg.[237] While most junior sisters did not engage in full-time study, they did take university courses.

On November 1, 1962, M. St. Conrad Normandin, provincial of the Eastern Province, called a special meeting of her councilors to discuss a surprise proposal from the superior general: to merge both provinces of the United States.[238] After considerable discussion, they sent their response to Rome outlining their views. First, sisters in the East were still adjusting to the disruption from the reunion of French- and English-speaking sectors of the province twelve years earlier. Would the addition of a "new and entirely different mentality" incur other wounds and create further painful divisions? Second, the added responsibility of four more communities could overtax the declining health and energy of the provincial. Finally, because the councilors had no familiarity with personnel or local situations in the West, they felt unprepared to offer counsel regarding issues or assignments there. Acceding to these concerns, the superior general tabled the proposal for several years. The primary focus for the Western communities in the 1960s would be the strengthening of instructional programs, providing education for teaching sisters toward undergraduate degrees, and improving the properties and buildings of their province.

With the progression of the sessions and decisions of the Second Vatican Council, gradual adaptations to rules and customs were introduced in the province. Correspondence in the 1960s makes reference—sometimes humorous—to modifications in the traditional habit, cap, and veil, changes in recited prayers, and adoption of the Divine Office, along with the "new liturgy" of the Eucharist. By October 1966, sisters were given the option of returning to baptismal names. Whether it referred to community living or apostolic service, change was the order of the day. In the spring of 1965, M. St. Dorothy attended the General Chapter in Rome with M. St. Vincent (Irene) Maynard, elected delegate of the province. One of the early volunteers from the East, M. St. Vincent was assistant superior in San Diego and principal at Santa Sophia elementary school in Spring Valley, CA, opened a year earlier. M. St. Dorothy welcomed the appointment in 1966 of M. St. Louis (Mary) Kenny as Director of Studies for both provinces, with oversight of educational ministries and teacher formation. Given the complicated problems in El Paso concerning financial debt, school accreditation, and teacher certification, sisters in the West were eager for her visit, which took place in the spring of 1966. M. St. Dorothy expressed the province's appreciation to M. Catherine Kenny for initiating the visit, as well as her apprehensions for the future. In a letter of June 17 that year, she wrote: "God alone knows our poverty from all standpoints . . . I feel so useless with so few houses, so few qualified nuns, and such a debt. I don't know where or how to turn." Early in 1967, Metzger asked M. St. Dorothy to close the academy's elementary school because it could not meet accreditation requirements. He offered to transfer the students to Holy Family School nearby and invited the Religious of Jesus and Mary to take over its direction. That change would also allow more space for much-needed high school programs toward accreditation. As one of the original network of Jesuit parishes, Holy Family had a large, well-equipped elementary school. It had ample space for the students from Yandell Drive. Permissions were granted for the change, and M. Maria (Yvette) Rondeau, was appointed the principal, having completed most of the requirements for a master's degree.

Two Provinces Become One (1968)

At the end of May 1968, after visiting both provinces and discussing their situations, M. del Rosario met with her council, who voted unanimously to unite them as the American Province, citing the financial and personnel challenges of the West and the support of provincial leaders. On June 14, 1968, M. Catherine Kenny, province leader in the East, in a letter of June 14, 1968, announced "a merging of the Eastern and Western American Provinces" to be put into effect during the summer months that year. She wrote that such a consolidation would facilitate the change of personnel and address financial concerns. The provincial center would be in Hyattsville, Maryland; she would serve as the provincial. The letter expressed deep gratitude to M. St. Dorothy, returning to Canada after generously serving the Western Province for eight difficult years. Finally, it announced a new "apostolic work other than schools, but in keeping with the spirit of our Mother Foundress." As a response to new ministries among the poor, the Religious of Jesus and Mary would begin a new mission in either Alabama or Louisiana. The date of its opening was for September of that year. While closing a chapter on a successful Mexican–American presence begun in 1926, the Religious of Jesus and Mary envisioned a new missionary outreach in the South and a life-giving response to the Church's call in the spirit of the recent council.

8

Pacific Patterns in Southern California

Joan of Arc Residence: San Diego, CA (1938)[239]

For millennia, indigenous Americans were living in the San Diego area of California prior to the European conquests of the sixteenth and eighteenth centuries. With the arrival of the Spanish explorers and the accompanying Franciscan friars, led by St. Junipero Serra, the Catholic faith grew with the colonization of the indigenous peoples. Serra is credited with founding twenty-one California missions throughout the territory, where the peasants and friars lived and farmed together. The friars preached the Gospel to the peasants and helped to improve their living conditions, while supporting the colonizing aims of the Spanish. Their actions brought them both praise and blame. Nevertheless, their missions grew: two (Alcala and San Luis Rey) were within what is now San Diego, a region with roots going back to the Spanish and Mexican empires. Situated in a mild climate bordering the Pacific Ocean, San Diego developed into a major naval and aviation center. Its importance grew during and after World War II, and the population doubled in size. What is now San Diego was first included in a diocese that took in most of California. In 1922, it was divided, with the southern portion becoming the Los Angeles-San Diego diocese; by 1936, the diocese was again divided to create the San Diego diocese. Its first bishop, Most Rev. Charles Buddy, served the diocese from his appointment to his death in 1966. Buddy would be a significant figure for the Religious of Jesus and Mary as they ventured to the Pacific coast for the first time.

Invitation to San Diego

The San Diego mission of the Religious of Jesus and Mary has its origins in a touching anecdote centered on one of Bishop Buddy's secretaries, Ms. Louise Vertefeuille. The good bishop had trouble pronouncing her name, so he called her "Miss Greenleaf." One day he asked where she lived, and she told him she was staying at the YWCA. When he commented that residing there seemed "inappropriate" for a young Catholic woman, she told the bishop that when she worked in New York City, she had stayed at Jeanne d'Arc, a Catholic women's residence directed by the Sisters of Providence. She bemoaned the fact that there were no such places in San Diego. The bishop promised he would try to rectify the situation. The province annals report that Buddy contacted Bishop Schuler of El Paso, who told him of the good work being done by the Religious of Jesus and Mary at Queen of Angels Residence. He was predisposed, then, to receive a letter from M. Dulce Nombre Reventós on December 8, 1937, asking for permission to open a residence for working women in San Diego. His response was welcoming: "You have my cordial permission, and with all my heart I approve that you undertake the foundation of a residence for working women in the city of San Diego." He promised whatever assistance he could offer for their project to be successful, confiding it to Our Lady's protection.[240] With gratitude, the sisters assured Buddy they would also offer catechism and pastoral outreach in Spanish to Mexican colonies in the region, a ministry they fulfilled for several years.[241]

Seeking and Finding (1938 to 1940)

On January 31, 1938, two sisters bound for California boarded a train from El Paso to San Diego. M. Dulce Nombre Reventós and M. Guadalupe Maria Perez, the original foundresses in El Paso, spent the night traveling and arrived at noon the following day. There was no one to meet them, but they bolstered their flagging spirits, reminding themselves of early Spanish missionaries who suffered to bring the faith to California. At first sight, they found San Diego to be "a colorful, charming city, bordering the shores of the mighty Pacific." They consulted with the local Augustinian Fathers, who advised they seek lodging at Mercy Hospital, directed by Sisters of Mercy. The weary travelers appreciated the welcome of a community "who received us with great charity and kindness." On February 2, they met with the bishop, who warmly welcomed and blessed them, promising his support and assistance. The "Sisters of Jesus and Mary" were the first congregation Bishop Buddy invited into the diocese.

M. Dulce Nombre undertook a search for a spacious and convenient house where they could begin to receive residents. At first, possibilities seemed few and those they did investigate lacked sufficient space. They struggled to decide their best approach. Would it be better to return to El Paso while waiting to find an appropriate setting, or should they settle for a less suitable residence to begin with? The sisters wanted to find a proper residence; they worried that they might be overstaying their welcome at Mercy Hospital, and were eager to begin their own ministry. When Buddy visited them, he asked them not to rush into an unsuitable situation. He reminded the pioneers that they were planning not for a year but a lifetime. They had recourse to prayer, and while they felt awkward about prolonging their stay at Mercy, the superior "kept reassuring us that we were welcome to stay as long as necessary. We shall never be able to repay their immense charity."[242] They lived there for almost four months. In March, M. Dulce Nombre, suffering from a chronic health issue, was hospitalized for surgery from which she recuperated rapidly.

True to his promise, at the end of March, Buddy offered the sisters a temporary site for their residence in a house owned by the diocese and occupied by priests. The clergy moved nearer to the cathedral to accommodate the newcomers. For the next two years, the residence for women was located at the corner of Third and Cedar Avenues. On May 1, 1938, the bishop formally opened the house and named it "Joan of Arc Club," in honor of its forerunner in New York. A month later, a bronze plaque bearing that name was attached to the house. Of the two first residents, one was the bishop's secretary, Louise Vertefeuille, who found a home at Joan of Arc until her death. Within weeks, four more sisters arrived to complete the pioneer community: M. Claudina Contreras, M. Reparación Terrazas, Sr. Rosa Gaona, and Sr. Refugio Aguilar. M. Dulce Nombre was the community superior and enthusiastic director of the work, despite her recurring health issues. Buddy arrived on June 26 to bless the residence and offer the first Mass. Two Sisters of Mercy from the hospital and four Sisters of St. Joseph, who had a school nearby, came to the ceremonies and shared the joy of the new community and residents. The following year, there were seven sisters in the community, six Mexicans and a Canadian.

Their stay was a brief one. On April 18, 1940, Buddy asked them to vacate the house in a week's time, as it was needed for the priests in service at the cathedral. For the second time, the small community moved into temporary lodgings—"an old house devoid of many amenities"—on Georgia Street, near 12th Avenue. Buddy advised them to purchase available land across the street from St. Joseph's Cathedral and begin to build there. Obtaining the necessary permissions, they acted on his counsel. Together with their four residents, they accommodated to a makeshift situation while construction began on a new residence at the corner of Third and Beech Streets. Their community life in those days was marked by poverty and humor. At one point, all their meals consisted of donated tomatoes and eggs. The building project was supervised by M. Dulce Nombre, whose father was an architect from whom she had learned much. The Sinner Brothers (!) were contractors and builders. A new Joan of Arc Club would be ready for occupation by the New Year.

The Logan Avenue House (1941–42)

Short-lived and relatively unknown, another ministry began in San Diego along with the women's residence. At the request of the bishop, the Religious of Jesus and Mary were asked to take charge of a home for young girls who were orphaned or from broken families. In June of 1941, the sisters received the keys to a house on Logan Avenue, which was in very poor repair and needed work all through the summer before they could begin to receive children. Three were selected for this ministry, arriving in September to set up the house. They planned to begin with only four or five young girls, but even that number were challenging in terms of their behavior. On September 28, Buddy blessed the house, and the work was under way. There are no extant accounts of the ministry or the girls who came to live there. On July 23, 1942, the annals indicate that "despite high hopes, due to many difficulties," which are not specified, the Logan Avenue house was closed. It may well be that the sisters were not trained for this ministry in which "the girls needed special guidance." Throughout the war, Buddy offered it as temporary housing for military nurses waiting for deployment overseas.

A "New" Joan of Arc Residence (1941)

By 1940, the city of San Diego had grown into a large and bustling center for the World War II military effort, with its ship-building industry and burgeoning factories. This brought a swelling population of workers and military personnel, along with a severe housing shortage. The new residence opened at an opportune time. The community moved gradually into the building at 1510 Third Avenue in December and celebrated their first Christmas midnight Mass together. An article in the diocesan newspaper, *The Southern Cross*, praised this new ministry. Buddy dedicated the new Joan of Arc Club on January 6, 1941, encouraging the community to "watch it grow." His prophetic hope was soon realized. Designed to provide a "home-like atmosphere for young ladies who work away from home," the residence was two stories high, with provision for the future addition of another floor. The building included modern safety standards and earthquake proofing. There were fifty or so bedrooms equipped with modern conveniences and large casement windows. Laundry and ironing facilities were provided. Guest rooms had private entrances. The facility included a large reception room, a beautiful chapel open for use by all the residents, and a dining room near a fully equipped kitchen. Guests could choose to take their meals at the residence. Rates for the rooms varied according to size and meal plans, but they were reasonable, "within easy reach of each working girl." In no time, all the rooms were occupied, despite the stringent admission policy requiring "girls of irreproachable character." That same year, one of the residents converted to Catholicism; she was baptized and made First Communion in the convent chapel. Thanks to the ministrations and instructions of the sisters, several other residents chose to take instructions and become Catholics.

During the war years, Joan of Arc experienced the impact of the city's large military presence in a unique way. Soldiers and sailors awaiting orders arrived, seeking spiritual guidance and comfort. Priests from the cathedral offered Mass in the residence chapel three or four times daily. Communion was distributed at any time of the day or evening to accommodate those preparing to ship out to the war fronts. In 1944 alone, more than 5000 military personnel received communion in the chapel.

Post-War Years of Change

On August 19, 1945, seven years after founding the California mission, an ailing M. Dulce Nombre returned to El Paso as superior of Queen of Angels. Her companion, M. Guadalupe Maria, took over the direction of the residence and the community, which numbered eight choir

sisters and four auxiliaries. The residents' dining room was enlarged, and
the bishop gave the community more land near the residence to provide
a garden. On January 15, 1947, news came that M. Dulce Nombre had
died. This was a loss not only for the residence "where everything speaks
of her," but also for the province and its southwestern mission she had
helped to found. Buddy celebrated a solemn requiem Mass at Joan of
Arc on Saturday, January 18. In his sermon, he "praised the spirit of self-
sacrifice and sweet resignation" that had seen her through years of exile,
physical suffering, and pioneering a new mission. The flourishing residence continued to grow in the post-war years. In 1952, M. Guadalupe
Maria purchased a half-acre of land from the diocese to build a simple,
ten–room edifice abutting the residence. This expansion offered better
accommodations for residents and sisters alike. The community that year
welcomed an additional sister.

In February 1955, the Mission Club at Joan of Arc, organized to
assist foreign missions, decided to focus its activity on helping the Indian
mission of the Religious of Jesus and Mary, where a number of American sisters were serving. They collected funds and sent them to missions
where the superior general had determined areas of greatest need. That
same month, the bishop proposed a new spiritual project involving the
sisters at Joan of Arc. The community organized a day-long spiritual retreat for sixty residents and other young women, with private prayer, the
Way of the Cross, two conferences, and benediction. It was so successful
that Buddy organized a second one for ninety women and girls in July,
beginning with Mass at the Cathedral and breakfast at the residence.
During the summer months, sisters from other houses lived at Joan of
Arc while taking courses at San Diego College for women. Members of
the community traveled daily to Del Mar and Otay for two-week catechetical missions in Spanish.

In 1955, the Religious of Jesus and Mary in the southwestern United
States became a part of the new independent province of Mexico. Their
headquarters were transferred from El Paso, Texas to Mexico City, and
M. Guadalupe Maria became their provincial superior. This restructuring
resulted in a smaller community presence at Joan of Arc, since Mexican
sisters now had a choice to return to their home country. In 1961 the sisters had to give up a favorite catechetical parish outreach. They continued
inviting the residents to daily evening rosary in the chapel and promoted
among them the devotion to the Eucharistic Heart and Immaculate
Heart. The social room offered older women a place for conversation and

mutual support of each other. Despite herculean efforts on the part of the sisters, the sixties presented them with serious challenges in the areas of finances, language, and lack of personnel. In 1966, the separate class of auxiliary sisters was suppressed. Superiors made efforts to offer educational opportunities to former auxiliaries. For a residence like Joan of Arc, this change meant fewer sisters available for the essential domestic work, and the need to hire paid staff. On December 12, 1967, the superior general sent a letter to Most Reverend Francis J. Furey, then bishop of San Diego, stating that "we are not too optimistic . . . I wonder if we have any apostolate in the Residence." It seemed to her that a sale or transfer to another congregation would be a better choice. Furey asked that the general leadership begin by having the property assessed and postpone any further decision on Joan of Arc. As time would show, the following year offered a new and broader future for the community and residence.

Los Angeles, CA: San Antonio de Padua School (1950 to 1957)

While it was yet an unfamiliar mission region for the Religious of Jesus and Mary, the "city of Angels" had welcomed large populations of Mexicans and Mexican Americans throughout its history. Originally a Spanish colony town, by 1940 Los Angeles numbered more than a million people. Shifting urban realities and the "Americanization" of the church among its Spanish-speaking residents redefined the city that attracted them by its job prospects and their desire to escape Mexico's ongoing conflicts. These Mexican immigrants, like their compatriots in Texas, turned to their religious faith for support. Many of their pastors were themselves exiles; as such, they were welcome in southern California to serve the growing Mexican-American population at the border, where priests were too few in number. The people's national devotion to the Virgin of Guadalupe always played a significant role in their domestic lives, as well as in their public processions and protests.

Our Lady of Guadalupe also became an important political and religious symbol in Los Angeles. Its first archbishop, Most Rev. John J. Cantwell, hoped to promote her cult as "Queen of the Americas" in the archdiocese.[243] In 1941, he was invited to lead a diocesan pilgrimage to the Mexican shrine; despite his initial hesitation, he conducted a successful and highly publicized pilgrimage in October 1941, two months before the attack on Pearl Harbor. To commemorate that historic visit and strengthen cultural bonds, the archbishop of Mexico City sent to Los Angeles a silver reliquary containing a fragment of Juan Diego's miraculous *tilma* (cloak) for veneration. Once it arrived, it was entrusted to Rev. Fidencio Esparza, a Mexican priest and pastor of San Antonio de Padua Parish since 1938. It is likely that he kept the relic in his parish for almost forty years.[244]

Soon after these significant events for the Catholic Church of Los Angeles, Esfarza met M. del Sagrado Corazon Nandin at a conference in El Paso sometime in 1947. It seems this was the occasion for him to invite her community to teach in the parish school he was building in East Los Angeles, along with a convent to house eight sisters. Late in March 1949, a draft contract was drawn up, delineating the rights and duties of both the pastor and the religious congregation, according to the guidelines of the archdiocese. It stipulated a monthly salary of $50 for each teaching sister. It stated further that the pastor could request changes in personnel as he saw fit. In addition to directing the school, the sisters were to teach Sunday school, and direct parish youth groups, including the children's choir. They were not permitted to have bazaars, sales, or raffles to benefit the community.[245] After a visit from the provincial early in 1950 to inspect the site and study architectural plans, permissions were granted to open the school that September. It was an attractive possibility. A community in Los Angeles would simplify arrangements for sisters studying at Immaculate Heart College in the city and provide a wider field for their educational ministry.

The Foundation at San Antonio[246]

The sisters planned to move to their new convent on Bridge Street in June 1950 and to prepare the school for its opening. From the outset, they were met with difficulties. A three-month strike of construction workers caused serious delays, thwarting hopes for a September opening. Authorities refused to accept Esfarza's appeal for a delay with a January opening date. The pastor hastily decided to open the school on schedule in rooms of a CYO (Catholic Youth Organization) building nearby, with arrangements for the sisters to board in a neighboring convent of Sisters of the Immaculate Heart of Mary (IHM). On September 10, the first three Religious of Jesus and Mary arrived: M. Guadalupe Maria Perez, M. Herminia Rangel, and Sr. Bernadita. They learned that there were seventy-two students enrolled "and the number was growing daily." Most of the children were Spanish speaking, with origins in Mexico. The spaces assigned as classrooms were small and without proper instructional materials. The sisters traveled daily from their temporary convent to the makeshift "school," then to dinner at 4 PM in the rectory, and by evening back to the convent.

Esfarza created a "big problem" for the teachers by asking them to begin classes with the older children rather than the primary grades. As one of the foundresses recalled, these pupils "had already acquired bad habits . . . it was difficult for us to control and change them." In the absence of desks, blackboards, and proper facilities, the teachers made do with folding tables they needed to clean off from meetings of the previous evening. This was the instructional environment until January of1951. The convent was finally ready by September 22, and two more sisters came to complete the community. On Saturdays, they took courses toward college degrees at Immaculate Heart College.

In January, the school was ready for occupancy, if not yet fully furnished. M. Guadalupe Maria returned to San Diego and was replaced as teacher by M. del Sagrario (Eva) Garcia. A Spanish sister became the community superior. By September 1951, the community was complete with eight members. There were now 300 students enrolled, many having come from public schools with "no notion of religion." Thanks to the pastor's generous offer of his car, student-sisters were able to get to the college without difficulty.

Instructional Issues and Closing

Despite their best efforts to meet the educational standards of the city and archdiocese, English-language deficiencies and lack of certification continued to challenge the sister-teachers at San Antonio. Shortly after her election as superior general, at a meeting with her councilors on May 16, 1953, M.M. del Rosario brought up the issue of withdrawal from San Antonio School. Two more teachers had been requested for the coming year. English language instruction was mandatory. "Since our Spanish [speaking] sisters are not competent enough to teach in English, and the authorities find them wanting in that respect, it would seem preferable to . . . let other religious communities take it over." The council approved her proposal; they would inform Cardinal McIntyre of their decision.[247]

Shortly after, however, they were informed by the chancery that their decision was "almost impossible because of some major problems . . ." The general leadership agreed to stay only if the pastor hired lay teachers for English instruction. They revisited and renewed their decision in August 1955, with the stipulation that if another community could not be found to take the school, the Religious of Jesus and Mary would remain for only one more year.

One of the auxiliary bishops contacted the provincial, indicating that he wanted to improve the situation of the sisters at the school. A month later, the provincial sent Rev. M. M. del Rosario a report of her meeting with Esfarza, who resisted hiring lay teachers. Instead, he proposed reorganizing the student body into two language groups and split sessions. At their meeting, the general council began a process of prayer and discernment, weighing the pros and cons of the proposal. On September 28, 1955, they voted to accept Esfarza's proposal, contingent on his hiring of four teachers. There is no further information about its implementation. By October of 1956, however, the general leadership learned that Esfarza had found a community to take over his parish school.

Auxiliary Bishop Timothy Manning wrote to M. Guadalupe Maria with the offer of a newly opened school in the San Fernando Valley region of Los Angeles, in exchange for the school at San Antonio. Named Guardian Angel, the new school was in Pacoima, one of the oldest and fastest growing neighborhoods of the city's sprawling suburbs. Its pastor, Rev. Paul E. Stroup, wrote to M. Guadalupe Maria on December 19, 1956, that he hoped she would be able to respond affirmatively to his request for sisters to teach in the school he had just finished building, along with an adjoining convent. He guaranteed transportation to and from the college when the sisters had to travel there for studies.

By January 1957, the provincial wrote to Rome urging prompt acceptance of the offer. The problems between the pastor and sisters at San Antonio continued, she wrote, while the pastor at Pacoima was eager to have the community in his parish. She made a further case that the air in Pacoima was healthier, being less polluted than in the city itself. She listed two disadvantages of the move: greater distance from the college for studies, and a need for more teachers than at San Antonio. The general council voted unanimously in favor of the transfer. On May 21, 1957, they received a second letter from the provincial announcing that the community would leave San Antonio in the summer and move on to Pacoima. She reported that earlier difficulties between Esfarza and the teachers had improved. The pastor of Guardian Angel prepared for the sisters' arrival in September and had begun to furnish their new school building and convent. As they bid farewell to one Los Angeles neighborhood and prepared to move to another, the Religious of Jesus and Mary ended a brief period of their southwestern ministry.

Pacoima, CA: Guardian Angel Parish (1957 to 2013)[248]

The indigenous meaning of Pacoima is "land of rushing waters," an appropriate description of the rapidly growing suburb of Los Angeles. One of the oldest neighborhoods in the San Fernando Valley, Pacoima boasted a 200-year history as part of a vast Spanish mission. Prior to 1950, it was also one of the poorest areas of the metropolis, lacking paved streets and sidewalks. The post-war years brought a transformation to Pacoima: almost overnight, it changed from a dusty farming community to a bustling bedroom community of Los Angeles, creating better-paying jobs and opportunities. Its blue-collar population, predominantly African American and Hispanic, had materially improved their lives as factory and construction workers. They lived in small homes or in the San Fernando Gardens public housing project. This was the urban setting of Guardian Angel Parish, established in 1929 on a donated piece of land. After its founding, it provided for the spiritual needs of about 100 Mexican American families as a mission church for St. Ferdinand's Parish in San Fernando, California. The missionary community of Oblates of Mary Immaculate (OMI) served the mission for twenty-seven years. Its second pastor, Robert Koerner, OMI, raised the funds to purchase land for a parish school and convent, and construction began in the 1950s. The status of Guardian Angel evolved from mission church to diocesan parish in 1956, with Rev. Paul Stroup as its first pastor. Within that year, he completed the building project so that the school and convent were ready for occupancy. Because the Religious of Jesus and Mary were unable to begin that year, Stroup hired two lay teachers for about eighty children who had transferred from the local public schools.

Founding and Early Years

The community arrived from the San Antonio Parish in June of 1957, having transported their belongings in several successive, difficult journeys. M. Agnes of the Cross(Josefina) Delgado was the local superior and principal of the pioneer group, with M. Sagrario Garcia, M. Rose Gomez, M. Ana Felisa Bernal, M. Mary Sanchez, M. Gonzaga Maria, and Sr. Paulina completing the community. An undated personal account relates that they began classes in September with 400 children, with the majority being African Americans. The second largest group was Mexican-American, complemented by an ethnic mix of Asians and Europeans.

In the first year, they registered children for the first six grades, planning to add another grade each year. M. Agnes was sixth grade teacher as well as principal. She was surprised that some of her students were yet unable to write their names. In the early weeks, sisters often had to intervene in the boys' regular fights with one another, arriving home as bruised as their students. Along with daytime class instruction, they held evening classes for the parents to help them learn the "new math" along with their children. There were weekly CCD classes for neighborhood public school students, with sessions held in two private homes. Catholic parents were encouraged to attend Mass with the children and involve themselves in various parish activities.

The first years offered a steep learning curve for the sister-teachers, acquainting them with new cultures and children whose religious knowledge and practice were limited. The sisters employed tools of positive reinforcement and gentle persuasion, kindness and understanding, toward students and families: "This way we were able to reach them." At the end of a year, the pastor and school supervisors noted the gradual progress with satisfaction. One of the sisters initiated a school band for first and second graders, which became quite an attraction! In time, the students wore uniforms; the group performed at school meetings and parish social events. For the upper grades, there was a parish choir to sing at the religious ceremonies, especially at Christmas. Along with the church services, they performed Christmas carols in homes of senior parishioners. There were as well the annual *fiestas* so popular with Mexican Americans: celebrations for *Cinco de Mayo* and the Day of the Dead, as well as for Our Lady of Guadalupe. The sisters helped plan these events alongside the parishioners and participated fully in them. They were truly part of parish life at every level. By 1959, there were five sisters and three lay teachers staffing grades one through six.

Signs of Change and Growth (1964 to 1987)

In a 1964 report prepared for the General Chapter, the Religious of Jesus and Mary stated that "with the help of God, our work in Pacoima has been fruitful." An average of 320 students registered each year, evenly divided between girls and boys. The pastor, Rev. Mario Matic, decided which children were to be admitted. He gave preference to Catholics without excluding non-Catholics. In general, the children were studious and able to pass high school entrance exams without difficulty. By 1964, teachers were proud to look back on their first students at Pacoima, now graduated from high school. School sports teams were very successful, and many trophies lined the school display case. The school Sodality was active, adding sixteen new members in 1965.

For the sisters, serving at Guardian Angel linked them to the early southwestern mission work with which they were familiar. It was an impoverished setting in which they worked with parents and children to instruct, console, and support them. In the first six years, more than thirty children were baptized and the sisters instructed many converts preparing for the sacraments. From 1957 to 1962, the sisters did parish catechetical work in Osborne, a small town five miles from Pacoima. Then they relinquished it to others because their undergraduate studies required more of their time and attention. The annual parish *fiesta* for Our Lady of Guadalupe was greeted with solemnity, beginning at 5 AM with the singing of *"Las Mananitas"* in the parish church, accompanied by the local *mariachi* band. One sister wrote, "There is nothing more typical and heartfelt than the love the [people] have for their *Morenita* [dark-skinned girl]." In this Marian image, Mexican Americans recognized themselves and their hopes. The parish came under the care of Spanish Vincentian priests in 1966, with Rev. Narciso Gonzalez as pastor. Two more priests joined him in succeeding years. In 1973, Guardian Angel again became a diocesan parish, with a ministry team of three priests; by 1981, just a single pastor would be appointed. With the merging of the Eastern-and Western-American Provinces of the Congregation in 1968, the community at Guardian Angel grew to nine sisters, among whom were two of the original founding group. Thanks to grants from the Parent-Teacher Organization and the government, the school had a functioning library under the direction of M. Stella Herrera, the eighth-grade teacher. With more than ninety percent minority students, it was important to have a diverse faculty. Along with dedicated laywomen, a few men were hired to teach or coach; a number of Hispanic and African-American teachers were hired, including non-Catholics.

By the 1980s, school reports and census information reveal a demographic shift from a majority of African Americans to predominantly Hispanic students. In 1985, the staff included three sisters, two African-American women, and four Hispanic women, with a sister as principal. Economic decline in these years made it difficult to collect tuition from parents who had been laid off or whose language deficits limited their opportunities. The school was, however, partially subsidized by the archdiocese, which "helped to continue serving poor families in the area while benefitting from near-capacity enrollment."[249] Under the leadership of Sr. Joan Faraone as principal, the school made academic strides, especially in curriculum development. By 1988, Guardian Angel qualified for funding of a full-day kindergarten, which had capacity enrollment; it also received grants that year to set up a computer-based reading program for the primary grades.

Despite those early struggles and challenges, the Religious of Jesus and Mary celebrated with gratitude their thirtieth anniversary in the parish on May 17, 1987. Auxiliary Bishop Armand Ochoa presided at the Eucharist, and the provincial, M. Gertrude Bélanger, offered a reflection. For three decades more, the ministry flourished, providing a home for the community, a staff for the school, and pastoral service to the parish community, known for its deep faith and dedicated families.

Changing Context, Painful Decision

With the new century, the province entered a period of questioning and challenge. This arose out of the evolving context of the American church and society, with fewer women entering, a higher median age, and growing health concerns for some of the twelve sisters in California. During her annual visit to Pacoima in the spring of 2012, the provincial, Sr. Eileen Reid, met with the community and raised the possibility of leaving Pacoima. Along with the considerations mentioned above, she spoke of the 160-mile distance between Los Angeles and San Diego, where their regional superior lived. While this proposal called into question their apostolic presence in California, it also revealed the critical need to plan for its long-range future. The sisters were invited by the general leadership to enter a process of discernment regarding the future the California region. Sr. Françoise Barras, secretary general, sent the sisters possible steps for discernment, requesting that the region "identify a number of alternatives for the future." Sr. Françoise planned to meet with them in December, but that meeting was postponed until March 2013.

There are no extant records of any meeting with Sr. Françoise, of local or regional discernment meetings, or of any proposals regarding the future of the California region. In June 2012, Sr. Rosemary Nicholson, the regional leader, and another sister from Pacoima met with the pastor, Rev. Steven Guitron, to discuss the situation. In the summary report she sent to the provincial, it was clear that the sisters' situation was an issue for the pastor. The five sisters in the convent were retired from teaching but were still engaged in volunteer pastoral work at his other parishes. While he appreciated their presence, he too had concerns for their growing medical needs. Furthermore, he pointed out that they were no longer teaching in the school and suggested that their "mission has come to an end."

Guardian Angel Parish was growing. Guitron viewed the convent as offering possibilities for meeting space, additional rooms for clergy, and new pastoral ministry programs. In the pastor's communication, the province leadership saw clear signs of how to proceed. On January 24, 2013, the provincial wrote to Archbishop José H. Gomez, laying out the reasons for withdrawing the sisters in the coming summer and relocating them to settings that were more conducive to their needs. It was a long and sad "*adios*" for the community, who spent their final day at Guardian Angel on June 28, 2013. Their legacy included fifty-six years of educational ministry at the school they had founded, and a living memory of generous service and ministry to the people of their beloved parish community.

Spring Valley, CA: Santa Sophia Parish (1959 to 1993)[250]

Situated in the Casa de Oro section of Spring Valley, California, the parish boundaries of Santa Sophia were once part of the eighteenth-century Franciscan mission foundations. Before World War II, Spring Valley was rural farmland; its population exploded as the military and war workers rushed into the area and thus contributed to the economic growth of the county. In October 1956, Bishop Buddy established Santa Sophia Parish, bringing together three small faith communities from neighboring districts. Masses were first celebrated in the homes of families and in a community center. Thanks to generous land donations, work began on a church and rectory in June 1957. With its unique shape and construction, including a towering crucifix behind the main altar, the architecture and furnishings of Santa Sophia displayed an open, contemporary design. On June 29, 1958, Msgr. John Verhoeven was appointed pastor and celebrated the first Mass in the church one week later. It was dedicated to "Holy Wisdom,"– Christ as the Word of God—and consecrated by Buddy on May 3, 1959.

Within a year of his arrival, Verhoeven founded Santa Sophia Academy, encouraged by Buddy, who invited the Religious of Jesus and Mary to direct and staff the new parish school, still under construction. For the first five years, the sisters assigned to the school lived at the Joan of Arc Residence and commuted thirteen miles daily to Spring Valley. Four unnamed sisters formed the pioneer group; they taught in temporary classrooms because the school building was still unfinished. These "classrooms" actually were designated areas within the church, from the entrance to the nave, which housed grades 2, 3, and 4. Kindergarten sessions were in the rectory; grades 5 and 6 used the spacious garage, which also served as a cafeteria. With an average of thirty children in each class, teachers needed the energy of St. Paul and the patience of Job! In the sanctuary, a curtain hid the tabernacle during class sessions. One sister reflected in the convent annals that God who became tiny must have smiled lovingly on these little ones learning in that sacred space. Despite the space issues, the teachers worked with a committee of parents to plan a successful initial Open House Week. The occasion allowed parents see the progress of their new school building and to meet the staff. At the end of the week, the annalist wrote of the "remarkable cooperation among parents, teachers and pupils." With time, another tradition developed: the annual "Silver Tea" in November, an invitation for parent involvement in the school. During their first year in the parish, the sisters displayed materials at the Vocation Day rally of the diocese, sharing information on the congregation, overseen by a life-sized standing image of the Foundress.

New School, New Convent

By Easter of 1960, classrooms in the school were ready for occupancy and provided better educational accommodations for all. The dedication and blessing took place at the end of May, marked by a living rosary, a crowning of Our Lady, and a procession. It was an occasion for thanksgiving to

God and for prayer that the educational future of Santa Sophia Academy would be successful. Enrollment in the school that year was 246, and there was hope for greater numbers. Space constraints meant that the rectory garage continued serving as a permanent classroom setting for grades 7 and 8. Parents and sisters realized how dedicated their pastor had been in achieving this milestone; in October, everyone gathered to celebrate Verhoeven's twenty-fifth ordination anniversary. At Christmas, there was the traditional Mexican ceremony of "*Las Posadas*," followed by a school party. Cultural and civic opportunities increased as the Academy became better known; children were competing successfully in various diocesan activities and contests.

In 1962, the school's first principal was transferred and another sister took her place.[251] By the following June, faculty prepared for its first eighth-grade graduation, marking another milestone. That September, M. St. Vincent (Irene) Maynard arrived from the Eastern province in September, 1963, as principal of the school and assistant superior in San Diego. An energetic and experienced educator, she brought new ideas and instructional concepts to the staff. She introduced the "Spalding Reading Method," with its accompanying reading laboratory, to help students improve their language and reading skills. New science learning kits were provided for the primary and intermediate grades. Progress was noticeable within that year, and the parents responded with generous donations for additional projects and supplies. M. St. Vincent also organized a Mothers' Club, with monthly meetings, offering another opportunity for parents to engage with teachers.

On December 10, 1963, Verhoeven wrote to the superior general, calling attention to a problematic situation with the teaching staff. While he appreciated M. St. Vincent and her contribution to improving the school, he stated that the sisters on the faculty were "very fine religious, but as teachers they do not qualify." In addition to some English language deficiencies, there were issues with classroom discipline. Standardized test results were not encouraging either, with many students falling below national averages. The school board of the region was requiring well-qualified teachers, and as pastor he wished to comply. In closing, he expressed gratitude for the principal and hoped that his school might welcome some prepared faculty in the future. Her response has not been recorded, but changes took place the following year, when a community of six was assigned to reside in an on-site convent.

On September 8, the parish celebrated the opening of a new convent at 9810 San Juan Street, which was the former rectory, remodeled and newly furnished. Verhoeven had moved into a bungalow nearby. The sisters were delighted to live where they served. With their usual liberality, the parishioners offered household gifts and furnishings for the sisters' new home. With M. St. Vincent as superior and principal, a young and vibrant community of sister-teachers looked forward to meeting their students: Sisters Mary Vianney (Rose) Gomez, Maria Stella Herrera, Dina Marie Garcia, Mary Alfred (Ann) Dewar, and M. Helen of the Cross (Alicia) Salcido. On September 14, school opened with a total of 247 students, with the largest number—fifty—in grade 3. Grade 8 had the fewest, with only twenty students because many had transferred to junior high schools in the area.

The Advent season of 1964 marked the introduction of the "new" liturgy of the Mass mandated by the Second Vatican Council and introduced throughout the United States that year, with readings and prayers in English and the presider facing the congregation for the first time. At Santa Sophia, the students entered this new era with celebrations of Advent and Christmas using the updated ritual. For the sisters, this period of renewal marked many changes in prayer forms, customs, and religious dress. Given the option, most returned to their baptismal names. Various styles of approved habits and headpieces appeared in the next few years as the sisters adapted to the external forms of renewal for religious life mandated by the Council. Sister Claire Lebreux arrived in 1967 to replace M. St. Vincent as superior and principal, a service she generously offered for the next six years. At the province level, the sisters began a two-year preparation for a special General Chapter of 1969, engaging the Congregation and its members with their "sources" and history, and propelling them into an unknown future.

Changing Times

On April 6, 1977, Verhoeven died suddenly, just short of twenty years as pastor of the church, school, and convent complex he had built and treasured. Alongside the parish community, the sisters mourned the passing of their beloved pastor. Three months later, Msgr. Thomas E. Prendergast arrived as the new pastor and took up the responsibilities of his growing parish community and school. On May 7, 1978, the sisters at Santa

Sophia hosted a centenary celebration of their arrival in the States. They invited the communities of California to join them during a special Mass at church. Several sisters joined the Santa Sophia community, renewing their vows publicly in the parish, after which they showed slides of the Foundress and the Congregation. They received a check for $1200 from the parishioners, another sign of the appreciation and generosity so evident at Santa Sophia. In 1982, two new school buildings were completed, comprising seven classrooms; the original classrooms were completely remodeled and refurbished as meeting rooms for parish activities. The next year, the parish hall underwent a transformation: an air-conditioned, large auditorium was added, along with a full-service kitchen and new restrooms. By 1985, Santa Sophia Academy would add a preschool to the plant, repurposing a small house on a corner of the property.

With the diminishing number of available teaching sisters in the 1980s, the Religious of Jesus and Mary struggled to honor their commitment to the ministry at Santa Sophia. Sister Vivian Patenaude, the provincial, wrote to Prendergast with concerns that the province was having difficulty filling certain positions but that they hoped replace the principal, Sr. Mary Ellen (Patricia) Scanlon, reassigned that year. Novices were missioned to the community as teaching interns, but by 1988 only three sisters remained in the parish. Sr. Rosemary Nicholson, the principal, had eleven laywomen on her teaching staff, with a student population of 285. The tuition had risen to over $1200 annually for parishioners. One sister directed the extended-care program; the other oversaw the RCIA program and religious education. A flyer distributed at the Open House on April 30 stated the underlying philosophy of the school, "that each child is a special person loved by God," and its role was to assist and augment the efforts of parents as primary educators. Part of the spiritual formation of the students was helping them become aware of peace, justice, and service. Along with helping students develop basic skills and critical thinking, teachers aimed to provide a positive climate for learning. Religious instruction had pride of place and was integrated into other aspects of student life and learning.

On May 20, 1990, the sisters celebrated thirty years of service in the parish, marking the occasion with a special Mass and reception for 220 alumni. Among the esteemed visitors was the much-loved Sr. Irene Maynard (M. St. Vincent), who said how pleased she was "to be back among people I love." She added that she would gladly return if she were forty years younger! The sisters looked back with gratitude and affection, even as they realized that their numbers were insufficient to continue there as they once did. That year the school staff had successfully undergone a regional accreditation process. Prendergast sent the provincial a check for $10,000 in recognition of the community's faithful service to the school and people for most of the parish's existence.

Early in June of the next year, pastor, sisters, and other people marked the thirty-fifth anniversary of Santa Sophia Parish. They celebrated with a dinner dance, a Family Day of games and activities, and the time capsule they buried on the grounds. A new pastor, Rev. Mark Campbell, had arrived, and a new era was underway for the sisters. With the exception of the principal, the remaining sisters announced their departure at the end of the school year. One was assigned to pastoral ministry in the diocese, the other to a much-needed sabbatical. On July 31, 1993, Sr. Rosemary Nicholson wrote to the parishioners announcing the withdrawal of the community from the parish. On Sunday, August 1, there was a farewell Eucharist at 9 AM. Sr. Rosemary reflected that all growth was dependent on change and that their convent-home could serve new parish programs: "When we were informed of the parish needs for convent space, we recognized that your ministries are growing and changing also." More than three decades after they arrived, the Religious of Jesus and Mary left Santa Sophia with grateful hearts, the legacy of their educational style, and lasting memories of a vibrant parish faith community in "the valley."

M. St. Cyrille Reynier, founder,
RJM mission to the United States

M. St. Jerome Fortier and Sr. St. Sabine Marion,
Fall River, MA, 1913

El Paso RJM with children at a southwestern summer mission

M. St. Mathias Bonin with French class, Villa Augustina, Goffstown, NH

M. Gertrude Jalbert with children in Mariakhel, Pakistan, c. 1960

M. St. Charles Collins with student at Thevenet
Montessori, Highland Mills, NY, c. 1980

M. St. Vincent Ferrer, founding provincial,
Hyattsville, MD, 1955

Sr. Yvette Beaulieu with Algebra student,
Regina High School, c. 1970

RJM Missionaries to Haiti with Sr. Eileen Reid, Jean Rabel, HAITI, 2009
Srs. Isabel Sola, Rose Kelly, Patricia Dillon, Vivian Patenaude,
Eileen Reid, Jacqueline Picard, Nazareth Ybarra.

Part Three

Weaving Fresh Fabric

9

New Beginnings

Maryland and the South

Hyattsville, MD:
Provincial House, Regina High School (1955 to 1991)[252]

THE BACKSTORY OF THE transfer of the American province headquarters to Maryland is recounted in chapter 6. The decision of the Religious of Jesus and Mary to undertake a major geographical relocation for their headquarters resulted in a significant socio–cultural shift for the province and its members. For over seventy–five years, from their founding mission in Massachusetts through their growth and extension in New York, the sisters had been identified with the urban Northeast, where they directed academies, parish elementary schools, high schools, and a residence for working women. The move to Maryland impelled them southward, where history, living conditions, and socio–economic realities differed from those in the familiar regions they had known. For the first time, they would experience issues of racial diversity, inequality, and the struggle of African Americans. Likewise, the move expanded their horizons, inviting new apostolic opportunities and possibilities they had not imagined. In short, the journey to the Mid–Atlantic region marked a new beginning, a transformation for the Religious of Jesus and Mary in the United States. This chapter recounts their southward movement and their encounter with the challenges of a rapidly changing society and church. In new times, they learned to weave hope with unfamiliar threads and fabrics, in an evolving pattern of lifestyles and ministries.

Historic Location

One of the thirteen original colonies and a Mid–Atlantic state, Maryland borders Pennsylvania, Delaware, Virginia, West Virginia, and Washington, DC, the nation's capital district. From its founding, it was one of the few predominantly Catholic colonial regions. Featuring a variety of industries, climates, and topography features, as well as a diverse ethnic and racial population, it was sometimes nicknamed "America in Miniature." As a slaveholding state when the Civil War broke out, Maryland nonetheless chose to remain in the Union; thus, it was a "house divided," and large numbers of its young men chose to fight for the Confederacy. With time, its culture shifted away from agriculture and a tidewater industry to thriving centers of manufacturing. A remarkable growth in Maryland's population occurred in the 1940s, when federal and civil–service workers arrived in the capital area as part of the surging post–war government expansion. Agricultural tracts were turned into suburban residential communities in Maryland. Many—including Hyattsville — were in Prince George's County, a convenient and affordable destination for relocating families, most with children. By 1950, the county population had reached almost 350,000 residents.

The historic city of Hyattsville, incorporated in 1886, had much to offer its residents. Still growing in the 1950s, it had lovely parks, churches, shopping areas, and public transportation to Washington. Several religious communities had found suitable properties on which to build formation houses in Hyattsville, located less than 10 miles from The Catholic University. Among them was a fifty–acre property at 8910 Riggs Road, purchased in 1950 by the Assumptionist Fathers for use as a formation center. Four years later, however, the priests moved their formation programs to Saugerties, NY.[253] On June 9, 1954, during an initial visit with Archbishop Patrick O'Boyle and chancery officials, the superior general and M. St. Vincent Ferrer toured several sites suitable for their building plans. They chose to purchase twenty–five acres of the property belonging to the Assumptionists, an order familiar to the Religious of Jesus and Mary in New England and New York City. Late in September, the sisters returned to sign the transfer of deed and settled on the purchase price of $100,000. O'Boyle had been generous in his offer to "ask the cooperation of some of the banks here in Washington" to assist the leadership as they sought loans for new construction. At the end of his June welcoming letter he added a significant postscript: "I was indeed pleased when you said you would take colored [sic] pupils. It is the policy of the diocese to accept all races in the schools."[254] O'Boyle was a strong opponent of racism and at the forefront of the school desegregation movement, having experimented with integrating Catholic schools in Washington, thereby contributing significantly to passage of the first Civil Rights Act of 1954.[255]

Breaking Ground, Blessing of Cornerstone

On November 11, 1954, the provincial leadership was joined by community superiors of the province and representatives of local religious communities of women, along with a large crowd from the area, to witness the groundbreaking ceremony for the convent and school. O'Boyle presided, accompanied by a number of ecclesiastics. At the ceremony's closing, the sisters sang a *Magnificat* of thanksgiving. The estimated cost of building was $860,000, a figure that would increase with time. Bids for contractors arrived through December; on January 18 the provincial council decided to give the contract to the lowest bidder, a Mr. Victor Beauchamp. Large loans were taken out to cover building costs, but it was clear they would need to borrow even more as time went on. There were several trips back and forth to Hyattsville during the construction, which began in February of 1955. Thanks to the hospitality of the Sisters of Charity of Cincinnati, who directed the parish school at St. John Baptist de la Salle, M. St. Vincent Ferrer and her companions were welcomed to the guest rooms in their convent. The annals report gratefully that "everything was done to help them in every way." Their hospitality was later extended to the pioneer group of Religious of Jesus and Mary arriving in August of the following year.

As the academic year got underway, M. Mary Armand (Agnes) Desautels was named the first principal for Regina High School.[256] She wrote an open letter to local pastors, principals, and seventh- and eighth-grade Catholic students in the area, announcing the opening of the school for September of 1955. The first year would be limited to a freshman class, with a new class added each succeeding year. The letter described three courses of study: academic, toward college studies; commercial, as a foundation for "work in the business field"; and general, with a concentration on homemaking and home economics within a framework called "Christian Family Living." Extracurricular offerings were in the

plans: classes in physical education/health, along with basketball, vol-
leyball, and softball teams. Music courses would offer opportunities to
join Glee Club with regular concert performances. There would be an
option for private piano lessons. Students could participate in a drama
club and contribute to school publications through classes in journalism.
A strong emphasis would be given to each girl's spiritual growth through
daily religion classes, regular conferences and retreats, and participation
in the sacramental and liturgical life of the school.

The annual tuition was set at $150. The school would offer a limited
number of scholarships each year. An artist's sketch published in a local newspaper on February 3, 1955, revealed the extent of the completed
complex, designed by the architectural firm, Johnson and Boutin. Including the novitiate, the convent would house eighty sisters and provide
large dining and community rooms, an infirmary wing, and two chapels.
Separated from the convent by a glass–enclosed central foyer entrance,
the school would have fourteen classrooms, two science labs, two rooms
for bookkeeping and typing classes, a large library, gymnasium, and a
"model home" for domestic science. A separate wing contained administrative offices, counseling rooms, and a teachers' lounge.

During a snowstorm on February 12, 1955, 210 interested applicants took scholarship and placement exams for Regina at a local high
school in Washington. Because of the poor weather, a second session
in March was scheduled, at which forty–two students presented themselves. Scholarships would later be awarded on a parochial basis. From
May 17 to 23 that year, the Religious of Jesus and Mary held a centenary
celebration of their arrival in North America. Delegations from Rome
and several provinces traveled to the founding house in Lauzon, Québec, for the festivities. Taking advantage of the occasion, some chose to
visit a few New England communities, and remained for the laying of
the cornerstone in Hyattsville. On Sunday afternoon, June 12, a global
representation of the Congregation, including the superior general and
her councilors, with several provincials from France, Spain, England,
and Canada, gathered for the "imposing ceremony," with O'Boyle presiding. Religious of Jesus and Mary from the province, and sisters of other
communities in the archdiocese, were joined by large numbers of clergy,
neighbors, and families of prospective students to pray for God's blessing on their newest mission to the United States. The prelate cardinal
welcomed the sisters cordially, wishing grace and benediction on their
enterprise. In his moving sermon, Msgr. John S. Spence, archdiocesan

director of education, spoke of the sisters' "indomitable spirit as being a passport of welcome to this archdiocese," and referred to their "tremendous confidence in the Almighty" already expressed in "assuming a colossal task" that others might be loath to undertake. The ceremony closed with Benediction of the Blessed Sacrament and several traditional hymns by the sisters' choir.[257]

Unfinished and Underway: The Beginning (1955)

Early in the morning of August 17, a Wednesday, the annalist reports that "three cars, loaded with all kinds of furnishings, left Highland Mills for Hyattsville." They arrived in a downpour and trekked through the oozing red mud of the new property to unload their cargo into the unfinished building. Returning to New York, they had reason to wonder how they possibly could make the definitive move to Riggs Road the following Monday. Undeterred and enthusiastic, on the feast of the Immaculate Heart, August 22, a pioneer group of six set out in two cars to take up permanent residence in Maryland. They included M. St. Vincent Ferrer, M. M. Armand Desautels, M. St. Thomas More (Anne) Wallace, M. St. Louis (Mary) Kenny, M. M. Cecilia (Catherine) Dowd, and M. St. Philomena (Anne Marie) Lusignan, who was sent on loan to help with organizing the house and setting up furniture. M. St. Hilda (Eva) Beaulieu, the future school librarian, arrived a few days later. For the first week, without electricity or doors in much of the building, they improvised for meals, using the community room as storage space for over sixty beds and mattresses, nightstands and library chairs. On the first night, gathering around the statue of the Sacred Heart they had brought, the little group sang hymns and improvised a semi–serious "address" to the provincial. Their spirits made up for the absence of some basic necessities, and the picnic–style meals were enjoyed with laughter, as they shared each day's discoveries.

Every morning, the sisters went to Mass at St. John Baptist de la Salle and enjoyed breakfast with the sisters there. Within a few days, they bought a small refrigerator and set it in the jam–packed community room, which also served as chapel and dining area for the group. Cars traveled from New York daily with more furnishings, and truckloads of school furniture began arriving. The challenge of each day was where to put everything, as they had to negotiate space around workers who were busy installing, building, and finalizing the construction. Every evening, there were "inspection tours" of the school to mark its progress, "at times quite visible, at other times quite hidden."

Before long, the community got a taste of southern hospitality and warmth from neighbors and benefactors. Especially welcome was a daily supply of milk from the Harvey Dairy, as well as a generous supply of ice cream from Hensler's Creamery and "daily bread" from Sunbeam and Blossom Bread companies. There was no charge for these lavish marks of goodness, which continued arriving throughout the first weeks. Needless to say, such generosity created good relations, resulting in profitable business partnerships at a later date.

On September 1, twenty–one novices arrived from Goffstown, New Hampshire, and Highland Mills, New York. Their youthful energy was welcome for the heavy lifting and back–breaking chores ahead. From 4:00 to 8:00 PM they arrived, making their way gingerly through the red clay around the building, hiking up the skirts of their habits, and changing into their oldest shoes or boots! Two dormitories of curtained cells had been prepared for them by the pioneers. Here, novices and postulants were to gather, sleep, and pray until their quarters were complete. M. St. Martial (Evelyn) Massé, the novice director, arrived that day as well, along with M. St. Denis (Fedora) Jutras, sewing mistress and sacristan. Perhaps most welcome of the newcomers was Sister St. Flavie (Doris) LaBrèche, a very fine cook—but as yet without a kitchen! Her culinary skills were tested by the small, electric double–burner that served as stove for feeding a group of thirty daily for a few weeks. Soup and sandwiches were the most frequent menu items, enjoyed by all. In the morning, novices breakfasted on rolls and coffee in the second–floor sewing room.

On September 2, the community gathered for their first Eucharist celebrated in Hyattsville. It took place in the school principal's future office, the only available room for such a gathering. The novitiate altar from Goffstown was set up; the annalist commented that the "congregation overflowed into the corridor, with more overflow than anything." Fr. Matthew, ST, one of the priests from the Missionary Servants' Seminary behind the Regina property, presided. Thus began a long and grace-filled friendship with the neighbors "up the hill" who became friends and brothers to the Regina community. From then on, one of these men arrived daily to celebrate daily and extraordinary liturgical services.[258] Within a few days, the provisional "chapel" moved to a larger classroom space where there was room for everyone. On September 4, seventeen postulants arrived throughout the day to begin a new life in an unfinished home. Any homesickness they may have felt was quickly dispersed by the tasks they soon learned to master: unloading trucks and setting up furniture, cleaning windows, washing and waxing classroom floors, and moving hundreds of desks into allotted class space.

September brought daily signs that the buildings were nearly ready for occupancy, despite the presence of almost fifty sisters going about their daily lives in the midst of workers with sawhorses and tools, and red clay dust appearing everywhere. The dining room was finally ready, except for the tile flooring, and everyone enjoyed sitting down to sandwiches and ice cream, as the kitchen furnishings had not yet arrived. With her skill and patience, Sr. St. Flavie provided one hot dish per day, mostly a nourishing soup or stew prepared on her portable burner. The long refectory tables were delivered in mid–September, and a few days later, tile flooring was installed. Sisters from New England and New York, assigned to serve as faculty or community service staff, arrived to complete the community of seventeen professed sisters. On their nightly tours of the buildings to mark all signs of progress, M. St. Vincent Ferrer would open her arms wide and exclaim enthusiastically, "Oh, my dream is coming true!"

School Opening, Shocking Death

On September 19, ninety–one freshmen entered the doors of Regina High School, with its fresh scent of drying paint and newly waxed floors. It was a disappointing number, because almost a quarter of those accepted had transferred to other schools, discouraged by the appearance of Regina's unfinished construction. The daring ones who came showed courageous and adventurous spirits. They proudly displayed their tan and brown uniforms with the new school seal, *Caritas et Veritas*, emblazoned on their jackets. These first "Reggies" would trace the path for hundreds to follow after. On opening day, however, they were newcomers, participating enthusiastically in orientation and organization sessions within a school environment as new to their faculty of five sisters as it was to them. In addition to M. M. Armand Desautels, the faculty included M. St. Hilda (Eva) Beaulieu, for business subjects; M. St. John of the Cenacle (Rolande) Robillard for religion and French; M. St. Louis Kenny for social studies and drama; and M. Cecilia Dowd, for English, journalism, and music. Creative energies and endurance on the part of both groups would be tested in the coming months.

Wednesday, September 21, began for M. St. Vincent Ferrer with a visit to the chancery, where O'Boyle granted her permission to have a cemetery on the property. Returning home at lunch time, she was delighted with the news that there was hot water at last. After the meal, she toured the convent to check on shower curtains, and began to feel ill. Blaming her discomfort on having eaten too hastily, she went to her room but was unable to lie down because of severe chest pain. A local physician was called, and he decided to administer a bedside cardiogram. Its results indicated the need for immediate hospitalization, an option M. St. Vincent Ferrer did not favor. While waiting for an ambulance, she rose from her bed and collapsed, gasped a few times, and stopped breathing. Her great heart had stopped, felled by the disease she had suffered for years. In the ambulance, there were attempts to revive her, but to no avail. M. Mary Aquinas (Mary Agnes) Doyle, her assistant, sent a circular to the province on September 24 recounting the details of the sad day. She indicated that "we are all sure she was already dead, that she had died in the unfinished home of her dreams." Msgr. Spence, who had rushed to the hospital at the news and anointed her, offered to direct all the funeral arrangements, including the use of his parish for the Mass. He gently reminded the three grieving councilors: "You know what Mother wants you to do. You must carry on the work." The shock of their loss reverberated in the province and at the school, including the contractors and workers. Religious communities and clergy in the area offered their sympathy and support, as did O'Boyle, who promised to preside at the funeral liturgy.

Monday, September 26, the solemn Mass of Requiem took place at St. John Baptist de la Salle Church at 10 AM. In the presence of O'Boyle and a large number of clergy, religious, and lay people, the Religious of Jesus and Mary laid their beloved provincial to rest after her long and arduous labors. The mourners included some of her immediate family members, forty-one novices and postulants who were given special permission to attend, and the student body of Regina High School, a living memorial for which she had laid down her life. A year later, her remains were transferred from Mt. Olivet Cemetery to a permanent resting place in the Regina cemetery, beneath a large crucifix donated by her family. During their sad days of mourning, it became a nightly ritual for the community to gather and recite the *De Profundis* in the provincial's memory, closing with one of her favorite hymns, "Mother of Christ." The singing brought her back among them again, with her "off-key but on–trust" lines: "When the voyage is o'er / Oh stand on the shore /And show him at last to me."

Carrying on the Work: Dedication and Open House

The voyage was far from over for the pioneer community, who were left to continue setting up new provincial headquarters and directing a high school that had just opened its doors. Separations, celebrations, and "firsts" followed in swift succession that first year. In mid–October, M. St. Martial left for a two–month stay in Rome, with a thirty–day retreat followed by an intensive program of preparation to be novice director. M. Consolata (Rita) Valcourt was named as the interim director, having just returned from her tertianship renewal in Rome. On October 21, the first Mass was celebrated in the convent chapel, in remembrance of the deceased provincial. An inaugural issue of the school paper, *The Reginalog*, appeared at the end of October. Articles included remembrances of M. St. Vincent Ferrer, news of student council elections, plans for the Drama Club, and a "Sports Special" with news of physical education activities in expectation of the gym's completion by November. On the last page was a full calendar of school events through the Christmas season, including the Glee Club Concert on November 22, at which the official school song was introduced. It would be sung from bleachers, on buses, at assemblies, and at alumnae events for decades to come: "Regina High, proudly we acclaim you; / Within your peaceful realm / Joyful we live and serve."

The first Thanksgiving at Regina was a true feast, made possible by the newly arrived kitchen appliances. The school library flooring, recently laid down, still needed washing and waxing; what better time for novices and postulants to do the job prior to all the community festivities? As the novitiate annalist reported, "The work made us appreciate the turkey and fixin's all the more." Despite their early challenges, the sisters expressed deep gratitude for the generosity and kindnesses offered them since their arrival. Another celebration—the dedication and open house of the complex—was just around the corner. Late in November they received word that M. St. Conrad (Leonie) Normandin was appointed the provincial. Her arrival was set for December 10, the eve of the dedication.[259]

A preliminary open house took place on December 3 for all the religious of the archdiocese, and on the Feast of the Immaculate Conception, the chapel pews arrived and were installed. The morning of December

11 dawned bright and cold; convent accommodations were filled with dozens of visiting Religious of Jesus and Mary from New England and New York. In the afternoon, the archbishop presided over an impressive ceremony of blessing every room in the convent and school and dedicating the building to the honor of God. A crowd of over 600 gathered in the auditorium, including clergy, families of the sisters, students and their parents, and neighbors from the area. In his opening address, Spence described Regina as "a blend of the time–tried and the new."

He praised the qualifications of the faculty and the aesthetics of the building as characteristics of Catholic education in the archdiocese. In his brief remarks after Benediction at the end of the ceremony, O'Boyle reminded the audience that Regina was a monument to the memory of its late foundress who had given her life for it. Following the ceremony was the official open house for all visitors, who were welcome to walk through the entire complex, including areas usually reserved for the sisters. At the end of the day, the community had welcomed over 1000 people who rejoiced with them at the completion of this daunting project.

As the eventful year drew to a close, the Regina Drama Club performed an operetta and one–act play for the Christmas season. They would present *Little Women* in February, under the direction of M. St. Louis, their moderator. Students gathered for a special Mass in the convent chapel on December 22, at which they presented Christmas offerings for the poor. The community welcomed the Lord's Nativity with a sung Midnight Mass and traditional French *"reveillon,"* followed by two morning Masses. The holiday season, with its relaxing schedule and festive gatherings, provided the community with much–needed respite.

Highlights of the First Decade

Early in 1956, the community celebrated a clothing ceremony for twelve postulants, presided over by O'Boyle. That summer, sisters traveled away for study or arrived from other houses to take courses at Catholic University. In July, many sisters traveled to participate in the initial province jubilee celebration, with Mass and banquet. At the end of the annual retreat directed by John W. Chapman, SJ, eight second–year novices made their first profession on August 14. The original February date had been postponed due to the unusual nature of circumstances during the transition. They were joined for the ceremony by three sisters taking final vows in the Congregation. In September of 1956, M. St. Louis was appointed Regina's second principal, a post she would fill with skill and vision for the next decade. Inspectors from Catholic University came to evaluate the programs of instruction for Regina and the province Thevenet Teacher Training Institute established earlier for sisters in formation. Their report was supportive and provided helpful recommendations toward affiliation of the Institute with the university, granted in 1956. M. St. Louis and her staff prepared materials toward the school's Maryland State accreditation, approved in 1958.

The opening of the third academic year at Regina showed an increase in students, with 132 freshmen and a faculty of thirteen, two of whom were laywomen, hired to direct the drama and physical education programs. The Regina Mothers' Club, begun in the school's first year, evolved into a Home and School Association by 1958, with fathers fully incorporated. Over forty percent of the fathers were government employees; others were in business or technical professions. The majority of Regina's mothers were homemakers, some were clerical workers. Meeting five times annually, the purpose of the parents' group was for "mutual understanding and cooperation" between the families and school. They organized and participated in the annual "Back to School Night" programs. With time, the Association became active in fundraising and support of programs in the province as well as the school.

The following month, the first organized juniorate program began for the newly professed sisters, under the direction of M. Consolata Valcourt. For several months, sisters would receive intense spiritual, theological, and academic formation. Thirty–one sisters formed the Regina community. Seventeen novices and thirteen postulants were following a formation program that included philosophy and theology courses given by Jesuits from their seminary at Woodstock College near Baltimore. The canonical visit of the superior general, Rev. M. del Rosario, took place at year's end. She arrived in Hyattsville in time to celebrate Christmas; on December 27, 1957, the Regina Glee Club dedicated their holiday concert to her. In her meetings with the province leadership, the superior general stressed the need to free younger sisters to follow the juniorate program, as well as complete their degree requirements for teaching. She raised the possibility of opening a college in the area, something the province had considered in the past. She supported the hiring of more lay teachers to facilitate sisters' participation in the congregation's juniorate and tertianship programs. To alleviate some personnel requirements, she suggested closing one of the parish schools to allow for adequate professional preparation of the sisters, who were often underprepared and overworked. While this seemed a feasible decision, the process would be delayed by several years, as it always involved dialogue with clergy and parishioners who were not ready for such a major change.On June 3, 1959, Regina High School celebrated its first graduating class of seventy young women, with O'Boyle in attendance and Spence giving the commencement address. In four years, zealous principals and faculty could point to a growing student body of over 400, a successful academic program, vibrant student council, several extracurricular programs, the *Reginalog* newspaper, and *Tiara*, the school's first yearbook. Two years later, the Drama Club performed "Cyrano de Bergerac," directed by Ms. Charlotte Renna, one of three lay teachers hired that year. In September of 1961, the community roster included forty–three sisters, with nine in the juniorate program under the direction of M. St. Rose (Rita) Bergeron. The Thevenet Institute, whose curriculum was also affiliated with Catholic University, was offering college courses to those in formation, with M. Mary Catherine Kenny as its new dean.

A Building Campaign and "Singing for a Home"[260]

From the outset, the province leadership had hoped to build a free–standing chapel behind the rotunda entrance, but sufficient funds were lacking. The number of entrants was encouraging, although the influx had already created some overcrowding. Clearly, the community would soon need more living space and larger novitiate quarters, along with the long–desired chapel building. Inspired by Mr. George P. Morse, attorney for the community and father of a novice from Regina's first graduating class, several parents and friends of the sisters formed a Community Development committee in October of 1960. Its purpose was to organize a building campaign in the province. They also aimed to raise funds from proceeds of a recording by the Jesus–Mary Choral Group, a choir of postulants, novices, and junior professed that included professional musicians and singers.[261] By November, the committee decided to have the group record fifteen of their songs and sell them throughout the province. Local committees were organized in New York, Fall River, Woonsocket, and Providence. The central committee worked out of Hyattsville, assuming responsibility for publicity and promotion of the record in local and diocesan papers. From that time on, advertising and publicity of the recordings became one of the ministries of M. Mary Immaculata (Margaret) Paul, journalism teacher and faculty adviser for Regina's award-winning newspaper and yearbook.

Thousands of letters were mailed announcing the release of the LP album for November. An initial contract was signed with Empire, a company in Takoma Park, Maryland, a convenient location for the group to record their album. A small group from the committee made promotional trips to communities and schools of the Northeast, encouraging sales and publicity for the recording. Most of the seventeen singing sisters were from Rhode Island and Massachusetts; three were graduates of Regina. The official opening of the Community Building Program took place in the Regina Auditorium on December 2, 1960. With Archbishop O'Boyle and several local personalities in attendance, the Choral Group performed seven of the selections from *Patterns in Song*, which was formally presented for sale and distribution that Christmas. Upon hearing the group, Dr. John Paul, head of the music department at Catholic University, commented that "they are an inspiring group in their disciplined musicianship and seriousness of purpose . . . They bring joy to the heart." The large group in the novitiate provided a labor force for sending out various appeal letters. The annalist wrote that if the records sold well, "it could mean breaking ground for our new chapel before long."

Within a year, the group had a contract from Columbia—one of the largest recording companies—for a Christmas album, *Gesù Bambino*, which they taped from the convent chapel during three intensive days in May. By the end of November 1961, more than 17,000 copies were sold.[262] In her communication with the province, M. Mary Immaculata stated that while the main purpose of the project was to raise funds, "we have learned . . . that God has given us a tremendous apostolate which complements our daily tasks as educators." She commented on the privilege it was through their singing to let the larger world taste the "precious treasure behind the cloister door." As sales mounted, a Record Office was set up to respond to mail-order requests. In two weeks, more than 800 were mailed out. Where would it all lead? That remained to be seen.

The number of applicants for entrance to the community increased for the next three years, providing an impetus to fundraising for a freestanding chapel and expanded quarters. Appeals letters advertising the recordings went out regularly, aiming at a goal of $500,000. In February of 1962, recording sessions began for a third album, *These Things I Wish for You*. The Choral Group performed that summer at a concert to promote the forthcoming album, which was finalized in November. More than 15,000 promotional envelopes were mailed out, advertising it as a Christmas gift. By the end of 1963, two more albums were recorded, and the popularity of the "singing nuns" grew to national status. The long-term consequences of this publicity for the spiritual formation of junior sisters, however, raised concerns for general and provincial leadership. Moreover, the sisters from the original group were making profession and moving on to ministries in various regions of the province, depleting the musical talent pool in Maryland. While financial records for proceeds from the sale of albums have not been found, a brief statement in the Minutes of the Provincial Council for March 25, 1964 states that more than $300,000 would be available for the new construction.

Marywood: Brookeville, MD (1961 to 1966)[263]

Having considered a number of options for expansion, the province leadership assessed that their financial situation, including debts, pledges, and funds raised from the building campaign, prohibited any large-scale construction for a new novitiate or chapel. They made inquiries and visited numerous properties, settling on a historic stone mansion situated at 20015 Georgia Avenue, Brookeville, Maryland, a rural township about twelve miles north of Washington, DC. Over 200 years old, it had once served as the Brookeville Academy for boys, and later as a public high school. The building underwent several changes until the twentieth century; in 1930, it was bought as a private residence known as Cedarstone. Sold in 1941 to Dr. and Mrs. Mark V. Ziegler, the house was renovated and restored, including its gardens and gazebo. On September 8, 1961, the Religious of Jesus and Mary purchased the twenty-acre property, with buildings, for $120,000. It would serve as a provincial residence and juniorate, making additional space at Regina for community and novitiate needs. The sisters hoped that in time Brookeville could be the site for a new novitiate.

On September 9, the provincial began to reside there, along with M. St. Rose Bergeron, juniorate director, and M. M. Adrian Etzel, community driver. They would later be joined by M. St. Aloysius Frégeau, province treasurer, and Sr. St. Flavie, the cook. They spent most of that month preparing the house to receive a group of ten junior sisters. There was as yet no convent chapel, so the sisters attended daily Mass at the local parish, St. Peter's (Olney), a ten-minute drive from their house. The pastor, Rev. William J. Awalt, welcomed them graciously, giving them a key to the church for their use at any time. By October 1, their community number was complete; on October 13, they gathered for the first celebration of Eucharist in their chapel. On November 18, fourteen members of the executive committee for the building campaign spent an afternoon at the property and were impressed with its possibilities. On December 9, O'Boyle and several clergy arrived for the blessing of the house and benediction of the Blessed Sacrament, followed by dinner. They were impressed with the beauty of the property, now called Marywood. In September of 1962, the local community of Hyattsville became an autonomous entity, separate from the provincial community, with its own schedule, councilors, and budget. It was home as well to a growing number of retired sisters and those in the infirmary.

The sixties were filled with formation activities and studies for the juniors, and with the usual travel schedules for provincial councilors, three of whom still lived in Hyattsville. In 1962, M. M. Loretta (Thérèse) Benard was appointed juniorate director. The peaceful setting of Marywood offered junior sisters a rhythm of community prayer, meetings, classes, and outdoor activities. Likewise, it replaced Hyattsville as the site for "probation," a month's preparation for sisters making final vows. In addition to directing the changes in sisters' assignments, the provincial leadership was asked in 1962 to send personnel to the Western–American Province to bolster communities and schools in Texas and California.

By 1963, the community had purchased an adjoining property with a small cottage on the grounds, to serve as sleeping quarters for the overflow of junior sisters expected that September. Moreover, the house offered space for a small kindergarten, opened in September of 1963, under the direction of M. Martin (Alphonsine) Langlais. Discussions for the building of a novitiate continued. The leadership initiated an assessment of Marywood's sewage and water systems, which were not connected to any public service. On January 14, 1964, during another visit from the superior general, a meeting took place at which architectural plans for a new construction were examined in light of the province's general financial status. Because of extraordinary expenses foreseen to provide access and sewage at Marywood, "It was decided the building would not be erected in Brookeville, but in Hyattsville."[264]

Not long after, the province leadership was invited to participate in a residential intercongregational Religious Educators Center on the campus of Trinity College, situated near Catholic University. It was an attractive offer for the Religious of Jesus and Mary, one that could provide first-rate degree programs for juniors.[265] If a participating congregation could provide a professor for the faculty at Trinity, there would be no cost for their sisters' tuition. That year, three sisters were assigned to doctoral studies in view of future participation in the program. At Trinity, efforts were multiplied to obtain government loans to fund their project, and a first group of junior sisters from five congregations met in September of 1966 for an orientation. With the changes effected by the Second Vatican Council, however, educational opportunities for women religious had opened up to include professional preparation in secular colleges and universities. Plans at Trinity for a separate sisters' educational program were tabled. The property at Brookeville was put up for sale. The province leaders decided to build an extension to the Regina property, known from then on as the "Provincial Wing." In June of 1966, the Council Minutes report receipt of $100,000 for the sale of the Brookeville property to Mr. Joseph Reitman, of Maryland. The amount would be used to reduce the debt on the provincial house.

Statistics of the Eastern–American Province were encouraging. In 1964, there were twelve houses with 316 sisters, seventeen novices and nine postulants. Two–thirds of the sisters were under the age of sixty. They directed six secondary schools and nine parish elementary schools along the Eastern seaboard. Two years later, in the wake of conciliar renewal, the Congregation suppressed its class of auxiliary sisters, encouraging educational and professional training opportunities for them. While this was a welcome and overdue change for the American provinces, it also created additional financial burdens as they began hiring more lay personnel for household tasks like cooking and cleaning.

New Provincial Wing (1966)

At a General Chapter of the congregation in the spring of 1965, M. St. Conrad was elected to the general council. On June 3, the superior general sent a letter appointing M. Mary Catherine Kenny as the new provincial superior; she assumed her responsibilities in July. Work on the new wing at Regina was in progress, assuring the resident community that the meanderings of recent years were over. On Sunday, October 16, 1966, O'Boyle arrived to preside at the blessing and dedication of the new provincial headquarters, including a larger chapel space where Mass was celebrated with solemnity. A crowd of 400 attended the ceremonies, followed by an Open House and reception. Regina High School Alumnae provided hospitality assistance. Connected to the original convent building, the wing boasted several amenities: across from the chapel at the end of the main floor corridor were the spacious Thevenet Institute library; an archives room, several parlors, dining areas for the provincial councilors. The second floor held a lecture room, province offices, and bedrooms for the councilors. On the third floor, a conference room offered space enough to hold large meetings. In the basement, Sister Lilian (Rita) Rochon directed an art studio, a project that attracted adult students for classes in drawing and ceramics. As the new center of province events, the new wing would be used regularly in the next several years for provincial chapters, meetings, and conferences; for ceremonies, professions, and funerals; for community discussions and celebrations. The convent building had reconfigured spaces for a proper infirmary wing, a novitiate sewing room, and classrooms in the basement for the use of the high school, where numbers and programs had grown.

Regina High School:
Years of Growth and Challenge (1962 to 1989)

As the school's second principal and beloved history teacher, M. St. Louis brought to her leadership role the creativity, initiative, and discipline that would impact the school for decades to come. She established high standards of academic excellence for faculty and students alike. The epitome of a Catholic educator, M. St. Louis combined formidable instructional skills with humor and whimsy. In September of 1961, only seven years since Regina's opening, she initiated the project to seek its accreditation with the Middle States Association of Colleges and Secondary Schools. With a faculty of twenty–eight, ten of whom were lay teachers, M. St. Louis led the faculty committees through the intense self–study prior to the visit of the Evaluation Committee, held February 13 to15, 1962. The members of the team visited every classroom and teacher, sometimes twice; they carefully examined every nook and cranny of the building for a week, including its guidance and extracurricular programs. Their "care and feeding," their housing and travel, were the responsibility of the school personnel. In their final evaluation, they commended the school for having accomplished so much in a few years, but most of all, for the spirit of the Regina community and students: "It has been said that the effectiveness of a system of education is judged by its end product. The students . . . speak well for you. Their friendliness, spirit of cooperation, their love and loyalty are remarkable." The evaluation experience, while rigorous, was successful. It also created bonds of loyalty and friendship among faculty and staff. Regina received its prized Middle States accreditation that year, securing a reputation and academic future in a region where secondary education was highly competitive.

In February of 1966, M. St. Louis was appointed the province director of studies and supervisor of schools. After a decade of strong, inspirational leadership, her legacy was profound and lasting. Parents, teachers and students had come to see in her the personification of Regina's academic and religious ideals: truth and love. Her replacement at Regina was Sr. Janice Farnham, formerly a secondary–school English teacher in New England. With a graduate degree in philosophy, she had no experience in school administration; her four–year tenure presented a learning curve at many levels. Academically, Regina continued in the pattern set for the first decade, emphasizing academic excellence and participation in civic and community affairs. Athletic programs and student groups, including drama and the debate club, were thriving. Culturally, the sixties had inaugurated an era of Catholic experimentation, student protests, anti–war movements, a new feminism, and marches against racism. Innovation and change were in the air. In response to the times, Regina introduced course offerings in comparative religion and African–American history. Elective courses in German, Russian, and Chinese took place on Saturday mornings. The Vietnam War became personal for staff and students in February of 1968. Sgt. Roy O'Keefe, husband of Michelle Bourdeau, a math and science teacher as well as a Regina alumna, was killed in battle.

Early in April that year, following the assassination of Dr. Martin Luther King Jr, riots and fires broke out Washington. That event had a profound impact on students and teachers, many of whom gathered at the school to send food and supplies to those affected by the widespread destruction. The "Poor People's Campaign" initiated by Dr. King opened on on May 12, 1968. Thousands of indigent people, predominantly African American, arrived in caravans from the South and West for a March on Washington to demand from the government better wages and living conditions. The archdiocese encouraged private schools to offer space to the busloads on their way to temporary tent–shelters on the Washington

Mall, later named "Resurrection City." On May 11 and 12, Regina's gym became a cafeteria and shelter for more than 150 African–Americans and other minority groups en route from Philadelphia. Younger sisters on the faculty, students, novices, and juniors helped with meals for the crowd, offered childcare, and set up sleeping bags. The Trinitarian Brothers helped secure the property from intruders. Sisters and students heard the passionate rallying speeches of young black leaders to the hopeful people gathered in their gym.

Some sisters and parents resisted this use of the school property, fearful of its implications. A few neighbors protested what they perceived as an invasion, with unwanted media attention for which they were not prepared. Sixteen students at Regina that spring were African American. For them, the issues were personal. In school publications they had expressed strong feelings of sympathy with protesters. Issues of racism and discrimination were now real at Regina, and they could not be ignored. A new social awareness surged among the faculty and students. Within two years, it evolved into a full–scale service program in which students volunteered in various service programs in the Washington area.

To honor the inauguration of Earth Day, on April 22, 1970, staff and students of Regina held outdoor events, joining with millions nationwide to demand government action over pollution. This movement contributed to legislation for clean air and water protection. In May, Regina hosted a three–day "Experiment in Free Form Education" (EFFE) with active participation from neighboring Academy of the Holy Names. Student-led and organized, this non–traditional approach to learning incorporated interests of faculty and students that were not in the curriculum, and invited instructors from the larger community to participate. Courses were offered in banner–making, karate, ethnic cuisines, inner–city life, blues music, computer science, crochet, and the Arab–Israeli crisis, to name just a few! So well received was EFFE that other high schools began similar programs.

In 1970, Sister Janice was assigned to a theological renewal program in Rome. The school welcomed its first lay principal, Ms. Marcia Saunders, a teacher from the Academy of the Holy Names. In her three–year tenure, she initiated an innovative approach to learning with its flexible modular scheduling. The new structure offered more student responsibility and choice of courses, with forty percent of class time given to independent study. In their ten–year report, the Middle States visiting committee noted that such a move required courage on the part of faculty and administration. They commended the school for its high morale and the involvement of students in the preparation and development of the program. They recommended work on sustained curriculum development, possibly with a consultant.

In 1973, Regina hired its second lay principal, Ms. Nancy Cavey. A visiting committee report for the following year revealed concerns around the new model. The issue of "unstructured time" had begun to raise questions among parents and students; some spoke of losing a sense of community with the increased individualization of instruction. There was likewise confusion about grading and evaluation in the new system. In its report of April 1974, however, the committee once again commended the excellent dedicated faculty as "one of the greatest assets of Regina."

Adaptation and Evolution of a Tradition

With the onset of changing demographics, diminishing enrollment, and financial insecurity, in 1975 the province leadership appointed Sister Anne Magner, a Regina alumna (Class of 1961), as its sixth principal. Already familiar with the school as a student and former member of the English department, Sr. Anne was comfortable and effective in leading the school community with competence and clarity. Addressing concerns about flexible scheduling, she initiated a return to the disciplined structures of a more traditional model, while keeping what seemed best about the innovative modular system. For the next five years, Regina renewed its commitment to academic excellence and involvement with the larger church and civic community. Advanced Placement and Honors courses were added to the curriculum.

These were years as well when the Religious of Jesus and Mary faced major internal change, a change reflected in Regina's profile. In 1975, there were 487 students; the faculty numbered fourteen sisters and seventeen lay faculty. Five years later, the student population was stable, but the faculty picture had reversed: eighteen lay teachers and nine sisters. Province life and planning were affected by the recent departures of several younger sisters, and the Regina staff felt the impact. There were efforts to increase the number of sister–teachers, and a salary–scale was set in place for the entire faculty. Student demographics and religious preferences were likewise changing. By 1983, almost half of the 310 students were African American, and more than 100 were non–Catholic. Declining numbers and improved salaries meant frequent and necessary tuition increases for the school, which depended on tuition for its operating budget. Deficits were reported annually. Tuition costs grew from $650 in 1974 to $1800 in 1983, an increase that proved excessive for many Regina families and may have contributed to the continued decline in student numbers.

On November 29, 1980, many alumnae and former teachers gathered to mark Regina's twenty-fifth anniversary with a liturgy of thanksgiving and reception. The program of the event noted that 2400 young women had passed through Regina's halls into further education, professional careers, and home-making. Their high-school years had encouraged them to pursue Regina's motto, "truth and love," by committed administration, staff, and teachers, three of whom received Jubilee Awards at the November ceremony in recognition of their significant contributions.

In 1982, Sister Janet Stolba, another Regina alumna (Class of 1960), assumed the school's leadership with enthusiasm. She oversaw the planning and execution of a five-year development program, which included an office of development and intensive recruitment efforts. To address the challenges of the new decade, in 1981 the administration published a revised faculty handbook. Its statement of philosophy and its objectives state that the school community strove to develop intellectual faculties and to foster a sense of values based on Catholic teaching and the community's statement of mission. In its School Philosophy statement for 1981–82, Regina hoped to "foster concern for social justice ... and care for each other, for those outside the community, and to be of service to those in need." Open to all races and religions, the statement stressed a desire to "apply Christian values to contemporary problems." Another important shift in school policy is outlined in the role of the new Board of Trustees as its chief policy-making body, responsible for long-range planning, development, and budget approval. Composed of parents, professionals, and sisters, the Board worked assiduously with Sister Janet to secure Regina's future, including the creation and implementation of the five-year plan, and a project to include seventh and eighth graders, which they hoped would enhance the dwindling population and help balance the budget.

New Program, Dwindling Numbers, Financial Deficits (1987–89)

In December of 1986, Sister Janet sent a memo to the school community announcing a new program for twenty gifted and talented students of seventh and eighth grades. Approved by the Board and province leadership, the program would be underway by the following September. The target population was to come from Catholic feeder schools, and applicants would need to demonstrate advanced abilities in reading and math. In addition to academic ability, they would be selected for superior motivation, creativity, and "identifiable personal interests." The enriched curriculum was to include foreign languages, laboratory sciences, music, and art. It would offer advanced instruction to prepare students for Regina's honors programs, taught by its faculty. Under the leadership of Dr. Robert Ledbetter, the school's academic dean, the program was designed to break new academic ground in girls' education, easing pressure from peers that might dissuade them from excelling in academic areas. Several positive articles appeared in diocesan and area newspapers. Applications arrived, interviews took place, and in September of 1987, fourteen eager seventh graders were enrolled in Regina's innovative program. Tuition was set at $3000. Despite a hopeful and creative start, the program hardly got underway. The next year brought critical budget issues and concerns about Regina's future and its possible closing. With the exception of the 1989 graduation program, listing fifteen eighth–grade graduates, there are no extant records or reports of this project.

On January 5, 1988, a special meeting took place in the school library to discuss concerns about the ongoing deficit, capital outlay needs, and "steps that must be taken to make Regina financially sound." Representatives of the province leadership, including Mr. Gerald Amelse, the province business manager, were in attendance, as well as Sr. Janet Stolba and the president and finance chair of the Regina Board.[266] After several years of deficit spending and taking out large loans to cover operating expenses, the school faced an uncertain future. That September, the Adelphi Friends School leased classroom space in the buildings. Yet, Regina's drastically cut projected budget for 1989 indicated a deficit of over $100,000. There had been several unsuccessful attempts to raise funds and stabilize the school's financial situation, with herculean efforts on the part of Sister Janet and the faculty, the provincial council, the Board, alumnae, along with substantial loans from the congregation's headquarters in Rome. A series of meetings took place, exploring alternative programs that included substituting province sponsorship rather than ownership of the school. Facing its own financial concerns, the province leadership decided to withdraw all financial support of Regina within a year. They requested that the school be separately incorporated. The province was willing to repay loans made to the school and cover costs for major repairs to its roofs. A letter was sent to the province informing sisters of the serious situation, despite the untiring efforts of many to turn things around. The Board faced their own decision: whether or not Regina could continue as a girls' secondary school. On December 20, 1988, Ms. Sonia Leon Reig, Board President and alumna, wrote to Sr. Eileen Reid, the provincial, with a report of the latest Board meeting. It stated that they had regretfully come to a difficult decision: "we are unable to prepare a tuition–funded balanced budget" that would provide quality education at Regina. The Board hoped to explore further options, but these would not include a fully funded budget for the near future.

January of 1989 brought a flurry of meetings with parents, faculty, board members, and province leadership. At the Board Meeting of January 4, after a lengthy review and discussion of matters that had been frequently revisited, the Board presented a motion to close Regina in May of the current academic year. By mid–January, the provincial council sent a unanimous recommendation to the congregational leadership that the apostolic service at Regina High School be terminated, due to "progressively declining enrollment, increased financial deficit, and province assets placed at risk." Painful and difficult as it was, the decision was a necessary one. Rumors had already spread that the school's closing was imminent. It became part of a years–long pattern of girls' high school closings in the archdiocese: Holy Names Academy in 1988; Notre Dame Academy, All Saints, and Holy Spirit in 1989. The remainder of the academic semester would be spent communicating with sisters, officials, parents, and high school administrators.

At the end of January, Sr. Eileen sent a moving letter to the sisters of the province, and another to parents, staff, and alumnae to announce the closing, reminding them of Regina's thirty–four years of remarkable service: "All of us are deeply grateful for the expanding community of knowledge and love that Regina has become for the Church and society." She singled out the special contribution of Sr. Janet Stolba, the principal, as the embodiment of the best of Regina's tradition. She assured everyone that the enrolled students would find a welcome in area Catholic high schools. On February 3, 1989, a formal announcement was made to the public. For her part, Sr. Janet wrote to various constituencies of the Regina school community, thanking them for their services, contributions, and support. On March 20, she sent a poignant message to the alumnae. The sentiments reflected her experience both as an alumna and Regina's last principal. "I need not dwell on the deep and abiding sorrow in my heart . . . Rather, I prefer to think with joy of what the school has meant to its alumnae and what it will continue to mean as an abiding presence in their lives." She then invited them to join in the thirty–first and last of Regina's graduation ceremonies, to be held on May 30, at the National Shrine in Washington. Prior to that, several closing events took place: a Mass of Thanksgiving and dinner honoring past principals; Senior farewell and Awards assemblies; graduation services for grade 8, and commencement for fifty–seven seniors; and a final school picnic on the first of June. Catholic high schools in the area were generous in offering to admit Regina students to complete their high school programs.

On June 3, 1989, the Board of Trustees held a final gathering that included a liturgy of thanksgiving in the community chapel. In his homily, Reverend Milton Jordan reminded the members that "none of us is truly happy living with a decision that has severed a truly vibrant reality from the world . . . the life we ended was dear to us and so many others." Yet he also called them to rejoice that the Religious of Jesus and Mary, "a noble group of women," had dedicated themselves to the formation of young women and had become a part of so many lives in Adelphi and Hyattsville. In its thirty–four years, Regina had left a lasting mark and legacy.

In April of 1990, Prince George's County leased the property that housed the school, community, and provincial offices. It was a five–year agreement, at $400,000 annually, to be used for educational purposes, its most suitable use. During that time the Regina site housed sixth– and seventh–grade classes from local schools with buildings under renovation. The province offices, staff, and archives moved to the St. James Convent in Mount Rainier, Maryland, a neighboring suburb. Twenty sisters remaining at the Riggs Road convent were gradually relocated to the retirement and infirmary communities in New England. Late in May of 1991, the province celebrated a two–day "Farewell Pilgrimage" to Regina as a final tribute to its ministry and to the Religious of Jesus and Mary who had lived and served there. On October 3, 1992, a special liturgy took place at Mt. Olivet Cemetery, where the remains of the deceased sisters had been transferred from the Regina cemetery. On March 31, 1993, a sale agreement with the county was finalized for five million dollars, and the Regina site became Cool Spring Elementary School, a comprehensive program for students from kindergarten through grade 6. With forty–four classrooms for 900 students, the school has developed

a bilingual and multicultural program for 600 students, most from Spanish–speaking immigrant families.

Hyattsville, MD: St. Mark's Parish (1958 to 1977)[267]

Three years after their arrival in Maryland, the Religious of Jesus and
Mary accepted the direction of St. Mark's Parish School, also in Hyattsville and not far from Regina. The parish was new, and its pastor, Rev.
Louis W. Albert had asked for sisters to staff an elementary school under
construction. Two sisters, M. St. Rose (Rita) Bergeron and M. St. Michel
(Rita) Bellenoit, were assigned to teach at St. John's, Chillum, in view of
their future mission under construction at St. Mark's. On September 12,
1958, the newly finished school building opened for children of the first
four grades. M. St. Michel was the principal; teachers were M. St. Agnes of
Jesus (Ruth) Bell, Mary Martin Langlais, M. Martha (Estelle) Haché, M.
St. Charles Marie (Loretta) Roberts, and a laywoman. The teaching sisters
lived at Regina and traveled daily to the school until 1968, when they
moved into their new convent, erected behind the school. On January
21, the first resident community of eleven—formerly living at Regina—
arrived to begin their ministry on site at St. Mark's. Sr. Margaret Mary
Quinn was the superior; Sr. Catherine McIntyre became the school's second principal. The community was made up of younger sisters, including
a novice and Sr. Eileen Reid, a nursing student at St. Joseph's College in
Emmitsburg, Maryland.

On January 29, 1968, the first Eucharist was celebrated in the convent chapel. Various groups of sisters from other houses came to visit,
joining them for a meal or prayer. On February 11, the community hosted a Valentine open house and buffet supper for more than forty from
the Regina community, followed by another for the lay faculty three days
later. In April, the community was deeply affected by the rioting, looting,
and arson in the aftermath of Martin Luther King's assassination. The
annals describe the curfew in Washington and the presence of troops of
National Guardsmen and soldiers. Sisters traveled to Regina to help at
the emergency food shelter set up there. They spent several days packing
goods donated by local churches and students' families, which were sent
to distribution centers in the city. The widespread outpouring of generosity impressed the communities in Maryland and energized their efforts.

The official Open House at St. Mark's Convent took place in the afternoon of Sunday, May 19, when O'Boyle officiated at the prayers and blessed the house. Many parishioners visited the beautiful quarters to which they had contributed so much. The first summer found the community traveling and welcoming visitors from New England and New York. In September of 1968, they welcomed Sr. Mary Ellen, RSM, from Baltimore, and Sr. Rita, CSJ, from Minnesota to live at St. Mark's while they pursued graduate studies at the neighboring University of Maryland. This inclusion of resident sisters from other religious communities marked the beginning of experiences in intercommunity living and support that later became part of the sisters' lives and ministry in various parts of the province.

Sometime in the sixties, sisters' annual stipends were set at $2000. In January of 1968, the Religious of Jesus and Mary entered a new contract describing the responsibilities of both sisters and pastor. The community was to furnish "trained and qualified teachers," but the sister–principal would not teach. Sisters' duties were defined by their educational purpose and did not include janitorial work, sacristy duties, or counting parish collections. They would offer instruction in Catholic doctrine to public school students in the area. They would not, however, engage in fundraising for their community without the pastor's approval. Included in the parish's responsibilities were provisions for maintenance and utilities in the convent, including "the salary of a housekeeper." A notice of six months was stipulated for termination of the contract.

In October that year, the community annals described its participation in a weekend of renewal in preparation for the forthcoming Special General Chapter of 1969. Several sisters served on commissions to prepare position papers, summarizing their ideas on renewal; these would be synthesized with other reports to express the thinking in the province. The sisters appreciated an opportunity "to share personal reflections and insights which contributed to a greater understanding of renewal." Four of the community attended the Special Provincial Chapter held at Regina after Christmas, preparing proposals on spiritual and apostolic renewal, as well as adaptation of lifestyle. The annals report that realizing the diversity in the congregation, this community hoped "many decisions will be left to the provincial level." In 1966, a minor but significant change was implemented. The form of address would no longer be the traditional "Mother," but "Sister." Simple as it may have seemed, the modification received mixed reviews, as did the return to sisters' baptismal names. For many former students and parents, these symbolized unsettling changes to a beloved culture that signified stability and religious values. Mixed reactions from the public were common with many of the adaptations chosen by the Religious of Jesus and Mary as part of their renewal efforts, including the many iterations of religious dress!

Signs of Growth and Crisis (1970 to 1977)

November 1970 brought a surprise announcement to the parish and community. Fr. Albert, the founding pastor of St. Mark's, was transferred to St. John the Evangelist in neighboring Silver Spring, Maryland. Along with parishioners and students, the sisters were saddened at the departure of a pastor whose devotedness and concern, faith and courage, had inspired them all. Their new pastor, Rev. Richard A. Hughes, arrived soon after. He found a vibrant parish community and eleven sisters, part of a faculty of nineteen at the school, with 768 students. The numbers reflected considerable growth since 1959, when six sisters and two lay-women directed and taught 450 students. In 1970 the community proposed that two sisters be assigned to pastoral work rather than classroom teaching. One of them, Sr. Thérèse Benard, had graduate training in adult faith formation from Leuven, Belgium. Their ministry would include adult education and training of instructors, along with outreach to the poor, sick, and elderly in the parish. This expanded sense of ministry reflected a desire to extend the sisters' presence beyond the institutional setting of the classroom. Whether or not their idea became a reality is not reported; however, the new pastor did not seem to favor these or similar alternatives. Communication was a neuralgic point of tension with Hughes, whom the sisters perceived as lacking trust and confidence in the faculty "and a general disapproval of what we are trying to accomplish, especially in the Religion program." In an announcement to a Home and School Meeting, the pastor told parents he would be raising all class sizes to forty-five students. Neither Sr. Catherine nor the teachers had been consulted; for their part, they felt some classes were already overcrowded. His insistence on certain religious practices for the whole school, without considering other possibilities with the teachers, created confusion and negative reactions. A report on the school in March of 1971 sums up their concerns about the pastor: "lack of communication, consultation, trust and support."

That September, Sr. Catherine was transferred, and St. Mark's hired a lay principal, Ms. Marguerite D'Amico. Thirteen sisters formed the community, with nine serving at the school. The difficulties with Hughes had not been resolved. In December of 1973, Ms. D'Amico shared the annual visitation report from the Archdiocese, with detailed statistics, priority of needs, and space issues. There were seventeen full-time teachers for 656 students. Academic requirements were well maintained and records kept up to date. The faculty developed scope-and-sequence charts for all grades; these would serve as curriculum guides. The religion program was strong, with emphasis on involving students and clergy in school liturgical celebrations. Without the required building facilities, the school had no physical education classes. A fine arts curriculum was in the planning. General maintenance and cleanliness in the building was rated "poor," despite chronic complaints in former years. The final section of the report, "priority of needs," gives first place to the need for "pastoral openness to new ideas" and mutual trust and communication. In a December 10 letter to Rev. Francis Murphy, the archdiocesan Superintendent of Schools, Ms. D'Amico reported her frustration, along with that of the teachers, because the pastor "does not hear our needs, nor answer our requests." She indicated that the negative comments of the pastor contributed to a morale that was "at very low ebb." On reading the visitation report, Sr. Mary Kenny, province director of education, wrote to Murphy, supporting the principal's comments. Addressing the "unfortunate" situation of the sisters, she stated that they "would need the assurance that their contribution to the educational mission at St. Mark's has the potential for influencing policy in critical areas and furthering genuine Christian community." In response, Murphy met with Sr. Mary Kenny and the faculty to discuss the situation, but no decisions were made.

Thanks to funding from annual drives, construction began in April of 1974 for a new parish center to ameliorate space problems and address the need for additional classes and activities. The auditorium would undergo remodeling and construction toward a hoped-for new church building. The parish council sent out a long questionnaire to families concerning church and school activities in May. That June, after just one year as the Coordinator of CCD instruction at St. Mark's, Sr. Thérèse Benard was removed from her post, having been told by the pastor that adult faith formation was not included in her duties. Over the summer, Ms. D'Amico left St. Mark's and was replaced with Ms. Madelaine Ortman, a teacher and vice-principal at the school. At the end of the month, the faculty sent

Hughes a letter reiterating their concerns for good administration and the qualities needed in a principal. Moreover, they expressed appreciation of Ms. Ortman's abilities; they requested her permanent appointment as principal as soon as possible, to ensure a smooth transition. Their request was granted. With renewed energy, Ms. Ortman began to address academic and pastoral needs of students. In several memos, she reminded Hughes of the need to meet deadlines when sending reports and expressed concern over ongoing janitorial problems. Early in January of 1975, in a letter to the pastor, Ms. Ortman stated how distressing it was for her that he failed to appear at a scheduled weekly meeting with her, despite his stated desire to be informed on administrative matters at school.

On November 25, nine sisters at St. Mark's wrote to the recently appointed Archbishop, Most Rev. William W. Baum, who was to visit the parish early in December. Their letter reiterated former concerns for the parish community under the leadership of Hughes, and the "growing frustration and apathy" on the part of its laity. They mentioned the ongoing strained atmosphere between the school staff and pastor that had resulted in a communication impasse. They clarified that their letter was not in any way a personal attack on the pastor, whom they described as eager to serve his parishioners while failing to understand their needs. They were open to meeting with Baum during his visit to St. Mark's. The extant documents do not include any communication from him, nor is there a report of a meeting with him. The situation seemed to improve the following year, as did the financial situation of the parish, with higher tuition rates and increased salaries for staff.

In May of 1977, however, Ms. Ortman resigned, having been hired as principal at another school. The Religious of Jesus and Mary were not able to offer a sister to replace her. Two difficult meetings with the pastor took place on May 17 and 18. At the Home and School meeting there were serious divisions among parents, and the discussions were emotional and directionless. The meeting with faculty on May 18 was equally problematic. Two faculty members were permitted to serve on the search committee for a new principal, and two sisters were accepted. The pastor wished to choose a "person of his thinking" to serve as well. At the first committee meeting, Hughes presented his candidate, a priest and secondary school principal. Most of the committee was not impressed with his presentation or responses to their questions; they knew he was the pastor's personal choice in his hope that "religion would be brought back" to the school with a priest–principal.

After a period of prayer and discernment, on June 6 the local leadership of St. Mark's Convent met with Sr. Gertrude Bélanger, the provincial, and Sr. Mary Ellen Scanlon, director of education. Sr. Gertrude informed them that the sisters from St. Mark's would withdraw at the end of the current school year. While the contract stipulated a six–month notice, they hoped this could be resolved to the benefit of both parties. They communicated that decision to archdiocesan authorities, who were already aware of the existing conflicts and frustrations. While church leaders were sympathetic, they made it clear that nothing could be done to alleviate the circumstances. On Wednesday, June 8, Sr. Gertrude wrote to the pastor with the request "that you release us from our contract which was signed on March 8, 1968." She requested a written response as soon as possible, but it was communicated orally. That evening, at a Parish Council meeting, the pastor announced the sisters' withdrawal. The local superior, Sr. Rosemary Mangan, was the community's representative at the meeting. She explained their reasons for withdrawal from St. Mark's, adding that they were doing so with genuine sorrow and regret.

On June 9, the provincial sent a letter to the parents communicating the decision and indicating that Hughes had released the community from its contractual obligations. The letter was countersigned by the four sisters on the faculty. In closing, it reiterated the profound gratitude of the sisters: "It has been our joy to work with you in the education of your children." They asked for prayer, understanding, and support. Facing a situation of professional placement for the sisters, Sr. Gertrude contacted Rev. Aldo Petrini, pastor at St. John Baptist de la Salle Parish nearby, who said he would welcome Religious of Jesus and Mary to teach in his school, from which another community had recently withdrawn.

The St. Mark's parish bulletin for June 12, 1977, announced the news to the parishioners as something "none of us wanted to think about." It spoke of the several thousand children who had received the care and benefit of instruction from the Religious of Jesus and Mary. With reduced numbers, the sisters were discerning "where they can work more effectively elsewhere." Prayers and good wishes were expressed. By August of that year, a new community of seven religious brothers had moved into the convent, renamed "St. Mark's Villa." They announced an open house for late September. With little fanfare, the community of ten sisters took their leave, after nearly two decades of educational service at St. Mark's. Grateful memories of their ministry and mutual bonds of friendship were visible in the church for several years: the reconciliation room, with its statue of St. Claudine Thevenet, was dedicated in honor of Sr. Elizabeth "Betty" McGreevy.

Chillum, MD: St. John Baptist de la Salle Parish (1977 to 1996)[268]

Well-known to the Religious of Jesus and Mary since their arrival in Hyattsville, St. John Baptist had provided them with hospitality on several occasions, most importantly with an offer of the church for funeral services of their deceased provincial in 1955, when the Regina construction was incomplete. The church first opened its doors in 1951, and construction on the parish school and convent was ongoing when five Sisters of Charity of Cincinnati arrived to teach more than 500 children in September of 1952. Like other religious congregations of that era, their community numbers began to decline; by 1975, only two sisters remained serving at the school. Rev. Aldo Petrini, appointed pastor in 1971, made it clear that unless the congregation could provide a sister–principal, he could not meet the financial cost of their support. After twenty–five years of service, in the summer of 1976, the Sisters of Charity withdrew from the parish.

The school continued with lay leadership and faculty, but the convent stood empty. Sisters at Regina were familiar with the parish and its pastor. Some of them were hoping to experiment with smaller, less institutional settings. The empty convent at St. John's offered an ideal possibility. Sisters may have approached Fr. Petrini with their proposal, which he enthusiastically agreed to rent at a reasonable rate. In June of 1977, several Religious of Jesus and Mary moved into St. John's, which provided them a fully furnished residence and good location for parish ministry. The province community directory that year lists fifteen sisters residing in Chillum, with Sr. Eileen Reid as the first superior. Several commuted to Regina High School daily, others were graduate students. Sr. Elizabeth McGreevy taught first grade at St. John's, and Sr. Grace Manley became the parish coordinator of religious education. Sr. Natalia Mejia was a childcare specialist at St. Ann's Infant Home in Washington, while Sr. Mary Leonard Haché worked as a visiting nurse.

This community was in one of the first examples of a "new style" of ministerial presence for Religious of Jesus and Mary in a parish setting. Sisters lived in a rented convent or home setting, reflecting a lifestyle marked by community prayer and reflection, open communication, shared meal preparation, and household chores. Their apostolic service was diverse, including pastoral ministry and an educational service expressing a shared mission: "to make Jesus and Mary known and loved." At St. John the Baptist, the stated community aim included a phrase from the 1977 Province Statement of Mission: "We commit ourselves to a simple lifestyle in which mutual support and reconciliation are ongoing means of . . . vitalizing our shared mission." The sisters joined in parish liturgical celebrations and served as lectors and Eucharistic ministers. Overall, the Religious of Jesus and Mary were re–discovering their call to a common mission through diverse ministerial responses to local and diocesan needs.

The extant community annals are sparse, covering just one year from August 1981 through July 1982. They detail the travels and special occasions for the community, including the beatification of the foundress and a number of jubilee celebrations. The sisters welcomed many guests at their table, celebrated many liturgies to mark special occasions, and traveled extensively. These activities reflect an engaged and joyful group of sisters that included graduate students, who led busy apostolic lives within a well–planned community structure. With time, however, their numbers changed and diminished, as sisters moved to new ministries and communities in the province. By 1995, the Chillum convent was too large for the four Religious of Jesus and Mary in residence. A new pastor, Rev. Robert Richardson, was seeking someone to lease the space and pay a higher rent for its use. In May of 1996, three remaining sisters collected their belongings and community property and closed the doors of their beloved home in Chillum to move to a residence purchased in neighboring University Park. All three were from the original community at St. John's: Sisters Mary Leonard Haché, Grace Manley, and Margaret Perron.

Takoma Park, MD: Our Lady of Sorrows (1978 to 1990)[269]

In the spring of 1978, the province leadership approved opening a new novitiate house. With fewer numbers of applicants to the Religious of Jesus and Mary, the novitiate space had been allocated for expanded use for students at Regina. The convent at Our Lady of Sorrows Parish in Takoma Park was vacant, and Rev. Robert Wummer, the pastor, was happy to welcome a community of sisters to live there. Located two miles from Regina, off New Hampshire Avenue, the convent had three stories and a finished basement. In addition to a chapel, dining room, and living room with fireplace, there were nine bedrooms and additional storage space. Five Religious of Jesus and Mary arrived on September 7, 1978, to begin this new venture: Sr. Rita Ricker, vocation and Quest Volunteer director, along with four sisters employed at Regina: Rachel Croteau, Anne Egan, Cheryl Nichols, and Mary Ellen Scanlon. On the celebration of its feast day, September 15, the parish welcomed their new community with a special Mass and reception, when parishioners met the sisters. Sr. Rachel volunteered to teach in the parish CCD program as a service to the parish. At the first Mass in their convent chapel on September 19, the pastor "expressed his joy at having sisters occupy the convent" and thanked them for their witness in the parish. As they continued to settle in, members of the teen club arrived to paint rooms on the first floor. Furniture was moved from one of the small community rooms set up at Regina. Visitors arrived in quick succession, including some Quest volunteers from New York. Over the Thanksgiving holiday that year, there was an open house for sisters from the province.

Early in January of 1979, Sr. Margaret Mary Quinn arrived to serve as community superior and formation director for the single postulant, Ms. Joan Faraone, who had begun formation at St. John's, Chillum. Ms. Faraone was well known to many sisters, having spent six years as a teacher at St. John's in the Bronx. A second candidate, Ms. Cloe Charpentier, arrived in late January to begin her formation program. A nurse who had lived in the New York Christian Community, Cloe would work at Children's Hospital in Washington, and take courses in science toward a nursing degree. In March, Joan began her novitiate program, followed by a summer of teaching in a special program for challenged students. The formation group was complete in September, with the arrival of candidate Ms. Deborah LaFontaine, a nurse from DeLisle, Mississippi, who also had spent two years in the New York Christian Community. Nine members in all, the community set a schedule for twice-weekly Masses in the convent, and weekly community meetings. Those in formation attended the Baltimore–Washington intercommunity novitiate program with members of other congregations. They also visited the communities of New England, an exchange that proved mutually enriching and encouraging.

At Christmastime several went out caroling to the homes of families and friends nearby. On January 1, 1980, there was an official open house for friends in the area. Later in the month, a group of volunteers on a "winter Quest" arrived to serve at Catholic Charities for a few weeks. With the arrival of summer months, sisters in formation participated in

the summer Quest volunteer programs. In 1981, the community numbered nine, with the addition of two new candidates from St. John's in
Kingsbridge: Ms. Margaret O'Toole and Ms. Mary Louise Scanlon. During the Christmas season, special courses were prepared for those in
formation on the history and spirituality of the Congregation. By 1982,
there were eleven sisters, with three novices and a new candidate, Ms.
Patricia Brito, also from Kingsbridge.

The following year, a Christian Community opened on Quincy
Street, near Catholic University in northeast Washington, DC. Until 1987
it served also as a house of studies for sister–students, including those in
formation. Nevertheless, the declining pattern of applicants to the province persisted; by 1987, there remained only two women in formation.
With the closing of Regina High School in 1989 and the changes occurring as a result of that decision, province leaders decided to consolidate
the residences in the Maryland region and to close the formation house
in Takoma Park. From that time on, women who entered received formation in one of the houses of the province and participated in regional
intercommunity formation programs.

Having informed the pastor of the decision to withdraw on July
31, 1990, the sisters once again prepared to disperse. Three among them
moved to a row house in Northwest Washington, on 13th Street, to serve
as a Christian Community; two others formed part of the founding community of the new provincial residence at St. James Parish in Mt. Rainier,
Maryland. On May 26, the Takoma Park community gathered for one
last time to share a meal and memories; early in June, they had a farewell
evening celebration for friends, parishioners, and sisters who had lived at
Our Lady of Sorrows. Summer was spent packing, moving furniture and
personal belongings. On July 30, Sisters Janice Farnham and Lois Kimber
closed the doors on twelve years of residence, formation, and community
life. The "pilgrim people" described in the documents of Vatican Council
II became an apt description of the province membership as they lived
through these times of change and renewal.

Mt. Rainier, MD: St. James Parish (1990 to 2005)[270]

For over three decades, the Regina property offered ample space for provincial offices, activities, and archives. It had likewise provided a stable
welcoming community to host countless meetings, chapters, conferences,

and celebrations for the province. With its closing and the subsequent relocation of sisters, the focus of province leadership included locating adequate and appropriate space for living quarters and administrative offices. They found what they were seeking in a recently vacated convent at St. James Parish in Mt. Rainier, Maryland, about six miles from Hyattsville. Begun as a small mission church in 1908, St. James became a parish in 1946 and welcomed a large Catholic community, including a parish school, until 1978. That year the school closed and the Sisters of Notre Dame de Namur (SNDdeN) withdrew. In the following decade, the parish faced diminishing finances and attendance. By 1990, when the Religious of Jesus and Mary learned that the convent was available to rent, they approached the pastor, Rev. Peter Aliata. He generously welcomed their proposal and the prospect of having sisters living in the convent. The official transfer of the provincial offices and residence took place on July 9, 1990.

Four sisters formed the first resident community: Sr. Eileen Reid, provincial; Sr. Alice Coté, province treasurer and superior; Sr. Yvette Beaulieu, and Sr. Helene Dussault, staff secretary. Sr. Yvette worked at the Washington Theological Union as a librarian. In 1991, she was appointed province archivist, replacing Sr. Irene Rhéaume, and dedicated every Friday to archival management. The following year, the community had grown to six in number; by 1994, there was a full complement of eight sisters with diverse ministries in province administration and archdiocesan offices, as well as Sr. Helen Scarry ministering as Secretary for Women Religious in the archdiocese. One sister offered her services to the parish catechetical programs. An ongoing shared ministry at St. James was hospitality, as sisters from the province and international visitors came to Washington for meetings or tourism. Two new councilors were appointed in 1992 to oversee ministry and membership, as well as communications and formation. A third, Sr. Rosemary Nicholson, the regional councilor for houses of the West, lived in Spring Valley, California. A welcome announcement came from Rome of the canonization and beatification ceremonies for their foundress, Blessed Claudine Thevenet, and Sr. Dina Bélanger (M. St. Cécile de Rome), to take place in March of 1993. Thanks to the generous gift of a benefactor, seventy sisters from the province and a delegation of their associates flew to Rome for the occasion. A province celebration took place at Notre Dame Parish in Fall River, Massachusetts, on July 31.

In 1994, the St. James community had eight members. Two years later, a new provincial, Sr. Rosemary Mangan, began her leadership service and moved into St. James. The resident sisters there continued to provide supportive administrative services for the province as well as other ministries for the archdiocese. With continued demographic changes in the area, the parish suffered another decline in Mass attendance and financial support. In 2004, a new community of priests and brothers, members of the Institute of the Incarnate Word, were invited to staff St. James. Seeking to set up their formation house on the site, they moved into the convent the following year. The four remaining sisters from St. James rented a private home in University Park, Maryland, which they named "Miriam House." The administrative offices, since 2002 under the provincial leadership of Sr. Janet Stolba, were relocated to a small office park in nearby Riverdale, Maryland. In 2005, the province archives were moved to a rented storage facility. In December of 2007, the Religious of Jesus and Mary entered a loan agreement with the French Institute at Assumption College in Worcester, Massachusetts. It would house the historical section of their province archives in the D'Alzon Library on the campus. From this time on, the province offices were a pilgrim enterprise, moving as need dictated. The absence of permanent official headquarters was a source of unease and insecurity. At the same time, it offered the province leadership freedom to choose innovative and creative spaces for larger gatherings, meetings, and celebrations. Times had indeed changed since the sisters' arrival in Maryland fifty years earlier.

The Lure of the South:
RJM Missions in Alabama and Mississippi (1968 to 1986)[271]

Heeding the calls of the Council, and having witnessed the assassinations of national leaders and civil rights protests of the sixties, sisters of the province were eager to respond with action on behalf of social justice. They turned to inner cities and the rural South, where poverty and racism were written large. As early as 1966, there were calls for sisters to assist with urban summer programs set up by church authorities. Requests to M. Mary Catherine Kenny, the provincial, had poured in from New York and Washington "that we provide volunteers for inner–city apostolates." In response, fourteen Religious of Jesus and Mary were sent in the sixties and seventies as summer volunteers to programs in Providence, New York City, Washington, and the South. The "cry of the poor" was finding an echo in their hearts and lives and changing their style of service. It is probable that province leaders asked about possible apostolic sites from their friends and chaplains, the Trinitarians. As part of the province outreach to the South, M. St. James Marie (Janice) Farnham and M. of the Eucharist (Margaret Theresa) Guinan were sent in the summer of 1966 to volunteer at St. Bede's Parish in Montgomery, Alabama, where they directed a Bible School and lived in the parish convent with two sisters from the Missionary Servants of the Blessed Trinity (MSBT). Two years later, the Irish–born pastor of St. Bede's, Rev. Eugene O'Connor was assigned to St. Leo's Catholic Church in Demopolis, Alabama.

As a mission of the French colonists as early as 1817, St. Leo's had held services in homes and a small wooden structure until 1905, when Catholics built a church. It continued as a mission church until 1936, when it became a parish in the diocese of Mobile–Birmingham. Once settled in Demopolis, O'Connor wrote to the provincial on May 3, 1968, requesting two sisters for pastoral work and catechetical education at St. Leo's. Two Sisters of the Blessed Sacrament had recently retired and moved, leaving the small convent available. O'Connor wrote that it had three bedrooms, a small chapel, dining and living areas. He could provide a car for the sisters and a monthly stipend of $100. The apostolic work included catechetical instruction at St. Leo's and at three mission churches attached to it. Home and hospital visits were included in the sisters' ministry. O'Connor described the parish as having 150 white families with segregationist views, residing largely in rural areas. Churches and schools of Alabama were still segregated. He added that "the diocese is taking a stand on these matters now."[272] If the sisters came, "it would be the greatest boost in many a long day."

In her response of May 15, M. Catherine expressed concern that the congregation generally preferred four or five sisters at one site in order to "maintain some form of community life." She also raised the possibility of having sisters teach in local public schools, an idea that proved inappropriate at the time. In response to her letter asking permission to open the mission in Demopolis, Archbishop Joseph Toolen wrote on July 2, 1968 that he was happy to welcome new sisters. While describing the Catholics at St. Leo's as white and conservative, he indicated that there were several mission areas where the sisters would get the "chance for missionary work with the poor and with Negroes." He encouraged the sisters to be engaged in that type of outreach.

Early in September, the two first Religious of Jesus and Mary to serve in Alabama arrived: Sisters Norene Costa and Estelle Haché. Settling into their small, tidy house at 302 South Walnut Avenue, they were welcomed with gifts of food and other signs of southern hospitality by the good parishioners of St. Leo's. On September 12, one of the patronal feasts of the Congregation, O'Connor offered the first Eucharistic liturgy in the tiny convent chapel. Their letters and reports are filled with accounts of their home visits to people, Catholics and non–Catholics alike; of attendance at Baptist services; of relationships with African Americans. They drove regularly to the three mission churches, appreciating the close community relationships with clergy and sisters of other communities. They learned that "southern hospitality" was more than a popular description. In rural Alabama, it was an essential component of every encounter, and it helped the sisters overcome the loneliness they sometimes felt being separated from other Religious of Jesus and Mary. They appreciated the pastor's generosity; he was grateful for their work and open to their initiatives.

Within a year, however, Sr. Norene was missioned to Spring Valley, California. Sr. Estelle was joined by Sr. Mary Leonard Haché, her own sister, for the second year. A nurse–midwife, Sr. Mary Leonard had spent seven years in the Christian desert village of Mariahkhel, Pakistan, where the sisters had a dispensary. There was a hope that she might be able to work in a local hospital setting in Demopolis, in addition to offering health education in the parish and missions. For unknown reasons, that did not come to pass. In June of 1970, the parish bid farewell to these sisters. Sr. Mary Leonard was assigned care for the sisters in the province infirmary, while Sr. Estelle moved to El Paso, Texas, and resumed classroom teaching in the Southwest. That fall, a new pair of Religious of Jesus and Mary arrived to begin their service in Demopolis: Sisters Denis Jutras and Rose Alice Bishop. Since neither had a driver's license and a car was essential to their ministry, the first order of business for them was to take a driving course. For the next two years, they continued the catechetical and pastoral work begun by their predecessors in the parish. They also did pastoral outreach in missions of Uniontown, Eutaw, Greensboro, Camden, and Livingston, Alabama.

In a letter of July 14, 1972, M. Catherine wrote to O'Connor that two new sisters would be arriving in Demopolis at the end of the summer. Sisters Ursula Hamel and Annette Vanasse were "starting out with a fairly good idea of what is expected of them." Sister Ursula was an experienced educator, certified in remedial reading. She was hoping to focus on service to African-American children in need of additional reading skills or help with other subjects. She would continue pastoral ministry in the parish. A registered nurse, Sister Annette was a veteran of several years in India, ministering in the sisters' dispensaries for the poor. She was eager to fulfill earlier hopes of healthcare outreach by applying to the local hospital and working with local medical personnel there. She would likewise be a presence in the parish and participate on the pastoral team as often as she could. M. Catherine's letter stipulates that "the situation of these sisters will be a little different from that of their predecessors" and suggests a new contract with the parish might be in order.

In fact, they would be the last Religious of Jesus and Mary sent to the Demopolis mission. In 1973, O'Connor became pastor of a large parish with a school in Embrey, Alabama. At St. Leo's, Rev. Henry McDaid assumed leadership for two years, during which time the sisters tried new ways of raising social awareness among the parishioners. By 1975, yet another pastor arrived in Demopolis, Rev. Jack Ventura. There were tensions between him and one of the sisters, reinforcing the concerns of the leadership about the feasibility of keeping two sisters in the parish. On February 17, 1976, the new provincial, Sr. Gertrude Bélanger, wrote to Ventura that she felt obliged to withdraw the sisters from the mission. She concluded with gratitude to God for the privilege it was for the community to have served in Demopolis, "and for the beautiful collaboration among the priest, people, and sisters."

Since 1972, Sr. Laura Dulude had lived in Mississippi, sent as a missionary to help the local pastor of DeLisle, Rev. Abram Dono, ST.[273] The Missionary Servants had arrived there a decade earlier, replacing the Josephite priests who had served African-American Catholics in the area since 1922. Opened for Black children in 1927, the school was directed by the Trinitarian sisters, with whom Sr. Laura lived in nearby Kiln, where the same congregation staffed Annunciation Parish and School. A province bulletin for August of 1976 includes a letter from the provincial announcing a new community of Religious of Jesus and Mary in DeLisle. Four sisters were moving into the renovated former parish rectory on Notre Dame Avenue, to begin their ministry. Sr. Laura, a veteran in the parish, would have a teaching companion in Sr. Margaret Theresa Guinan; Srs. Annette Vanasse and Mary Coyne, both health-care professionals, were to dedicate themselves to nursing and healing services in the area. The sisters who worked outside the parish contributed to its ministry by assisting with community outreach, liturgical services, and religious education programs. Their stay in DeLisle, however, was brief. Within a year, the Religious of Jesus and Mary left the area, which saddened diocesan officials, who praised their service to Catholic education and expressed the hope that the community would return to Mississippi, where there was need for religious who wanted to serve poor and marginalized people, especially children.

On October 20, 1979, Austin Walsh, ST, the pastor at Annunciation Parish in Kiln, wrote to Sr. Gertrude Bélanger asking for sisters to staff the parish school.[274] The Trinitarian Sisters were withdrawing from the school at the end of the academic year. They would continue to offer pastoral services in the parish. Walsh had contacted Sr. Laura Dulude, asking her to return as principal; he had been impressed with the spirit and dedication of the sisters in DeLisle. His invitation was broad: in addition to classroom teaching, parish ministries for sisters would include religious education, health services, and parish visiting. The convent had room for seven sisters. In view of diminishing resources and schools having closed elsewhere in the province, the province leadership decided to consult the sisters in each community and engage them in discernment toward a decision. There was substantial support from province membership, because the ministry in Kiln offered new possibilities for community living and broader ministerial opportunities, especially among the poor. In a letter to the province on March 10, 1980, Sr. Gertrude announced that sisters would be sent to Annunciation School in September, with the hope that in 1981, five Religious of Jesus and Mary would live and serve in Kiln. Grateful and relieved, in June the pastor drew up a contract for the sisters employed at the school.

Early in September, three sisters arrived in Kiln to form the initial community of "Mississippi Missionaries." Sr. Margaret Theresa Guinan returned to the area as principal of Annunciation School, with its 125 students. A year earlier, the school had undergone a successful self-study toward state accreditation. Sr. Claire Lebreux arrived to be a classroom teacher. Another veteran of the area, Sr. Mary Coyne, offered nursing services at Coastal Family Health Center in nearby Biloxi. The sisters were all included on the pastoral team, another aspect of mission life in Kiln. Two Trinitarian Sisters and a Dominican shared the community's life and prayer as they ministered in the area. Intercommunity living had become an acceptable option for women religious whose ministries intersected for the good of a community they served.

Sr. Claire left after the first year, replaced by Sr. Lorraine Blanchette as kindergarten teacher. Sr. Mariette Dignard completed the group in 1981, arriving for a brief period to do practical nursing and health ministry in the parish. Notwithstanding much good will and creative efforts, by

1984 the parish team faced financial problems affecting the school. The Missionary Servants planned to turn the parish over to the diocese by 1987. Toward that end, in 1985 they withdrew funds that subsidized the school, leaving its future in jeopardy. They called for a school evaluation, in view of its foreseen closure; meanwhile, concerned parents rallied with a variety of efforts to keep the school open. Tuition was raised to $65 a month. The focus of the pastoral team for the future, however, was on lay formation and adult education.

In the fall of 1984, Walsh left Annunciation for another pastorate. He was replaced by Antone Lynch, ST, who knew and appreciated the work of the Religious of Jesus and Mary. That year, there were only two sisters serving in Kiln. Sr. Lorraine Blanchette, near completion for her degree in education, had become school principal; and Sr. Antoinette Gamache, who taught in a neighboring school. As members of the pastoral team, they served as Eucharistic ministers and participated in adult faith formation. For these two sisters, ministry in rural Mississippi was unfamiliar, requiring cultural and religious skills for which they were not adequately prepared. The pastor hoped to have an additional sister to direct religious education in the parish. The following year, tensions grew between him and the sisters, which he expressed at length in his correspondence. These tensions were summarized on November 18, 1985, in a letter to Sr. Vivian Patenaude, the new provincial: "There is a mismatch between the Religious of Jesus and Mary sent in ministry and the needs of Annunciation Parish." Lynch asked that the sisters withdraw from the parish; he did not request others to replace them. In further communication with the provincial, he expressed disappointment that there had been no attempt to discuss with him the issues raised. By the end of February 1986, he wrote that he did not "wish to pursue present or future ministerial personnel." While the bishop and diocesan officials offered the community other ministerial possibilities, it was clear that rural ministry to the poor in isolated situations required cultural preparation, along with specialized education and skills. On April 17, Sr. Vivian wrote to the province, announcing the termination of the Mississippi mission for the Religious of Jesus and Mary. The two remaining sisters would leave at the end of the academic year, bringing to a sad ending fourteen years of teaching and learning among people the sisters had grown to know and love deeply. While their hope for a lasting presence in the South was unfulfilled, their experience contributed to weaving fresh fabric for themselves and others.

The southern communities that first lured them revealed living threads for new patterns of living and serving.

10

Re-weaving and Re-woven

Tapestry for a New Age

Celebrating a Centenary: 1977–78[275]

As DUSK FELL ON May 23, 1977, several hundred guests joined scores of
Religious of Jesus and Mary for a solemn Mass of thanksgiving and "home-
coming" at Notre Dame Church in Fall River, Massachusetts. They had
gathered to mark the anniversary of the sisters' arrival in the United States
a century earlier and to usher in a year of programs, renewal days, alumnae
gatherings, and a major fund-raising project for the province. The presider
and homilist, Most Rev. Daniel A. Cronin, bishop of Fall River, praised the
service of the sisters in the United States, referring to the founding days
when they tended to "over 100 young women employed in factories . . .
and provided them with nourishment, comfort, and security." He prayed
that this good work begun by God at Notre Dame Parish would be brought
to fulfillment. There was great cause for rejoicing: from fragile beginnings
in 1877 with three sisters, the Religious of Jesus and Mary now numbered
275 sisters sharing a common mission from coast to coast. At Notre Dame,
they still directed the flourishing parish school. The academy and boarding
school had been closed a few years earlier. After major redesigning and
renovating of the entire third floor of the convent, it now served as a province infirmary and retirement center.

A year later, on a windy Sunday morning, April 20, 1978, Msgr.
Alfred Gendreau, pastor of Notre Dame Parish, hosted the closing Centennial Mass and banquet, attended by five bishops, forty priests, and

more than 1600 well-wishers from families, friends, alumnae from many
schools, and religious communities. Bishop Cronin again presided at
the Eucharist. Among the special guests were Bishop Thomas W. Lyons,
auxiliary bishop of Washington and longtime supporter of the community, who gave the invocation; Sr. Irene Léger, RJM, a member of the
General Council from Rome; and a delegation of sisters from Canada,
the "motherland" that sent so many forth to the New England mission.
Several Religious of Jesus and Mary sang and performed at the Mass
along with the parish chorale and folk group. At the banquet, the main
speaker was Dr. Ellen Roderick, a graduate of Regina High School (1961)
who had attended Stella Viae International School in Rome. Sr. Gertrude
Bélanger, the provincial, pointing to the sisters' ministries and new endeavors, thanked the many donors present for their support. Cronin and
civic leaders offered remarks and testimonials. Everyone agreed that the
festivities were a fitting conclusion to the centenary, an occasion to move
into the future with trust and faith.

The Call of Vatican II

If the centennial celebrations were occasions of joy and renewed hope,
they were also the culmination of a year's reflection on the previous decade. Earlier chapters of this book have referred to the tumultuous years
of the sixties and seventies and their impact on the local churches and
communities in the province. For the Religious of Jesus and Mary of the
United States, the era ushered in a period of unprecedented change, a
rollercoaster of events and experiences at once inviting and unsettling.
The years following the Second Vatican Council provide an apt setting for
this concluding chapter.[276] First, it aims to summarize the province's response to conciliar calls for a "return to the sources" and "*aggiornamento,*"
a transformed religious life in a renewed Church. Second, it outlines an
evolution in the sisters' spirituality, community lifestyles, and expressions
of their shared mission. Finally, it points to the power of their communal
hope as a resilient thread that "stays as everything else falls away."[277]

When the Council ended in December of 1965, it inaugurated an
exceptional period of reform and renewal in the Church and religious
life. For the American provinces of the Religious of Jesus and Mary—East
and West—it opened a heady time of experimentation, encouraged by
Church leaders and the "signs of the times" that they were called to heed.

There were 362 professed sisters; more than seventeen percent of them were newer members, with temporary vows. Twenty-seven novices and eighteen postulants comprised the novitiate community. The province was ready to engage both its youthful energies and mature experience in a vigorous, ongoing response to the Council's calls for change. Two conciliar documents had the strongest effect on the sisters: the Decree on Religious Life, *Perfectae Caritatis*, and the Pastoral Constitution on the Church in the Modern World, *Gaudium et Spes*. The first stated that the primary and highest Rule for religious was the Gospel of Christ. It insisted on a program of institutional adaptation and renewal that included continuity and change: "The up-to-date renewal of religious life comprises a constant return both to the sources of Christian life and to the primitive inspiration of the institutes and their adaptation to the changed conditions of our times" (No. 2). To this end, the Council mandated special chapters and meetings for all congregations to inaugurate the renewal process.

In the opening lines of *Gaudium et Spes*, the sisters heard a clarion call to seek, find, and follow Christ by engaging the contemporary world as their founding sisters had done: "The joys and the hopes, the griefs and the anxieties of [people] of this age, especially those who are poor or in any way afflicted, these are the joys and hopes, the griefs and anxieties of the followers of Christ. Indeed, nothing genuinely human fails to raise an echo in their hearts." The Religious of Jesus and Mary welcomed the Council's challenge and took its mandates fully to heart. Unhesitatingly, they embraced programs of liturgical, biblical, and spiritual renewal and undertook experiments in new styles of community living. Their apostolic commitments included a fuller engagement with the needs of their society. They rejoiced at the "new Mass" in English, with the priest facing the congregation. They welcomed the beginnings of women's inclusion in sacramental ministry; many trained as lectors and Eucharistic ministers. They found more freedom in new directives for personal prayer and shared recitation of the Liturgy of the Hours.[278] Most approved the gradual modifications of their religious dress into more contemporary styles that were "simple, poor, and modest." They were encouraged to question outdated practices and customs and to experiment with new ones. One sister recalls that when she first read the document on the church and the modern world, she wept for joy and hope, believing that its vision of the Church would soon become a reality! Many in the province shared that hope. They discovered with time that its fulfillment lay far into the future, along a path that exacted a high price of suffering and loss.

Chapters of Renewal: 1969 to 1972

The congregation's general leadership announced an extraordinary General Chapter of renewal, mandated by the Council for all religious, to be held in Rome from September to November of 1969. In preparation for this unique meeting, provinces were invited to form commissions and prepare documents with proposals on each of six major topics. These provided the agenda and discussion matter for special chapters in the provinces. At the preparatory province chapter for the American Province, held from December 26, 1968 to January 3, 1969, five delegates were elected to represent the province in Rome, a departure from a long-established custom of permanent "electresses" at chapters. Summer meetings took place at Highland Mills as preparation for the Special General Chapter. These comprised the "First Summer" of renewal sessions. With hope that the American experience could offer ideas at the international level, the delegates carried their proposals and position papers to Rome.

The second session of the special provincial chapter opened in Hyattsville on December 27, 1969.[279] The delegates reported on the General Chapter process and presented interim documents and "Norms" issuing from their discussions in Rome. These framed the two-year period of experimentation that followed. The provincial council set up a Religious Life Committee to assist local groups with implementing Chapter directives. A series of local and regional meetings then took place, designed to engage all the members in addressing the topics contained in the interim documents. They covered general areas of apostolic religious life: nature and spirit (charism), community life, prayer, formation, and government. The area of apostolic ministry was not included on the agenda at this time. Delegates at this second session, however, chose to name all houses of the province "mission centers." This decision reflected a deeper awareness that as apostolic women religious, their mission was fundamental to all aspects of their lives. The specific residence where sisters lived was a center from which they were sent on a shared mission, regardless of their individual service. In her opening address, M. Catherine Kenny, the presiding provincial, had set a challenging tone: "God is pushing us toward freedom, and some of us are afraid to accept it . . . Rules which are not relevant to contemporary situations must be adjusted. We must free ourselves from restrictions that hamper us in the labor of our apostolate." Thus began a two-year process of renewal toward eventual revision of their Constitutions.[280]

Working with a post-chapter committee, Sr. Mary Kenny, director of education, led an in-depth evaluation and assessment of the twelve schools in the province. A special committee on retirement and pre-retirement worked toward a province plan for these areas. The words of Martin Buber, "All real living is meeting," aptly describe this period of dialogue, questioning, and exploring options for the future. In addition to chapter committees, there were gatherings of age groups, regions, formation personnel, local and province leadership. These were the initial years for "experimentation" with smaller communities, styles of prayer, changes in religious dress, creative models of governance, and apostolic outreach. A number of sisters participated in national and international programs for renewal. In 1970, Sisters Janice Farnham and Rosemary Mangan were sent to take part in the first Apostolic Religious Communities (ARC) program in Rome.[281] These developments energized province members, but statistics for this period also revealed institutional diminishment and loss. A number of schools had closed or were facing closure. Several younger members were leaving the Congregation, a fact that created more pressure on those teaching in the schools. As a result of province reorganization, eleven sisters in the West chose to return to their home province of Mexico, while six in the East decided to go back to Canada.

From April 12 to 18, 1971, delegates gathered again for a province chapter meeting. They elected five of their number to the coming General Chapter, which would include election of new general leadership. In addition to M. Catherine Kenny, the provincial, Sisters Eugenia Castonguay, Agnes Desautels, Janice Farnham, and Rosemary Mangan formed the delegation from the States. The chapter finalized its documents and proposals for renewal, issuing from their period of experimentation. Remarkable for its brevity and originality, the United States province statement of priorities—distilled from its "nature and spirit" document—reflects a new self-awareness as an "essentially apostolic community whose special mission is to make God known according to the charism of Claudine Thevenet." It stresses the conviction of a shared mission expressed by a diversity of service, and the need for a supportive community of love.

Among the reports and documents the province sent to Rome for consideration was a four-page assessment of apostolic "Goals, Resources and Needs," prepared by Sr. Mary Kenny and the evaluation committee. Referring to a questionnaire sent to every community, the report notes the "deep effects that the whirlwind of change in the Church and world have had on us as a community." It asks whether "our apostolates are designed to meet yesterday's problems" and expresses a concern about the province schools, which were struggling for survival. There were signs that parish schools were foundering nationally, partly because of the exodus from their communities of so many teaching sisters. Recent experiments with regional elementary schools in Rhode Island seemed to offer some promise, as did schools with diverse urban populations. The province's high schools were at a crossroads, based on shifting demographics and the quality of their programs. Some sisters had begun serving in diocesan schools, where they taught and shared with members of other congregations. Others moved into pastoral ministry and community outreach, services with opportunities for a broader educational service. With each change, the province moved gradually from a private, self-sufficient educational network to more collaborative ministry with others. These were new times, calling for novel approaches. One of these was the founding of Thevenet Montessori School at Highland Mills in 1971, highlighting the importance of early childhood development. Begun in the basement of the convent, Thevenet Montessori grew and flourished well into the twenty-first century.

The General Chapter of 1971 met from August to November. Its sixty-plus delegates represented diverse cultures of five continents, and their experiences of conciliar renewal were equally diverse. It became clear that opinions on the "how" of renewal were as varied as the number of sisters in attendance. Few delegates knew each other, and most were unfamiliar with cultures other than their own. Thus, the process was slow and tedious, made more so by the diversity of languages despite some simultaneous translation. The work entailed long hours of recording and reporting. Technology was limited to telegrams, mimeographing, and unreliable postal services. Sisters worldwide engaged the chapter as they could and received information from letters, weekly reports, and summaries, which were slow to arrive from Rome. On October 19, the delegates elected a new superior general: M. Thérèse Poulin, provincial of Québec, Canada.[282] Among her four councilors was Sr. Mary Consolata (Rita) Valcourt, the local superior in Highland Mills who was on the staff of the Montessori program.

The General Chapter closed with few decisions. The interim documents continued to serve as guides as the sisters lived out the Council's challenges and spirit. On their return to the States, the American delegates drove cross-country to every community in the South and West, sharing in person the results of the Chapter. From the end of December through February 12, 1972, they met with community members to discuss implementing the Norms. Later that spring, they held regional meetings for the communities in the East.

Choosing Life: 1972

At the spring session of their province chapter, held in Fall River, Massachusetts, March 24–28, 1972, sisters gathered with energy around the theme "Choose Life." In addition to forty-nine delegates, for the first time, sixty–eight observers attended the sessions. They participated fully in all sessions with voice, but no vote. M. M. Catherine's opening address identified the task ahead as "negotiating the shift from one age to another." Speaking of a contemporary world marked by violence and rebellion, she pointed to these dark realities as possibilities for mission. Christ, St. Ignatius, and Claudine, she reminded the delegates, were all rebels. Now, it was their turn to be a "minority of rebels." They were to choose life as Christ did, serving in love, with shared power, creativity, and service. "Our institutions are not our mission," she concluded. With their disappearance, "the life that inspired them takes on a deeper dimension and finds new expression." A renewed sense of mission would be imbued with the social consciousness articulated in conciliar and post-conciliar statements. M. Catherine referred to the recent World Synod of Bishops, "Justice in the World," calling for action on behalf of justice as a "necessary feature in the task of evangelization." She reminded the delegates that religious were expected to be "at the pinnacle of social consciousness."[283]

Three days of sessions afforded time and space for reports on activities and programs, as well as the introduction of new projects for consideration and support. Six "experiments" in intentional community living had taken place; in their evaluations, sister-participants noted enjoying easier and better communication within a smaller group. For groups set up within bigger communities, a few reported a sense of estrangement from the large group, and some expressed confusion around roles and shared responsibilities. One new project elicited enthusiastic support: over fifty were interested in joining the "Second Summer" of prayer and study in the history of religious life, to be held at Highland Mills, with presenters that included Mary Milligan, RSHM, and William Yeomans, SJ. Animated discussions also took place on retirement planning and possible models of religious dress. In the area of vocation promotion, there was a promising report on the province Quest volunteer program, then in its second year.

Perhaps the most original idea came up during the last session, held on Monday of Holy Week. Sr. Antoinette Jacques, who had spent a sabbatical year of prayer in Highland Mills, presented a proposal from that community intended to revitalize its ministry. The aim was to set up the convent as a "House of Prayer" where sisters and others might spend time renewing their spiritual and physical energies. A discussion ensued of the proposal's pros and cons, with the majority speaking against it. Surprisingly, in the final vote it was unanimously supported on a trial basis. At the closing Mass after the session, the Gospel centered on Jesus being welcomed at Bethany, inspiring a name for the new project. Thus, did Thevenet become Bethany House of Prayer, and later, Bethany Spirituality Center. The beloved site in Highland Mills had reoriented its mission and service once again to meet the needs of a new time.[284]

The 1972 Chapter launched an intense period of study and reflection in the province. Renewal efforts for the next decade centered on key elements of the sisters' lives: a "return to the sources" by exploring their historical origins and the charism of Claudine Thevenet; a deeper understanding of the Ignatian tradition informing their spirituality and service; an expressed need for community life informed by the apostolic mission; a renewed sense of mission and service for a contemporary Church and world.

Returning to the Sources

The first compilation of historical documents toward the canonization of Claudine Thevenet was published in 1967. The cumbersome volume, required to initiate the Church process, was called a *Positio*, a term that became part of renewal vocabulary in the province. It first appeared in Latin and Italian; the documents concerning the foundress were in French. Accessible to very few of the sisters in the United States, the *Positio* nevertheless provided the basis for their initial exploration of the historical context of their founding years.[285] It became a primary source to check historical facts and documentation on the origins and early history of the institute. The *Positio* was a tool for a better understanding of the congregation's spiritual and ministerial wellsprings. A more accessible if uncritical source appeared in *Return to the Sources*, a small volume published in 1968. It contained incomplete portions of founding documents, along with excerpts from letters of the foundress. Other historical sources in English were few and largely inspirational; the most recent had been published in 1953.[286]

Their recent research had led many sisters to outline an original idea for the 200th birthday celebration of Claudine Thevenet, to be held in 1974. Why not produce a new biography of Claudine that spoke to contemporary readers? With the permission and support of M. Catherine, a group of interested sisters began a study of materials at hand. They sought the guidance and expertise of James Walsh, SJ, then editor of the British journal on spirituality, *The Way*. He invited them not only to read the sources but to try to read Claudine's heart and inner experience from the historical events and context of her apostolic calling. A series of meetings began in December of 1973, during which Walsh suggested they produce a "Spiritual Profile" of Claudine rather than a biography. Sisters were assigned research topics and reported on their findings, sometimes working late into the night.

A challenge to their work was the absence of any writings from the foundress, except for a few family letters. Further study and discussion showed that their most complete and helpful source was the documentation on a parish sodality, the "Pious Association of the Sacred Heart," which Claudine had led as president for ten years. Their Rule and the minutes of their meetings provided many clues to her inner life and service as a lay leader prior to the founding of the Congregation. Those years served as framework for the document and followed the traditional spiritual pattern of "dark nights" in the founder's life. Walsh was a critical editor and inspiring director throughout the process, agreeing to write an introduction. Sisters Janice Farnham and Rosemary Mangan drafted several versions of a text, with the group offering suggestions and revisions.

In the summer of 1974, the Profile was ready for publication. Copies were sent to Rome as information on the province's celebration. Before printing began, word came from the general leadership that the forty-five-page document could not be published. The sisters learned much later that this particular phase of the canonical process did not allow for any new documentation. For the drafting group, this was a painful rejection of a creative attempt to bring the foundress to life for the post-conciliar era. At the suggestion of M. Catherine, the Profile began a long afterlife in a series of editions entitled "Working Draft." It was sent first to sisters in the province and later shared with other English-speaking provinces. Thanks to this short work, the sisters of the American Province came to better know and love their foundress through her historical and spiritual journey. Rather than focus on "works" and institutional growth, they understood Claudine's charism as a unique complex of gifts she received for mission and shared with all who came after her. They rediscovered the compelling nature of that charismatic grace in lines from an early history: "For [Claudine], the greatest misfortune was to live and die without knowing God." This insight informed their apostolic choices and discernment for years to come.

In 1975, the core group met again to plan for critical translations of the earliest documents of the Congregation. Now known as the "Institute of Sources," they planned to translate and edit short primary texts for English speakers. Sr. Gertrude Bélanger, now the provincial superior, gave enthusiastic support to the endeavor. To mark the centenary of the Religious of Jesus and Mary in the States in 1977, a slim annotated collection volume of the foundress's sixteen extant letters was translated and distributed. Other historical studies followed, highlighting the role of the Pious Association and early rules of the Institute. Beginning in 1991, the province sponsored a series of "charism retreats" in various locations, including a summer venue in Ireland. Sisters making these retreats aimed to deepen their spirituality and mission through the lens of Claudine's charism as the source of their life as apostolic women.

Another lasting insight from these years of rediscovery was an essential element of the charism: Claudine's gift of forgiveness. She received it in the aftermath of her brothers' cruel execution; the Congregation reclaimed it as a call of the Church and an apostolic priority for the twenty-first century: "to incarnate forgiveness, reconciliation, and healing for a wounded world."[287]

Reclaiming the Ignatian Tradition

From its origins, the Congregation was marked by the influence of Jesuit spirituality and the Spiritual Exercises of St. Ignatius. Prior to the Council, American sisters always knew they were Ignatian but were hard-pressed to identify specific aspects of their spirituality linking them to that tradition. Their annual eight-day retreats were most often preached by Jesuits; they were considered the primary expression for the congregation of Ignatian influence. That slowly began to change. As superior general since 1953, M. del Rosario Araño had initiated renewal efforts in Ignatian spirituality and studies, providing each province with updated versions of the text of the Ignatian Spiritual Exercises. She encouraged and gave high priority to programs of renewal with an Ignatian focus: the full Exercises in a thirty-day directed retreat, the tertianship renewal program in Rome, the training of sisters as spiritual directors. Between 1970 and 1976, nineteen sisters of the province made the full Exercises, usually at Bethany in Highland Mills. Following that, several went to Guelph, Ontario, at the Loyola House Training Centre, where they trained in spiritual direction and retreat work. The ministry at Bethany expanded to include programs in Ignatian spirituality, regular spiritual direction, and every summer, a number of Ignatian directed retreats. Sisters gathered for conferences and weekends on the centrality of Christ in the Gospels as well as the importance and practice of discernment for their apostolic choices. They rediscovered the importance of the examen in daily life as a personal practice, and they grew together in the practice of discernment for apostolic choices.

Together with shared experiences of biblical and liturgical renewal, their exploration of the Ignatian spirit and tradition was one of the lasting aspects of the province's post-conciliar transformation. Linking their origins to Jesuit sodalities of the eighteenth century, sisters discovered in the Rule of the Pious Association and other documents strong links with the Jesuit "style" of spirituality and service. The associates, for example, were to emulate the early Christians by mutual support and affection, with "one heart and one soul" (Acts 4:32). This strongly reflected the union of minds and hearts enjoined by Ignatius in his Constitutions. Seeking and finding God in all things, they were to live and serve as a community of friends, with "joy of heart, liberty of spirit, confidence and generosity" (Rule, Pious Association), a phrase that later appeared in the revised Constitutions. They were called together to be sent to others as communities for mission. These insights became central to province efforts at the revision of constitutional texts during the seventies. In late November of 1998, the province sponsored an assembly in Highland Mills, to mark the 150th anniversary of the first Constitutions. Sisters from Mexico, Canada, and the Middle East attended, along with lay associates. Part of the program included a presentation on the Ignatian spirit, "Living out Discerning Love," by Howard Gray, SJ. In another, Sr. Catherine McIntyre addressed the topic of the "RJM Spirituality in the

Constitutions." Referring to the 1977 revision of these texts, to which she had contributed, she recalled that "we wrote our Constitutions, painfully and joyfully, out of our shared experience. [They] invite us to drink from the well of our experience and convictions." Reclaiming the Ignatian heritage, distilled through their unique province experience, served as a powerful source for renewal. It offered rich insights and challenging possibilities for the future.

Forming Communities for Mission

Earlier chapters have shown that the sisters in the United States succeeded best when they had adapted their lives and ministry to local and regional situations. The internal structures of their common life, however, had remained constant. In large institutional settings, communities could number more than sixty sisters, living a quasi-monastic lifestyle with fixed schedules. In parish settings, community numbers were smaller, and the sisters' lives afforded more flexibility because of their involvement in parochial life. Maintaining the rhythm of prayer and silence mandated by the common rule, community life for sisters in a parish setting could be more relaxed and familiar. In both cases, however, opportunities for conversation or spiritual sharing were few, and "recreation" times and places were set twice daily for all. Otherwise, sisters maintained a monastic silence through the day. The Council's call for dialogue and better communication in communities was the catalyst for province experiments in community life. Four small intentional groups were formed within larger communities (El Paso, Fall River, Maryland, and Woonsocket) where members met together for prayer, relaxation, and faith sharing. There were likewise independent communities with three to eight sisters. Between 1971 and 1976, the province opened eight small communities. Their objective was to offer a simple community lifestyle marked by mutual support and reconciliation, and centered on their shared mission. The members were encouraged to evaluate their experience and send regular reports to the province. Each small community required that all share responsibility for household duties, engage in open and honest dialogue, and extend hospitality. With time, many sisters found this style suitable to the active ministries in which they were engaged. It was more conducive to mature and responsible participation, engaging the voices of all in discernment and decision making. In successful communities of this type, the role of superior shifted away from household management to a listening and discerning style of leadership. Province leadership initiated regular superiors' and principals' meetings to educate sisters and address their challenges in various community settings.

In 1976, as the province prepared to celebrate its centenary and work toward revised Constitutions, the leadership set up an Office of Research and Planning, initiated and led by Sisters Margaret Perron and Eileen Reid. They began by organizing task forces to address areas of province need: recruitment, apostolic service, human resources (retirement and pre-retirement), finances, health care, and community life. Their role was twofold: to set up programs, policies, and procedures in those areas; and to formulate a Statement of Mission that expressed province commitment to a discernment process culminating in more authentic prayer life, community living, and apostolic service. It was an ambitious and intensive project in which all the sisters engaged their energies. To promote ongoing communication, the first issues of a province newsletter, *Focus*, appeared.[288] After every community had reviewed drafts and sent comments, the text was printed and distributed. A brief but strong statement, it summarized the work of the task forces and impelled the province forward. It acknowledged "our need to re-evaluate our present situation . . . and establish a clear direction for our apostolic service." It committed the province to a prayer life rooted in the Word and Eucharist, to community life calling for mutual support and reconciliation, to ministry inspired by "the greatest misfortune," and to a process of ongoing discernment. In a real sense, this Statement of Mission of 1977 distilled the province's contribution toward revised Constitutions, which were approved at the General Chapter later that year.

Christian Communities

Another form of group living emerged, known in the province as Christian Communities. An outgrowth of the successful summer volunteer program, Quest, the idea grew from an awareness of the role of laity in the post-conciliar Church, as well as the need to provide a lived experience of community-in-service for women discerning a call to religious life. Several of the original Quest volunteers wanted to extend the time of their service to deprived communities because they found summer programs to be too brief. Early in 1976, a group of six or seven Questers met with Sr. Janice Farnham and Sr. Margaret Mary Quinn to pray and discern about a year-long Quest community in service to the poor. They were unanimously in favor of the project, with site and specifics to be worked out subsequently. By June of 1977, at another meeting, enthusiasm was still high, but financial realities prevented anyone of the original group from committing herself. Sr. Janice sent out flyers to potential volunteer sites and explored service alternatives in the metropolitan New York area. Providentially, the small community of sisters at Godwin Terrace had disbanded that year, leaving the house available as a possibility.

With the eventual approval of Msgr. John Doherty, pastor of St. John's, and the wholehearted support of the sisters' larger community, the first year-long Christian Community opened its doors in September of 1977. The group included four women volunteers, two of whom were interested in religious life, and four Religious of Jesus and Mary: Sisters Janice Farnham, Estelle Gravel, Estelle Haché, and Margaret Theresa Guinan. The shared life of sisters and volunteers included a commitment to simple living and concern for the poor. Based on their professional training, volunteers found positions in advocacy, nursing, and social service programs in New York. With the exception of Sr. Janice, who was Quest and Vocation Director, the sisters ministered at St. John's School. Gradually the community became involved in parish life and outreach. Their life included daily prayer together, weekly Eucharist, shared meals and household duties, as well as regular meetings for faith sharing. They welcomed many guests and women interested in joining the group. Two of the first women, Ms. Debbie LaFontaine, from Mississippi, and Ms. Mary Scanlon, from St. John's in New York, later entered the Religious of Jesus and Mary. Prior to her senior year at Georgetown, Ms. Diane Williams joined the community in 1978 while participating in an urban advocacy program in the city. Her personal reflection concludes: "I have no doubt that I grew stronger as a woman of faith, more self-assured in the work world, and gained clarity of vision for my future in the time spent at Godwin Terrace." Following this initial experiment of shared community life for sisters and young women in discernment, at least eight other communities were formed throughout the province in the next decade. For RJM women in formation, regular participation in a Christian community often provided a supportive setting in which to test their calling.

Renewing the Sense of Mission, Weaving a New Pattern

In his 1971 exhortation to consecrated religious, Pope Paul VI issued a challenge to hear again the anguished voices of Christ's privileged members: "How then will the cry of the poor find an echo in your lives?" (*Evangelica Testificatio*, #18). For the Religious of Jesus and Mary, that cry echoed the cries prompting Claudine's mission: "The lot of those thousands of poor children . . . who were destined to grow up perhaps without ever hearing the name of God, made her tremble."[289] Their lot became hers; henceforth her preferences were for the "weakest, most shameful, most abandoned" of God's little ones. Throughout its history, the Congregation had been called and sent to those on the margins of their societies. The sisters' concept of mission was shaped by a universe of need, and their response grew into an international service of education. In the nineteenth century, a central element of their apostolic spirit was a strong emphasis on foreign missions to promote the Church's aim to "make disciples of all nations." From the first courageous group of sisters who left France for India in 1842, the Religious of Jesus and Mary identified themselves as a missionary institute. Three decades later, the sisters from Canada who arrived in Fall River came as foreign missionaries to protect Catholic children from the evils of Protestantism and godlessness in a secular republic. In a few decades, the mission in the United States grew into a large province, with sufficient numbers to send sisters to far-off lands where they were to "make Jesus and Mary known and loved." In fact, many women entered the community with a desire to "go to the missions." Between 1921 and 2017, thirty-four sisters from the United States were sent to thirteen countries. Their stories and self-sacrifice were continuous sources of inspiration to sisters and their students and attracted others to do as they had done.[290]

In the conciliar call for a pilgrim church of *all* the People of God, the Church shaped another new expression of its mission. The Church was a sacrament of God's love revealed in Christ and the Good News he proclaimed. It was never static but always on the move; not identified with one culture, but open to all. As a result of their prayerful discussions in the post-conciliar years, sisters in the United States learned to distinguish their mission from its expression in schools or other apostolic service, which they now expressed as "ministry." They described it succinctly as sharing in the one mission of Jesus: "to make known the Father's love to all who hungered for God, especially the poor" (Statement of Mission, 1977).

Whatever the individual ministries of sisters, their unified response was to be directed by the Gospel message, the tradition of the Congregation, and the context of the American church. The province sought creative responses to the call of the poor and the promotion of justice recommended by its recent chapters. Some dedicated themselves to health care with the homeless, others to advocacy and social ministries, including older sisters who had retired from full-time ministry. Sr. Delvina Poulin, whose religious life had been spent in domestic service, discovered a new calling as a "grandmother" at a boys' home in Fall River. "What a grace," she wrote, "that in my eighties I can share Claudine's service to the poor"! In addition to sending sisters as members of intercongregational projects to the urban poor, the province sought to attract students from their secondary schools to join outreach efforts. It was an appealing idea and, as some hoped, a way to attract new candidates to the community. So far, their efforts at recruitment had been sporadic and unsatisfactory.

Quest Volunteers

In June of 1970, Mr. J. Tedd Kelly, an educational consultant to the province leadership, wrote a proposal oriented to vocation promotion for the province. Its aim was to present religious life as "quest that never ends" and to provide a flexible base from which to attract young women to the Religious of Jesus and Mary through programs and a summer service project. Sr. Janice Farnham was appointed the Vocation/Quest Director; she was at the ARC renewal program in Rome and was unable to initiate the Quest Program. Sister Anne Magner directed the first summer Quest in July of 1971, serving the migrant community in Warwick, New York. Three Religious of Jesus and Mary volunteered to pioneer the project: Sisters Stella Herrera, Rita Ricker, and Janet Stolba. They were joined by three young women: Andrea Klaus, Pauline Thibault, and Saylor Wright. For the month of July, they lived at Highland Mills and travelled daily to help in the clinic and children's program. For the next seven years, traveling from St. John's Convent in New York, Sr. Janice set up future sites and living quarters for a growing number of volunteers. In 1974, her first report to the province described Quest as a "means of reaching young women between the ages of 18 and 25 . . . to help them in their own personal quest." The program did this by opportunities for sharing in prayer and serving the poor through their summer service projects.

Depending on the service sites, each community had from five to fifteen members. In 1975, eight graduates of St. Clare's in Woonsocket prepared to leave for summer Quest communities in upstate New York, Harlan, Kentucky, and Olive Branch, Mississippi. There were annual gatherings and weekend retreats for present and former Questers. The Quest office published a quarterly newsletter, *The Windmill*, which provided news of former volunteers and plans for future project sites.

By 1976, thirty-four sisters (eight from other congregations) and fifty-six volunteers had formed Quest communities in six states. Novices frequently were part of summer Quest projects. In addition to their services for migrant workers, the volunteers tutored in day camps and summer schools; they taught Bible school and offered sacramental preparation; they engaged in recreation projects along with arts and crafts. At some sites, they visited hospitals and homes of the sick. Thanks to province financial support and small donations, annual expenses for summer programs never exceeded $3000. In 1977, Sr. Rita Ricker became the second director of Quest, serving for the next nine years. Ms. Caroline Masciale, the first lay director, then led the program for two years and was replaced by Sr. Mary Bourdon. As time went on, young men applied and were accepted as volunteers. In 1986, the program welcomed year-long volunteers. Another first was an international Quest program of 1989 in Galway, Ireland, with a community of volunteers from both sides of the Atlantic. They worked among the Travelers, a nomadic pre-Celtic people who lived in camps and were subject to discrimination. That year, there was also a shared project at the Mexican border in Tijuana, Mexico. When the province undertook its new mission in Haiti, the Quest program narrowed its recruitment efforts to volunteers for service to that mission. From the few Questers pursuing an "impossible dream" in 1971, close to 500 volunteers have partnered with Religious of Jesus and Mary in responding to the Church's call in the cry of the poor.

Re-woven in Hope, Weaving a Future[291]

After celebrating God's goodness and presence for a century, province membership could point to creative and life-giving patterns emerging, even as they mourned diminished and aging numbers of sisters and fewer institutional settings for ministry. The ministries at Highland Mills were thriving. In the first seven years of its spiritual ministry, Bethany

Retreat House had welcomed close to 4000 guests. Programs offered included Ignatian Retreats, Prayer Weekends, Province Meetings, Marriage Encounters, and various group sessions. On October 15 of that year, sisters gathered for the blessing and dedication of Welch Hall, the new Montessori school building. Its construction meant that more children could be admitted, allowing for capacity enrolment. There was enthusiasm over the regionalization experiments in New England, seen as successful examples of collaborative efforts to maintain Catholic elementary education. Sisters were teaching in eleven schools from East to West, where the future seemed more assured than in the recent past. In 1997, Sr. Mary Bourdon, trained in sociology and pastoral counselling, set up an after-school program for girls from economically disadvantaged communities in southeast Washington, DC. Thanks to her dream and labor, it grew into the Washington Middle School for Girls, welcoming about thirty-five students in Grades 3 through 8. It was sponsored by the Religious of Jesus and Mary, the Society of the Holy Child, and the National Council of Negro Women. Sr. Mary led the school with passion and vision for twenty years, directing its growth and expansion. At the invitation of the province, many alumnae of Regina High School offered their support, encouraging school programs with financial contributions, as Board members and volunteers. Through them, the spirit of Regina and its legacy were secure at their "little sister" school.

After the beatification of Claudine Thevenet in 1981, the General Council introduced the idea of a lay association in the Congregation, to share its founding charism, spirituality, and mission. Such associations of lay faithful had a long history in the Church. After the Council, they became one expression of the apostolic calling of the entire people of God. In the revised Code of Canon Law of 1983, members of associations are called to "live the charism in the first person and share the gifts of the Spirit in full co-responsibility" (No. 287). The General Chapter of 1983 voted to accept the "Family of Jesus and Mary" as a congregational project and encouraged provinces to set up their own groups. In the United States, there were several efforts to establish groups in different regions of the province. Some sisters volunteered to direct the groups; others were welcome to join their gatherings. Four groups flourished in the province: in Goffstown, New Hampshire; at St. John's, New York; in Warwick, Rhode Island (St. Timothy's), and in Tijuana, Mexico. Groups that thrived combined a common apostolic outreach with meetings for prayer and spiritual growth. Full recognition of the associates came with the addition in 1995 of an article in the Constitutions of the Congregation. Governed by their own statutes approved that year, the Family of Jesus and Mary has developed globally. In 2002, it numbered 1600 members worldwide, some of them non-Christian. All desired to share the spirituality and service of the sisters. After the founding of the Haiti mission, the American Province added its first Caribbean group of associates in Port-au-Prince.

An Uncertain Future

In July of 2000, over 120 Religious of Jesus and Mary gathered at a retreat center in New Jersey to celebrate "Charism 2000." The assembly was memorable. It included sisters from seven other provinces as well as lay friends and associates. Together they worshipped, prayed, shared, sang, and danced in gratitude for an international expression of their shared gifts, in many languages and styles. They experienced the blessing of their global communion, rich in diversity and cultural traditions; it renewed all present in the grace of Claudine's charism.

Despite bright signs of life for the province, the years leading to the new century were shadowed by stark realities. From their peak numbers in 1968 of 346 members with a median age of forty-eight, the membership of the American province in 1980 had dropped to 226 sisters, including eight missionaries and three others living outside the province. By 1992, there were 186 sisters; their median age had risen to sixty-seven. They continued to be engaged in ministry but with a different profile: by 2000, only thirteen sisters were teaching in community-owned schools. There were no novices or postulants. In May of 1991, a large number from the province made a final journey to Hyattsville for a farewell pilgrimage. With the loss of that cherished high school and national center, it seemed that the province's recent past in the United States had receded into history. It was a time to grieve the loss of former certainties, the fraying of parts of a rich tapestry woven in former times. It was also a period to assess and question: to what future was God calling them now, as their youth, resources, and energies dwindled? Where would they find hope in such uncertain times? True, the Apostle reminded them that "hope that is seen is not hope" (Rom 8:24). They were invited to trust and move forward into wilderness, as Abraham and Sarah did, "hoping against hope" (Rom 4:18) that God would once again provide what they needed.

Haiti: Surprise of the Spirit (1996)

For some time, there had been a sense in the province that it was time to explore areas of need beyond those they already served. In 1991, some members of the province leadership had read shocking articles about the treatment of young girls in Haiti known as *restaveks*, poor children who were loaned out to rich families as servants and suffered all kinds of mistreatment. Were they hearing in this story a contemporary echo of the call to Claudine and her friends, asking them to respond? The question persisted and came up at a number of meetings. In 1993, in gratitude for the canonization of St. Claudine, a letter arrived from the superior general, M. Lourdes Rossell, asking each province to undertake a mission among the poor. She suggested in a later message that the American Province undertake a mission in Haiti; she had received a request for teachers there from the Brothers of the Sacred Heart in Port-au-Prince. The province leader, Sr. Eileen Reid, took action. Sr. Laura Dulude, a provincial councilor, met a few times with a Sister of the Holy Names, Denise Girard, whose congregation had ministered in Haiti for some time. Invitations to "come and see" were extended. From June 2 to June 12, 1993, Srs. Mary Bourdon and Janice Farnham spent time seeking out possible sites, under the sponsorship of the Parish Twinning Program in Haiti. Their published reports, and their contacts with programs in Haiti sparked interest in the province. Because a bloody coup had overthrown the Aristide government in 1991, it was hard to formulate any action until 1995, when the situation stabilized.

A province Haiti Task Force was formed. Its members were to explore the most effective ways to respond to needs in Haiti, identify them, and develop action steps for implementation. Their report would be presented to the 1996 provincial chapter for consideration. As the task force began their research, it was clear they had insufficient information to move forward. The group asked to make an on-site visit. In April of 1996, three members of the task force, Sisters Patricia Dillon, Vivian Patenaude, and Mary Scanlon, spent a week in Port-au-Prince and ten days in Gros Morne, served by the Montfort Missionary priests. Each one was affected deeply by the experience. Their guide and mentor was Sr. Rose Gallagher, SNJM, who had worked at both sites, where her congregation did educational ministry. Clearly, Haiti presented a universe of need, and any response would be welcome. Sr. Patricia Dillon wrote that her experience "put faces on the statistics" about Haiti. She added her wish that "perhaps the dignity and culture of the Haitian people would help me/us to overcome the racism of our white normative society." She expressed a hope that the Religious of Jesus and Mary would take the risk to respond to the invitations they received. The group also sought information on the financial costs of supporting missionaries in Haiti.

In their final report to the province on July 22, they were unanimous in stating that a) the province should undertake a mission in Haiti, the poorest nation in the Western hemisphere; and b) it was essential to involve lay participation in the undertaking. Their proposal was simple: "That the USA Province send sisters to minister in Haiti." They presented it to the provincial chapter, held from August 16– 20, with each one recounting her experience as an invitation to conversion rather than an experiment in the "conversion" of Haiti. In vigorous discussions on the topic, delegates were torn between their desire to respond and the realities of an aging province with limited personnel and resources and an uncertain future. Some delegates made it clear that it would be foolhardy to undertake a Haitian presence when the province couldn't respond to "needs at home" that were equally compelling. Opposition to the proposal was outspoken, pointing to an uncertain outcome. Sr. Rosemary Mangan, the recently appointed provincial, reminded the delegates that if they approved the proposal, the province commitment would not only be for those few sent to Haiti. It would entail the sacrifice of sisters already actively engaged in ministry. It would require substantial financial support. Choosing a foundation in Haiti challenged every sister to own the decision and support the mission wholeheartedly as a province commitment. It was time to seek the Spirit's help toward a momentous decision.

At its final session on August 19, 1996, the delegates voted on fifteen proposals by secret ballot. The Haiti proposal was last on the page. As the final votes were tallied and announced, a communal gasp arose in the room: the Haiti proposal received fifty-two affirmative votes. A unanimous choice, despite their reticence and uncertainties. There were tears of joy and gratitude at this "new Pentecost" for the province, a surprise of God's Spirit who had reminded them: "I am about to do a new thing; do you not perceive it?" (Isa 49:13). As delegates returned home, the question in the province was a more practical one. Who would be chosen to begin this new venture? Who was willing and able to offer herself? In a post-chapter letter to the province, Sr. Rosemary invited sisters to a time of prayerful discernment and dialogue. It was decided to accept the invitation of the Montfort Missionary parish in Gros Morne, which offered a supportive and positive environment for sisters opening a mission. It had needs for services in health care, education, and general welfare. The chosen three were Sisters Patricia Dillon, Vivian Patenaude, and Jacqueline Picard, whose recent training as a nurse practitioner would find ample opportunities for service. As part of their preparation, they traveled to Queens, New York, in July of 1997 for a month's immersion course in Creole culture and language.

On a warm late summer day in September of 1997, a large group of sisters, lay associates, relatives of the new missionaries, and friends of the Religious of Jesus and Mary gathered in joy at St. Bernadette's Church in Fall River, the site of their founding parish of Notre Dame de Lourdes. They were celebrating the annual province jubilee as well as a solemn missioning ceremony for the Haitian founding sisters. The choir and congregation sang "Here I Am, Lord," as each one received her mission cross from a Religious of Jesus and Mary she had chosen. It was a deeply moving event, filled with prayers of gratitude, tinged with the sadness of separation and loss.[292] Time would confirm the shared conviction of the province that their decision had been in the Spirit. The Haitian mission grew to include two other sites in Jean Rabel and Port-au-Prince, attracting sister-missionaries from Ireland and Spain as well as countless associates and volunteers, to shape a truly multi-cultural, interprovincial presence among God's people in Haiti. It added a colorful Caribbean thread to the tapestry of hope they had woven since 1877.

The missioning ceremony was laden with symbolism for the Religious of Jesus and Mary. This parish, these grounds, held the memory of their first days and years in the United States. It was the thread "that stays as everything else falls away . . . as we follow our own small threads to the place where they merge with the boundless whole."[293] From such small and fragile threads they had begun to weave a pattern of prayer, community, and service. It grew into a strong, colorful fabric, woven from the hope of three courageous immigrant women in Fall River and all those who came after them. Their story reveals an intricate pattern of shapes and hues now stretching across the nation. It is still unfinished. The weaver-God of all history continues to move the Spirit's shuttle across the world's loom, humming with the hope that never disappoints (Rom 5:5), toward that "masterpiece in which we live forever."[294]

Endnotes

1. Canon law defines a "province" as a grouping of several houses of the same congregation under one superior, called a "provincial."

2. For an overview of Catholic immigration, see Dolan, *American Catholic Experience*, 127–37.

3. Fisher, *Communion of Immigrants*, 42.

4. Dolan, *American Catholic Experience*, 326.

5. Shelley, *New History of Archdiocese of New York*, 58.

6. Fisher, *Communion of Immigrants*, 74.

7. By mid-century, one-fourth of the population in the Québec region consisted of English-speakers, a total of over 125,000. Most of these were no better off than Francophones. Over half of them emigrated from Ireland during the Potato Famine. About 11,000 Acadians from Nova Scotia were expelled from Canada by the British and deported to their coastal colonies along the Eastern seaboard of the United States, from New England to Georgia and Louisiana. For a general article on French-Canadian migrations, see Janice Farnham, RJM, "French Canadian Catholics in the United States," in *The Encyclopedia of American Catholic History*, eds. Michael Glazier and Thomas Shelley (Collegeville, MN: Liturgical Press, 1997), 549–53.

8. Liptak, *Immigrants*, 65.

9. Liptak, *Immigrants*, 170.

10. Liptak, *Immigrants*, 164–70.

11. Fisher, *Communion of Immigrants*, 76.

12. Dolan/Hinojosa, *Mexican Americans and the Catholic Church*, 144.

13. Dolan/Hinojosa, *Mexican Americans and the Catholic Church*, 36.

14. O'Malley, "The Millennium and the Papalization of Catholic Church," 16.

15. Byrne, "American Ultramontanism," 301.

16. The Religious of Jesus and Mary, an apostolic congregation of pontifical right, was founded in 1818 at Lyon, France, by St. Claudine Thevenet (1774–1837), and Rev. André Coindre (1787–1826), a diocesan missionary who later founded the Brothers of the Sacred Heart. Both were dedicated to healing social and religious wounds in the wake of the French Revolution. The Congregation is marked by its Ignatian spiritual heritage, devotion to the Hearts of Christ and Mary, and commitment to educational and pastoral service, with a strong missionary tradition.

Originally a parish-based pious association of laywomen, with the founder as its president, the sisters began to assist orphans and the daughters of impoverished silk-weavers of the Lyon region in work schools known as "providences," and later undertook boarding schools for girls from more affluent families. At Claudine's death in 1837, her institute seemed to be in decline: of the five establishments she had founded, only three remained, all within a thirty–mile radius of Lyon. By 1842, however, a small band of sisters left for Agra, India, inaugurating the international missionary character of the congregation, and thus ensuring papal approbation of its Constitutions in 1847.

Foundations followed in Spain (1850), Eastern Canada (1855), England (1860), the USA (1877), Switzerland (1893), Italy (1896), Mexico/Cuba (1902), Ireland (1912), Argentina (1913), and Germany (1922). A second wave of expansion occurred in after 1950. By 1968 the congregation's membership reached a peak of over 2600 sisters, in 142 establishments worldwide. In 2018 the congregation numbered over 1000 sisters in twenty–eight countries on four continents.

17. O'Malley, *What Happened at Vatican II*, 53.

18. Byrne, "American Ultramontanism," 301–26.

19. Tanner, *Councils*, 96.

20. Walch, *Parish School*; and Dolan, *American Catholic Experience*, 263–93.

21. Walch, *Parish School*, 87.

22. Walch, *Parish School*, 151.

23. Thompson, "Adaptation and Professionalisation," 454–47; and "Sisters' History is Women's History, 182–90.

24. Founded in 1897, Trinity College in Washington, DC, was the first Catholic college for women. In 1911, a Sisters' College opened on the nearby campus of Catholic University. The University did not admit women as fully enrolled students in any graduate program until Sr. Marie Inez Hilger, OSB, from Minnesota, complained to her bishop that no Catholic college or university admitted females as graduate students. The issue came up at a bishops' meeting and in 1924, Sr. Hilger became the first woman admitted with permission to graduate studies in social work at Catholic University. A laywoman was admitted three years later. In 1928, the University began to admit female graduate students.

25. Weaver, *New Catholic Women*, 81.

26. Weaver, *New Catholic Women*, 81.

27. See Glisky, "Sister Mary Emil Penet, IHM:" *Catholic Education*, March 2006, 360–76.

28. O'Malley, *What Happened at Vatican II*, 311.

29. Coburn, "Ahead of Time?" 42.

30. Schneiders, "Ongoing Challenge of Renewal."

31. Congregational sources for this chapter were the General Archives, in Rome (AG), Province Archives (AP), and typescripts of the correspondence of the superiors general and provincial of the American mission.

32. [M. Aloysius Hugon and M. Joachim Creuzet], *Histoire de la Congrégation des Religieuses de Jésus–Marie d'après les témoignages des contemporains*. Lyon: 1896. This work, in two volumes, was translated and updated in a critical edition prepared by Sr. Antonia Bonet, RJM, and titled *History of the Congregation of the Religious of Jesus and Mary According to Contemporary Witnesses* (Pune, India: Anand Press, 1992).

33. The sisters had kept the French custom of addressing the choir professed as "Mother." The auxiliaries, those in domestic service, were called "Sister." A General Chapter in 1872 adopted the use of "Sister" for all. A later Chapter in 1897 reinstated the use of "Mother" for all choir sisters in Spain, England, North America, and India, where

it had not been in use. The title of "Madame" referred to sisters without final vows in the early twentieth century. The auxiliary sisters wore a simpler version of the habit. In 1966, following the Second Vatican Council, the second class of sisters was suppressed.

34. *First Constitutions and Rules of the Congregation of the Religious of Jesus and Mary*, with Introduction and Notes by Sr. Antonia Bonet, RJM. Trans. Sr. Thomas More Borrell, RJM (Barcelona: Private printing, 2006), 71 and n. 25.

35. See Notes of M. Cecilia Gaudette, RJM, "*La Dispersion*," December, 2011. The house at Our Lady of Peace opened in 1902. The name of M. St. Augustin Ferbeyre is listed in the professions in France for August 16, 1897. She died on September 18, 1926 in Goffstown, NH. Thanks to Jennifer Burke, RJM, for her research on these sisters in the French provincial archive.

36. AG: SIV/1: *Lettres, M. St Cyrille*, 1877-95, December 25, 1881.

37. AG: *Régistre*, 1840–92.

38. Letter of M. St. Pothin to M. St. Cyrille, December 28, 1879.

39. AG: SIV/1: *Lettres, M. St–Cyrille*, 1877–95.

40. AG: GII/1896–1965, 27.

41. AG: G–1/7, M. St. Clare Bray, 1911

42. AG: GIII/Reg. xxx, 25.

43. M. St. Clare Bray, *Cameos*, 134. This brief history of the Religious of Jesus and Mary is the first written in English. With the original title *The Congregation of Jesus and Mary. Cameos from its History*, it was published anonymously in 1917 by Burns & Oates, Ltd., with a foreword by Sydney Smith, SJ, editor of the Jesuit journal, *The Month*.

44. *Cameos*, 54– 55.

45. For a chronological listing of the Provincial Superiors, see Appendix II. See also Montesinos, *Life and Times*, 419–32.

46. AG: GI/, 4–6.

47. Eliane Pelletier, RJM, *Les filles de Claudine Thevenet*, 100.

48. AG: S IV/I: *Lettres, R.M. St–Cyrille*, June 24, 1870.

49. Pelletier, 97–103.

50. M. St. Clare Bray, "The High Vocation of Teaching," n/d.

51. On February 15, 1940, the General Council voted to name this province "Hispanic-American," but it was commonly known in the United States as "Hispanic-Mexican." Throughout this text, the latter title is used. See AG: Register xxx: GII/1.

52. See page 156.

53. "No parish is complete till it has schools adequate to the needs of its children." *Pastoral Letters*, I (1984), 225.

54. See AP: H 300.25. It contains detailed information on the foundation, development and growth of the convent, academy and parish school in Fall River.

55. AP: H300.25/1, "*La fondation*."

56. Virginie Fournier, sister of M. St. Benoit, had been educated with the Religious of Jesus and Mary at Lauzon, P.Q. and was assisting the pastor as a teacher and catechist. She also entered the community, but left as a novice because of serious eye problems. In 1892, she founded the Sisters of Notre–Dame du Perpétuel-Secours, under the religious name of M. St. Bernard. Overcome with blindness four years before her death (1918), she left a legacy of eleven foundations and a reputation for heroic virtue.

57. Hayman, *Catholicism in Rhode Island*, I, 266.

58. The two-story brick building known as the *"petit couvent"* was originally owned by Mr. J. Hayes, a friend and benefactor in the early years. He offered it to the foundresses as a temporary residence prior to their move to the Mason Street house. After his death, the Religious of Jesus and Mary acquired the building, which at various times offered additional space for classrooms, bedrooms, home economics lab, storage, and art studio for private lessons.

59. AP: H300.25/1, *"La fondation."*

60. *The Providence Journal,* Dec. 11, 1879.

61. AP: H300.25: "Orphans Home, Flint Village."

62. AG: G/1, *Lettres, M. St-Pothin.*

63. For a full account of this incident see Philip Silvia, Jr., "The "Flint Affair": French-Canadian Struggle for "Survivance," in *The Catholic Historical Review,* 65:3 (1979) 414–35.

64. *Fall River Evening News,* February 13, 1885.

65. AG: IV/1: *Lettres, M. St. Cyrille.* See Chapter 3 for the full story of the Newport property. The deed of sale was signed in May, 1886. Dr. Horatio Storer, a trustee in the parish of St. Joseph, acted as the sisters' agent for handling the sale.

66. In 2010, Brother André Bessette (1845–1937) was canonized by Pope Benedict XVI.

67. AP: H 300.1, "Manchester, Closed Houses."

68. Chevalier to M. St. Cyrille, June 1, 1881.

69. In the 1840's, the Irish Sisters of Mercy laid an American foundation in Pittsburgh, under the leadership of M. Frances Xavier Warde (1810–84), one of the original founders of the Mercy Sisters in Dublin. At the invitation of Bernard O'Reilly, bishop of Providence, she and four sisters began their New England mission in that city in 1851. Seven years later, she came with another group to begin educational and social work in Manchester. She often returned to Manchester, retiring there in the 1880's. As superior general of the congregation, she founded twenty–seven convents of Mercy in ten states.

70. AP: H 300.1, *Historique,* 2.

71. AP: H 300.1, *Historique,* 2

72. While she did not herself come to meet with Chevalier, M. St. Cyrille sent the convent chaplain from Sillery with plans for the new convent and school building. He arrived on August 30 and returned the next day.

73. AP: H 300.1, *Historique,* 4.

74. AP : H 300.1, *Historique,* 4.

75. Convent Annals, 39.

76. Convent Annals: July 12, 1895.

77. See Verrette, *"Messire Joseph Augustin Chevalier,"* and *'Cinquantenaire 1881–1931."*

78. *"Cinquantenaire,"* 170–73.

79. Chevalier to M. St. Thérèse Chapleau, November 6, 1924.

80. See AP: H 300.1/11, "St. Theresa Parish, 1926 to 1934."

81. AP: H 300.1/ 11, *"Fondation."*

82. Letter of Boire to M. St. Peter Claver, December 21, 1935.

83. Circular letter of M. St. Borgia, June 3, 1936.

84. Cited in *Historique,* 41.

85. See AP: H 300.1/10.

86. Bradley to M. St. Cyrille, March 7, 1890.

87. Grace Hanley (b.1867) was the daughter of Civil War veteran Colonel Patrick T. Hanley and his wife Sarah, both devout Catholics. At the age of four, Grace fell from a carriage and injured her back. She suffered crippling injuries to her spine, causing excruciating pain, chronic headaches, and ineffective treatments. Until she was twelve, Grace's family exhausted all their medical options, consulting Boston's most-respected doctors. The family had recourse to novenas and prayer. In August of 1883, a Redemptorist priest from the Mission Church of Roxbury, Our Lady of Perpetual Help, came to visit the child and advised the family to make a novena at Our Lady's Altar there. Carried by her father, Grace joined her relatives for the novena prayers and rosary, convinced that she would be healed. On the ninth day, she rose to walk to the altar without crutches or any other support. She knelt at Our Lady's shrine, offering thanksgiving to Our Lord and the Blessed Mother for her recovery, and walked out of the church unaided. News of her healing spread like wildfire in newspapers and Catholic circles. To remove her from curious crowds and notoriety, her parents sent her to the RJM convent–school in Sillery, Québec. From there she was accepted into the Congregation, made her novitiate and was professed in August of 1890, a month before coming to Claremont.

88. Convent Annals, 118.

89. See AP: H 210.12, "Villa Augustina," and H 300.1, "Manchester: Closed Houses."

90. Verrette, *Un Cinquantenaire*, 88.

91. Verrette, *Un Cinquantenaire*, 85.

92. Verrette, *Un Cinquantenaire*, 89.

93. Hadley, *History of Goffstown*, 262.

94. Marie-Clarisse Gaudette, daughter of Oscar and Léocadie Guite, followed the commercial course at the Villa but her education was interrupted by the influenza epidemic in 1918. She had taken music lessons at the Villa and returned there to teach music and French. She entered the novitiate in Sillery at the age of twenty-one, took the name Marie Cecilia, pronouncing first vows on August 12, 1925. Furthering her violin studies, she received a certificate from the music institute at Laval University, Québec. M. Cecilia taught music and other subjects to students in several convents of Canada and the U.S. From 1934 to 1948, she served as choir director and teacher at the boarding school of Fourvière in Lyon, enduring hardships and dangers during the Nazi occupation in France. After the war, she returned to apostolic work in the States, including a brief time as superior in Fall River. In 1958, she was assigned to the general headquarters in Rome. There she assisted the secretary general and undertook the research she would continue well into the 21st century. Her prodigious memory and capacity for detailed work resulted in extensive findings on the early congregation, its first missionaries, and the early foundations in the United States. She labored well beyond her hundredth birthday, a legend in the Congregation as well as a certified "super centenarian." She died in Rome on July 13, 2017.

95. The *Prima Primaria*, or first Jesuit Sodality of Our Lady at the Roman College, dates back to its sixteenth-century foundation by Jean Leunis, SJ. Sodality groups all over the world sought affiliation with this "first of the first" and sought to live by its rules and spirit: frequent communion, devotion to the Mass and to Mary, and service to the poor. From their early foundation in Lyon, the Religious of Jesus and Mary established sodalities in their schools. Since 1967, these Ignatian groups are called Christian Life Communities.

96. Benoit, *L'Avenir Nationale*, October 10, 1943.

97. See AP: H 300.7, "Precious Blood." Collection includes convent annals, historical and commemorative booklets, photo albums, and academic information from 1881 to 1973.

98. Convent Annals, 3.

99. Souvenir Booklet, 1930.

100. See Hayman, *Catholicism in Rhode Island*, I, 240–41; 264–65.

101. Kennedy, *Québec to New England*, 94.

102. On their arrival at St. Charles, the Sisters of Mercy were responsible for both French and English-speaking children of the parish, offering bi-lingual instruction at Sunday school and an "Academy" for French-language students until the Religious of Jesus and Mary settled at Precious Blood.

103. Convent Annals, 2.

104. Convent Annals, 6.

105. Hayman, *Catholicism in Rhode Island*, I, 241.

106. Kennedy, *Québec to New England*, 96.

107. See Combes, *Retraite prêchée*.

108. Four sisters named in this period bear the family name of "Bilodeau." They were all blood relatives who served at Precious Blood in the early twentieth century. M. St. Etienne (Vitaline: 1843–1908) was the aunt to the other three, all children of her brother Georges Bilodeau. Marie-Louise (1876–1953) known in religion as M. St. Peter Claver, served as the provincial of Canada (1926–47), and then of the newly formed Franco-American province (1947–51). Gratia, M. de la Colombière (1880–1916), died at Precious Blood. The youngest, Clara, took her aunt's religious name of St. Etienne (1887–1980). She was among the first novices in New York, and served for many years in Woonsocket. Canadian-born, the three nieces spent part of their childhood in Wisconsin and were fluent in English.

109. Hayman, *Catholicism in Rhode Island*, II, 568–70.

110. Rhode Island diocesan web page: www.dioceseprvd.org/history. See also Sorrell, "The *Sentinelle* Affair," 67–80.

111. Most citations in this are from the Convent Annals.

112. Convent Annals, 9.

113. *Album Souvenir, Jubilé d'Or.*

114. M. Maria de la Luz Castrejón (1900–89) was one of the first sisters to serve in El Paso, Texas (1927–34) until she was moved to Cuba. She was a catechist in San Diego, CA, from 1939 to 1948, and then returned to her native Mexico as a teacher. M. Maria de la Trinidad Samperio (1898–1994) taught in Barcelona and Havana (1927–36) before the expulsion. In the States, she ministered as a catechist in rural missions of El Paso, New Mexico, and San Diego before returning to teach in Merida, Yucatan.

115. Convent Annals, 13.

116. AP: H300.7/5: "Letters of M. Pia."(1880–1968). A German citizen, M. Pia made her novitiate in Rome during World War I and was professed there in 1915. She pronounced final vows in Willesden, England. How she came to know M. St. Peter Claver is unclear. In 1955, she wrote an account in English of her harrowing journey through the Black Forest.

117. See ADRI: "Newport Property," Papers of Bishop Harkins.

118. Boston native Horatio Robinson Storer, MD (1830–1922), was a renowned gynecologist, author and early anti-abortion activist. A graduate of Harvard Medical

School, in 1857 he led a "physicians' crusade against abortion" that resulted in stricter laws nationwide. Following a life-threatening illness, Storer moved to Newport in 1875. A convert to Episcopalianism in 1869, he became a Catholic ten years later, influenced by his devoutly Catholic wife. As one of the first trustees of the new parish of St. Joseph, Storer helped to build its infrastructure. He was articulate and generous in his various relationships with the Church. When he died at the age of ninety-two, he had outlived all his Harvard classmates.

119. ADRI: Papers of Bishop Harkins, 6–32.

120. See ADRI: Harkins Diary, 1889–1914; AP: H.300.6, "St. Charles"; and Hayman, *Catholicism in Rhode Island*, II, 120–22; 169.

121. AP: H 300.6, Convent Annals, 4.

122. AP H 300.6, Convent Annals, 4.

123. ADRI: Harkins Diary, 1895.

124. M. Eufemia Mandri to Harkins, April 21, 1899.

125. M. Eufemia to Harkins May 25, 1899.

126. See Hayman, *Catholicism in Rhode Island*, II, 164–71.

127. ADRI: Harkins Papers, Meeting of Board of Consultors, March 20, 1914.

128. ADRI: Harkins Diary, March 9–11, 1914.

129. AP: H 300.6

130. AP: H 300.6, Letter of November 12, 1925.

131. See AP: H300.6. I am indebted to Sr. Antoinette Jacques, a co-founder of the residence, for her contribution. See also David McCarthy, "From Humble Origins," *The Providence Journal*, December 7, 2007.

132. As of 2000, the parish had 200 registered families, by whose efforts a church was built to house the worshipping community every Sunday.

133. See AP: H201, "Centreville."

134. AP: H 201, "*Fondation du Couvent*," 3.

135. AP: H 201, "*Fondation du Couvent*," 7.

136. AP H 201, *Conventions*, 8.

137. AP: H 201, M. Eufemia to Harkins, July 13, 1900.

138. See AP: 300.30/1, "Holy Family."

139. Hayman, *Catholicism in Rhode Island*, II, 102–4.

140. See AP: H 300.4. Documents from several parish communities contain examples of contracts between parish corporations and the Religious of Jesus and Mary, outlining the rights and duties of each party.

141. Hayman, *Catholicism in Rhode Island*, II, 121–22. See also AP: H300.4, for annals, photos, and contracts.

142. AP: H300.4/1, #3. A marginal note on the contract supports this requirement: "None of the sisters knows English; this needs to be changed. The pastor mentions it frequently."

143. AP: H 300.4, "*Historique de N.D. de Lourdes*," 2.

144. Plante, "Native Son," 26.

145. Plante, *American Ghosts*, 3–18.

146. Plante, *American Ghosts*, 6.

147. See Shelley, *Bicentennial History of the Archdiocese of New York*. For administrative and historical records on the New York foundations see AP: A 101; A 203/204; A 223; H 210; H300.3.

148. See AP: H300.3, "Our Lady of Peace." The extensive collection has materials

on the foundation and early years: photos, correspondence, annals, and historical accounts, most written in French.

149. Born in Québec on Christmas Day, 1849, Catherine Letellier de St-Just was one eight siblings. Professed in 1872, she was a teacher, directress and superior in a few houses in Canada. M. St. Euphémie was acquainted with the convents of the mission in the States, having served for short terms in Manchester, Woonsocket, and Fall River. Called to the General Chapter as an electress in 1901, she spent time in a New York hotel before boarding the ship to Rome. She felt a strong distaste for the many sights, smells and sounds of the city, its "feverish activity."

Rev. Arthur Letellier, SSS, became the pre-eminent benefactor and protector of the first community in New York. Québec-born, he had studied in Paris and Rome prior to his ordination. When the Blessed Sacrament Fathers arrived at St. Jean-Baptiste Parish in 1900, he was named its pastor and superior of the mission. His tact and influence with diocesan authorities, along with legendary generosity, were a support to his sister and her young community in its first years. They felt a deep loss in August 1921, when they got news that Letellier had died suddenly of a stroke while attending a retreat in Montreal.

150. Opened in 1902 by the Assumptionists, the parish of Our Lady of Guadalupe, at 229 W 14th Street, was the first Spanish-speaking Catholic parish in New York City. Its parishioners were working-class immigrants from Spain. The church was situated in a converted brownstone row house. Darbois served as superior of the mission and pastor from 1902 to 1908.

151. The Religious of the Sacred Heart came to New York in 1881, opening a convent and Academy at Madison and 54th Streets. Like most French convent schools, it attracted students from upper classes and offered a high level of women's education. Farley undoubtedly wished to avoid competition among communities with academies. He also recognized a greater educational need in the immigrant populations.

152. See AP: H 300.12,4. An undated typescript of the foundation, "*Bref Historique*," contains an account by M. St. Euphémie of her dream-vision. "I was in Rome, still fearful and overwhelmed at the thought of a foundation in New York. One night, I seemed to hear a strong but gentle voice say to me: 'Don't be afraid. Follow me.' . . . I did this without seeing my guide. We came to the sea in the midst of a violent storm. We boarded a boat that was tossed by furious waves and surrounded by ice floes. My guide calmed the storm and soon we neared a large island. As we approached it, the first thing I saw on the shore was a statue of the Madonna, opening her arms in welcome. This dream gave me such peace and courage that no challenge seemed beyond my abilities." The dream also gave her a name for the new mission: Our Lady of Peace.

153. AP: H 300.3, "*Bref Historique*," 13.

154. AP: H 300.3, "*Bref Historique*." The text has recollections of the founding journey for the Spanish sisters. It also covers the later voyage of the exiled sisters from Mexico and their dispersion to various communities, including Our Lady of Peace, where they recalled the generosity of M. St. Euphémie who had welcomed them warmly.

155. The Jesuits first arrived in New York City in 1846 as part of their Canada-New York Mission. In 1850, the cornerstone was laid for what would become the College of St. Francis Xavier. The Jesuit community on 15th Street included communities at St. Francis Xavier Parish and College, with David Hearn, SJ, as president-rector. When the New York Province was formed in 1879, the College had become the second largest Jesuit school in the United States. The community on 15th Street served as province

headquarters. From 1901 to 1906, Thomas Gannon, SJ, was the provincial, to be succeeded by Joseph Hanselman, SJ.

156. Extraordinary confessors were appointed by the diocesan ordinary to hear the confessions of women religious three times annually, to insure the sisters' freedom of conscience. M. St. Euphémie's oversight in this matter was clearly unintentional.

157. See AP: H 300.3, Convent Annals. See also *Woodstock Letters,* 179–80.

158. Loreto School for boys had opened in 1892, using two converted tenement houses. Walsh built a small addition connecting both buildings, thanks to the generosity of a rich property holder in the neighborhood. This allowed for an additional classroom and space for a girls' school. The boys' school was under the direction of lay teachers.

159. *Woodstock Letters,* 179–80.

160. AP: H 300.3/1. An account of this period is handwritten in a black spiral notebook, "*Journal de la Maison de New York.*" It has many corrections in pencil. It may have served as a first draft for the history of the house. It also contains the convent annals from 1916 to 1936.

161. Still offended by the chaplaincy incident a year earlier, Darbois complained to the chancery about the sisters' move into a house he had hoped to buy for the parish. Suspecting a "devious plot by the Jesuits who were now the nuns' chaplains," he expressed an unfounded fear that "enclosure" rules would not be observed in the fenced garden between the communities, and that the sisters' chapel would attract worshippers away from his parish.

162. AP: H 300.3. Unsigned and undated, the typescript has four pages, titled "West 14th Street, New York."

163. See AG: GIII. One of the sisters living at 14th Street recalled that the first domestic helpers were teenage girls from rural French Canada who worked as waitresses and house maids for one year. They were offered free room and board, a small stipend, and instruction in religion, etiquette and good manners under the supervision of M. François de Sales. They wore a simple black uniform with white apron, and ate in their own dining room.

164. Sr. M. du Bel Amour Hamelin held interviews with these sisters in 1978 and 1981.

165. Bernadette Letourneau (1900–1977) became a Religious of Jesus and Mary, making profession with Dina in August 1923; Aline Canac-Marquis (1893–1958), another Québec native and former classmate, entered the Congrégation de Notre-Dame (CND) in 1918, receiving the name Sister St. Frédéric-Marie. She spent a long and fruitful ministry as composer and teacher of music in several Canadian convent schools. At her death, she is reported to have said "Dina is coming to get me."

166. Born in Québec City, Dina Marie was the only child of Séraphia Matte and Olivier Bélanger. She attended elementary and secondary school with the Sisters of the Congrégation de Notre Dame, and at one time had hoped to enter with them. Her music studies completed, she was assured by Jesus that God "wanted me at Jesus-Mary." She entered in 1921, finished novitiate training, and made temporary vows on August 15, 1923. That September, she was assigned as a music teacher at the convent school of St-Michel, but had to interrupt her ministry because of chronic bouts of illness. She pronounced perpetual vows on August 15, 1928. Eight months later, she moved permanently into the convent infirmary, suffering from pulmonary tuberculosis. At the direction of her superiors, she wrote an account of her spiritual experiences, published

as "A Canticle of Love." She died on September 4 1929, at the age of 32. Beatified by Pope St. John Paul II on March 20, 1993, Dina's cause for canonization is in process.

167. AG: GII, 1931, 127. The report to the 1931 General Chapter from Canada listed 370 choir professed and 145 auxiliary sisters. Eleven sisters of the province were serving in Europe or India, and the novitiate had a total of sixty in formation. It was one of the largest, most prosperous and promising provinces in the Congregation.

168. AG: GII, Report of 1931 General Chapter, 48.

169. *The New York Times*, November 24, 1967, 74.

170. See AP: H 210.9. The collection includes community annals from the foundation, correspondence, two large ledgers and several envelopes. Handwritten notes and a draft typescript prepared by Sr. M. du Bel Amour Hamelin provided additional details for this narrative.

171. See "The Story of the 'People by the Bridge'—A Tribute to the Parishioners of St. John's Parish." A popular historical account of St. John's Parish, it was published in1986 to celebrate its centennial. Written by Msgr. John T. Doherty, pastor at St. John's from 1971to 1982, it contains anecdotal information from various sources as well as references to the development of the educational mission of the "Ladies of Jesus and Mary."

172. AG: "*Fondations*," II, 478.

173. The Highland Mills property was closed for two years (1912 to 1914). A small group in formation moved to Kingsbridge temporarily, from 1912 to 1916.

174. AP: H 210.9, undated by-laws of Alumnae Association, Article 1, Section 5.

175. John Farley was elevated to the cardinalate in 1911, nine years after his appointment as Archbishop of New York.

176. AG: GIII/Register xxx, 56.

177. A foundation of the Congregation in Ireland dates back to 1912. Sisters in Ireland and England were dependent on the Mother House until 1931, when England became a province that included the houses of Ireland. Not until 1949 did Ireland become an autonomous province. The three Irish missionaries to the States, with the exception of M. St. Charles Collins, were sent from the English province. M. St. Charles (1905–95) was assigned to the Kingsbridge mission for one year, the day after her profession in 1925. She stayed for the next thirty-four years, teaching middle and upper grades until her retirement in Highland Mills in 1959. Galway-born M. St. Camillus (1904–2001) made her vows in 1926, taught in Ireland and England until her final vows, after which she sailed to New York. From 1931 until her retirement in 1975, she taught three generations of St. John's children, who treasured memories of her skills as an educator and her gentle ways. She lived in the Kingsbridge community until just before her death, a wise and humorous presence. M. St. Gabriel (1912–94), from Killarney, arrived at St. John's in 1934, two years after her first profession. She spent thirty-three years teaching and helping with administrative tasks in the school and community. In 1967, she moved on to Hyattsville, Maryland until her retirement in Rhode Island. True to their missionary tradition, these Irish women never looked back. They left at St. John's a legacy of faith, love for Christ and Mary, and apostolic zeal.

178. AP: H 210.9. Excerpt from typescript of Scanlan's remarks, dated April 12, 1950. The "glory" refers to the logo of the Congregation.

179. Founded by St. John Baptist de la Salle, the Christian Brothers were known as educators. From 1950 to 1972, fifty-four brothers were teachers, coaches, and friends to their students at St. John's, whose appreciation for them was deep and long-lasting.

Their vital contributions were cherished by their alumni, many of whom went on to study at nearby Manhattan College, founded by the Christian Brothers in 1853.

180. See H210.5/9. There are two handwritten copy books with Minutes of the Mission Club from 1948–57, the only extant written material on the student group. Anecdotal evidence suggests it was influential beyond those years, contributing to many religious vocations. Likewise, most of the information on the Friends' Group was from memories of sisters and former students. Envelope #5 contains lists of names and addresses of well over 100 parishioners contributing financially to the sisters' apostolic work.

181. H210: 9/3, "Contract."

182. Apart from the contract, the archival collection from St. John's has no information on the high school. I am indebted to the recollections of Ms. Cathy Reid Egan, one of the students in the first class of freshmen. Ms. Egan recalled clearly many details of that year, including the names of each sister, and related her deep disappointment at the announcement of the school closing. She praised the principal, M. St. Rite de Cascia (Sr. Cora Mercier), for organizing a special closing assembly for the girls and their families. Along with distribution of awards, there was a student-led play, "Seven Nuns in Las Vegas," that lifted spirits and softened their feelings of disappointment. At the time, no reasons were given publicly for the closing. Several factors may have contributed to it: the death of Scanlan, a paucity of teachers and finances, and lack of a gymnasium.

183. For a fuller account of the development of Christian Communities, see page 308.

184. AP: H 210.1. The collection contains material about the Highland Mills foundation and development. Early documents include annals written in French from 1911 to 1914.

185. See *Country Life in America* Magazine, January, 1907.

186. Lindsay, *Pioneer*, 80.

187. See AP: H 241. The box contains information on the novitiate in Highland Mills, complete with annals through 1955, when the novices moved to Hyattsville, MD.

188. Frances V. Raymond (1881–1947), daughter of Francis and Jennie Hodgson, was born in New York City. At the time, the family lived near the Jesuit Parish of St. Francis Xavier. She was one of four siblings, two boys and two girls [two were half-siblings from an earlier marriage]. In 1902, Frances entered the Sisters of Charity of Convent Station, New Jersey, made profession two years later, but withdrew from that community in 1907.

She spent her entire life as a Religious of Jesus and Mary in Highland Mills, most of it as the local superior of the community [1920 to1931]. In 1931, when the first American Province was created, she was appointed provincial, a post she held until her death. One of her brothers was Edward W. Raymond, SJ (1865–1924), whose life was spent in Jesuit schools, parishes, and hospital chaplaincy.

189. While the novitiate was located in Kingsbridge, two sisters were professed there: M. Marie-Eymard (Aline) Gendreau, and Sister St. Laure (Wilhelmina) Simard. Two postulants were also admitted and made profession in Kingsbridge in 1914: Sr. St. Casilda (Marie Laure Caron) and M. St. Etienne (Clara Bilodeau), sister of M. St. Peter-Claver.

190. Ellen Sutton (1867–1955), daughter of Michael and Catherine Fitzpatrick, was born in Québec. At the age of twenty, she entered the Religious of Jesus and Mary

in Sillery and professed her vows in 1889 as M. St. John of God. She taught in Sillery, Manchester, NH, Woonsocket and Fall River. In 1910, she became a provincial councilor and electress; in that capacity, she was instrumental in organizing the college at Sillery, and spent years as directress of its boarders, where she was known as "a cornerstone" of the institution.

Assigned to Highland Mills at its reopening in 1914, she was superior and principal through 1920 and again from 1926–31. When the new American Province was established, M. St. John of God served as assistant provincial, a post she kept until 1949. In her later years, she was known to all as "Granny dear," and appreciated by students as a teacher of French and English. Her death in 1955 came just after the transfer of the province headquarters to Maryland. She is buried in Highland Mills.

191. M. St. Cuthbert (1881–1967), born Zoe Lindsay in Québec, was educated in Sillery. A gentle, cultured woman with considerable writing skill, she served as general archivist, companion and private secretary to Rev.M. St.Clare for over two decades. She authored several works on the history and life of the Congregation, especially in India. After the death of M. St. Clare, she went to England, becoming superior at the convent school of Willesden Green. In 1939, she went as a missionary to India, where she was mistress of novices until 1950. She died in Pakistan at the age of 86.

192. AP: H 210.1, "Convent of Jesus and Mary," undated twelve-page Prospectus.

193. Almeda Raymond [1873–1920], elder half-sister of Mary of Good Counsel, was born and lived in Manhattan, working as a salesperson. At an unknown date she took up residence at the convent in Highland Mills, where she died and was buried in the convent cemetery.

194. AG: G 1/7, "Letters of M. St. Clare."

195. An eyewitness account of the event was typewritten two days later by M. St. John of God and glued to page 289 of the community annals book.. Attached to it is a news article from *The New York Times*, dated November 6, 1932. It gives the names of the men involved, referring to the shooter as a "maniac" and "madman." He had been institutionalized for a short time prior to this incident.

196. See AG: GII, Register of General Chapter, 3 May 1931.

197. See ADNY: "Convent of Jesus and Mary, Highland Mills".

198. Francis Joseph Spellman (1889–1967), a Massachusetts native, rose quickly in ecclesiastical circles. After serving as auxiliary bishop of Boston for seven years, he was appointed in 1939 as sixth archbishop of New York and military apostolic vicar for the US forces. In that capacity, he made several visits overseas to American troops.

Spellman was a friend of Pius XII, politicians and celebrities. He exercised considerable national influence in religious and political matters, raising large sums of money for various causes. His financial skills earned him the nickname, "Cardinal Moneybags." His leadership in the archdiocese led to extensive construction projects of the Catholic infrastructure and a consolidation of all parish building programs. A controversial figure, Spellman disapproved of some liberal leanings at Vatican II, including use of the vernacular in the liturgy; to his credit, he brought as his theologian the Jesuit John Courtney Murray, architect of the council's declaration on religious freedom. At his death, Spellman's tenure as archbishop was the longest in New York's history.

199. See AP: A 202/203, for information on the Franco-American Province. Space had to be reconfigured in Goffstown to receive the new provincial and her council. M. St. Peter Claver took up temporary residence at Precious Blood, assuming the role of local superior for that time. The definitive transfer to Goffstown took place in 1948.

200. The future of the American Province was discussed at the General Chapter. Because of its limited size and growth, the idea was raised of a merger, or "reunion," with the newly-formed Franco-American Province, eliciting a negative reaction from M. St. John of God.

201. See AP: H 241: "Novitiate Annals, Goffstown, 1948–54," and the incomplete collection of a newsletter, "*La Maison Blanche*," Volumes 1to 3. Beginning in 1949, candidates entered in Goffstown or Highland Mills. Boxes AP: P 243 to 245 contain registers of ceremonies, and lists of entrance and profession of sisters from Canada, Highland Mills, and Hyattsville. They cover dates between 1859 and the 1970s.

202. Two postulants were admitted in Highland Mills in 1948, and one in 1949. From 1949 to 1953, a small number of novices were sent annually from Goffstown to increase the group in New York.

203. As Vicar for Religious, Nelson would have been familiar with both communities in the American province.
Information about his visit was taken from unpublished, handwritten notes summarizing each interview at Highland Mills. I am indebted to Msgr. Thomas J. Shelley, historian of the New York archdiocese, who found the material in uncatalogued papers of archives from religious congregations in New York. Nelson probably made a similar visit to the St. John's Community in Kingsbridge, but neither his notes nor any report have been found.

204. AP: A 240, "Minutes, Provincial Council, 1949–67." The visit in 1951 was the only time M. Luisa Fernanda came to the United States. It was then that she allowed shorter meditation periods (1/2 hour) for students and relaxed schedules during the summer. While the annual retreats at the time were only for six days, she reinstated the full eight-day retreat for the sisters, preferably under the direction of a Jesuit Father.

205. Editorial, *The Woonsocket Call*, September 14, 1953.

206. AP: A 240.1, "Minutes, Provincial Council, 1949–67." One of the proposed plans for Highland Mills included a residence for women, "in order to assure the survival of the provincial house." The minutes for October 11, 1951, refer to "all that is necessary for the community, the novitiate, and a college." The province would borrow the funds for construction.

207. AP: A 240, Statement of fiscal status, April 1952.

208. It was the policy of the Archdiocese to allow mortgages only if the borrower had half the amount on hand of planned construction costs.

209. Born in Barcelona, Spain, Ma. Angeles Araño (1906–95) was the eldest of four children of an upper middle class family. She entered the Congregation and was professed as M. del Rosario in 1930. Some years of teaching followed in the community at San Gervasio (Barcelona) until the Spanish Civil War (1936–39), when all convents were closed and sisters went into exile or hiding. M. Rosario moved back into her family home, exercising clandestine ministry and serving the community in various ways. After the war, she was appointed superior, then assistant provincial and provincial of Spain.
Elected as eleventh superior general in 1953, she brought her creative energy and vision to the Congregation through eighteen years of growth, making fifty new foundations. She presided over its post-conciliar period of turbulence and renewal, encouraging deeper study of Ignatian spirituality and promoting the practice of the full Spiritual Exercises. In 1954, she initiated an eight-month Roman tertianship program in ongoing formation. She oversaw publication of Directories of Spirituality and

Education, and furthered the historical preparation of documents for the beatification of Claudine Thevenet. After the Council, she was elected the first president of the International Union of Superiors General (UISG) from 1966–71. As congregational leader, she presided at its Special General Chapter (1969) and the first stages of revision for the Constitutions. With the election of her successor in 1971, she moved to the community's retreat house in Nemi, Italy, where she offered spiritual counsel and direction until her retirement to the infirmary in Barcelona where she died.

210. AP: A 240, Minutes of May 4, 1952. The search for alternatives to building at Highland Mills included purchasing an empty public school and using it as a Catholic high school for girls in Auburn, NY, where the sisters had recently moved to direct an elementary school in St. Francis Parish

211. AP: A 240, Province Annals, 1954, 11.

212. Although the Archdiocese of Washington was created on July 29, 1939, it shared its first archbishop with Baltimore—Michael J. Curley—who continued to administer both archdioceses as a single unity until his death in 1947. The first residential archbishop for Washington was Patrick A. O'Boyle.

213. A Pennsylvania native, Patrick.A. O'Boyle (1896–1987) was ordained in 1921, ministering in parishes and diocesan offices in New York where social concerns, labor rights, and racial equality became his key issues. He was director of Catholic Charities in New York prior to his Washington appointment. Known for his opposition to racism, in 1948 he led the way to desegregation of American schools by experiments with integrating Catholic schools and universities of Washington six years before the U.S. Supreme Court ruled segregation unconstitutional. His commitment to racial equality and civil rights was highlighted when he delivered the invocation at the 1963 March on Washington. Created a cardinal in 1967, O'Boyle was socially progressive and theologically conservative, ordering strict censures on his clergy who dissented from "*Humanae Vitae*" in 1968.

214. See AP: H300.5, for annals, photos, and statistics on the Auburn community and school. For the circumstances leading to its closing, see A 240: "Minutes, 1949–67." Between 1951 and 1969, twenty-three Religious of Jesus and Mary were missioned to St. Francis.

215. The Missionary Servants of the Most Blessed Trinity (MSBT) are an outgrowth of a lay apostolic movement for women and men, founded in 1909 by the Vincentian Thomas A. Judge, in Brooklyn, NY. Approved as a religious community in 1920, they received canonical status from Rome in 1931. The congregation has served in many dioceses where sisters work to develop a missionary spirit among lay people, and they excel in faith formation. These sisters served at St. Francis of Assisi for over twenty years.

216. In 1954, the pastor had announced plans to have a ninth grade, so that students would have Catholic education until the opening of Mt. Carmel High School (1956). The number of students warranted two classes.

217. See Dolan and Hinojosa, *Mexican Americans*, 31-64.. See also Fisher, *Communion of Immigrants*, 75–77.

218. Dolan and Hinojosa, *Mexican Americans* 41.

219. Liliana Owens, SL, et. al., *Anthony J. Schuler*, 328.

220. See Barrios, *Jesus-Maria in Mexico*, 81–125. See also AP: A 200 and AP: H300.16 (El Paso). Sr. Lorraine Genest, RJM, collected personal accounts from sisters in Texas and translated several Spanish texts.

221. Romualdo Benedet (1880–943) was a Spanish Jesuit ministering to Holy Family Parish in El Paso. He had been a friend to the Religious of Jesus and Mary in Mexico since 1914, and became their intermediary with Bishop Schuler. Other friends of the founding sisters were Cruz-Maria Garde, SJ, pastor of Sacred Heart Parish, and Ronald MacDonald, SJ, the driving force behind the Carlsbad mission.

222. Founded in 1812 in the hills of Kentucky, the Sisters of Loretto were the first American congregation with no foreign affiliation, and the first to bring Catholic education to the Southwest. They ministered along the Santa Fe Trail. In the 1920s, the Loretto sisters directed eight schools in the city.

223. *Las Posadas*, ("The Inns") is a religious festival celebrated in Mexico and some parts of the United States between December 16 and 24. *Las Posadas* commemorates the journey that Joseph and Mary made from Nazareth to Bethlehem. Each evening a small procession reenacts the journey, stopping at various homes—"inns"—where lit candles and food offerings welcome the pilgrims. After prayers and songs, the children break open the *piñata*.

224. *El Paso Herald-Post*, March 10, 1938, 2.

225. For information on Queen of Angels, see AP: A 300. and *Jesús-Maria en México*, 97.

226. See AP: A200. The document traces the development of the province through 1953.

227. In addition to "Hispanic-Mexican," the province was called "Hispanic-American" or "Spanish-American," in recognition of the contributions of Spain to its early foundations.

228. See AP: A200.1, and *Jesús-Maria en México*, 116–21.

229. See *"The Franciscan Missions of the Southwest,"* Franciscan Fathers at Saint Michaels, Arizona, 1917. Accessed April 16, 2019: https://newmexicogenealogy.com/carlsbad.

230. AG: A141, "General Chapter Report, 1946."

231. AG: GII, Meetings of General Council, 1949.

232. AP: A 200, *"Historique de la Province de El Paso,"* 1938.

233. See AG VI: 5/7, and AP: A 200.2, containing circular letters of M. St. Dorothy Boivin, and correspondence from sisters sent to help in El Paso from the eastern communities.

234. Blanche-Irene Boivin (1901–92), a native of Fall River, MA, made profession in Highland Mills, NY, but spent most of her religious life in the missions of Canada, mostly in New Brunswick. She was a strong advocate of quality education for students and sisters alike. She knew little Spanish when she became the provincial of the Western-American province.

235. AP: A 200, Prospectus, Jesus and Mary High School, c.1972.

236. Metzger was the first non-Jesuit and third bishop of El Paso from 1942 to1978.

237. The term "juniorate," introduced into religious formation programs in the 1950s, refers to a period of about two years after first profession. Intended as an intensive time of spiritual and professional formation, juniorate programs were organized to provide personal integration for the newly professed.

238. AP: A 240.1, "Minutes, Provincial Council (1949–67). M. St. Conrad (Leona) Normandin was appointed provincial following the sudden death of M. St. Vincent Ferrer Ducharme in 1955. She served the province until 1965, when she was elected to the General Council in Rome.

239. See *Jesus- Maria en México*, 106–16. Joan of Arc Residence continues its ministry at this writing, so processed archival materials are incomplete. For the founding years through the 1950's, a good source is the Hispanic-Mexican documentation in AP: A 200.1.

240. See *Jesús-Maria en México*, 107–8.

241. See AP: A 200.1. The house annals mention catechetical work in Otay, Chula Vista, National City, and "Eden Garden" in Del Mar. This outreach was to public school children and farmworkers who cultivated tomatoes, celery and limes.

242. AP: 200.1, Annals, Joan of Arc, 1938.

243. Prior to his arrival in Los Angeles, Irish-born John Joseph Cantwell served as bishop of the Los Angeles-San Diego diocese from 1922 to 1936, when the diocese was split and Los Angeles became an archdiocese. At its first archbishop, Cantwell founded two seminaries, over 200 parishes, several hospitals and clinics, and close to fifty parish schools. Known for his sensitivity to the needs of the Hispanic community, he created fifty Spanish-language parishes and missions promoting devotion to the Virgin of Guadalupe. Cantwell offered refuge to exiled Mexican clerics, who in turn served the city's immigrants and refugees.

244. See Noreen, "The Virgin of Guadalupe," 502–3. Rev. Fidencio Esparza, himself an exile from the Mexican religious persecution, came to Los Angeles in 1929. As pastor at San Antonio from 1938 through 1976, Esparza oversaw the construction of the parish school, and conducted a yearly pilgrimage to the Shrine of Guadalupe in Mexico City. While documents of proof and the usual paper trail are missing, it is probable that Esfarza kept the relic in his parish until the 1980s, when it was hidden in the Historical Museum of the archdiocese. Since the canonization of Juan Diego in 2002, the relic is enshrined at the Cathedral of Our Lady of the Angels.

245. AG VI: 5, "*Contrato.*"

246. AG: II/2, "Minutes of General Council, 1949–57." Materials on San Antonio are scattered and incomplete. An undated and unsigned account of the first years was written by one of the founding sisters, probably Sr. Herminia Rangel.

247. AG: II/2. Since 1948, the Archbishop of Los Angeles was James Francis McIntyre, created a cardinal in 1953. A strong proponent of Catholic schools, this proposal may have been untimely

248. See AP: H 210.16. While there are general accounts of the foundation, these are incomplete. From 1957–60, the mission was part of the Mexican Province.

249. AP: H 210.16, Undated Prospectus.

250. See AP: H 210.19. Information is incomplete and sketchy.

251. Names of the first two principals are not recorded in the province documents. Before 1963, all the sisters teaching at Santa Sophia were Mexicans or Mexican-Americans. The Western-American province was created in 1960. From that time on, sisters from the East were sent to help bolster the schools in the Southwest.

252. Sources for information on Hyattsville are collected in the province archives. Chief among these are the Provincial Council Minutes, AP: A 240.1; AP: H 201.3. Province Annals, See AP: H 300.31/2, for material on Regina High School from 1955 to 1989.

253. See "Assumptionists in the US," 1994, https::/www.assumption.us/virtual history. Accessed November 6, 2019.

254. AP: A 240.1, 49–50.

255. Berdes, "Catholic School Integration," 55.

256. The school's Marian title reflects one of the special devotions of the Congregation, as well as the celebration in 1954 of the Marian Year promulgated by Pope Pius XII.

257. Rev. John S. Spence (1909–73), was also pastor of St. John Baptist de la Salle Parish, in nearby Chillum. He was consecrated an auxiliary bishop in 1964. His kindness and hospitality to the sisters in the early years would long be remembered.

258. Founded in 1921 by a Vincentian priest, Thomas Augustine Judge, the priests and brothers of the American Missionary Servants were dedicated to pastoral service of rural and marginal communities in the South. Familiarly known as "Trinitarians," by 1953 they moved their seminary to the corner of Metzerott Road and New Hampshire Avenue, up the hill behind the Regina property.

259. A Woonsocket native, Leonie Normandin entered the congregation in Sillery. Once professed, she taught in the boarding schools of New England. At the time of her appointment as provincial, she was the superior at Fall River. In 1965, M. St. Conrad was elected as a general councilor and moved to Rome until her retirement and return in 1971. She died in Providence, Rhode Island, at the age of 91.

260. See AP: H 201.3 for information on the Record Group.

261. M. Marie Laetitia (Muriel Blain), from Woonsocket, was a professional concert singer and soloist. She made her first vows in February, 1960, after which she enrolled in a graduate degree program at the School of Music at Catholic University. She directed all the albums the group recorded. M. Mary of Joy (Elaine) Saulnier, an accomplished pianist and degree student at the school of music, performed solos and accompanied most of the songs. M. St. Denise (Muriel) Renaud the third sister–student at the School of Music, was accompanist for several of the album songs and a soprano in the choral group. Dr. John B. Paul, head of the School of Music and program consultant for the albums, was an encouraging mentor in the project.

262. Five albums appeared from 1960 to 1963: "Patterns in Song," "*Gesù Bambino*," "These Things I Wish for You," "Life of Love," and "Joyfully Yours."

263. See AP: H 300.2. See also Province Annals, AP H201.3.

264. AP 240.1,197.

265. Founded by the Sisters of Notre Dame de Namur (SND), Trinity College was the nation's first Catholic college for women. At a time when most universities were for men only, Trinity provided women with an excellent liberal arts education within the Catholic tradition. Beginning in 1969, men's colleges began accepting women, and the enrollment at Trinity suffered a major decline. With creative leadership and restructured programs, by 1997 Trinity Washington University was the private college of choice for women from DC public schools.

266. The province leadership hired its first lay business manager in May, 1968. Retired Army Colonel Bernard G. Teeters served from 1968 to 1979; Mr. Gerald A. Amelse, the second layman, served from 1979 to 1989. From that time on, the position was held by a Religious of Jesus and Mary.

267. See AP: H 300.13.

268. See AP: H210.32.

269. See AP: H 300.33. It contains house annals, information on the novitiate and minutes of community meetings.

270. See AP: H 210.50 for the local community at St. James. For Province Annals, Council Minutes, and activities for this period, see AP: A211 and A 211.1.

271. AP: H 300.11, H 300.12, and H 300.27.

272. O'Connor was probably referring to the actions of Archbishop Joseph Toolen, who led the diocese for 22 years. A strong advocate of Catholic schools and of a non–confrontational approach to racial integration, Toolen opened a large number of schools, churches and other institutions for African Americans. In 1964, acknowledging significant opposition, he integrated all Catholic schools in the diocese, leading his critics to call him "the nigger bishop."

273. DeLisle is part of a historic section of the Mississippi Gulf Coast, which includes Kiln, Pass Christian, Biloxi, and Gulfport, part of the Biloxi Diocese. Until 1922, the parish was integrated, with both races worshipping together in harmony. Due to misunderstandings and the ill health of the founding pastor, the Josephites took over pastoral care of the African Americans. They built a new church, calling it St. Stephen's. In April 1963, the Missionary Servants arrived to replace the Josephite community and lead a racially–divided community. Hurricane Camille tore into the Gulf Coast in 1969, destroying Our Lady of Good Hope Church and leaving white parishioners without a place of worship. They were welcomed by the black community at St. Stephen's. Three years later, tensions were resolved by frank and painful discussions between both groups. In December 1973, after a half–century of separation and segregation, the Catholics of DeLisle became one inter-racial community again.

274. The Missionary Servants had staffed Annunciation since 1945. By 1980, Walsh had been there for nine years.

275. See AP: A143.2, 144, 145.2 (General Chapters); A302, 303,304, 307.3 (Provincial Chapters); AF 201; H 201.

276. Vatican II, as it came to be known, was the 21st Ecumenical Council of the Church. More than 2000 bishops met in four sessions from October 11, 1962 to December 8, 1965. They produced sixteen documents, addressing topics from Scripture and liturgy to ecumenism and the primacy of conscience. In its wake, Catholics experienced a sea change in the way they thought of themselves, their church, and the world.

277. Parker Palmer, "Everything Falls Away," from his Facebook Page. Accessed May 18, 2020.

278. Their custom had been to chant the Office of the Blessed Virgin Mary in choir, on one note (*recto tono*).

279. Since Vatican II, the Religious of Jesus and Mary have held two sessions of provincial chapters. One is preparatory to the general chapter; the second session is held after the general chapter.

280. The activities of these years are chronicled in the Province Annals: AP: AF 201.

281. Begun in 1970, The ARC Program (Apostolic Religious Communities) was conceived and initiated by Sr. Joan Bland, SNDdeN, with the guidance and co-direction of Rev. Paolo Molinari, SJ, one of the theological experts on religious life at the Council. It was housed at the large generalate of the Sisters of Notre Dame de Namur, on the outskirts of Rome, where Sr. Joan was a general councilor. ARC provided an eight-month, international program of renewal in Scripture and theology for English-speaking women religious. Molinari secured some of the finest scholars and teachers in Rome as instructors in the program, which continued for almost two decades. Several sisters from the American Province participated in the ARC program in the next decade.

282. M. St. Thérèse Poulin led the Congregation from 1971 to 1989. She encouraged fidelity to Church teachings and the congregational texts issued by Chapters. She stressed the need for a "new evangelization" and encouraged provinces to hear "the

cry of the poor" in their communities and ministries. Following her three terms as superior general, she served as provincial superior in Bolivia. Her last years were spent in retirement at the community in Sillery, Québec.

283. "Justice in the World" was the document produced by the World Synod of Bishops in 1971. It dealt with issues of justice and liberation of the poor and oppressed; as such, it is part of official Catholic social teaching.

284. M. Catherine Kenny has been considered the founder and leader of Bethany, which she directed until her death there in 1998. She left personal notes on its origins and development in the early years, providing details for this narrative.

285. An English translation of the *Positio* was published in Ipswich, England, in 1983; the Canadian province published a complete French edition in 1999.

286. [A Religious of Jesus and Mary], *Life and Work of Mother Mary St. Ignatius, Foundress of the Congregation of Jesus and Mary*, Dublin: Clonmore and Reynolds, 1953.

287. "Called to Prophetic Mission," General Chapter 2013.

288. The newsletter later became *Update*, appearing monthly, until it evolved into its present weekly online format, "Bridges."

289. *Positio*, 540.

290. See Appendix III.

291. See AP: A307.3. Special thanks to the personal contributions of Srs. Patricia Dillon, Mary Bourdon, and Vivian Patenaude regarding the Haiti Task Force and the ensuing Chapter decision.

292. Srs. Vivian and Jacqueline arrived in Gros Morne late in September; Sr. Patricia Dillon delayed her flight by six months, as she underwent cancer surgery and therapy. Sr. Mary Scanlon, who had shown interest from the beginning, developed terminal cancer and died at Calvary Hospital, Bronx, in March, 1988.

293. Palmer, "Everything Falls Away."

294. Palmer, "Everything Falls Away."

Appendix I

Foundations in the United States

1877–2017

NOTE: FOUNDATIONS IN THE US have been of two types: those combining apostolic work and residence, and those serving only as sisters' residences.

> #—residence for sisters with no corporate apostolic work attached
> +—house belonging to Mexico

1877–1982   Fall River, MA: Notre–Dame Parish

1881–1936   Manchester, NH: St. Augustine Parish

1884–1973   Woonsocket, RI: Parish of *Précieux–Sang* (Precious Blood)

1886–88   Newport, RI: St. Joseph Parish

1887–1972   Providence, RI: St. Charles Parish

1889–1900   Centreville, RI: St. Jean–Baptiste Parish

1890–1895   Claremont, NH: St. Mary Parish

1902–1967   New York, NY: Our Lady of Peace, West 14th Street

1903–1995   Bronx, NY: St. John Parish (Kingsbridge)

1904–1919   New York, NY: Our Lady of Loreto School

1902–1989   Woonsocket, RI: Parish of Holy Family (*Ste–Famille*)

> 1902–11: sisters travelled daily from Precious Blood;
> 1911: sisters moved into parish convent.

1911–1912	Highland Mills, NY: Summer Residence and Novitiate
	1912–14: house closed; novitiate at St. John's, Kingsbridge
1906–1969	Providence, RI: Parish of Our Lady of Lourdes
	1906 to 1912: sisters lived at St. Charles
1914– 2017	Highland Mills, NY: Thevenet Hall Academy (1931–71)
	1911–12; 1914–55: Novitiate 1931–47: Provincial House, American Province 1972–2016: Bethany Retreat House, Spirituality Center
1917–1919	Chester, NY
1918–2003	Goffstown, NH: Villa Augustina Boarding School (1918–1979)
	1918–68: Academy, Secondary School 1947–52: Provincial House, Franco–American Province 1948–55: Novitiate
1929–1978	El Paso, TX: Jesus Mary Academy, Yandell Boulevard
	1938–55; 1960–68: Provincial House, Novitiate
1936–2004	+ El Paso, TX: Our Lady of Angels Residence, Nevada Street
1936	San Diego, CA: Joan of Arc Residence
1938–1950	Carlsbad, NM: Mission of San José/ Catechetical Center and School
1950–1957	Los Angeles, CA: San Antonio Parish School
1951–1969	Auburn, NY: St. Francis Parish
1955–1991	Hyattsville, MD: Provincial House, Novitiate, Juniorate, Infirmary, Regina High School (1955–89)
1957–2013	Pacoima, CA: Guardian Angel Parish
1958–1977	Hyattsville, MD: St. Mark's Parish
1960–1977	Swansea, MA: Stella Maris (Summer House)
1961–1966	Brookeville, MD: "Marywood": Provincial House/Juniorate
1959–1993	Spring Valley, CA: Santa Sophia Parish
1968–1976	Demopolis, AL: St. Leo Parish

1971–1982   El Paso, TX: Our Lady of the Assumption Parish

1972–1977   # Providence, RI: Seaman Street

1972–1973   # Wheaton, MD

1973–1974   # Karlson Court, MD

1973–1974   # Takoma Park, MD

1973–1979   # North Smithfield, RI

1973–1981   North Providence, RI: Marieville

                1982–1998: Jesus–Mary Cenacle (Province Infirmary)

1974–1976   #Adelphi, MD: Dana Drive

1974–1977   # Bronx, NY: St. John's Community (Godwin Terrace)

1976–1996   #Chillum, MD: St. John Baptist de la Salle Parish

1976–1978   DeLisle, MS: St. Stephen Parish

1976–1982   # Goffstown, NH: Emmaus House (small community of Villa)

1977–1982   # Adelphi, MD: St. Joseph's Mission Center

1977–1986   Bronx, NY: St. John's Christian Community (Godwin Terrace)

1977–2004   #Fall River, MA: Thevenet Mission Center, Highland Avenue

1977–1979   # El Paso, TX: Skylark Drive

1978–1979   # El Paso, Texas, Mundy Lane

1978–1996   #Takoma Park, MD: Our Lady of Sorrows Parish (Novitiate)

1979–1981   # El Paso, TX: North Stanton Drive

1979–1985   # Cumberland, RI: Mercymount

1980–1986   Kiln, MS: Annunciation Parish

1981–1985   # Johnston, RI

1982–1987   # Providence, RI: Our Lady of Lourdes Parish

1982–1985   # El Paso, TX: Beverly Court

1982–1985   # Fall River, MA: Eastern Avenue

1983–1987   #Washington, DC: Quincy Street Christian Community

1985–1995   # Providence, RI, Webster Avenue

1985–1989	# El Paso, TX: Rio Grande (Assumption Mission Center)
1987–2017	#Bronx, NY: St. John's Mission Center (Godwin Terrace)
1986–1995	#Bronx, NY: St. John's Christian Community (Corlear Avenue)
1987	#Washington, DC: 13th Street Christian Community
1988–1997	# College Park, MD: Christian Community, Larch Avenue
1989	# Warwick, RI: St. Timothy Mission Center
	2013: Archives Repository
1989–2002	# Woonsocket, RI: Dina Mission Center, Woodland Road
1990	Plainville, MA: Jesus–Mary Mission Center, Retirement Community
1990–2005	Mt. Rainer, MD: St. James Mission Center, Provincial Residence and Offices
1990–94	#Los Angeles, CA: Nativity Mission Center
1991–94	#Manchester, NH: Christian Community
1992–1999	#Los Ángeles, CA: Casa Claudina
1992–2003	Tijuana, MEXICO: Quest Community, RJM Border Mission
1993–1997	# La Mesa, CA: RJM Mission Center
1994–2012	# Goffstown, NH: Emmaus Mission Center
1995–1997	Bronx, NY: Farrell Hall Christian Community
1996	# University Park, MD: 41st Avenue
1997–2007	# Chula Vista, CA: Casa de la Esperanza
1997	# College Park, MD: Clemson Road
1997	Gros Morne, HAITI: Kay Jezi Mari
1997–2006	Bronx, NY: St. Claudine Christian Community (Corlear Avenue)
2002	#Woonsocket, RI: Dina Mission Center (2016: Lincoln, RI)
2002	Jean Rabel, HAITI: Kay Klodin
2003–2009	# Manchester, NH: St. Joseph Mission Center
2003–2007	+ El Paso, TX: Blessed Sacrament

2004–2013	Arlington, MA: Sophia House Discernment Community (Novitiate, 2005–7)
2005–2008	# University Park, MD: Miriam House
2005–2008	Riverdale, MD: Provincial Offices—no residence
2007	# San Diego, CA: Casa de la Esperanza
2008–13	Washington, DC: Provincial Offices (Trinity University Building)
2008	Port-au-Prince, HAITI: Barbiole 2011: severely damaged in earthquake
2008–2017	#Yonkers, NY: Woodlawn Community
2013	Washington, DC: Provincial Offices (Stuart Center)
2016	#Highland Mills, NY: Thevenet House (Martin Cottage)
2017	#Monroe, NY: Convent of Jesus and Mary
2017	#Yonkers, NY: Nimitz Community

Appendix II

Provincial Superiors in Canada, Mexico and United States

Province of Canada:
Houses of Canada and United States (1877–1931)

M. St-Cyrille (Irenée Reynier): 1869–91

M. St-Ephrem (Marie Blacheyre): 1891–94

(Eleven months—vacant)

M. Eufèmia (Rosa Mandri): 1895–1901

M. St. Augustin (Adelaide Hatschemberg): 1902–4 (died in NY)

French General Secretary, M. St. Anastasie (Virginie Gallien), interim provincial

M. St. Croix (Artémise Tanguay): 1904–18

M. St. Thérèse (Laure Chapleau): 1918–26

M. St. Peter Claver (Marie–Louise Bilodeau): 1926–47

American Province: 1931–49

M. of Good Counsel (Frances Raymond): 1931–47

M. St. Peter Claver (Marie–Louise Bilodeau): 1947–49 *

* M. St. John of God (Ellen Sutton), interim provincial of New York

Franco–American, Eastern–American Province: 1947–1968

M. St. Peter Claver (Marie–Louise Bilodeau): 1947–51

M. St. Vincent Ferrer (Flore Ducharme):1951–55

M. St. Conrad (Leona Normandin): 1955–65

M. Mary Catherine (Patricia Kenny): 1965–68

Houses of the Southwestern United States, dependent on Spain: 1926–1939

M. St–Ignace (Concepcion Morell): 1926–36

M. Ma.de Jesús (Mercedes Catarineu):1937–39

Hispanic–Mexican Province (also called Spanish–American)

Houses of Mexico; El Paso, TX; San Diego, Los Angeles, CA: 1939–60

M. Maria de los Angeles (Teresa Mancheño):1939–55

El Paso, TX:	Jesus–Mary Academy
	Queen of Angels Residence
Carlsbad, NM:	Mission school and catechetical outreach
San Diego, CA:	Joan of Arc Residence for Women
Los Angeles, CA:	San Antonio Parish School

1955: Establishment of Province of Mexico

Provincial house transferred to Mexico City (Mexico, Cuba, Colombia, and southwestern US)

M. Guadalupe–Maria (Soledad Perez): 1955–60

M. Margarita del Divino Corazon: 1960–62

Western–American Province: 1960–68

1960: Houses of Southwest (Texas, California and New Mexico)

M. Guadalupe–Maria (Soledad Perez): 1960–62

1963: Queen of Angels Residence reattached to Mexican Province

M. St. Dorothy (Blanche Irene Boivin): 1963–68

1968: United States Province:
Union of Eastern and Western–American Provinces

Mary Catherine (Patricia) Kenny:	1965–72
Gertrude Bélanger (Marie Assumpta):	1972–80
Vivian Patenaude (Mary of the Visitation):	1980–86
Eileen Reid (Mary of the Holy Spirit);	1986–95
Rosemary Mangan (Mary Kathleen):	1996–2001
Janet Stolba (M. St. Francis of Assisi):	2002–2008
Eileen Reid (Mary of the Holy Spirit):	2008–2013
Margaret Perron (M. St. Edward–Marie):	August 2013

Appendix III

Sisters Sent Abroad from the United States

1921 to 2017

Sr. Mary of Bethany (Charlotte) Bazinet	Pakistan: 1968–88
Sr. Agnes of Jesus (Ruth) Bell	Lebanon: 1964–76; 1977– 83
Sr. Lorraine Blanchette	France: 1997– 98
Sr. St. Mathias (Beatrice) Bonin	Manitoba (Norway House), Canada: 1950–51
Sr. Claudette Charpentier	Bolivia: 1986–88
Sr. Mary Crepeau	Colombia: 1970–73
Sr. St. Wilfrid (Alida) Desmarais	Manitoba (Norway House), Canada: 1951–53
Sr. Patricia Dillon	Haiti: 1998
Sr. Cecilia (Clarisse) Gaudette	France: 1934–49; Rome : 1959–2017
Sr. M. Thérèse (Irene) Gendreau	Lebanon: 1965–83, 1988–89 ; Syria : 1984–86
Sr. Estelle Gravel	Saskatchewan, Canada: 1987–95
Sr. Mary Veronica (Jeannette) Grisé	India : 1937–57
Sr. Mary Leonard (Claire) Haché	Pakistan: 1963–69

Sr. Marie du Bel Amour (Regina) Hamelin	Pakistan : 1975–77
Sr. St. Thérèse (Jacqueline) Jacques	Ireland, 1966–67
Sr. Barbara (Alice) Jalbert	India, 1934–82
Sr. Bernadette (Cecile) Jalbert	India: 1947–79
Sr. Mary Gertrude (Beatrice) Jalbert	Pakistan: 1955–94
Sr. Mary Roland (Julienne) Jalbert	India: 1950–66; Lebanon: 1974–85
Sr. St. Kevin (Adele) Kelly	Pakistan: 1953–58
Sr. Mary Catherine (Patricia) Kenny	Rome: 1961–62
Sr. Claudette Lapointe	France: 1990–99
Sr. St. Philip (Doris) Lavoie	Lebanon: 1966–67
Sr. St. Luke (Hermine) LeBoutillier	India: 1937–55; Pakistan: 1955–69; Lebanon: 1963–64
Sr. St. Luke (Grace) Manley	France: 1964–65
Sr. Mariam (Evelyn) Norick	Pakistan: 1965–2018
Sr. Vivian Patenaude	Haiti: 1997–2016
Sr. Jacqueline Picard	Haiti: 1997
Sr. Eileen C. Reid	Thailand: December, 1979 to April, 1980
Sr. Mary Magdala (Germaine) Schnitzler	Pakistan: 1961–63; India: 1964–71
Sr. St. Stanislaus (Vivian) St. Pierre	Rome: 1954–58; Switzerland: 1958–61; Germany: 1962–66
Sr. St. Pierre Chanel (Gilberte) Valois	Pakistan, Lebanon, England: 1953–83
Sr. M. of the Purification (Annette) Vanasse	Pakistan: 1964–1969
Sr. Mary Xavier (Florence) Weiss	India: 1921–1964
Total: 34	*Countries served: 15*

Bibliography

Archival Sources

AG: Generalate Archives, Religious of Jesus and Mary

AP: Provincial Archives, United States Province

ADNY: Archives of the Archdiocese of New York

ADRI: Archives of the Diocese of Providence, Rhode Island

Secondary Sources

"A Short History of . . . Our Lady of Loretto." *Woodstock Letters* 46 (1917), 172–87.

Alberigo, Giuseppe. *A Brief History of Vatican II*. Maryknoll, NY: Orbis, 2006.

Barrios, Josefina Maria, and Constanza Aguilar. *Jesús–Maria en México*. Mexico City: Religiosas de Jesús–María, 2002.

Berdes, Jane. "Catholic School Integration in Washington, DC." *Integrated Education* V (1976) 55.

Bray, Emily (M. St. Clare). *The Congregation of Jesus and Mary. Cameos from its History*. London: Burns & Oates, 1917.

Burns, Jeffrey M. "Religion and Immigration, 1865–1945." *The Cambridge History of Religions in America*, 457–78. Cambridge University Press, 2000. https//doi.org/ CHOL

Byrne, Patricia. "American Ultramontanism." *Theological Studies* 56 (1995) 301–26.

Byrne, William, et.al. *History of the Catholic Church in the New England States*. Boston: Hurd and Everts, 1899.

Coburn, Carol K. "Ahead of its Time . . . Or, Right on Time? The Role of the Sister Formation Conference for American Women Religious." *American Catholic Studies* 126 (2015) 25–   44.

Combes, André. *Retraite prêchée aux Religieuses de Jésus–Marie, Woonsocket, États-Unis, du 17 au 26 juillet 1902*. Paris: Vrin, 1966.

Doherty, John T. "The Story of the 'People by the Bridge.' A Tribute to the Parishioners of St. John's Parish." Bronx, NY: 1986.

Dolan, Jay P. *The American Catholic Experience: A History from Colonial Times to the Present.* NY: Doubleday, 1985.

Dolan, Jay P. and Gilberto Hinojosa, eds. *Mexican Americans and the Catholic Church, 1900 – 1965.* Notre Dame, IN: University of Notre Dame Press, 1995.

Fisher, James T. *Communion of Immigrants. A History of Catholics in America.* NY: Oxford University Press, 2002.

Flannery, Austin. *Vatican Council II: The Basic Sixteen Documents: Constitutions, Decrees, Declarations.* Dublin, Ireland: Dominican Publications, 1996.

Foisy, J. A. *The Sentinellist Agitation in New England, 1925–1928.* Providence, RI: Providence Visitor Press, 1930.

Foley, Nadine. *Journey in Faith and Fidelity: Women Shaping Religious Life for a Renewed Church.* New York, NY: Continuum, 1999.

Glazier, M. and Thomas Shelley, eds. *The Encyclopedia of American Catholic History.* Collegeville, MN: Liturgical Press, 1997.

Glisky, Joan. "Sister Mary Emil Penet, IHM: Founder of the Sister Formation Conference." *Catholic Education* 9 (2006) 360–76.

Hadley, George P. *History of the Town of Goffstown, 1733–1920.* Concord, NY: Rumford Press, 1924.

Hayman, Robert W. 1982. *Catholicism in Rhode Island and the Diocese of Providence, 1780–886.* Vol. I. Providence, Rhode Island: Diocese of Providence, 1982.

———. *Catholicism in Rhode Island and the Diocese of Providence, 1886–1921.* Vol. II. Providence, RI: Diocese of Providence, 1995.

History of the State of Rhode Island and Providence Plantations: Biographical. New York: American Historical Society, 1920.

Jacobs, Richard A. "U.S. Catholic Schools and the Religious Who Served in them: Contributions in 18th and 19th Centuries," *Catholic Education* 1 (1998) 364–83.

Jésus–Marie, Religieuses . *Album Souvenir des Noces d'Or du Couvent de Jésus–Marie, 1884–1934.* Woonsocket, RI: 1934.

Lindsay, Zoe (M. St. Cuthbert). *A Pioneer. Life of M. St. Clare Bray.* Rome, Italy: Religious of Jesus and Mary, 1930.

Liptak, Dolores Ann. *Immigrants and their Church.* New York: Macmillan, 1988.

Montesinos, Gabriela Maria (Clotilde). *The Life and Times of Claudine Thevenet.* Translated by Catherine Dell. Pune, India: Religious of Jesus and Mary, 1977.

Messire Joseph–Augustin Chevalier. Jubilé de Diamant Sacerdotal, 1867–1927. Manchester, NH: L'Avenir National, 1927.

"More on Our Lady of Guadalupe." *Assumptionists in the United States.* Brighton, MA: Assumptionist Center, 61–65.

Nolan, Hugh J., ed. *Pastoral Letters of the United States Catholic Bishops.* I, 1792–1940. Washington, DC: United States Catholic Conference, 1984.

Noreen, Kirstin. "The Virgin of Guadalupe, Juan Diego, and the Revival of the Tilma Relic in Los Angeles." *Church History* 87 (2018) 487–514.

O'Malley, John. "The Millennium and the Papalization of Catholicism." *America* 182 (2000) 8–16.

———. and David G. Schultenover. *Vatican II: Did Anything Happen?* New York: Continuum, 2007.

———. *What Happened at Vatican II.* Cambridge, MA: Harvard/Belknap, 2008.

O'Toole, James M. *The Faithful. A History of Catholics in America.* Cambridge, MA: Harvard/Belknap, 2008.

Owens, Mary Lilliana. *Most Rev. Anthony J. Schuler, First Bishop of El Paso, and Catholic Activities in the Diocese, 1915–1942.* El Paso, TX: Revista Catolica, 1953.

Plante, David. *American Ghosts. A Memoir.* Boston: Beacon Press, 2005.

———. "Native Son." *Boston College Magazine* (1995) 24–27.

Paradis, Wilfrid H. *"Upon This Granite." Catholicism in New Hampshire, 1647–1997.* Portsmouth, NH: Randall, 1998.

Pelletier, Eliane. *Les Filles de Claudine Thévenet en Terre Canadienne. Histoire des Fondations, 1885–1985.* Québec: Religieuses de Jésus–Marie, 1990.

Rausch, Thomas P. *Catholicism at the Dawn of the Third Millennium.* Collegeville, MN: Liturgical Press, 1996.

Silvia, Philip T. "The "Flint Affair": French-Canadian Struggle for 'Survivance.'" *Catholic Historical Review* 65 (1979) 414–35.

Sorrell, Richard. *The Sentinelle Affair (1924–1929) and Militant "Survivance." The Franco-American Experience in Woonsocket, Rhode Island.* PhD diss. SUNY/Buffalo, 1975.

Schneiders, Sandra Marie. *Finding the Treasure: Locating Catholic Religious Life in a New Ecclesial and Cultural Context.* New York: Paulist, 2000.

———. *New Wineskins: Re–Imagining Religious Life Today.* New York: Paulist, 1993.

———. "The Ongoing Challenge of Renewal." Working Paper, CORI Conference: Malahide, Dublin, 2014.

Shelley, Thomas J. *The History of the Archdiocese of New York.* Strasbourg: Editions du Signe, 1999.

Tanner, Norman P. *The Councils of the Church.* New York: Crossroad, 2001.

Thompson, Margaret Susan. "Adaptation and Professionalisation: Challenges for Teaching Sisters in a Pluralistic Nineteenth–Century America." *Paedagogica Historica* 49 (2013) 454–70.

———. "Sisters' History is Women's History: The American Context." *Journal of Women's History,* 26 (2014) 182–90.

Vermette, David. *A Distinct Alien Race: The Untold Story of Franco–Americans. Industrialization, Immigration, Religious Strife.* Québec: Baraka Books, 2018.

Verrette, Adrien. *Un Cinquantenaire: Académie Notre–Dame, 1881–1931.* Manchester, NH: 1931.

Walch, Timothy. *Parish School. American Catholic Parochial Education from Colonial Times to the Present.* Washington, DC: NCEA, 2003.

Wall, Barry W. *Bearing Fruit by Streams of Waters: A History of the Diocese of Fall River.* Strasbourg: Editions du Signe, 2003.

Weaver, Mary Jo. *New Catholic Women: A Contemporary Challenge to Traditional Religious Authority.* San Francisco: Harper & Row, 1985.

Index

CPSIA information can be obtained
at www.ICGtesting.com
Printed in the USA
LVHW011505120121
676309LV00011B/1027